Organic Gardening FOR DUMMIES®

by Sue Fisher, Ann Whitman, Suzanne DeJohn
and the Editors of the National Gardening
Association

Organic Gardening For Dummies®

Published by
John Wiley & Sons, Ltd
The Atrium
Southern Gate
Chichester
West Sussex
PO19 8SQ
England

www.wiley.com

About the Authors

Sue Fisher began her horticultural career in 1980, training in commercial horticulture and working in the nursery and garden centre industry. It was her initial training that sowed the seeds for a lifetime passion for organic gardening, with the conviction that putting so many chemicals on plants just could not be healthy!

For much of the first part of her career, Sue was plant buyer for the Frosts group of garden centres and landscape company, and the winner of many top industry awards. But promotion brought with it distance from the plants that she loved, so in 1990 Sue struck out on her own as a garden writer and designer. The BBC spotted Sue's passion for her subject and commissioned her first book within a year, and her features in the press won her the coveted Garden Writers Guild trade press Writer of the Year award. Now her published work spans ten solo books, including the UK adaptation of *Gardening For Dummies* (she has also acted as technical editor for several other titles in the *For Dummies* series); contributions to a number of other books with top gardeners including the late Geoff Hamilton, Alan Titchmarsh and Carol Klein, and a wealth of articles in newspapers and gardening magazines. Sue has broadcast on radio and TV, and lectured to many audiences, from garden clubs and societies to tour groups. Her designs have transformed numerous private gardens, using planting styles from contemporary to cottage. With memories of the birth of her own love of gardening, she also advises schools on garden management and design.

Recently, Sue moved to Devon where she is currently transforming a half-acre plot above the Tamar Valley into a haven for all the family, using a contemporary approach to wildlife and sustainable gardening design.

Suzanne DeJohn describes her fascination with all things botanical as encompassing a curiosity about the natural world and a passion for the science that explains what she sees, all wrapped up in an aesthetic sensibility that inspires her to find beauty in the simplest expressions of nature. 'As gardeners, we must take our cues from nature and follow the principles that govern healthy ecosystems. It's the only way we can create an environment that can sustain us now and for generations to come.'

Suzanne has worn a variety of hats in her twelve years with the National Gardening Association, including work in the education, editorial and IT departments. She coordinated NGA's online question and answer service for six years and has answered literally thousands of gardening questions. Convinced that gardeners are curious and love to learn, she was inspired to create the *Exploring the Garden* series of in-depth, online courses that teach the principles of botany in the context of the garden. Suzanne also does Web- and print-based graphic design work for NGA, takes photos for the websites and creates illustrations to accompany articles.

Suzanne's varied background includes a BS in geology from Tufts; university courses in botany, soils and plant pathology; a stint as a research assistant in plant pathology; and several years as a self-employed artist and graphic designer. She's worked on a landscape crew, as well as on a dairy farm and an organic vegetable farm, and spent several years as a cook at a natural foods store. The common themes running through these seemingly disparate vocations are plants, beauty, nature and healthy food. Suzanne strives for balance in her life by combining time spent outdoors in her gardens with time spent at the computer, communicating what she has learned about plants and gardening.

Ann Whitman earned a Bachelor of Science degree in Plant and Soil Science at the University of Vermont. She also completed a Master of Arts degree in Landscape Design from the Conway School of Landscape Design in Massachusetts. Ann is the author of *Trees and Shrubs For Dummies* (Wiley Publishing, Inc.) as well as *How-To Landscaping Basics* and *Water Gardens: Simple Steps to Adding the Beauty of Water to Your Garden*, both published by Time Life. She also contributes to several gardening magazines and websites. When she's not writing, Ann gardens on fertile river-bottom soil in Vermont where the winters are long and the summers are short, but worth it.

The National Gardening Association (NGA) is committed to sustaining and renewing the fundamental links between people, plants and the earth. Founded in 1972 as 'Gardens for All' to spearhead the community garden movement, today's NGA promotes environmental responsibility, advances multidisciplinary learning and scientific literacy, and creates partnerships that restore and enhance communities.

NGA is best known for its garden-based curricula, educational journals, international initiatives and several youth garden grant programmes. Together, these reach more than 300,000 children nationwide each year. NGA's websites, one for home gardeners and another for those who garden with kids, build community and offer a wealth of custom content.

To find out more about the National Gardening Association, write to 1100 Dorset St., South Burlington, VT 05403, USA, or visit its website at www. garden.org or www.kidsgardening.com.

Publisher's Acknowledgements

We're proud of this book; please send us your comments at http://dummies.custhelp.com. For other comments, please contact our Customer Care Department within the U.S. at 877-762-2974, outside the U.S. at 317-572-3993, or fax 317-572-4002.

Some of the people who helped bring this book to market include the following:

Acquisitions, Editorial, and Vertical Websites

Project Editor: Steve Edwards

Commissioning Editor: Kerry Laundon

Assistant Editor: Ben Kemble

Development Editor: Andy Finch

Technical Editor: Ian Spence

Proofreader: Kim Vernon

Production Manager: Daniel Mersey

Publisher: David Palmer

Cover Photos: © iStock/intst

Cartoons: Ed McLachlan

Composition Services

Project Coordinator: Kristie Rees

Layout and Graphics: Lavonne Roberts, Corrie Socolovitch

Proofreader: Melissa Cossell

Indexer: Estalita Slivoskey

Publishing and Editorial for Consumer Dummies

　　Kathleen Nebenhaus, Vice President and Executive Publisher

　　Kristin Ferguson-Wagstaffe, Product Development Director

　　Ensley Eikenburg, Associate Publisher, Travel

　　Kelly Regan, Editorial Director, Travel

Publishing for Technology Dummies

　　Andy Cummings, Vice President and Publisher

Composition Services

　　Debbie Stailey, Director of Composition Services

Contents at a Glance

Introduction *1*

Part 1: Understanding the Basics of
Organic Gardening *5*

Chapter 1: Gardening Organically: The Basic Techniques 7

Chapter 2: Benefiting You and the World: Great Reasons to Go Organic.................17

Chapter 3: Understanding and Planning Your Site 27

Part II: Getting Stuck into Soil,
Compost and Fertilisers *37*

Chapter 4: Digging Beneath the Surface: Soils 39

Chapter 5: Building Healthy Soil 49

Chapter 6: Composing Great Compost: Let the Rotting Begin! 65

Chapter 7: Enriching the Earth with Organic Fertilisers 81

Part III: Growing Organically in Your Garden *95*

Chapter 8: Settling in Plants and Keeping Them Happy 97

Chapter 9: Enjoying Home-grown Feasts 113

Chapter 10: Raising Organic Vegetables 125

Chapter 11: Growing Herbs for the Home and Garden 151

Chapter 12: Picking from the Berry Patch 163

Chapter 13: Cultivating Fruits and Nuts for Your Organic Orchard.......................175

Chapter 14: Saying It With Flowers 189

Chapter 15: Managing Garden Trees and Shrubs 205

Chapter 16: Creating and Caring for Your Organic Lawn 219

Part IV: Managing Problems *233*

Chapter 17: Creating a Natural Balance: Preventing Pests and
Diseases Organically 235

Chapter 18: Managing and Controlling Insect Pests 251

Chapter 19: Battling Plant Diseases 269

Chapter 20: Outwitting Invading Creatures 287

Chapter 21: Weed It and Reap! 299

Part V: The Part of Tens 313
Chapter 22: Ten Best Organic Gardening Practices 315
Chapter 23: Ten Ways to Be Eco-Friendly 319

Index 323

Table of Contents

Introduction *1*

About This Book.. 1
Conventions Used in This Book... 1
What You're Not to Read.. 2
Foolish Assumptions.. 2
How This Book Is Organised 2
    Part I: Understanding the Basics of Organic Gardening 3
    Part II: Getting Stuck into Soil, Compost and Fertilisers............. 3
    Part III: Growing Organically in Your Garden......................... 3
    Part IV: Managing Problems 3
    Part V: The Part of Tens 3
Icons Used in This Book 4
Where to Go from Here.. 4

Part 1: Understanding the Basics of Organic Gardening... 5

Chapter 1: Gardening Organically: The Basic Techniques 7

Defining Organic Gardening 7
Building Healthy Soil.. 8
Planting Wisely 9
    Ensuring diversity of plant types.................................... 10
    Encouraging animal and insect diversity.............................. 11
Using Integrated Pest Management.. 13
Managing Nutrients 14
Reducing, Reusing, Recycling 15
    Conserving water 15
    Considering the source 15

Chapter 2: Benefiting You and the World:
Great Reasons to Go Organic 17

Growing Organically for Your Health... 17
    Selecting alternatives to synthetic chemicals....................... 18
    Getting more nutrients from organically grown foods 18
    Using fewer genetically modified organisms.......................... 19
Considering the Environment 20
    Protecting wildlife... 20
    Helping insect pollinators.. 21
    Minimising water contamination 22
    Preventing soil erosion 23
    Conserving water 24
    Predicting the future for organic gardening......................... 24

Chapter 3: Understanding and Planning Your Site. **27**

Knowing Your Garden's Conditions..27
    Understanding soil assessment 27
    Considering your region's climate..28
    Thinking about your microclimates 28
Getting Started on Your Garden Design 30
    Using basic design principles...31
    Landscaping and arranging 32
    Putting pencil to paper...33
    Making a map 34
    Putting it all together..35

Part II: Getting Stuck into Soil,
Compost and Fertilisers **37**

Chapter 4: Digging Beneath the Surface: Soils **39**

Excavating Soil Components..40
Digging into the Topsoil..42
    Turning over the composition of soil...42
    Uncovering soil structure 44
Creating Fertile Ground 46
    Understanding what plants need 46
    Grasping how soil affects fertility...48
    Measuring soil acidity or alkalinity: pH 48

Chapter 5: Building Healthy Soil **49**

Knowing Your Soil 49
    Testing your soil type: Sand, silt or clay?.....................................50
    Checking your soil drainage 51
    Measuring the soil pH 52
    Assessing the nutrient levels..53
Adjusting Your Soil's pH...54
Adding Organic Matter: The Soul of the Soil..54
    Becoming gung-ho about dung 56
    Using compost: The prince of organic matter 58
Cultivating Your Soil 59
    Understanding why cultivating is necessary 60
    Digging: How deep to go 61
    Getting help: Mechanical cultivators 63

Chapter 6: Composing Great Compost: Let the Rotting Begin!. **65**

Understanding Why Composting is Common Sense................................66
Situating and Arranging Your Compost Area..66
    Buying or building compost bins..67
    Selecting solutions for small spaces 69

Getting Started: From Refuse to Riches 70
    Choosing ingredients for your compost recipe 70
    'Cooking' your compost heap 72
    Speeding up the process: Compost activators 73
    Loving leafmould 73
    Working with wiggly wormeries 74
Handling Problematic Materials 77
    Composting food waste . . . safely 77
    Recycling woody prunings 78
    Dealing with non-compostables 78

Chapter 7: Enriching the Earth with Organic Fertilisers 81
Becoming Familiar with Fertilisers 81
    Debating organic versus synthetic fertilisers 82
    Choosing between fast-release and slow-release fertilisers 83
    Considering the big three nutrients 84
    Providing secondary nutrients 86
    Avoiding trace element deficiency 86
    Applying fertilisers 87
Getting to Grips with Types of Organic Fertiliser 88
    Buying organic fertilisers 88
    Rocking-on with mineral-based fertilisers 89
    Boosting your soil 90
    Producing your own liquid fertilisers 91
    Growing green manures and cover crops 92
Finding a Sustainable Source of Fertiliser 93

Part III: Growing Organically in Your Garden 95

Chapter 8: Settling in Plants and Keeping Them Happy 97
Planting Knowledge: Getting to Know Plant Types 97
    Appearing here only once: Annual plants 97
    Checking them out every two years: Biennial plants 98
    Counting on them every spring: Herbaceous perennials 98
    Persisting year on year: Woody perennials 99
Starting from Seed 99
    Sowing seeds directly in your garden 100
    Starting seeds indoors 102
Buying as Plants 103
    Knowing your sources 103
    Picking winners 104
Preparing and Planting 105
    Putting in container-grown perennials,
        annuals and vegetables 106
    Settling in bare-root plants 107
    Planting trees and shrubs 109
Feeding, Watering and Maintenance 110

Chapter 9: Enjoying Home-grown Feasts....................113

Going Your Own Way: Good Reasons for Growing Your Own Grub.....113
Deciding What Plants are Suitable for Your Patch....................114
Selecting the Best Varieties....................116
Understanding What Crops Need....................116
 Supplying soil, sun and shelter 116
 Watering and feeding....................118
Succeeding in Small Spaces....................118
 Cultivating crops in containers....................118
 Producing fruit pots 119
 Going up: Growing plants vertically 119
 Using frames and supports....................120
 Raising windowsill crops 120
Extending the Season: Growing Early, Late and Exotic Crops....................122
 Starting early 122
 Warming the soil....................123
 Using cloches and crop covers 123
 Growing in a greenhouse 123
 Putting polytunnels into service....................123

Chapter 10: Raising Organic Vegetables 125

Planning Your Vegetable Garden....................125
Rotating Crops: Problem Avoidance in Action 126
Gardening the Easy Way: No-Dig Beds....................128
 Grasping the benefits of 'going to beds' 129
 Sizing and shaping up....................129
 Preparing the ground properly....................130
 Choosing crops for raised beds 130
Determining What Veg to Plant . . . and When....................131
Sowing, Planting and Caring for Your Veg....................133
 Sowing seeds and setting out plants 133
 Fertilising: Feed me, feed me!....................133
 Weeding and watering....................134
 Harvesting time....................134
Vegging Out With Veg Varieties....................135
 Alliums: Onions, shallots, garlic and leeks 135
 Asparagus 137
 Brassicas: Broccoli, cauliflower, cabbage and company....................138
 Legumes: Peas and beans 139
 Lettuce and leafy salad friends 140
 Peppers and their aubergine cousins 141
 Potatoes 142
 Root crops: Carrots, parsnips, beetroots and radishes 144
 Sweetcorn 145
 Swiss chard and spinach 145
 Tomatoes 146
 Vining crops: Cucumbers, squash, pumpkins,
  courgettes and marrows 148

Chapter 11: Growing Herbs for the Home and Garden 151

Growing Herbs 151
  Fitting herbs into your garden 152
  Watching for invaders 153
Taking a Look at Some Common Herbs 154
  Basil 154
  Calendula 154
  Caraway 155
  Chamomile 155
  Chives 155
  Coriander 156
  Dill 156
  Fennel 157
  Horseradish 158
  Lavender 158
  Mint 159
  Oregano 159
  Parsley 160
  Rosemary 160
  Sage 161
  Sweet marjoram 161
  Tarragon 162
  Thymes 162

Chapter 12: Picking from the Berry Patch 163

Bearing Fruit: Berry Basics 163
  Choosing where to grow your fruits 164
  Controlling weeds 165
  Buying plants 165
Discovering the Delights of Soft Fruits 166
  Beautiful blueberries 166
  Ramblin' brambles: Blackberries and friends 167
  Keeping current with currants and gooseberries 168
  Going ape for grapes 170
  Robust raspberries 171
  Rhubarb rhubarb 172
  Sublime strawberries 172

**Chapter 13: Cultivating Fruits and Nuts for
Your Organic Orchard** 175

Getting to the Roots of Fruit Tree Anatomy 176
  Accepting that size (and shape) does matter 176
  Cross-pollinating: Sex and the single tree 178
  Budding genius 179
Looking After Your Fruit Trees 179
  Planting for success 180
  Pruning fruit trees 181
  Preventing pests and diseases 181

Coming Over all Fruity: Choosing Fruit Trees for Your Garden 182
    Adding apples to your plot 182
    Cheering up your garden with cherries 183
    Picking peaches and nectarines 184
    Peering into the world of pears 185
    Plumping for plums, damsons,
        gages and prunes 186
Going Crazy for Nuts 186
    Angling for almonds 187
    Craving cobnuts and filberts 187
    Waiting for walnuts 187

Chapter 14: Saying It With Flowers. 189
Mixing It Up with Flowers: The Basics 189
    Creating mixed borders 190
    Preparing your soil 191
    Planting and aftercare 192
Selecting and Growing Flowers of all Types 193
    Enjoying annual events 193
    Planting perennial favourites 194
    Blooming bulbs 196
    Fancying fantastic foliage 197
Running for the Roses 198
    Making the right rose choice 199
    Choosing disease-resistant roses 199
    Buying roses 200
    Planting roses 200
    Fertilising and mulching for roses 203
    Watering your roses 203
    Solving common rose troubles 203

Chapter 15: Managing Garden Trees and Shrubs. 205
Planning for Long-Term Success 205
    Putting everything in its place 206
    Avoiding troublemakers 206
Giving Your New Trees and Shrubs the Best Start 207
    Selecting the right season 207
    Picking out healthy plants 208
    Getting short-term care right 208
Taking the Long View for Trees and Shrubs 209
    Fertilising follies 210
    Practising pruning 210
Choosing the Perfect Trees and Shrubs 211
    Painting your garden with flowering and ornamental trees 212
    Filling your garden with flowering and foliage shrubs 213
    Considering conifers 215

Chapter 16: Creating and Caring for Your Organic Lawn **219**

Getting Down to Grassroots...219
Choosing the Right Grass 220
Preparing the Soil 220
Planting the Lawn 221
    Going for turf 221
    Creating a lawn from seed 223
Maintaining Your Organic Lawn 224
    Grasping the full importance of mowing 224
    Watering your lawn 225
    Avoiding lawn problems with cultivation, not chemicals 226
Switching to Lawn Alternatives 229
    Growing ground covers...229
    Converting a lawn to something wilder 230
    Making a meadow 230

Part IV: Managing Problems... *233*

Chapter 17: Creating a Natural Balance:
Preventing Pests and Diseases Organically....................**235**

Dealing with Pests the Organic Way 235
    Choosing pest- and disease-resistant plants...........................237
    Making your garden less inviting to pests...............................237
    Identifying culprits and problems 239
    Establishing thresholds 241
    Preventing and controlling pests...241
Welcoming Natural Pest Controllers into Your Garden 243
    Identifying beneficial insects...243
    Attracting beneficial insects..245
    Encouraging other natural predators 246
Observing Commonsense Organic Pesticide Use 247
    Knowing pesticide types...248
    Protecting yourself, the plants and the environment 248
    Keeping records 249

Chapter 18: Managing and Controlling Insect Pests **251**

Understanding Insects 251
Managing Insect Pests..252
    Removing pests manually..253
    Barring the way with barriers 254
    Resisting with repellents...256
    Tricking with traps 256
    Controlling pests biologically 257
    Cleaning up pests with soaps and oils 258
    Using plant-based insecticides...259
Getting Rid of Common Insect Pests...260

Chapter 19: Battling Plant Diseases **269**

Diagnosing What's Wrong with Your Plant 269
Understanding Plant Diseases 270
    Finding the fungus among us 271
    Battling bacteria and viruses 272
Protecting Your Plants Against Disease 272
    Choosing plant varieties wisely 272
    Keeping plants dry and mulched 273
    Preventing plant disease in other ways 273
Getting to Grips with Disease-Control Techniques and Products 274
Combating Common Garden Diseases 276
Rooting Out Environmental Problems 282
    Dodging weedkiller damage 282
    Avoiding lawn-mower and strimmer damage 283
    Defending against leaf scorch 283
    Fortifying against nutrient deficiency 284
    Steering clear of salt damage 284
    Fending off frost and winter injury 284

Chapter 20: Outwitting Invading Creatures **287**

Gearing Up For Battle 288
Combating Larger Animals 289
    Defending against deer 289
    Battling beastly badgers 291
    Warding off those wascally wabbits 292
    Guarding against grey squirrels 292
    Fighting off feline foes 293
Vanquishing Voles and Mice 295
Defending Against Lofty and Low-down Creatures 296
    Beating the birds 296
    Maintaining your defences against moles 297

Chapter 21: Weed It and Reap! **299**

Winning the Weed Wars 299
    Knowing your enemy 300
    Facing up to wicked perennial weeds 301
    Mulching for weed prevention 302
    Pulling and cultivating 306
    Firing weeds with flame guns 308
    Resorting to organic herbicides 309
    Covering the ground with cover crops 309
    Clearing overgrown ground 310
Spotting Problems that Weeds can Hide 311
    Providing homes for insects, good and bad 311
    Harbouring diseases that spread 312

Part V: The Part of Tens 313

Chapter 22: Ten Best Organic Gardening Practices 315
Enriching Your Soil...315
Mulching Early, Mulching Often 316
Choosing Healthy, Disease-Resistant Plants 316
Putting Plants in the Right Place 316
Using Organic, Slow-Release Fertilisers................................317
Encouraging Beneficial Organisms..317
Practising Integrated Pest Management................................317
Trapping and Blocking Pests 318
Avoiding Toxic Pesticides 318
Promoting Diversity 318

Chapter 23: Ten Ways to Be Eco-Friendly 319
Letting Perfection Go 319
Reducing, Reusing and Recycling..319
Composting Kitchen Scraps and
    Garden Debris...320
Reducing (Or Eliminating) Your Lawn...................................320
Planting a Tree...321
Choosing Human-Powered Equipment 321
Minimising All Forms of Pollution 321
Teaching Your Children Well..322
Sourcing Your Food Locally...322
Considering the Seventh Generation 322

Index 323

Introduction

*I*f you want to grow food and maintain your garden without using synthetic garden chemicals and fertilisers, this book is certainly for you. But organic gardening is about much more than just producing safe food and chemical-free lawns. To garden organically and successfully, you need to enlist the help of nature and roll out the welcome mat to billions of soil bacteria, pest-munching birds, amphibians and other creatures. Organic gardening is also about making conscious decisions on sustainability and taking responsibility for actions that affect the world outside your back door, past the end of your driveway and beyond the boundaries of your home town.

Many people proudly claim to be environmentalists, while knowing very little about how to be a good steward of their own garden. This book gets you started on the path to making healthier choices for your own garden and the world, while having a lot of fun and exercise and gaining the satisfaction of carrying out informed and eco-friendly gardening.

About This Book

Organic gardening covers a lot of ground, so to speak – from maintaining a lawn and growing roses to harvesting fresh fruits and vegetables. This book takes you step by step through building and maintaining healthy soil, encouraging helpful insects and other organisms, choosing problem-free plants and getting them off to the right start. In addition to the basic concepts of organic gardening, we also include information about how to grow fruit and veg for eating, flowers for beauty, trees to sit under and lawns to stretch out on – without harmful chemical pesticides, fungicides or weedkillers, or synthetic chemical fertilisers.

Conventions Used in This Book

Here are a few conventions we use in this book, designed to help you navigate your way through the content:

- ✓ *Italic* is used for emphasis and to highlight new terms that are defined.
- ✓ **Boldfaced** text is used to indicate the action part of numbered steps.
- ✓ `Monofont` is used for website addresses.

We give measurements in metric, followed by imperial equivalents.

An 'x' in a species name indicates a hybrid cross: *C.* x *lavalleei*, for example, indicates the Lavalle hawthorn, a variety of Hawthorn (*Crataegus* species).

What You're Not to Read

Although we want to believe that you're going to pore over every word in this book, we know that you may be in a hurry or just want the basic information. Therefore, we make any 'skippable' information easy to recognise by placing it in sidebars or marking with a Technical Stuff icon. Although interesting and related to the topic at hand, such info isn't essential to succeeding as an organic gardener.

Foolish Assumptions

In writing this book, we make some assumptions about you:

- ✔ You want to create a safe, beautiful and healthy place for your family to work and play.
- ✔ You want to harvest the freshest, tastiest and most nutritious fruits and vegetables possible.
- ✔ You care about the environment and want information that helps you care for your garden or allotment in an ecologically sound way.
- ✔ You've heard about organic gardening but you need more specifics and perhaps convincing that organic is right for you.

Whether you come to this book in total gardening ignorance or have some experience under your fingernails, you can find plenty of hands-on, how-to information to make your organic garden better than you believed possible.

How This Book Is Organised

To make navigating through this book easier, we divide it into the following parts, each one containing relevant chapters.

Part I: Understanding the Basics of Organic Gardening

If you think that you want to become an organic gardener but aren't sure what that entails, start with this part. It contains plenty of detail to get you up and running, covering the basic concepts of organic gardening, from soil health to planning low-maintenance gardens.

Part II: Getting Stuck into Soil, Compost and Fertilisers

The foundation of organic gardening is creating and maintaining a rich and healthy soil. Turn to this part to get started on testing soil; recycling your garden and household waste to make your own compost; and buying and using natural, organic fertilisers.

Part III: Growing Organically in Your Garden

The chapters in this part describe how to grow the most popular vegetables, herbs, berries, fruits and nuts, trees and shrubs, flowers, bulbs and lawns. In each chapter, we offer advice about how to choose the best plants, how to plant and maintain them, and where to obtain more information.

Part IV: Managing Problems

Turn to this part whenever you spot trouble in paradise and want to discover what to do about it. Here you can find everything you need to know about insects, diseases, animal pests and weeds, including specific control measures and products. Most importantly, as an organic gardener you can find how best to avoid trouble in the first place.

Part V: The Part of Tens

Use these two handy chapters to impress your friends at parties and win them over to an organic lifestyle. You can find the best organic practices and ten ways to have an eco-friendly home and garden. Go spread the word!

Icons Used in This Book

This book uses a variety of icons to highlight neat tips, common pitfalls and interesting and helpful information. Here's what they mean:

If something saves you time or money, or helps you make a better decision, we flag the paragraph with this icon. This icon also appears by sources that help you find particular plants, equipment or help.

This icon indicates key organic gardening principles and practices.

This icon alerts you to actions that may be dangerous to you, your plants or the environment. Proceed with caution!

If an action, technique or idea is especially good for the environment, we use this icon. Although, of course, just about everything in this book is eco-smart.

This icon marks more in-depth information for readers who want to dig a little deeper into the subject. If you just want to know the basics, feel free to ignore the info you find here.

Where to Go from Here

We design this book so that you can dive into any chapter that grabs your interest. If you're new to organic gardening, start with Chapter 1 or Chapter 22's summary of organic practices. If you're experienced and can't wait to plant veggies, go straight to Chapter 10. Or thumb through the Table of Contents or index for specific topics, until something catches your eye.

Part I
Understanding the Basics of Organic Gardening

'They may be slow but they're eco-friendly
and they also fertilise the lawn at the
same time.'

In this part . . .

If you're unsure what organic gardening is all about, jump right into this part for an overview. Chapter 1 introduces the foundations of organic gardening and living sustainably at home, along with basic organic planning techniques that you can use whether you're growing edible crops, flowers or border plants. Chapter 2 describes the benefits of gardening organically, right at home and in the wider environment. If you need to justify your organic preferences to chemically orientated gardeners, you'll have plenty to say after reading this chapter.

Evaluate your own garden's conditions, such as sun or shade, frost and soil conditions, with help from Chapter 3. And if you've ever wondered about climate and microclimates, this chapter is the place to turn. After gathering this information and more, you can match the right plant to the right place and begin planning your organic oasis. (Chapter 3 also covers creating a basic garden plan.)

Chapter 1

Gardening Organically: The Basic Techniques

· ·

In This Chapter

▶ Understanding the organic gardening philosophy

▶ Nurturing your soil

▶ Managing pests

▶ Practising conservation

· ·

*E*veryone agrees that organic gardening means avoiding the use of synthetic fertilisers and pesticides. But the theory and practice of organic gardening go far beyond that simple concept. Growing organic food and flowers, and managing your whole garden on organic principles, represents a commitment to a sustainable system of living in harmony with nature. For many people, organic gardening is a way of life.

In this chapter, we deal with the fundamentals of organic growing, including the philosophy behind organic gardening and the specific techniques that lead to success.

Defining Organic Gardening

The ways in which people use – and misuse – soil, water and air affect the lives and habitats of plants, insects, birds, fish and animals, as well as humans. Organic gardening is all about preventing and treating problems in the least obtrusive, most nontoxic ways. Dedicated organic gardeners adopt methods that use cultural and natural biological processes to do the following:

> ✔ **Improve soil health and fertility.** A healthy soil is the foundation of every organic garden. Organic gardeners nurture the soil ecosystem by adding organic matter, such as compost or manure, and avoiding chemicals and synthetic fertilisers that can harm soil life. In turn, soil organisms consume and break down the organic matter, making the nutrients it contains available to plants.

✔ **Decrease erosion.** Exposed soil is vulnerable to erosion by rain and wind. When organic gardeners cover soil with mulch, cover crops or other protective materials, they preserve the integrity of this precious resource.

✔ **Reduce pests and diseases.** Organic gardeners minimise problems and reduce the need for pesticides or fungicides by relying on cultural techniques, such as proper pruning, removing dead or diseased plant material and using crop covers or barriers. Organic gardens can also use biological controls when pest problems occur.

✔ **Encourage plant and animal diversity.** Through diverse plantings and avoidance of harmful chemical products – even organic ones – organic gardeners promote healthy ecosystems that invite beneficial organisms, including pollinators and predators of garden pests, to take up residence.

Organic gardeners take their cues from nature. Instead of relying on the spray schedules promoted by pesticide manufacturers, organic growers observe what's going on in their gardens and intervene to prevent pest problems. When you see white butterflies fluttering around your garden, for example, you know that you need to protect your brassicas from cabbage whitefly, by covering your crops with fine insect mesh to prevent the butterflies from laying eggs in the first place.

Organic growers view their gardens as living ecosystems and work with nature to produce beautiful borders and healthy crops. No matter what plants you're growing – vegetables, fruits, herbs, trees, flowers, grasses – the same basic techniques apply, as the sections in this chapter demonstrate.

Depleting soil fertility, damaging and polluting ecosystems, and consuming excess water threaten the future of the Earth's safe and abundant food supply. The ways that farmers and individual gardeners and homeowners choose to farm, garden and maintain their land make a difference in whether the land can continue to house, feed and clothe people.

Gardeners around the globe have adopted organic gardening techniques to help nurture the health of the Earth and all its inhabitants. (If you need more convincing that organic is the way to go, turn to Chapter 2.)

Building Healthy Soil

Just as a durable house needs a strong foundation, healthy plants require soil that can provide their roots with nutrients, water and air. Few gardens are blessed with perfect soil, and even if they are, keeping soil healthy and able to support plants is an ongoing process.

Creating and maintaining healthy soil is the single most important thing you can do to ensure the success of your garden plants.

Building soil means providing soil life – microbes, worms, fungi – with the materials and environment these creatures need to do their jobs. Taking from the soil without giving anything back breaks the natural cycle. Harvesting crops, bagging lawn clippings and raking fallen leaves removes organic material that's ordinarily destined for the soil on which it falls. If the organic material isn't replenished, soil health declines. Substituting synthetic (non-organic) chemical fertilisers for naturally occurring nutrients may feed plants, but doing so starves the soil and reduces the mineral content of crops.

Adding organic matter is the most common – and most important – part of building healthy soil. Compost (which we discuss in Chapter 6) is a perfect source of organic matter; other sources include well-rotted manures and crop residues. Maintaining proper soil pH (a measure of acidity/alkalinity) is also vital, because it affects soil life and the ability of plants to use nutrients (flip to Chapter 5 for more on pH values).

Avoiding activities that damage soil is just as important. Compaction from heavy foot or vehicle traffic and misapplied fertiliser and pesticides, for example, can harm the soil's ability to support plant life. Part II contains everything you need to know about your soil and how to improve it in an organically sound way.

Planting Wisely

Organic gardens strive to maintain healthy, balanced *ecosystems* (communities in which each part contributes to and affects the lives of the other parts). Because plants evolved over millennia to adapt to specific growing conditions, they thrive when those conditions are met. When you choose plants that match your site's sun, shade, climate, soil type and soil moisture, you're well on your way to creating a healthy, thriving, problem-free garden.

The first step in planting wisely is understanding your region's climate, as well as your garden's particular attributes, which then allows you to match plants to planting sites effectively (Chapter 3 contains more about evaluating your garden in this way). For specific planting information and the low-down on growing a wide variety of plants organically – vegetables, herbs, berries, fruits, nuts and flowers – read the chapters in Part III. More precisely, we cover long-lived trees and shrubs in Chapter 15 and apply organic principles to lawn care in Chapter 16.

The second step is ensuring that your garden cultivates stable plant and animal communities. In nature, plants and animals live in balanced ecosystems (see Figure 1-1) in which each plant and animal species has enough food, water and *habitat* (place to live).

Figure 1-1:
Plant and animal communities extend above and below ground.

In a balanced ecosystem, the predators have enough prey and the prey have enough predators. When one part of an ecosystem dies out or becomes too scarce, the plants and animals that depend on its function in the environment get out of balance, too. If honeybees disappear, for example, the plants that need bees for flower pollination can't produce seeds. If predators such as ladybirds become scarce, the insects they normally prey on – aphids – may become so numerous that they seriously injure or even kill the plants on which they feed.

Ensuring diversity of plant types

Organic gardeners mimic nature by encouraging diversity in their gardens. Natural plant communities contain many species of trees, shrubs and perennial and annual plants. This rich diversity helps each plant species survive in many ways:

- ✔ **Mixed populations** avoid insect and disease devastation because all the plants of a particular species aren't located next to one another. Although pests damage or kill some plants, they overlook others.

- ✔ **Deep-rooted plants** often bring soil nutrients to the surface, where they're released as the plant foliage dies and gets recycled into the soil, benefiting more shallow-rooted species.

- ✔ **Nitrogen-fixing plants** can take nitrogen from the air and deposit it in the soil, thus benefiting other species nearby.

- ✔ **Tall, sun-loving species** provide shade, shelter and support for lower-growing, shade-preferring species.

When plants grow artificially in *monocultures*, which are large colonies of a single species, they lose the benefits of a diverse plant community. Pests and diseases spread easily from one plant to the next, and plants rapidly deplete the soil of nutrients.

A good example of a monoculture is the old-fashioned rose garden, which grew little else but masses of rose bushes and required gardeners to spray pesticides and fungicides on a regular basis to avoid aphids, blackspot, mildew and so on from devastating the plants. Now most gardeners grow roses in a mixed border along with other plants that attract natural predators or repel diseases, as well as growing varieties that are disease-resistant.

Growing plants that mutually benefit one another makes sense and is simple to do in home gardens. You can add clover to your lawn, for example, because clover takes nitrogen from the air and adds it to the soil. Also, you can plant shade-loving, ground-covering plants under leafy trees to protect soil and tree roots from erosion.

Encouraging animal and insect diversity

A variety of plants naturally invites a variety of wildlife and insects. Berry-producing trees and shrubs attract birds; nectar-rich flowers draw butterflies, bees and other insects. Why, you may ask, do you want to encourage wildlife and insects in your garden? Answer: your garden needs them. Beneficial insects and other creatures prey on plant pests and *pollinate* plants – that is, they transfer pollen from one flower to another, fertilising the blooms so that they develop into fruit or vegetables. Some of a gardener's best friends include ladybirds, lacewings and hoverflies that are voracious munchers of pests, especially aphids.

As an organic gardener, you want to provide different habitats to encourage beneficial creatures to take up residence. Plant a variety of flowers so that something is in bloom all season long. Particularly good choices are herbs, such as marjoram and hyssop; plants with tiny flowers, such as alyssum and thyme; and plants whose small blooms are arranged in flat-topped flower heads, including fennel, yarrow and dill. Avoid spraying insecticides – even those classed as 'organic' – because most of them harm beneficial creatures too (as we describe in Chapter 17).

Here are other ways to encourage diversity:

- Build or install homes designed for birds, butterflies, native bees, frogs and toads.
- Install a bird feeding station to help entice birds into your garden, especially in winter when times are hard; doing so also helps to boost healthy populations of birds that are likely to remain in or near to your garden in future.
- Mimic nature by creating a layered garden with tall trees, medium shrubs and lower-growing perennials and annuals.
- Include a variety of different plants, including some evergreens, to provide winter habitat and food.
- Provide a source of fresh water: a pond is ideal – the bigger the better.
- Leave some parts of your garden undisturbed, or at least minimally cultivated.

In most natural ecosystems, pests and predators are in a balanced but dynamic relationship. Foxes and buzzards keep rabbits and rodents in check; without these predators, the rapidly reproducing prey would soon overpopulate, leading to death by starvation. In the same way, pests have a place in your garden because they provide food for beneficial organisms – if food is scarce, the beneficials starve or leave. Tolerating some pests assures predators that your garden is a good place to hang around.

Edible gardens

Gardeners have always combined plants grown solely for their beauty with those grown for food. Ancient Babylonians mixed ornamentals and edibles in their gardens; so did early American colonists. The trend to separate food gardens from ornamental plantings began in the Victorian era and culminated during the last few generations, when people began relegating food gardens to one corner of the back garden. But in the past few years, the enormous surge of interest in 'grow your own' has seen the development of *edible landscaping* – using edible plants throughout the garden, growing vegetables, fruits and herbs among flowers and shrubs, and even as part of large-scale landscaping in urban environments: in containers, on green roofs and as 'living walls'.

Using Integrated Pest Management

When faced with pest problems, many gardeners automatically reach for a poison spray. Using pesticides to kill insects, however, deprives the pests' natural predators of food, which causes the predators to decline, necessitating more pesticides to achieve pest control (refer to the preceding section for details of an unbalanced ecosystem). The whole system is a nasty, vicious cycle.

Even worse, pesticides often kill more than just their intended targets. Beneficial insects and spiders that prey on plant pests and pollinate flowers die, too. And if pesticides drift on the wind or water away from their target, they can poison fish and birds as well.

Humans aren't immune to pesticides: the fact is that what you do to your environment, ultimately, you do to yourself. People know comparatively little about the long-term impacts of these substances: just consider the chemical DDT, which was in widespread use until its dangerous side effects were discovered.

Organic gardeners choose a different approach. Instead of fighting pests and disease with chemical warfare, organic gardeners strive to create healthy, balanced ecosystems. If pest problems arise, the gardeners look for the least toxic, least environmentally disruptive solutions.

Integrated pest management (IPM) combines biological, cultural, physical and chemical strategies to control pests. In plain English, that means using the easiest, least environmentally harmful, cheapest methods first and using the more expensive, toxic methods only as a last resort.

Managing pests through IPM involves the following steps:

1. **Prevention:** Keeping pests and diseases out of the garden in the first place sees more than half the battle won. Inspecting new plants, cleaning your tools, eliminating weeds at an early stage and using best watering practices help prevent the spread of potential problems.

2. **Crop monitoring:** You have to know exactly what pest you're dealing with, when it appears, how many individuals you have and on what plants.

3. **Cultural controls:** Use strategies such as rotating crops to avoid planting related plants in the same spot each year and choosing pest and disease-resistant varieties in order to minimise problems.

4. **Mechanical controls:** You can employ certain techniques to prevent pests from getting on your plants, such as covering plants with special fabrics or using strong-smelling plants to repel pests: hand-picking and squashing pests is also highly effective.

5. **Biological controls:** Take advantage of nature's law that every organism has a natural control. You can buy and release many of these control organisms, such as ladybirds and beneficial nematodes, or encourage the ones that already exist around your garden.

6. **Chemical controls:** Even organic sprays are best used as a last resort, because some pest controls classed as organic – that is, derived from natural products such as pyrethrum – still harm the good guys as well as the bad. Be aware of this fact when looking for a quick-fix solution – and ponder whether, instead, you're better to put up with a few nibbled flowers, leaves or fruits.

We devote Part IV of this book to pests, diseases and garden problems.

Managing Nutrients

Plants need nutrients to grow, flourish and fend off pests, diseases and environmental stresses. Giving them what they need is key to successful organic gardening; in contrast, and as with humans, overdoing poor food choices spells trouble.

The best way to feed your plants is to feed your soil. Vast numbers of beneficial organisms call the soil home; nourish them, and you nourish the plants. Adding organic matter such as compost provides fungi, bacteria, earthworms and other soil dwellers with food and a hospitable environment. In turn, they break down this organic matter into nutrients that plants use.

In some cases, you may need to apply extra nutrients to keep your plants healthy. Using organic slow-release fertilisers encourages strong, steady, healthy plant growth. Most organic fertilisers provide a broad range of nutrients, and they don't harm soil life or hurt plant roots.

In contrast, the synthetic fertilisers that conventional gardeners use provide only a few specific nutrients in a form that plants take up immediately. They make plants grow quickly but don't necessarily make them grow strong and healthy, because fast-growing leaves and stems are soft and juicy – and inviting to pests. Plus, any applied nutrients that the plants can't use are wasted, sometimes running off to pollute waterways. Another problem is that synthetic fertilisers usually come in concentrated liquids or granules that gardeners must dilute in water, and improperly diluted solutions burn plant roots.

Turn to Chapter 5 for information on building healthy soil, and see Chapter 7 for information on organic fertilisers.

Reducing, Reusing, Recycling

Most organic gardeners are concerned with conservation – they reduce, recycle, reuse and in general try to limit what they buy. In the garden, *conservation* means reusing the nutrients contained in plant matter by composting kitchen waste and garden refuse, so that all those valuable nutrients go back into your own garden. Conservation also means taking care not to waste water and making sure that the products you use in your garden don't put an undue burden on the environment.

Conserving water

With increasingly erratic weather patterns, water supply is often 'feast or famine' – and gardeners can do their bit to ensure a minimal impact on water supplies. A well-designed organic garden adapts better to restricted watering because the soil is nurtured and mulched to reduce water loss, and the plants are well adapted to the location. Still, even organic gardeners have to water their plots occasionally.

The ideal watering system applies moisture directly to the areas that need it: the roots. Soaker hoses and drip irrigation are best because they apply water slowly, right to the soil, where it can soak in rather than run off.

Overhead sprinklers are the worst watering system, especially if they're used on a hot, sunny day: up to one third of the water applied is lost to evaporation.

Install rainwater storage systems so that you have your own water reservoirs: from simple water butts to tailor-made storage built under driveways and patios. Target scarce water supplies to plants in most need: vegetables that form fruits, such as tomatoes, courgettes and cucumbers; new plants, especially seedlings; and leafy salad crops.

You can safely ignore lawns unless they're newly turfed or sown; grass may brown during a drought, but soon greens up when rain arrives.

Considering the source

Look into where the products you use in your garden originate. You may be surprised. Is using bagged bark mulch shipped thousands of miles good for the environment, especially if local mulch is available? Does buying packaged soil conditioners make sense, when a local farm can supply aged cow manure?

As the price of fuel rises, the cost of shipping goods across continents is forcing consumers to look for products that originate closer to home. You may be surprised by what you can find just down the road: wood shavings from furniture factories; grounds from coffee shops; brewery waste; mulch from council Christmas-tree-recycling programmes and tree-trimming companies; and small-scale composting operations.

Think creatively! Use flattened cardboard boxes for mulch, make your own biodegradable paper pots and use anything that can hold compost and have drainage holes made in it as a plant container. One person's rubbish is the gardener's treasure!

Chapter 2

Benefiting You and the World: Great Reasons to Go Organic

In This Chapter

▶ Keeping your family healthy

▶ Protecting and preserving the environment

*Y*our interest in organic gardening may be due to many different reasons. Perhaps you believe (quite correctly) that eating organic produce and having an organic garden environment are better for your health and that of your family. Or you're concerned for wildlife and want to reduce the damage of chemical pesticides. Or perhaps you think that organic gardens are more productive and beautiful.

People grow organically for all these reasons and more. And by using growing techniques that are safe and sustainable over the long term, you too can become part of the legacy of people who honour the health of the Earth and all its inhabitants.

This chapter outlines some of the reasons why gardeners choose organic practices, which tend to fall into two general categories: an interest in personal health and a concern for the environment. If you're unsure about committing to organic growing or you need information to help you make the case to naysayers, this chapter can help.

Growing Organically for Your Health

Probably the main reason why many people garden organically is to provide their families with safe, wholesome food and a toxin-free environment. Many gardeners believe that organically grown foods taste better, and recent studies show that such foods may indeed have higher nutrient levels than their conventionally grown counterparts. Organic growers also steer clear of genetically modified plants, the health risks of which are still unclear.

Selecting alternatives to synthetic chemicals

As regards health and safety, synthetic (that is, nonorganic) chemicals pose the greatest concern in gardening. Despite a complex system of rules, regulations and labelling requirements, people still suffer from the effects of chemical residues in the environment because the residues of persistent chemicals such as DDT can last for many decades. This perhaps helps to explain why ever more people are adopting the precautionary approach! Like most gardeners, organic growers may occasionally need to use measures to combat problems, but they choose carefully, opting for the least-toxic organic sprays and only as a last resort when other control measures have failed.

Getting more nutrients from organically grown foods

Most organic gardeners say that the fruits and vegetables they harvest from their gardens taste better than their supermarket counterparts. Are the foods healthier, too? A multi-million-dollar, four-year study of the benefits of organic food, funded by the European Union (EU), suggests that some organically grown foods are indeed more nutritious than their nonorganic counterparts. The study – the largest of its kind – also found that in certain cases organically grown foods have higher levels of antioxidants, which are believed to be beneficial in fighting cancer and heart disease.

Scientists aren't sure why organically grown food is more nutritious, but here are a couple of tantalising ideas:

- **Nonorganic fertilisers may force rapid plant growth.** Research suggests that the soluble nitrogen fertiliser applied in nonorganic gardens forces rapid but weak plant growth, and that these plants contain fewer of the antioxidants needed to protect their own health – the same antioxidants that protect human health.

- **Higher nutrient levels in organically grown foods may be linked to healthier soil.** Several studies comparing the nutrient levels in different fruits and vegetables show an apparent decline in food nutrient content over the past 70 years. Research suggests that this decline may be the result of soils being depleted by an industrial agriculture system that relies on synthetic fertilisers instead of on the soil-building techniques favoured by organic growers.

> For this reason, replenishing the minerals in the soil is playing an increasing role in organic gardening.

Using fewer genetically modified organisms

Along with synthetic fertilisers and pesticides, organic growers avoid planting genetically modified organisms (GMOs) – organisms whose DNA has been altered through genetic engineering. Introduced to commercial farmers in the early 1990s, health activists and environmentalists have raised concerns about GMOs.

Historically, plant breeding was confined to *cross-pollination*: that is, the pollen of a flower from one plant was transferred to the stigma of a flower from another plant. If pollination was successful, the flowers produced viable seeds, and if the breeders were lucky, one of the plants that grew from those seeds contained the beneficial traits the breeders were seeking. The plants had to be compatible for pollination to occur; usually, that meant they had to be the same species. In this way, breeders created hybrid plants through complex, carefully controlled cross-pollination.

In contrast, genetically modified plants are created by introducing genes of completely unrelated species. The unrelated species don't even have to be plants!

The public's concern about genetic engineering reflects the notion that mixing the genes of entirely different organisms just feels wrong. Food activists coined the term 'Frankenfoods', and although the spectre of a fish with feathers is scarily evocative, the biggest health risks most likely lie in the potential for allergic responses when people consume foreign genetic materials.

GMOs pose environmental risks, too. Farmers regularly plant GMO varieties of soybean, corn, wheat and cotton. Some of these varieties have been genetically modified with DNA from a soil bacterium to resist the synthetic herbicide glyphosate so that farmers can spray fields to control weeds without damaging crops. The result has been the evolution of 'super weeds' that are increasingly resistant to the herbicide. How many more genetic mutations and rounds of super weeds are necessary before people accept that this strategy is flawed?

Similarly, scientists altered crops so that they contain the bacteria *Bacillus thuringiensis* (Bt), an important biological control that organic farmers have used for decades. Pests are quickly developing resistance to this formerly safe and effective control, leaving organic farmers searching for alternatives.

Although GMOs are currently marketed only to commercial growers, this situation may change. And if you live near a farm growing GMOs, pollen from those fields may contaminate your garden or allotment crop. The danger of genetically modified crops is hotly debated, and the EU has placed strong restrictions on growing GMOs.

Considering the Environment

The Earth's population continues to grow, but the amount of land available for growing food is disappearing rapidly. Erosion, development, pollution, dwindling water supplies and other human-induced and natural disruptions threaten safe food and water supplies. Plant and animal species continue to disappear at alarming rates as people damage and encroach on their habitats.

Organic practices help alleviate this situation because their long-term focus is on *sustainability* – the practice of using natural resources indefinitely without damaging the environment. For example, the nutrients in organic matter are recycled and fallen leaves are used as mulch. You do your bit when you use good, old-fashioned, elbow grease to cut your lawn, instead of petrol-powered mowers and trimmers.

In fact, all organic gardeners improve the prospects for the environment through their personal choices that, at the very least, do as little harm to the environment as possible. The way you choose to grow flowers and food and maintain your garden environment can improve the quality of the soil, air and water, as well as the lives of the organisms that depend on them. However small your plot, any positive actions you take can make a difference.

Protecting wildlife

Organic gardeners strive to maintain a balanced ecosystem in which all creatures, even garden pests, play a role. They rely on nontoxic techniques, such as crop covers, barriers and repellents to *manage* pests, not eradicate them. By allowing the presence of certain pests, organic gardeners encourage the pests' natural predators to take up residence – and indeed plant specifically to entice these predators. And when pests and predators are in balance, everyone wins.

Sometimes, even organic gardeners may need to use pesticides or herbicides as a last resort. When they do, they keep in mind that, although pesticides kill pests, they can harm innocent bystanders as well. When possible, organic gardeners choose products that affect only the pest they're trying to control.

Most organic pesticides break down quickly into harmless substances when they're exposed to air, sunlight and/or water. Many synthetic pesticides, on the other hand, are formulated to keep working – killing – long after the need is passed. These long-lasting pesticides not only continue killing pests, but can also accumulate in the bodies of animals, harming them over a long period. In the case of the infamous pesticide DDT, (which was banned in the United States in 1972 and phased out in the UK and Europe by 1986) the chemical accumulated in fish, rodents and other animals. When predators such as peregrine falcons ate those animals (which form most of their diet), they accumulated increasingly larger quantities of DDT and other persistent chemicals, too. As a result, they laid eggs with thin shells that broke before they hatched, destroying generations of birds and sending many species to the brink of extinction. By the early 1960s, peregrine populations were reduced by 80 per cent, and it took until the late 1990s for numbers to return to pre-decline levels.

Helping insect pollinators

Pollination occurs when pollen is moved within flowers or from one flower to another of the same species, leading to fertilisation and successful seed and fruit production. Some plants, such as sweetcorn, are pollinated by wind. However, nearly 80 per cent of the world's crop plants, including alfalfa, apples, blueberries, cotton and melons, depend on insects or other pollinators to transfer their pollen.

Although concern for the welfare of pollinating insects has been growing among scientists for decades, it took a global crisis dubbed Colony Collapse Disorder (CCD) to catch the media's attention and make the general public take notice. During the winter of 2006–2007, US beekeepers reported losses of 50–90 per cent of their hives. Researchers are still trying to determine the cause, but many think that a combination of disease-related and environmental factors are involved.

Whatever the cause, CCD awakened people to their utter dependence on the honeybee. Before that, plants relied on native pollinators, such as solitary bees, bumblebees, wasps, butterflies and beetles. Unfortunately, the populations of these native pollinators dwindled, due at least in part to pesticide use as well as loss of habitat. The warming climate may also be playing a significant role.

Organic farming offers the best, currently available, practical model for addressing the need for climate-friendly food production.

At one time, the UK had 25 species of bumblebee, a creature that dislikes warm weather. Three species are now extinct and seven are listed on the official Biodiversity Action Plan (BAP) as being in urgent need of help. Honeybee colony losses are running at 30 per cent a year, compared to just 6 per cent in 2003. To pollinate crops, farmers are having to import captive-bred colonies of bees, with their attendant risks of spreading diseases and pests.

Using organic growing practices can help reverse this worrying trend. By growing diverse plants, choosing varieties specifically to attract and feed pollinators, and avoiding pesticide use, you can play an important role in increasing the populations of pollinating insects and make a significant difference.

Minimising water contamination

Surface waters can become polluted from *runoff* – water that flows over the ground, carrying pesticides, herbicides, fertilisers and soil with it. Even at very low concentrations, these chemicals can harm aquatic life.

Fertilisers pose an additional threat as follows:

- ✔ Excess nitrogen and phosphorus fertilisers from lawns, farms and gardens wash into streams, lakes and oceans, where they contribute to excess algae growth. Densely growing algae depletes the oxygen in the water, which can kill fish and suffocate the native plant species.

- ✔ Nitrogen, the main element in most fertilisers, also moves easily through the soil – especially when mixed with water from rain, snowmelt or irrigation – and enters the groundwater, contaminating wells and other sources of drinking water. High concentrations of nitrate – a common nitrogen compound – can be toxic to children younger than 6 months' old and to cattle, sheep and horses.

Although you can't control what commercial farmers spray on their crops, you can choose to use safe products in your own garden and to support farmers who grow their crops in environmentally sound ways.

As an organic home gardener, you can avoid any toxic products as much as possible, because although the shops demand perfect-looking vegetables and fruits, you can be happy to overlook slightly nibbled leaves or oddly shaped fruit and concentrate on crops for their wonderful flavours. Also, you can choose to purchase organic food, particularly from local producers and farmers' markets to minimise 'food miles' (such a person is known as a 'locavore', and you can find more about this title in Chapter 23).

Preventing soil erosion

Topsoil is precious, containing the rich matrix of humus (which we discuss in detail in Chapter 5), minerals and micro-organisms on which plants depend for growth. In turn, plants hold the topsoil in place with their roots and shelter it with their leaves. Soil without plants erodes easily, washing away with runoff from rain and snow or blowing away in the wind.

When soil washes into streams, rivers and lakes, it significantly disrupts those ecosystems and pollutes the water. Erosion devastates farmland, too. The United States, for example, loses 2 million acres of *arable land* (that's suitable for growing crops) each year due to soil erosion. Experts report that 30 per cent of arable land was lost worldwide in the last 40 years of the 20th century, due in part to erosion.

What happens in your own small garden plot may seem insignificant compared with these mind-numbing statistics, but your gardening practices *do* play a role in the bigger picture. You can help reduce erosion by keeping plants growing on, or covering, the soil throughout the year; preserving and encouraging humus formation; and avoiding excessive cultivation, disruption and compacting of the soil.

Organic gardening and the Soil Association

Concern about soil erosion and the health implications of intensive agricultural systems in general led to the formation of the Soil Association in 1946. The Association founders' main areas of concern were erosion and depletion of soil, reduced nutritional quality of intensively farmed food, animal exploitation in intensive farms and the adverse impact of intensive farming systems on the wider environment.

Thirty years of basic research and a growing membership led to a clearer understanding of how people can efficiently combine old and new traditions in farming practices. The first Soil Association standards were drawn up in 1967, stating that any organic enterprise requires the creation and sustenance of a living soil: 'The use of, or abstinence from, any particular practice should be judged by its effect on the well-being of the micro-organic life of the soil, on which the health of the consumer ultimately depends.' These principles remain in place today.

Today, the Soil Association's certification system audits and tracks products from field to packing, covering over 80 per cent of all organic products sold in the UK. For more on the Soil Association, check out the website at www. soilassociation.org.

Conserving water

Fresh, clean water is a scarce and limited resource. Only 1 per cent of all the water on Earth is freshwater; the rest is saltwater in the oceans and ice in polar regions. The water cycle is a *closed system*, which means that the amount of water in the world remains the same and changes only its form, from fog to rain to rivers to groundwater.

Around a third of the water that homeowners consume in summer is used to water lawns and gardens. And when water is applied improperly, much of it simply runs off into sewers and storm drains, carrying chemicals, motor oil and rubber residues from driveways, and anything else in its path.

Of course, organic gardeners need to water their gardens, but they take steps to minimise use, waste and contamination. Collecting rainwater to use on plants is top of the list; as well as water butts, you can now buy a range of rainwater harvesting and storage systems. Grouping plants according to water needs, using drip irrigation and soaker hoses, applying mulch, reducing the amount of a water-hungry lawn and watering only when necessary are just a few ways to conserve water.

Some people even take the whole garden approach by building *rain gardens* – specially landscaped areas designed to collect rainwater and allow it to soak into the ground or be stored for re-use, instead of allowing it to run off.

Conservation of this precious resource just makes sense, and conserving water is especially critical with the increasingly extreme weather patterns that are now becoming the norm.

Predicting the future for organic gardening

Over the last couple of decades, organic gardening has moved from being seen as the province of cranks and crackpots to a mainstream method of gardening that is becoming a commonsense approach. Many people are prompted to go organic for some or all the reasons already covered in this chapter: climate change, sustainability, the threat to biodiversity and the issue of food safety. The credit crunch is playing its part too. While sales of organic products dropped by nearly 6 per cent in 2010, interest in 'growing your own' and levels of sales of edible seeds continues to increase.

Even traditional gardeners are likely to be going 'greener' than ever now because many garden chemicals are simply disappearing from the shelves. Tougher legislation means that licensing home gardening products is simply not economical for chemical manufacturers, so gardeners are going organic by default. The horticultural industry has no option but to come up with alternatives, particularly pest- and disease-resistant varieties and new forms of biological control. The future really does look very organic indeed.

Pioneers of organic growing

Advocates of natural farming methods eschew the 'chemical' way of doing things, believing that that it disrupts the natural ecological order, creating an escalating cycle of dependency on stronger and newer chemicals. The following are a few pioneers of organic agriculture and the systems they created in response to chemical farming:

- **Biodynamic agriculture, Rudolf Steiner:** Steiner, an Austrian philosopher, studied the relationships between plants and their environment to develop a holistic growing system called *biodynamic agriculture*, which made use of plants' rates of growth, favoured environments and relationships with other plants. He found, for example, that some plants grow better when planted next to certain other plant species. Biodynamic agriculture is still widely practised throughout the world. You can find out more about biodynamics from the Biodynamic Association (www.bio dynamic.org.uk).

- **Biointensive mini-farming, John Jeavons:** In the 1970s, Jeavons combined modern methods (including biodynamics) with sustainable agricultural practices from ancient cultures to create a new organic method called *biointensive mini-farming*. He wanted to find the smallest area needed to produce all his own food, clothing, income and building materials. Jeavons's techniques allow anyone, anywhere, to produce all the vegetables one person needs for a year with approximately 9 square metres (100 square feet) and a four- to six-month growing season. Discover more about biointensive techniques from Ecology Action (www.growbiointensive.org).

- **Permaculture, Bill Mollison and David Holmgren:** Mollison, an Australian ecolo-gist, and his student, David Holmgren, founded permaculture in the 1970s, based on the principles of living lightly on the planet, using sustainable alternatives and working the land or gardening in harmony with nature. The name is derived from *permanent agriculture* and *permanent culture*. In a permaculture system, the gardener designs the garden as a closed system. Collected rainwater irrigates the crops; plant and animal waste returns to the soil; plants and animals benefit one another by serving multiple purposes. Check out Mollison's book *Introduction to Permaculture* (Tagari Publications, 1997) and the Permaculture Institute website (www.permaculture.org.uk).

- **Forest gardening, Robert Hart:** Observing the food-growing practices of indigenous peoples in and near forests worldwide, Hart noted that traditional forest gardeners obtained their food from many layers of the forest and surrounding areas. Similar in many ways to permaculture, forest gardening creates an ecosystem that benefits plants and animals as well as humans. Find out more from Hart's book *Forest Gardening* (Chelsea Green Publishing, 1996). Inspired by Hart's work, UK Forest Gardening specialist Martin Crawford has spent 15 years creating a 0.8-hectare (2-acre) forest garden in Devon, and is the author of *Creating a Forest Garden* (Green Books, 2010).

- **Garden Organic/Henry Doubleday Research Association, Lawrence Hills:** The UK's largest organic gardening charity, based at Ryton-on-Dunsmere near Coventry, began due to the inspiration and work of organic enthusiast Lawrence Hills. A keen organic gardener and journalist, he came across the work of 19th-century

(continued)

(continued)

smallholder Henry Doubleday, who was so fascinated by the comfrey plant that he devoted his life to popularising it. Hills continued this work, eventually setting up a charity to research and promote comfrey, and improve organic growing. Alan and Jackie Gear joined the organisation in 1974: the charity grew and moved to its current base at Ryton in the mid-1980s. The extensive, beautiful and productive gardens demonstrate organic growing methods to many thousands of visitors each year. Garden Organic is involved in many research projects in the UK and overseas and holds the Heritage Seed Library that protects 800 rare vegetable varieties. The charity celebrated its 50th anniversary in 2008 (www.garden organic.org.uk).

By growing organically, you can join an international community of gardeners and farmers who are committed to protecting the Earth and growing wholesome, healthy food.

Chapter 3

Understanding and Planning Your Site

In This Chapter

▶ Making the most of your garden site

▶ Drawing up a useful garden plan

*W*orking with nature, not against it, is fundamental to organic gardening. As we describe in this chapter, the key to doing so successfully is carrying out a thorough assessment of your garden, and placing plants where they grow best or produce good crops. Well-placed plants can shelter your house; feed and provide refuge for wildlife; and give you fruits, vegetables, herbs and flowers.

This chapter's focus on putting plants in the right places and starting them off on the right foot may just make it the most important one in the book.

Knowing Your Garden's Conditions

Healthy plants suffer from fewer pest and disease problems than struggling plants, and also tolerate drought, heavy rainfall and other adverse situations more successfully. Therefore, putting plants in the right places to encourage their natural resilience is common sense. The natural rhythm of the seasons, including low winter temperatures and summer highs, sets the most obvious limits within which you garden. Other, subtler factors – including moisture, nutrients, soil and sun – also influence how and where plants grow best.

Understanding soil assessment

Getting up close and personal with your soil is the basis of successful organic gardening, and we provide lots of information in Chapters 4 and 5. Although all soils can be 'improved' to a certain extent, the best approach is always to assess your soil at the start, and choose plants that thrive there. For example, if your soil is stony or sandy, concentrate on drought-tolerant plants that have naturally adapted to cope with these conditions. If you plant drought-lovers on heavy, soggy clay, they're likely to struggle at best, or rot and die at worst.

If you find yourself having to deal regularly with heavy soil and too much moisture, which results in plant disease, you've a couple of options. As well as choosing plants that enjoy plenty of water, you can install buried drains to carry away excess surface water. You can also build raised beds. The soil in a raised garden drains more quickly than the surrounding soil, especially if you add plenty of organic material. Find out more about raised beds in Chapter 9.

Considering your region's climate

The predominating weather conditions of an area, measured over a long period of time, determine a region's *climate*. Factors affecting climate include seasonal temperatures; humidity; timing, amount and type of rain; length of growing season; and wind patterns. Closeness to hills and large bodies of water, distance above sea level and *prevailing wind* (the direction from which the wind usually blows) also influence climate. You need to match a plant to a site both on a large scale, in terms of the general climate, and on a small scale by looking at your garden's microclimates (see the next section).

Don't use geographic proximity alone to evaluate climate. Two places near each other geographically can have very different climates, for example if one is high on a hillside and the other is on the valley floor. Also, widely separated regions can have similar climates.

Thinking about your microclimates

Within larger climates, smaller pockets exist that differ somewhat from the prevailing weather around them. These *microclimates* occur wherever a building, body of water, dense shrubs or hillside modifies the larger climate.

Microclimates can be small, such as the sunny side of your house or the shady side under a tree, or as large as a village. Common microclimates around your property may include the following:

- **North side of house:** Cool and shady year-round
- **South side of house:** Hot and sunny all day; often dry
- **East side of house:** Warm morning sun and cool afternoon shade
- **West side of house:** Morning shade and hot afternoon sun

✔ **Top of hill:** Exposed to wind and sun; soil dries quickly

✔ **Bottom of hill:** Collects cold air and may be poorly drained due to rain that runs down the slope

No doubt you can find other examples on your site as you closely observe the patterns of sun, water, wind and temperature throughout the year.

Plan your garden (a subject we cover in the later section 'Getting Started on Your Garden Design') to take advantage of microclimates. Use wind-sheltered spots that hold the warmth, such as a sunny south-facing wall, to protect tender plants from drying winter winds in cold climates. Avoid putting frost-tender plants at the bottoms of hills, where pockets of cold air form.

Choosing the right plant for the right place: sun and shade

When you work out your garden plans, find out where the sun shines and shadows fall at different times of the year. In the summer, the sun rises higher in the sky, for example, and casts shadows differently than in the winter, when it rises lower in the sky.

Where you live also affects the sun's intensity. Gardeners in the south of the UK enjoy stronger sunlight than gardeners who live in the north. Garden books use terms such as *full sun* or *part shade* to describe where plants grow best, but full sun in Scotland isn't the same as full sun in Bournemouth. Plants that grow happily in the sun all day long in Scotland, for example, may prefer a little midday shade in the sunnier south.

Figuring out just what kind of sun and shade you have can be confusing. Plant descriptions in this book and many others use the following terms:

✔ **Deep or dense shade** occurs on the north sides of buildings and walls, and under trees with low branches and dense leaves. No direct sunlight reaches the ground.

✔ **Partial shade** occurs in places that receive direct morning or afternoon sun, but none at the midday hours, from about 10 a.m. to 2 p.m.

✔ **Light or dappled shade** falls under trees with high branches or sparse foliage.

✔ **Full sun** means direct sunlight for at least six hours each day, including some of or all the midday hours.

Use plants to create microclimates. Combine sun-loving and shade-loving plants so that one protects the other. In your vegetable garden, for example, you can plant leaf-lettuce seeds between the broccoli plants because the broccoli shades the sprouting lettuce, which prefers cooler, shadier soil.

Finding out about your local water patterns

Your climate and microclimate determines how much water falls on your garden, and the slope of the land and type of soil determine whether that water puddles or runs away. But you can also influence what happens to water after it falls from the sky or flows out of the tap by designing your garden to take advantage of natural conditions. Rather than sending rainwater down the drain, for example, you can direct it through a gully or 'stream' to keep a pond topped up or to gather in a low-lying spot where you can grow moisture-loving plants (known as a 'bog garden').

You can also make the most of rainwater by collecting and storing it to use during dry periods. Water butts linked to gutter downpipes are easy to install, but you can go bigger – and less obtrusive – with tanks installed under a patio, deck or driveway, for example.

Getting Started on Your Garden Design

You can find hundreds of garden design books and websites, but often the best place to start planning a design is in your own neighbourhood. What gardens take your fancy as you drive by? Visit public gardens in your area; they're ideal for getting ideas about plants that thrive in your local climate. Larger gardens open to the public are well advertised, though often the best sources of inspiration are smaller gardens that only open occasionally, usually for charity. The best source of information is the National Gardens Scheme (which publishes an annual guide affectionately known as the 'yellow book').

Keep a small camera with you as you travel around, and snapshots of plant groupings and colour combinations that you want to replicate in your garden. Tear pages out of magazines and catalogues, and start a scrapbook.

As you plan your organic garden, keep the following tips in mind:

- ✔ **Plan for convenience.** Common-sense design features can make garden tasks easier. Make sure that fence openings are wide enough for a lawn mower or wheelbarrow, for example. If you're creating a new garden, install soaker hoses or drip irrigation at planting time, the easiest time to tackle that task.

- ✔ **Plan for biodiversity.** Choosing plants in a range of types, sizes, colours and shapes makes for a more interesting garden, encourages wildlife and beneficial organisms and minimises pest problems.

- ✔ **Plan for low maintenance.** You can minimise gardening chores with careful planning. Choose hardy, reliable, easy-care plants and ensure that the mature sizes of trees and shrubs are appropriate to the site so that you have to do little pruning. Use easy-care ground covers in place of high-maintenance lawns. (We discuss lawns in Chapter 16.)

✔ **Plan for sustainability.** Think long term when designing your gardens; consider how plantings will look in five or ten years. (Visit botanical gardens to view mature specimens.) Choose well-adapted, long-lived plants that require minimal supplemental water and fertiliser. Composting garden and kitchen waste helps to minimise the need for outside sources of fertiliser.

✔ **Plan for abundance.** Think about how your landscape is going to look in all four seasons, and include plants that provide interest year-round. Consider all the things that gardens can provide: add a cutting garden for indoor bouquets; sow extra herbs for drying; plant gourds and berry-filled shrubs for crafts. If you install a cold frame, greenhouse or poly-tunnel, you can have fresh produce all year round. (Check out Chapter 9 for all about growing undercover.)

✔ **Plan for energy conservation.** Strategically placed trees and hedges create areas of cooling shade for summer and reduce the effects of cold winds in winter. (For details, see the 'Designing for energy conservation' section, later in this chapter.)

Before you start planning and planting, check local regulations and your property deeds for restrictions on aspects such as tree and hedge planting in open-plan front gardens. If you rent, check your tenancy agreement.

Using basic design principles

Mixing and matching plants is a creative and exciting aspect of gardening. Do this job in winter, when seed and plant catalogues land on the doormat and the weather is too bad to go out and garden. Whether you're designing a whole new garden, a new border or just adding or rearranging existing plants, keep the following design elements in mind:

✔ **Colour:** Gardeners usually make flower colour their top priority when deciding which plants to purchase, but the colour of foliage and bark can also add to a garden's overall palette. Consider that many plants bloom for only a few weeks, but you see their foliage and bark at other times of year. Sometimes, the most beautiful gardens have the simplest colour schemes. A garden filled with white flowers and silvery-grey foliage, for example, shimmers in the moonlight.

✔ **Cultural considerations:** An essential attribute for organic garden plants is disease-resistant varieties, especially in species that are vulnerable to particular problems. Many roses, for example, are prone to mildew and blackspot, but lots of newer varieties resist these fungal diseases. Look for 'disease-resistant' in the descriptions of all plants, but especially for roses, fruit trees, vegetables and berries.

✔ **Growth habit:** Growth habit can make a particular plant more or less suitable for a garden. Climbers, for example, take up little room in the garden and give an extra vertical dimension to the space. Trailing plants, such as creeping thyme and certain cotoneasters, carpet the ground.

✓ **Scale:** Look for trees and shrubs that complement the scale of your garden and its surroundings. A huge tree can overwhelm a small garden; a small shrub can look lost in an expanse of lawn. Keep scale in mind in individual gardens, too. You may want to arrange plants by height, putting short ones in the front and taller ones in the back. For gardens that are viewed from all sides, put the tallest plants in the middle.

✓ **Season-extending attributes:** Some plants offer good-looking seed pods, buds, bark or architectural shapes. Poppy seed heads, ornamental grass seed heads, curly willow stems, red dogwood shoots and silver birch bark take centre stage when foliage and flowers have faded. Plants with an extra-long blooming period or that have two seasons of interest (such as crab apples with spring blossom, colourful and long-lasting edible autumn fruit and wildlife appeal) offer good garden value.

✓ **Season of bloom:** A big mistake that many gardeners make is buying only what they see blooming in the garden centre in the spring. Their gardens look lovely in spring and early summer but lack interest during the rest of the year. Make a list: start by choosing plants that bloom in winter and then work backwards through autumn and summer to spring.

Landscaping and arranging

Landscaping can be more than making your garden beautiful. Many plants can serve double duty: for example, a fruit tree planted so that it shades your patio helps keep you cool while you savour its delicious fruits. When planning your garden, consider all the ways in which plants can enhance your life.

Designing for energy conservation

Common-sense landscaping can increase the comfort of a home, reduce heating costs and make a home cooler and more comfortable in summer. Here are a few energy-conservation tips:

✓ Plant deciduous trees and large shrubs on the southeast and southwest corners of a seating area – but not so close to your house that the roots interfere with foundations. They shade your house from summer sun but shed their leaves in the autumn so that the warmth of the winter sun can reach your home.

✓ Plant an evergreen or dense deciduous hedge on the north or northeast side of your house that faces the prevailing winter winds, in order to provide a buffer from cold gusts.

✓ Clothe house walls with climbers and wall shrubs to help winter insulation and summer cooling. Grow climbers and vines to shade sunrooms and porches, too, but choose deciduous ones that shed their leaves in winter.

Employing an integrated landscape

As an organic gardener, you're uniquely positioned to create integrated landscapes in which edibles and ornamentals share garden space. Why? Because you don't have to worry about pesticides sprayed on lawns and flowers contaminating your food plants.

Try using fruit trees as structure plants: they're attractive and low maintenance. Many vegetable plants are good-looking too: Rainbow Swiss chard, which has striking orange, pink, red and yellow stems, is a natural in flower beds and offers a nutritious harvest.

Knowing the rules of traditional garden design is all well and good, but you also need to know that you can break them!

Putting pencil to paper

Good garden designers observe and discover how the different parts of the landscape – home, gardens and other functional areas of a site – relate to one another, and they use those relationships to direct their designs. Think through each of the following items as completely as you can, using plenty of paper to take notes and scribble ideas:

- ✔ **What you want from your garden:** Your list may include a vegetable garden, herb patch, wildlife-attracting pond, flowers for bouquets, fruit trees or shrubs, compost bin, tool storage and recycling bins.

- ✔ **How the different items in your list relate to one another:** Consider the distance between places that depend on each other. Should you place the vegetable garden at the far corner of the garden or close to the kitchen and tool-storage area in the garage?

- ✔ **How often you visit each area:** Places that you visit daily, such as the rubbish, compost and vegetable garden, need to be located closest to the house. An area that needs infrequent maintenance, such as an orchard, can be situated farther away.

- ✔ **How many functions each element can fulfil:** Trees can provide shade, fruit, ornament and windbreak, among other things. Vegetable gardens can be ornamental and also provide food. Flowers attract bees, butterflies and other insects, and also colour the garden, furnish garnish for salads and bouquets for the table, and provide habitat for beneficial insects.

When you've brainstormed your list, you're ready to draw up a plan that makes sense on the ground.

Making a map

One of the most important ways that organic gardeners encourage healthy, pest- and disease-resistant plants is to plant them where they can naturally thrive. But you have to know something about your site before you can match the plants to their right places. Grab a friend, the longest tape measure you own (or can borrow) and a pencil and paper, and then head outside. This section leads you through a quick-and-dirty mapmaking exercise.

Step 1: Sketch the major features of your property

Start by drawing the outlines of major features of your property, including buildings and property lines. Use your tape measure and do your best to draw to scale, with everything in the correct proportion to everything else, but don't agonise: neatness doesn't count.

For long distances, measure the length of your stride, and multiply it by the number of strides you take to get from one end to the other.

Sketch the locations of important rooms, windows and exterior doors of your house. Remember to note permanent features, such as the driveway, paths, deck and shed. Note the location of water taps and electrical outlets. Make an arrow on your map to indicate the direction of north; you need that information as you plan your garden.

Step 2: Note natural features

Add the following natural features (shown in order of priority) to your map:

- ✔ **Sun and shade:** Label the sunny and shady spots around your garden so that you can take advantage of them. If you've lived in the house long enough, note the sun and shade at different times of the day and year.

- ✔ **Soil, slope and water:** Draw arrows on your map that point down slopes. Circle areas where water pools or runs after a rainstorm. Note places where your soil stays muddy or drains quickly.

- ✔ **Wind:** Note the direction and strength of the prevailing winds across your site at different times of the year.

- ✔ **Existing plants and natural features:** Use circles to draw existing trees and shrubs that you intend to keep. Record the width of the plant canopy by measuring from one edge of the *drip line* (where rain drips from the foliage to the ground) to the other. Note the locations and sizes of gardens, large rocks and other features you want to preserve.

- ✔ **Views:** If you plan to do landscaping, note the nice and not-so-nice views. Remember to check the views from your windows, too.

Your map should look something like the one shown in Figure 3-1 when you're done.

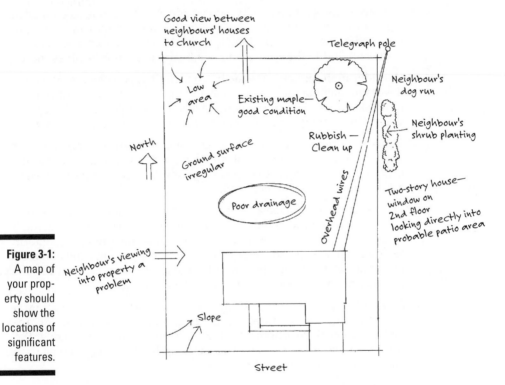

Figure 3-1: A map of your property should show the locations of significant features.

Putting it all together

Here's where your dreams meet reality. The idea is to take your list of projects and match them to the most appropriate places in your garden. To do so, lay tracing paper over your map (from the preceding section) or make photocopies so that you can doodle ideas without messing up the original. As you try out different combinations and placements, keep these tips in mind:

✔ **Prioritise your wish list.** Put your desires into a time frame or order of steps. You may have to build a rabbit-excluding fence before planting an orchard or vegetable garden, for example, and preparing soil comes before planting.

✔ **Think long term.** Some tasks take a day to accomplish; other projects stretch out for longer. Break long projects into shorter, prioritised steps.

✔ **Concentrate on the areas closest to the house first.** Put your most intensive gardens and use areas near the house, and plan to install them before you tackle the outlying areas.

✔ **Conserve energy.** Use gravity, sun, shade, wind and rain to your advantage. For example, moving a container of water or a barrow of compost downhill is easier than pushing it uphill. Note the places where soil warms up first in the spring, and plant early-season vegetables there.

✔ **Consider maintenance.** Decide how much time you can realistically devote to maintaining your garden and plants, and plan accordingly. Don't sketch in a 40-square-metre (420-square-foot) vegetable garden if you've only enough time to weed and harvest an area half that size.

✔ **Think multipurpose.** Make plants and built-in features serve more than one function. Use a fence or plants to support an ornamental or food-producing vine, screen an unpleasant view, prevent trespassing, enclose a private space and deflect wind.

✔ **Play matchmaker.** Make a list of plants that you want to grow. Next to each one, write down whether it needs full sun, part shade or shade (terms we describe in the earlier section 'Choosing the right plant for the right place: sun and shade). In another column, note soil and moisture preferences. Group plants with similar needs, and look at the places on your map where each group would be happiest.

✔ **Avoid obstacles.** Put trees, shrubs and perennial plants where they've room to mature. If you have overhead power lines, avoid planting trees under or near them. Choose climbers and shrubs that don't cover the windows of your house, and plant them so that they aren't going to rub on the guttering in five or ten years.

Now, with your plan in hand, you're free to dig in . . . literally!

Part II
Getting Stuck into Soil, Compost and Fertilisers

'He ain't singin' the blues – he's singin' the greens!'

In this part . . .

We hope that you're ready to get down and dirty, because healthy soil is at the root (groan!) of organic gardening and producing healthy plants. Chapter 4 describes just why you shouldn't treat soil like dirt (that's enough bad puns!). Healthy soil contains minerals, organic matter and the proper amount of air and water, and is also teeming with micro-organisms that help the soil support your garden plants.

Chapter 5 gives you details on how to evaluate your soil and good ideas about how to improve it. We get up close and personal with manure here, too (whew!). Flip to Chapter 6 to find out how to become an expert 'rotter' and make your own compost to improve your soil – and do the environment a good turn as well. Chapter 7 provides all the gen on organic fertilisers that come from plants, animals and minerals, and explains how to use them.

Chapter 4

Digging Beneath the Surface: Soils

In This Chapter

▶ Getting to know soil components
▶ Unearthing the importance of topsoil
▶ Understanding soil fertility

*S*oil may not seem like the most exciting part of gardening (perhaps the topic is too down-to-earth, if you'll forgive the pun), but soil is the foundation upon which you build everything else. Trying to create a garden without working the soil first is like building a house without any foundations, or without doing the wiring. Underground may be out of sight, but never out of mind.

Soil teems with all kinds of organisms – visible and unseen – which feed on and decompose organic matter and release nutrients for plants to use. Beneficial micro-organisms in the soil prey on harmful ones and protect plant roots from diseases and pests. Earthworms and other soil creatures tunnel through the soil, opening spaces for oxygen, water, nutrients and roots to move freely.

Organic gardeners and farmers encourage this naturally beneficial soil life and improve their soil by using the following methods:

✔ Adding organic matter, such as compost

✔ Employing practices that prevent damage to the soil habitat

✔ Avoiding synthetic pesticides and fertilisers that destroy subterranean life

To join the ranks of organic gardeners, you need to be up to speed on all things 'soily' – its composition, the vital role of topsoil and what it needs to produce healthy plants – which is where this chapter comes in.

Excavating Soil Components

The first step towards improving your garden's soil is to understand its composition. If you dig down deeply into the soil, you can see layers – known as the *soil profile,* and shown in Figure 4-1. From the bottom up, the layers are as follows:

- **Underlying rock:** About half the volume of most soils consists of small mineral pieces that originate in the underlying rock (sometimes referred to as *parent rock*). The composition of the rock partly determines the type of soil you have; for example, sandstone rock yields sandy soil. Impervious rock can lead to poorly drained soils, whereas porous or highly fractured rock usually contributes to good drainage.

- **Subsoil soil:** This layer is mineral-rich and largely undisturbed by cultivation and weather. Subsoils contain little organic matter and few micro-organisms. Sometimes, a hard, impervious layer called a *pan* forms in the subsoil; it prevents water from draining properly and needs to be broken up, or else all your plants may struggle to grow and even die.

- **Topsoil:** The top layer is the familiar one, which cultivation, gardeners and weather can alter. Most plant roots and soil micro-organisms live in this surface soil, and in addition to small mineral pieces, topsoil contains organic matter, air and water. The proper balance of these components is vital to the health of plants, which is why gardeners concentrate their efforts on topsoil.

If you do any large-scale earthmoving in your garden (perhaps for building work or level changing) always keep the excavated poor-quality subsoil separate from the good quality topsoil for future use.

Tradition says that a nation endures only as long as its topsoil. Without it little plant life is possible, and without plants, no animals survive. During the Dust Bowl of the 1930s in the USA, hundreds of millions of tonnes of topsoil blew off the land in the southern Great Plains, in part because farm fields had replaced the deep-rooted native prairie grasses.

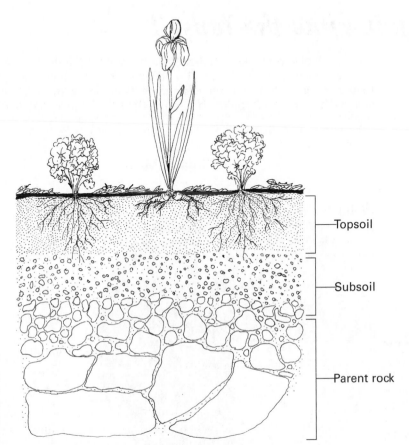

Figure 4-1:
Soil profile
showing the
various soil
layers.

Topsoil

Subsoil

Parent rock

Nature needs at least 500 years to create just a few centimetres of topsoil from subsoil.

Preserving and improving soil are among the tenets of organic gardening. You can't change the soil type, but you can improve its quality enormously. Most improvement efforts focus on the topsoil, but if this layer is thin, you may need to extend your efforts to the subsoil layer. Find out more about building healthy soil in Chapter 5.

Digging into the Topsoil

The health of garden plants depends on the soil having the proper balance of mineral pieces, organic matter, air and water (check out Figure 4-2). The key to improving the topsoil is understanding its nature; knowing what type of soil you have enables you to choose the right techniques to enhance its good qualities.

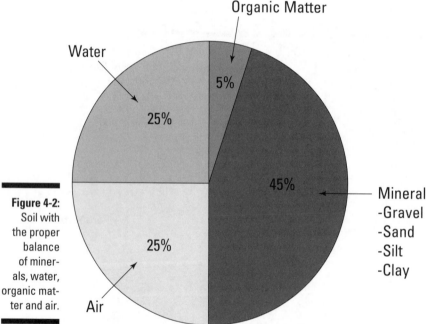

Figure 4-2: Soil with the proper balance of minerals, water, organic matter and air.

Organic Matter

Water

5%

25%

45%

Mineral
-Gravel
-Sand
-Silt
-Clay

25%

Air

Turning over the composition of soil

Clay, silt and sand particles, in different sizes and shapes, make up about half the volume of most soils, as shown in Figure 4-3. The relative amounts of these particles determine your *soil texture*:

- ✔ **Clay particles:** These smallest soil particles are microscopic and flat.
- ✔ **Silt particles:** These middle-sized particles are more angular and larger than clay, but still microscopic.
- ✔ **Sand particles:** These particles are the largest of the three types and can be angular or rounded.

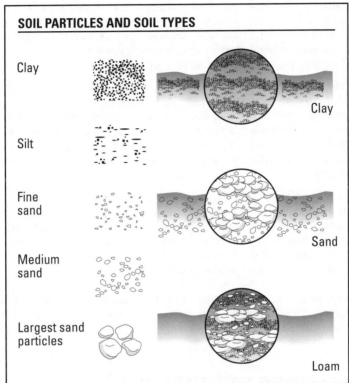

SOIL PARTICLES AND SOIL TYPES

Clay

Silt

Fine sand

Medium sand

Largest sand particles

Clay

Sand

Loam

Figure 4-3: Soil particles differ in size and shape.

The spaces between soil particles are called *pores*. Nutrient-rich water moves through these pores, as does the air on which roots and micro-organisms depend. When the soil contains little pore space, water and air can't move through the soil. But when it has too much pore space, water passes through too quickly.

For most plants, the ideal mixture is approximately 40 per cent sand, 40 per cent silt and 20 per cent clay. Soil with this makeup is called *loam*. Loamy soil is ideal because it provides a great balance of water-holding capacity, drainage and fertility. Alas, not all soils are loamy. Those composed of predominantly one particle type can pose challenges for gardeners:

✔ **Clay soils** are naturally fertile, but they can be difficult to work. Clay soil's individual particles are so small and flat that they pack tightly, leaving little room for water and air. On a practical level, this structure means that clay soil drains poorly, stays wet longer than other soils, contains little oxygen and dries as hard as concrete. A wet spring may mean a delay in planting; a dry summer causes the soil to crack and harden. Clay is often called a 'claggy' soil – which means that it sticks to your boots and tools when wet. Although this condition sounds like bad news, on the plus side clay's ability to retain moisture and nutrients makes for a highly fertile soil. When clay soil is improved, you can grow fantastic plants and wonderful crops in it.

✔ **Silt soils** have moderate fertility, medium-size particles and pore spaces that hold some water and air. Like clay soils, the particles can pack tightly, especially when wet, but they can get powdery or dusty when dry. Silt particles are easily carried away by rain that falls and runs off the ground (known as *runoff*) and are small enough to be blown away by wind. As with clay, silt can be hard to work initially, but is extremely fertile.

✔ **Sandy soils** contain few nutrients. Sand particles are large; water drains quickly from the pore spaces and any nutrients that are present tend to leach (wash) out. Sandy soils don't pack tightly like clay and silt soils, which makes them lovely and easy to work with – even soon after rain – but means that they need lots of bulky organic matter to improve their water and nutrient-holding quality and grow healthy plants.

Unfortunately, except by importing in huge amounts of soil, you've no way to change your soil's texture. You can take advantage of its natural assets, however, and compensate for its challenges by working on the soil structure.

Uncovering soil structure

The way in which soil particles align themselves or clump together is called *soil structure*. The best garden soils have a loose, crumb-like structure that water, air and plant roots can penetrate easily. *Unstructured soils*, such as beach sand, don't clump together, which allows water to flow through them too rapidly for most plant growth. *Poorly structured soils*, such as heavy clay, clump together so tightly that little water and air can pass through.

Two of the most important goals for organic gardeners are improving the soil structure and then maintaining that good structure. A better soil structure enhances the water-holding capacity in sandy soils and the drainage in clay soils.

Many things affect soil structure – for good and ill – but the most important ones from a gardener's point of view include the following:

- **Organic matter:** Gardeners go all shiny-eyed over bulky organic matter because such matter is a source of *humus* (decayed plant and animal matter). Soils that lack enough humus may clump together too tightly or not at all. Adding organic matter improves the structure of sandy, silty and clay soils. (Head to Chapter 5 to find out how to add organic matter to your soil.)

- **Rotovating and cultivating:** Churning the soil mechanically is a good way to break up compact soils and mix in organic matter. Of course, you can achieve the same result by digging by hand, but that's a lot harder!

Although rotovating can initially add more air to the soil, be careful not to overdo it. Too much mechanical cultivation pulverises the soil structure, damages soil life and promotes too-rapid breakdown and loss of organic matter. Be aware that on clay soils, the blades can smear the soil to form a solid layer or pan. We discuss rotovating in more detail in Chapter 5.

- **Soil organisms:** As they tunnel through the soil, earthworms, beetles and other organisms open spaces between soil particles, allowing air, water and roots to pass through easily. Earthworm *castings* (excrement) are also rich in nutrients.

Providing food and habitat in the form of organic matter encourages beneficial soil organisms.

- **Working with wet soil:** Quite simply, don't! Avoid walking on, digging in or rotovating saturated soil. Wet soil, especially clay, packs together tightly when compressed, forming clods that can bake to pottery-like hardness in hot sun. Allow garden soil to drain to the dampness of a wrung-out sponge before working in it – basically, if it sticks to your boots, keep off. Find out about building raised beds to improve drainage and minimise soil compaction in Chapter 10.

Improving and maintaining soil structure is an ongoing process no matter what type of soil you have. Adding organic matter to your soil every year is an important step, particularly for sandy or clay soils. Organic matter acts like a glue to help sandy soils stick together into aggregates that retain the proper amount of moisture. It also binds with the tiny particles to create larger ones with more pore space, which helps clay soils drain more effectively. Even healthy, loamy soils benefit from annual additions of organic matter.

Organic matter is vital to soil structure, but it also contributes to soil fertility. Again, Chapter 5 contains lots more useful information on organic matter.

Creating Fertile Ground

Fertility is the capacity of a soil to supply the mineral nutrients that plants need. Several factors influence soil fertility, as we reveal in this section.

A central element of organic practice is that if you feed the soil, the soil feeds the plants.

As an organic gardener, feeding plants isn't just a matter of you pouring on the fertiliser. Instead, you want to build the natural fertility of your soil by adding organic matter (as mentioned in the preceding section), preserving and improving the soil structure, and modifying the soil pH (we describe pH in the later section 'Measuring soil acidity or alkalinity: pH' and provide more details in Chapter 5).

Understanding what plants need

Overall, plants need 16 elements, or nutrients, for proper growth. Different soils contain differing levels of these needed elements. When enough of each element is present, plants grow optimally. If even one element is in short supply, plants can't grow as well. Think of the weakest-link theory, which says that a chain is only as strong as its weakest link. Your soil is only as fertile as its most deficient nutrient.

Nutrients for photosynthesis

The nutrients that plants need in the largest quantities are carbon, hydrogen and oxygen, which plants use for photosynthesis. During the process of *photosynthesis*, green plants take these nutrients from the air and from the water in the soil to produce sugars – the 'food' that fuels plant growth.

Mineral nutrients

Plants generally get mineral nutrients from the soil or from applied fertilisers. Mineral nutrients include nitrogen, phosphorus and potassium, as well as numerous others. When gardeners talk about feeding plants, they mean providing them with extra mineral nutrients.

Nitrogen, phosphorus and potassium are abbreviated to their chemical symbols 'N', 'P' and 'K' on fertiliser bags.

The term *feeding* is a bit of a misnomer because plants produce their own food – carbohydrates – during photosynthesis. The mineral nutrients that plants need are split into two categories:

TECHNICAL STUFF

Going nuts for soil elements

Plants may take up trace elements that they don't need – but that humans do. This is partly why fruit and vegetables are an essential part of a healthy diet – our recommended '5 a day'. The trace elements iodine, fluorine, selenium, cobalt, arsenic, lithium, chromium, silicon, tin and vanadium, for example, are considered to be essential for animals and humans but not for plants.

For example, Brazil nuts usually contain large amounts of selenium, which has no known nutritional value to plants but which is an important antioxidant for human health. The level of selenium in plants varies due to the selenium content in the soil.

✔ **Macronutrients:** These mineral nutrients are the ones needed in the largest quantities, and consist of nitrogen, phosphorus, potassium, calcium, magnesium and sulphur.

✔ **Micronutrients:** These mineral nutrients are needed in smaller amounts. The eight micronutrients considered essential for plant growth are iron, manganese, boron, copper, zinc, molybdenum, chlorine and nickel, and they all occur in small quantities in most soils. These micronutrients, and other substances found in low concentrations in soils, are sometimes called *trace elements*. In the future, scientists studying plant nutrition may well discover more micronutrients among the many trace elements in soils.

Organic fertilisers are derived from natural sources, which is why most contain an abundance of trace elements including important plant micronutrients. Synthetic fertilisers, on the other hand, often contain just nitrogen, phosphorus and potassium, and so they don't replenish or enhance the other nutrients and trace elements.

TIP

Researchers still have much to discover about soil and the interplay among minerals, organic matter, soil life and plant health. With this in mind, choose fertilisers and other soil additives that supply a broad range of nutrients, because what is certain is that plant – and human – health depends on healthy soil.

For more on plant nutrients and building soil fertility, flip to Chapter 5. In addition, Chapter 6 focuses on compost and Chapter 7 on organic fertilisers.

Grasping how soil affects fertility

The kinds and relative amounts of the particles you have in your garden soil influence how much food is available for your plants. Clay and silt soils have larger surface areas and smaller pore spaces and so tend to hold more nutrients than sandy soil, which drains quickly, washing the nutrients away.

Improving soil structure – the way individual soil particles bind together – can improve fertility. Organic matter in the soil acts like a sponge, holding on to nutrients ready for plants to use. Strangely enough, it helps improve drainage on clay and silt soils, by increasing the pore space, and also improves the water-holding capacity of sandy soils. For more information on soil texture and structure, take a look at 'Digging into the Topsoil' earlier in this chapter.

Measuring soil acidity or alkalinity: pH

One vital piece of information that you need to know about your soil's structure is its *pH* value; that is, the measure of its acidity or alkalinity. You need to know this measurement because the pH level can affect how effectively your plants take up nutrients.

The pH scale runs from 1 to 14, with 7 being neutral, but you never find soils at extreme ends of the scale. Most soils are between pH 5 (acid) and pH 8 (alkaline); regions with high rainfall tend to have acidic soils, whereas the soil tends to be alkaline in dry regions. This rule isn't a hard and fast one, though, so always test your garden soil. If your soil is too acidic or too alkaline, nutrients that are present can be bound up in compounds unavailable to plants.

Although the ideal pH for most plants is between 6 and 7, certain plants need an acid soil in order to thrive (you may hear these referred to as 'acid-loving' or 'lime-hating' plants – the meaning is the same). Read Chapter 5 to find out lots more about pH, including how to determine your soil's pH and modify it, if necessary, for optimum plant growth.

Chapter 5

Building Healthy Soil

In This Chapter

▶ Understanding the type of soil you have

▶ Adjusting the pH and nutrient levels

▶ Getting in touch with organic matter

▶ Working with uncultivated soil

*O*rganic gardeners know that when you feed the soil, the soil feeds the plants. Healthy soil supports an abundance of living organisms, including bacteria, fungi and earthworms, which together create a dynamic soil ecosystem. Many garden chemicals, synthetic fertilisers and other products, however, can damage or even destroy this subterranean life, and poor gardening practices can harm the soil structure. The organic gardening techniques that we describe in this chapter help you improve and maintain a healthy soil environment. Don't treat your soil like dirt!

To discover all about soil composition, check out Chapter 4, which describes all the different types.

Knowing Your Soil

Like the above-ground ecosystem of your garden, the underground ecosystem in the soil needs nurturing. Looking after your soil is somewhat akin to building a house: the foundations are the really important out-of-sight bits that need the most work (the initial soil cultivation), and then ongoing maintenance is also required (regular additions of organic matter).

Soil improvement isn't a one-time deal but an ongoing process of promoting the beneficial organisms on which your plants depend.

In the wild, soil life is sustained and nutrients are recycled through natural processes. Organisms known as *decomposers* – such as micro-organisms and earthworms – feed on organic matter and transform the nutrients it contains into forms that plants can use. The process is a slow, steady, ongoing one: plants grow, die and decompose, and the cycle continues.

When you maintain tidy borders, cut the lawn and remove the clippings, or harvest crops from your vegetable garden, you change this natural dynamic. Every time you rake up plant debris or pick produce, you remove organic matter – and the nutrients it contains – from the garden environment.

Gardeners also tend to grow plants much closer together than in the wild, which means that they need even more TLC from us.

To keep your soil healthy, you must put back nutrients and organic matter in ways such as mulching flower beds with manure or adding compost to vegetable gardens. For this reason, making your own compost from garden 'waste' is a vitally important part of organic gardening, because it helps replicate what would happen in nature before humans interfere!

Most of the soil-building techniques discussed in this chapter centre on nurturing beneficial soil life and maintaining this natural dynamic underground ecosystem.

The first step to improving your soil is knowing what kind of soil you're working with. (To discover how to alter your soil, check out the later sections 'Adjusting Your Soil's pH' and 'Adding Organic Matter: The Soul of the Soil'.) Different soils have different strengths and weaknesses as regards supporting plant life. The proper soil-building techniques depend on your soil's fundamental characteristics, such as its water-holding capacity and pH.

Testing your soil type: Sand, silt or clay?

To discover what type of soil you have, take a small amount of damp soil in your hand, as shown in Figure 5-1, and rub a pinch of it between your thumb and index finger:

- ✔ If your soil feels gritty and doesn't hold together, your soil is mostly sand.
- ✔ If your soil feels slick and slimy, your soil is mostly clay.
- ✔ If you can form a cylinder, but the material starts to crumble as you roll it, your soil is mostly silt.

Figure 5-1:
Testing
your soil by
squeezing
a clump in
your hand.

For a more accurate measurement of the amounts of clay, silt and sand in your soil, use the jar test as follows:

1. **Collect soil from several places in your garden and mix the samples thoroughly.**

2. **Take a cupful or so of the mixture and remove stones and debris.**

3. **Place a 5-centimetre (2-inch) layer of the soil in a tall, narrow, clean, clear glass jar (such as a large mayonnaise jar), and then fill the jar about two-thirds full of water.**

4. **Seal the jar and shake it vigorously to mix the contents: set it down and start a timer.**

5. **Measure after 1 minute and mark the level of soil that has settled to the bottom of the jar: this layer is sand. Use a permanent marker pen or a sticky label.**

6. **Measure again and mark the jar in two to four hours. The difference between the two marks is the amount of silt.**

7. **Measure again after several days, and subtract the sand and silt to find the amount of clay.**

8. **Divide the height of each level by the total height of the settled soil, and multiply by 100 to find the percentage of each component.**

   For example, if the total settled soil is 15 centimetres (6 inches) high and the sand portion is 7.5 centimetres (3 inches), the sand content is 50 per cent ($7.5 \div 15 \times 100 = 50$ per cent).

Checking your soil drainage

Knowing how well your soil drains helps you determine what to plant, or whether you need to take steps to improve drainage. Sometimes, drainage conditions are obvious: for example, puddles in your lawn a day or two after heavy rain indicate poor drainage. But a layer of clay may lurk underneath a loamy or sandy soil, causing water to linger in otherwise well-drained soil (see Chapter 4 for descriptions of loamy, clay and sandy soil). So especially before you plant trees and shrubs, dig a hole to see what lies beneath the surface. Wait until the weather has been dry for a week or so, though, in order to get an accurate picture of your soil's drainage potential.

Here's how to check your soil for its drainage, known as its *percolation*:

1. **Dig several holes in different sites around the garden, approximately 30 centimetres (1 foot) wide and deep.**

2. **Fill the hole with water.**

3. **Time how long the water takes to drain.**

If the water drains out within 10 minutes or less, your soil drains too fast and probably dries too quickly. In well-drained soils, the water drains within 10 to 30 minutes. If it drains within 4 hours, the drainage is okay for most plants. If it takes more than 4 hours, the soil is poorly drained.

Use this information to choose the most appropriate plants for your soil and, if necessary, amend your gardening methods and even the layout (such as creating raised beds for your herbs and vegetables if you've very poorly drained soil).

Adding bulky organic matter, such as compost, to the soil can improve the drainage of both sandy and clay-heavy soils (see the later section 'Adding Organic Matter: The Soul of the Soil').

Measuring the soil pH

As we mention in Chapter 4, finding out the pH of your soil is highly advisable. The *soil pH* measures the alkalinity or acidity of the soil. You need to know whether your soil is acidic (below pH 7 on a scale from 0 to 14) or alkaline (above pH 7), because some nutrients are available to plants only within a specific pH range.

Most plants grow best in a pH range between 6 and 7, with 6.5 to 6.8 considered ideal. Some plants, however, such as blueberries and rhododendrons, like a highly acid soil (pH below 5), and so you may need to adjust the pH to individual plants.

You can discover your soil's pH value in one of two ways:

✔ *Home test kits* give you a basic pH reading. You can buy test kits and meters, ranging from extremely simple to elaborate, with the more sophisticated tests costing more but giving you more accurate results.

✔ *Lab tests* give you more accurate and detailed results than home kits. Sending samples to labs for these more complex tests do, of course, cost a lot more than a simple home pH test. To give an example, the service offered by the Royal Horticultural Society (RHS) provides an analysis of soil pH, texture, organic matter and the three major nutrients, and costs £30 per sample.

The soil ecosystem changes constantly, and so a soil test is just a snapshot of your soil at the time you gather the sample. Although the soil pH (and many nutrient levels as we discuss in the following section) are relatively stable, other nutrient levels (such as nitrogen) can change depending on rainfall, temperature and crop cover. Use your soil test results as guidelines, but focus on building a healthy ecosystem rather than on simply adding nutrients.

Assessing the nutrient levels

A simple rule is that if your plants are growing, flowering and fruiting well, the nutrient levels are fine. Unbalanced nutrient levels, on the other hand, can result in yellow, stunted and unproductive plants. Unhealthy plants are more prone to insects and disease attacks, translating into more work for you and less satisfaction from your garden. Clearly, you don't want that!

The soil tests we describe in the preceding section – home and lab – also provide estimations of the major nutrients in your soil. The more sophisticated lab tests also look for organic matter and micronutrients, as well as heavy metals and other industrial residues.

The tests can also show the quantities of soil nutrients that are available to plants, especially the three nutrients that plants use in the greatest amounts: nitrogen, phosphorus and potassium. Soils also contain many other nutrients, such as magnesium and calcium, which plants need in smaller amounts. If any nutrient is insufficient, plants don't grow to their maximum potential. For lots more on nutrients and fertilisers, flip to Chapter 7.

Soils on old industrial sites can contain chemicals and metals that you may want to know about before planting a vegetable garden.

Lab reports can also offer specific recommendations about which nutrients to add to your soil (and in what quantity) for your plants' optimum growth. However, unless you've a problem with your plants that has no obvious cause, you're unlikely to have to go to the trouble and expense of lab tests.

Soil test recommendations may not follow organic principles. They may suggest, for example, that you add specific synthetic fertilisers to boost certain nutrient levels. You may need to look for organic alternatives in order to provide these nutrients.

Adjusting Your Soil's pH

When you've obtained the pH information on your soil, as we describe in the earlier section 'Measuring the soil pH', you can set about altering it as appropriate.

If your soil is too acidic, you need to add lime to raise the pH. The term *lime*, or *limestone*, refers to crushed calcium carbonate (calcite or calcitic limestone) rock. Soils that test low in magnesium benefit from dolomitic limestone (calcium–magnesium carbonate). The finer the dust, the faster it dissolves and begins to raise soil pH. Also look for pelleted lime, which consists of very finely ground limestone formed into easy-to-apply pellets. Apply the lime in autumn, adding 250 grams (or 9 ounces) per square metre.

The full effect of the lime occurs in the second year, so carry out a second pH test before reapplying.

Organic gardeners prefer these types of lime because they've a slow, gentle action. They avoid slaked or hydrated lime, which acts so quickly that it can harm soil life.

If you have alkaline soil, apply sulphur to lower the pH. Usually, you can buy this substance in the form of sulphur chips, which are slow-acting and last for 2–3 years. Soil bacteria convert sulphur to sulphuric acid, which lowers your soil's pH.

When adding lime or sulphur to your soil, be sure to wear gloves and a dust mask, because the material can be very dusty and irritating if inhaled. You can spread the material by hand or use a drop-spreader made to spread grass seed on a lawn. In the garden, work the lime or sulphur into the top few centimetres of soil with a rake or fork after spreading.

Don't expect results from the addition of lime or sulphur right away. They take at least a few months to react with the soil enough to change the pH to the desired levels – another good reason to prepare your soil a season before you plan to plant.

Adding Organic Matter: The Soul of the Soil

Organic matter – which consists of dead plant and animal waste, such as grass clippings, hay, leaves, manure, mushroom compost, pine needles, straw and anything else that used to be alive – is the mantra of the organic gardener. Organic matter is the 'soul of the soil', a universal component of healthy earth that improves soil in several vital ways:

- ✔ **Feeds micro-organisms and other soil life:** Beneficial bacteria, protozoa, fungi, beneficial nematodes and other soil microbes consume organic matter (and one another) and excrete that matter in a form that plants can use for growth. Earthworms, beetles and other creatures also eat organic matter and tunnel through the soil, creating beneficial air spaces and excreting nutrients.

- ✔ **Decreases harmful disease organisms:** Beneficial microbes prey on and control harmful, plant-damaging nematodes and fungi.

- ✔ **Improves the soil structure:** Organic matter helps sandy soils stick together better and hold water and nutrients. It also helps to open spaces between small, sticky particles so that clay and silty soils drain better and contain more oxygen.

- ✔ **Increases reserve of soil nutrients:** Soil microbes store nutrients in their bodies; they release those nutrients as they die or are consumed by other microbes. The more microbes the soil contains, the more nutrients it can store.

- ✔ **Feeds plants (sometimes):** Some bulky organic matter, such as manure or garden compost, contains nutrients, whereas others just improve the structure of the soil.

Add organic matter to your plantings any time you can, whether you use mulch between vegetable garden beds, compost around perennial flowers or bark mulch around trees or shrubs.

Some of these materials need to be left to decompose to a certain extent before you add them to your garden where plants are growing (a process known as *composting*, on which we focus in the later section 'Using compost: The prince of organic matter' and in Chapter 6). If you mix un-composted, carbon-rich materials such as sawdust or straw into the soil, you get a flurry of microbial activity. As the organisms reproduce in response to the influx of food, they tie up other nutrients, especially nitrogen.

Therefore, plan to wait at least several months before planting to avoid your plants showing signs of nutrient deficiency. After the microbes do their work decomposing the carbon-rich material, they die. Then the nitrogen and other nutrients tied up in their bodies return to the soil and become available to plants again. Carbon-rich materials applied on the surface of the soil as mulch decompose slowly and don't tie up nutrients.

The mysterious case of humus

One of the end products of organic matter decomposition is *humus*, a chemically stable material that contributes to good soil fertility and structure. Humus (which, unlike the Middle-Eastern dip, hummus, *isn't* delicious to eat!) is a sticky, shapeless substance in which no identifiable organic matter (leaves, stems and so on) is present. The actual properties of humus are still a bit of a mystery to soil scientists, but they agree that humus is an important part of a healthy soil ecosystem.

Humus helps soil particles stick together to form aggregates and acts like a sponge to absorb and hold water and nutrients. People sometimes use the terms 'humus' and 'organic matter' interchangeably, or describe good soil as 'humus', but technically humus is just one component of healthy, biologically active soil.

Sometimes, even the healthiest soil can't provide all the nutrients that garden plants need, and a boost of fertiliser is called for. For information on buying and using organic fertilisers, turn to Chapter 7.

Becoming gung-ho about dung

If you need persuading to become a connoisseur of manure, think of it as processed organic matter that has already begun decomposing. Manure does wonders for soil health and plant growth. You can add the droppings of different animals (rotted down with their bedding) to your garden, giving the soil all the benefits of organic matter plus a boost of nutrients. Like a fine wine, manure is best when aged before using (and not drunk!).

Fresh manure contains concentrated nitrogen. It may be too potent for tender plants and can 'burn' roots – just as too-concentrated solutions of synthetic fertiliser can.

Let manure age for 6 months to a year before using it on plants, or compost it along with other waste to speed up the rotting process (see Chapter 6 for more on producing your own compost). Manure that's ready to use straightaway is known as *well-rotted* or *composted* manure.

Here are several common types of manure:

- ✔ **Domestic pets:** The droppings and beddings of herbivores, such as rabbits and guinea pigs, can be composted and used on the garden.

  Avoid using cat and dog faeces, which may contain parasites that are a serious danger to health.

- ✔ **Farm livestock:** Look for animal manure that has been mixed with bedding and left to rot down. Chicken manure is excellent but is very strong, and so use sparingly.

- ✔ **Horses:** Stables exist even in the heart of cities as well as in the countryside, and so this option is likely to be your best bet. Horse manure nearly always contains a high proportion of bedding, which rots down to give a wonderfully fertile and moisture-retentive soil improver. However, although horses were traditionally bedded on straw, which rots quickly, an increasing number are now bedded on shavings, which take longer to rot down. The difference is important, as you can use 'strawy' manure on your garden after six months, whereas shavings need a year to break down first.

- ✔ **Human manure:** Solid waste is safe to use only if you've a composting toilet that is designed to rot down human waste to safe-to-use compost, as the name suggests. Urine, however, is another matter, as you can find out in Chapter 6.

- ✔ **Wild animals:** If you live near a zoo, you may have access to the manure of wild animals, such as elephants and giraffes. 'Zoo poo', as people often call it, can also be bought, pre-packaged, from garden centres or by mail order.

Keep these rules in mind when using manure:

- ✔ **Select manure from the oldest heap at the farm:** Many farm manure piles contain lots of additional organic matter, such as straw or shavings from horse or chicken bedding. Manure that contains shavings is best left to rot for at least a year before using directly on your garden, because the woody material takes longer to break down.

- ✔ **Buy in bulk:** By far the cheapest way to obtain manure is to get a trailer or truck-load delivered, but this approach only works if you've a good source and a friendly farmer nearby. In the countryside, try your local Scout or Young Farmers' groups, which often do once-yearly deliveries (usually advertised as 'dung runs') to raise funds. Otherwise, you need to 'pick your own', taking your own trailer (or bags) to the source.

- ✔ **Use packaged manures:** Garden centres and nurseries sell concentrated manure that's ready to use. If you need lots of manure, however, buying it this way in bags can be costly.

- ✔ **Apply composted manure annually:** In an ideal world, add a 5–8 centimetre (2–3-inch) layer of manure to garden beds and around trees, shrubs and perennial plants once a year, in late winter or early spring. If you want to use fresh manure, add it to your garden in the autumn (or whenever you can leave that part of the garden unplanted for six months or so), and mix it into the soil so it can slowly decompose. Don't use fresh manure directly on plants!

- ✔ **Use green manures or 'grow your own':** No, not another mention of composting toilets, but growing plants specifically to add their nutrients and organic matter to the soil. To find out more, go Chapter 7.

A few people have become ill after handling fresh manure. Wear gloves and shoes when working with raw manure, and wash your hands and clothing afterward to be on the safe side. If the manure is dry and dusty, wear a dust mask.

Using compost: The prince of organic matter

The best and most refined of organic matters is *compost*, which is organic matter and/or manures that have decomposed until they resemble lovely, dark, crumbly soil.

Whether you make your own compost or buy it ready-made, you can add finished compost to the garden or around plants at any time. Most gardeners apply compost in a 5–8-centimetre (2–3-inch) layer annually around plants and on garden borders. This procedure is best done in spring or early summer before too much plant growth is present to contend with, and when plants are growing strongly and can take up the nutrients straight away.

You may wonder why gardeners don't just add the raw materials (such as garden and kitchen waste) to their gardens. Well, composting the materials first has a number of advantages:

- ✔ The final product is uniform in colour, nutrients and texture.
- ✔ The final product is odour free.
- ✔ The final product contains fewer viable weed seeds and potential disease organisms (depending on how it was composted).

Believe us, your plants are sure to appreciate you composting and treating them so well.

As gardeners have become more aware of the value of compost, more sources of it have become available. Many councils now compost green waste and sell it: you can buy compost in bulk (loose, in 'dumpy bags' delivered or to collect yourself) or bagged, depending on where you live.

Organic gardeners never throw away any waste that's potentially compostable – it just doesn't make sense to chuck it out (via a council truck or in your own vehicle) and then make another fuel-guzzling trip to buy compost for your garden. To find out that we're not talking rot but making it, head on to Chapter 6.

Buying bagged compost

Bagged compost is the easiest form to buy, especially if you've a small garden or problems with access, such as in an older terraced house.

Look for the words 'certified organic', 'Soil Association approved' or some other indication that the contents are approved for organic growing.

Obtaining compost in bulk

For larger quantities of compost, buy in bulk. The price is lower and you can check the quality of the compost. Many private companies, councils and community composting groups make and sell compost. Often, they even deliver the compost to your garden for a fee.

Use these tips to evaluate bulk compost:

- ✔ **Consider the source.** Before buying the compost, ask about the primary, organic-matter sources that were used to make the compost. Compost made from garden or municipal waste (leaves and grass clippings) is considered to be the safest and best. Other compost may contain ingredients that had contaminants, such as chemicals from agricultural crop residues and heavy metals from municipal wastes, which may affect the growth of your plants or accumulate toxins in your soil. Spent mushroom compost is good quality, but is likely to contain chemical residues unless the crop has been grown organically.

- ✔ **Look at the colour and texture.** Finished compost should look dark and have a crumbly texture without any large pieces of undecomposed organic matter, such as branches or pieces of wood.

- ✔ **Squeeze it.** If water oozes out when you squeeze a handful of the material, the compost's too wet; if it blows away easily, the compost's too dry.

- ✔ **Give it a whiff.** The smell should be earthy, without a strong ammonia or sour smell.

Cultivating Your Soil

Unless you're lucky enough to inherit a well-*cultivated* (that is, soil which has been dug, improved, raked or rotovated to a stage where it can grow crops) garden or allotment you're going to have to cultivate your soil thoroughly at least once – even if you plan to grow veg in 'no-dig' beds (flip to Chapter 10 for more on no-dig beds).

The foundation for organic gardening is to create a healthy soil, and unfortunately the starting process is hard work – although well worth the effort because you reap the rewards for many years to come. Not for nothing did ancient civilisations revere the soil as 'Mother Earth'!

If you're confronted with an overgrown nightmare of a plot, flip to the end of Chapter 21 and discover how to get to grips with uncultivated ground.

Healthy gardening tips

Get any group of gardeners together and as well as talking about plants, they're likely to be complaining about bad backs and pulled muscles. Do yourself a favour and follow these guidelines for healthy gardening:

✔ Start gently if you're not used to digging, with just quarter or half an hour's work and build up over the following days.

✔ Warm up your muscles with a bit of bending or stretching first – just like going to the gym.

✔ Use a spade and fork that are the right size for you. As well as the height of the handle (which needs to be just above your hip level) the blades come in different sizes, which obviously influences the amount of soil being lifted at one time. Handle tools before you buy to test, and always get the best you can afford – they're better to work with and last for many years.

✔ Clean the blade of your spade occasionally as you work to keep it sharp.

✔ Dig little and often, rather than doing a whole day's work at once.

✔ Soak in a hot bath at the end of a day's gardening – perfumed with a bunch of organic herbs such as lavender, of course.

Understanding why cultivating is necessary

Apart from getting you fit and saving on gym fees, turning over your soil, by hand digging or using a mechanical cultivator, achieves several aims. It

✔ Increases the amount of air spaces in the soil

✔ Breaks up large lumps or clods

✔ Enables you to improve the structure considerably by mixing in lots of bulky organic matter

✔ Allows you to remove weeds, stones and other debris

If you've moved into a new house, chances are that you've plenty of builders' leftovers, such as cement bags and beer cans, so it goes without saying that you need to clear any such debris first. Although hand-digging gives the best results (as we describe in the later section 'Getting help: Mechanical cultivators'), if you've a large area to cultivate, go easy on your back and use a rotovator. After all, no point saving money on the gym only to spend it at the osteopath!

Digging: How deep to go

In most cases you can opt for the easier option of *single digging*: turning over the top layer of soil to one spades' depth, mixing in organic matter as you go. But if your soil has been compacted by builders' vehicles, is in very poor condition or you want to win all the trophies at the annual village produce show, consider *double digging*. This procedure isn't sharing the work with a friend, attractive though that may sound, but is digging the soil to two spades' depths.

Single digging

Here's the process for single digging, which is illustrated in Figure 5-2:

1. **Start by taking out a trench of soil equal to the width of the bed and the depth of your spade.**

2. **Put this trench-full of soil in a heap to one side, or in a barrow.**

3. **Spread organic matter (manure, compost or whatever you can lay your hands on) into the trench and onto the slope of the soil you've just turned over.**

4. **Slice into the adjacent portion of soil with your spade and flip that soil into your new trench and over the newly spread organic matter.**

5. **Use a digging fork to break up clods and mix everything together.**

6. **When you get to the end of your bed, use the soil you put to one side to fill in the final trench.**

During steps 4 and 5, annual weeds can be buried in the digging process and just left to die, but perennials are tougher nuts to crack. You need to remove every scrap of root or they cheerfully pop up again later in the season.

Double digging

The process starts in the same way as single digging (see the preceding section), by removing a trench-full of soil and putting it to one side. Make sure that the trench is at least 30 centimetres (1 foot) across though – if your soil is light and inclined to fall back in the trench, make it 60 centimetres (2 feet). Now things get harder:

1. **Using a digging fork, break up the subsoil in the base of the trench to the full depth of the tines, or prongs.**

2. **Spread plenty of organic matter across the trench (a barrow per square metre is a good general guide).**

3. **Dig the topsoil from the adjacent strip of ground (creating your next trench, in effect) and place it into the strip you've just worked.**

4. **Bash it with your spade to break up clods and turn it over as you work to mix in more of that gorgeous organic matter.**

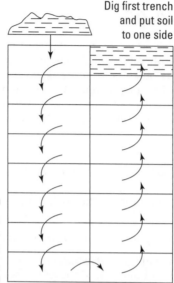

Dig first trench
and put soil
to one side

Figure 5-2:
The single-
digging
process.

And that's it really. Just keep working across your bed in this fashion, and then for the final trench, barrow in the excavated soil that you started with. See Figure 5-3 for more detail.

Don't dig too far in one go or you have to move the soil a long way.

Keep off the soil! After you've expended all that sweat and energy on digging your ground, don't ruin your work by walking on it and thereby compacting the soil, more than you have to. For sowing seed, planting and other close work, stand on a plank to spread your weight. No-dig beds are best of all – more on these in Chapter 10.

When to cultivate your soil

Timing is everything. Rather like the porridge in 'Goldilocks and the Three Bears', the ground has to be not too wet, not too dry – but just right. The state of the soil when digging is especially important with clay: too wet, and clay is impossible to work and you damage the structure; too dry, and it sets like concrete. Basically, if the soil sticks to your boots and tools, the soil's too wet.

Gardeners on free-draining, sandy or light soils can feel very smug because they've more flexibility as to when to dig, although light soil shouldn't be worked when dry because some of that precious topsoil can be blown away.

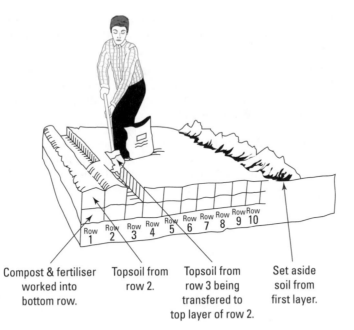

Figure 5-3:
The double-digging process.

Compost & fertiliser worked into bottom row.

Topsoil from row 2.

Topsoil from row 3 being transferred to top layer of row 2.

Set aside soil from first layer.

Getting help: Mechanical cultivators

Whether to use a rotovator is an ongoing philosophical debate among gardeners, with promoters and detractors arguing the issue. Rotovators are machines with blades or *tines* that chop into the soil, churning (or *tilling*) it and blending everything in the top 15–30 centimetres (6–12 inches) of soil. Following are factors to consider on both sides of the tilling debate:

- ✔ Tilling is an easy way to incorporate soil improvers, such as lime, bulky manure, compost and green manure crops into the soil.

- ✔ Tilling turns weeds under, facilitating their decomposition. But it can also bring weed seeds to the surface of the soil, where they can germinate readily. It can also chop and disperse roots of perennial weeds, and so you can end up with a much worse problem in the long run.

- ✔ Tilling can kill some insects and diseases that may be lurking around the soil surface. But it can also kill earthworms and beneficial soil creatures.

- ✔ Tilling makes for a clean, easy-to-plant garden bed. But it can damage soil structure, increasing the risk of creating a poorly drained and hard-to-work soil, especially if the area is tilled when the soil's still too wet.

- ✔ Tilling hastens the breakdown of desirable organic matter, and so you have to add organic material more frequently and in greater quantities.

✔ Tilling can loosen the soil so that it *erodes* (blows or washes away), especially when you're gardening on a slope or in a windy area, which isn't good news because soil should be conserved.

✔ Tilling repeatedly can create a compacted layer or *pan* just below the tilled layer, which is a particular problem on clay or silty soils. If you have such a soil, you may have to carry out deep digging by hand every few years to break up the pan.

If you've a large garden or are breaking new ground, a powerful, mechanical tiller can save time and effort. Instead of buying a small machine, hire in a large, powerful one that does a much better and more efficient job.

Chapter 6

Composing Great Compost: Let the Rotting Begin!

In This Chapter

▶ Getting the compost bug

▶ Managing your compost heap

▶ Cooking up great compost

▶ Dealing with difficult materials

*W*hen organic gardening enthusiasts get together, they often gravitate towards the compost area for a serious discussion about mixes, activators, bin designs and other such matters. But don't let this interest in putrefying matter put you off! The fascination and rewards of recycling your garden, kitchen and certain household waste into scrumptious rich, dark, crumbly compost, are immense. Despite often being tucked out of sight, compost heaps really are the heart and soul of an organic garden.

The great thing about compost is that it just happens, quite naturally: any pile of garden waste rots down all by itself – just think what happens in woods and other wild places. Most gardens, however, lack the space for large mounds of waste, or simply need to be tidier. Or, perhaps, the gardener wants to speed up the process a bit, hence the need for compost bins. In addition, certain waste ingredients, such as food, woody prunings and leaves, require specialist treatment. For all these reasons, gardeners need to give nature a helping hand, which is where this chapter is worth its weight in waste. We show you how to design and position your compost heap, what to include (and what to leave out) and ways to improve the process.

In Chapter 5, we describe the importance of compost to the soil, but this chapter is your chance to get your hands dirty as we delve more deeply into the compost heap itself. Read on for a fascinating foray into the world of rot!

Understanding Why Composting is Common Sense

Organic gardeners tend to look at both the small, local picture and the wider question of the environment, and the issue of compost is no different. On the one hand, the focus of their own garden is on creating healthy soil using organic matter – and nothing beats having your very own production line on site, in the form of compost bins. The warm, cosy environment is wonderful for wildlife too and makes the ultimate happy home for all kinds of creatures, from millions of microscopic organisms to hedgehogs, frogs, toads, newts and slowworms.

On the other hand, the concerns of sustainability in the wider world also often inspire gardeners to go organic, and the issue of rubbish disposal, such as the levels in landfill sites, comes ever higher on the domestic agenda. By cutting down on the amount of waste sent to landfill or incineration, you can do a really good turn for the environment. Recycling your waste on site means that you close the circle of nature in your own plot. And besides, wasting fuel by carting your garden waste to the tip, and then spending out on buying bulky soil conditioners, doesn't make environmental or financial sense.

Situating and Arranging Your Compost Area

Although stylish compost bins for small gardens are available (hop to the later section 'Buying or building compost bins' for more), in general a composting area is definitely something to tuck out of the way. Aim for making it tidy, because it certainly won't be good-looking.

When deciding on location, though, practicality is of prime importance. Garden waste is bulky, finished compost is certainly heavy, and sometimes you need to add water – which all demands that your compost heap be conveniently accessible. Instinct may tell you to put it right at the end of the garden, but if your plot is large – or on a slope – placing it in the middle or even near the house may be best. At the risk of stating the obvious, avoid spots right next to your patio or a seating area, because compost can whiff from time to time and may attract fruit flies.

The top-notch spot for composting is in the sun and with bins standing on soil for maximum micro-organism activity, but you still get good results – albeit slower ones – in shady spots or on a solid surface.

Allow enough space for at least two compost bins (so that one can 'cook' while the other fills); you may even need more if your garden is large and generates lots of waste. Large amounts of autumn leaves are best treated separately (see 'Loving leafmould' later in this chapter) and so take this consideration into account when deciding on compost capacity.

Your composting site is also a good spot for storing other bulky items, such as wheelbarrows, bags of compost and stacks of pots, and so if you're creating a screened-off area, make sure to create a sufficiently large site.

Buying or building compost bins

Although any pile of waste eventually rots down, a compost bin keeps your waste neat and confines to it a relatively small area. Some styles of bin also keep out animal pests, such as mice and rats. Most importantly, the structure of a bin retains heat and moisture, speeding up the 'cooking' process so that your waste turns to ready-to-use compost in the shortest possible time.

The hotter your waste gets, the quicker it rots, and so if time is of the essence, consider a well-insulated bin that speeds up the process.

Compost bins can be bought from lots of sources: garden centres, DIY stores, through mail order and sometimes at bargain prices from your local council. Figure 6-1 contains examples of bin designs.

The general principle of all compost bin designs is the same, although do have a particular look at the thickness of the walls with regard to their insulation properties. The old adage of 'you get what you pay for' applies just as much here as everywhere else: a large, stout, well-insulated bin makes better compost in a much shorter time.

Thin-walled bins (see Figure 6-1a) with a hatch at the bottom may not be as efficient to use as they seem. The intention is that as the waste turns to compost, you can remove it via the hatch and add fresh waste to the top. Although this design looks like a good idea, in practice you get only small amounts of compost at a time (and can add only relatively small amounts of waste). And because the pile doesn't get very hot, weeds, seed and disease spores may survive.

Tumbler compost bins (see Figure 6-1a) are designed to be rotated on a regular basis so that the compost inside gets mixed well, heats up and rots down evenly. Some tumblers have crank handles for turning and others are designed to roll along the ground, tumbling the compost as it goes.

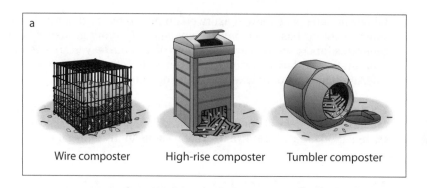

Wire composter   High-rise composter   Tumbler composter

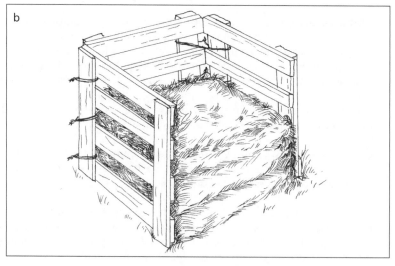

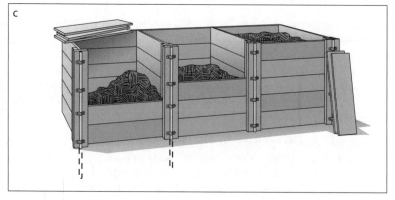

Figure 6-1:
A selection
of compost
bin designs:
(a) com-
mercial
composters
(b) a simple
wooden
compost bin
(c) the three
wooden
compost bin
system.

Ideally you need two or more compost bins, and so consider making your own to save money. Practicality is the main requirement: a compost bin doesn't have to be smart to work well. Here are a few ideas for DIY bins:

✔ **Wire bins:** These bins are the easiest of all to make, but you do have to buy a roll of 1-metre stout wire mesh. Simply bend the wire into a cylinder, or drive four stakes in the ground to form a square and then wrap the mesh round the outside (see Figure 6-1a).

✔ **Wooden pallet bins:** Shipping pallets make excellent and ultra-simple compost bins; simply wire four together to form an open-topped 'box' (see Figure 6-1b). Many retailers are only too glad to give away pallets because they usually have to pay to dispose of them.

When the waste rots down, simply unwire the pallets so that the 'box' falls open and you can easily get at the finished compost. The gaps in the pallets mean that the waste on the outside tends to rot more slowly, but all you need to do is chuck these bits into the next batch of waste. Alternatively, line your pallet bin with flattened cardboard boxes or polystyrene sheets, for extra insulation.

✔ **Wooden bin system:** This classic design (see Figure 6-1c) is the gardeners' favourite: sturdy, efficient, long-lasting and with good insulating properties. It enables you to fill one bin while the others are 'cooking'. Although you can buy these bins ready-made, save money by making your own.

When making your own compost bin, creating a double bin can save you money on materials as the two bins share the centre wall, and using reclaimed wood such as old floorboards also helps to keep costs down. Using timber that measures 15×2.5 centimetres (or 6×1 inches) to make the bin walls, which you nail or screw to sturdy uprights, make each bin around a cubic metre in size. So that you've easy access for filling and emptying the bins, make the fronts with loose boards that you can lift in and out of 'channels' made using 2.5×2.5 centimetre (or 1×1 inch) square timber. The wood should be pressure-treated, or thoroughly painted with wood preservative.

Selecting solutions for small spaces

Even the tiniest garden, backyard or balcony can accommodate a compost facility to suit. The waste from just a few containers, added to fruit and vegetable peelings, envelopes and cardboard, for example, can be recycled into rich compost to fill a tub or two.

Investing in a wormery (check out the later section 'Working with wiggly wormeries') is particularly worthwhile for restricted areas, allowing you to transform food waste into superb plant nourishment. In addition, decorative 'beehive' compost bins that have pitched roofs make handsome features that look right at home in a small garden border – and can be made even more attractive with a coloured wood stain, available in many shades.

Getting Started: From Refuse to Riches

In most literature about composting (and you'd be amazed at the extent of it), garden waste is often referred to as *browns* and *greens*. Although these terms relate to the colour of the waste, they're also a way of differentiating between dry, carbon-rich materials (*browns*), such as twigs, stems and shredded prunings, and moist, nitrogen-rich ones (*greens*) like grass clippings, leafy shoots and weeds.

Knowing the difference is important, because the best compost is made from a well-mixed dish of browns and greens.

Whether you're using a smart 'bought' compost bin, a homemade pallet box or are just making one big heap on the ground (as we describe in the earlier section 'Buying or building compost bins'), the approach to composting is the same:

1. **Mix roughly equal parts, by volume, of dry carbon-rich browns and moist nitrogen-rich greens.**

2. **Fill your container (or make a pile) and cover. While a lid for your bin is ideal, you can also use a piece of old carpet, flattened cardboard boxes or a sheet of thick polythene.**

3. **Leave for roughly six months, by which time you should have compost that resembles dark, crumbly soil.**

Basic composting really is that simple.

If after six months anything still resembles its original form (stems, cardboard and so on), simply chuck it into the next heap to 'cook' a bit longer. While the first heap is 'cooking', you can be filling the next one.

Choosing ingredients for your compost recipe

Here's a list of materials that you can safely compost (along with a few to avoid):

✔ Most garden waste composts well, including grass clippings, weeds, turf and dead plant stems.

Don't use diseased plant material or roots of perennial weeds (the spores survive unless your heap gets very hot) or any plant material recently treated with weedkiller.

Of course, your organic garden would never contain weedkiller, but the problem can arise if you're composting material from other nonorganic gardens.

Woody material and branches are best chopped or shredded because they take ages to rot down.

✔ Leaves, in small quantities, compost fine: handle large amounts separately.

✔ Manure from chickens and small pets such as guinea pigs and rabbits works well. (Chapter 5 guides you through the delights of manure.)

Don't use dog and cat faeces, however, which can contain parasites (but see the later section 'Working with wiggly wormeries').

✔ Cut flowers compost fine.

✔ Uncooked fruit and vegetable waste, such as peelings, stalks and salad leftovers, work well but don't use cooked food and meat scraps that are likely to attract vermin (though they can be composted in other ways: read the later sections 'Working with wiggly wormeries' and 'Composting food waste . . . safely').

✔ Crushed eggshells compost, but rinse first to remove egg white that can attract rats.

✔ Cardboard and paper that you don't recycle, such as packaging, envelopes, shredded paper and toilet roll inners, can be safely added to your compost heap.

Flattened cardboard boxes make good insulators to the sides and top of a heap, and eventually compost themselves.

A few, perhaps less obvious materials that you can also compost effectively are:

✔ Sawdust and shavings from untreated wood.

✔ Vacuum cleaner contents (so long as it doesn't contain dangerously sharp waste like broken glass).

✔ Wood ash (but not coal).

✔ Wool or cotton clothing, 100 per cent content only and chopped up small.

'Cooking' your compost heap

Although nature can generally be left to get on with composting, an occasional check is a good idea to make sure that your heap isn't too dry or too wet:

- ✔ If too dry, your compost lacks the sufficient microbial activity to rot successfully.

  You can easily correct dry compost by gently trickling water onto the heap, and then covering so that the moisture doesn't evaporate; this addition is most important in summer, of course.

- ✔ If too wet, the lack of oxygen results in a slimy, rather smelly mess (the most common occurrence is when green grass clippings are added in large quantities without enough browns).

  Over-wet heaps take a bit more work to correct than dry ones, because the waste needs to be taken out and mixed with easy-to-blend browns, such as crumpled newspaper, torn card or dry leaves.

Of course, if effective composting were that simple you wouldn't be able to fill your book shelves with an entire library on the subject. You can make faster, better compost in several ways:

- ✔ **Heating your compost:** Save up your waste and fill a bin in one go, so that it reaches a higher temperature. A hotter bin means faster composting, and also ensures that you stand a good chance of killing off weed seeds and diseases. Don't forget to mix, stir or ventilate it too (see the next three points).

- ✔ **Mixing your compost:** Regularly mixing your compost (preferably once a week or fortnight for the first couple of months) is a great way to get fit and make speedy compost at the same time! Empty out the contents of your bin (which is no mean feat with a cubic metre or so of waste) and chuck it back in again, mixing 'sides to middle' as you go. The waste heats up after each mix, speeding the process.

- ✔ **Stirring your compost:** If you find mixing too hard (mixing isn't essential after all), an easier option is to use a compost aerating tool: a basic stirring device that you can buy.

  Stirring may not be good for any snoozing wildlife, so check that you don't have hedgehogs, frogs and the like snuggled up in there.

- ✔ **Ventilating your compost:** Plenty of air in the heap speeds up decomposition, and so ensuring good ventilation at the base of your bin is a labour-saving alternative to mixing. Put in a layer of spaced-apart bricks or a 'mattress' of un-shredded woody prunings to allow air in.

Another method of speeding up composting is to add activators, as we describe in the following section.

Speeding up the process: Compost activators

Correctly made compost doesn't really need additional activators, but they can speed up the process a little. Manufacturers produce a number of products that are intended to accelerate the composting process.

Not all bought activators are suitable for organic gardening, and so do check the label carefully. Products based on chemical nitrogen can in fact have a detrimental effect on the organisms in your heap.

Instead of purchasing activators, you may want to consider several good organic alternatives that cost nothing at all:

- ✔ **Comfrey:** This plant is a favourite of organic gardeners because the foliage is particularly rich in nitrogen, potash and minerals. The young growth of nettles is also particularly good.

  Grow a patch of comfrey near your compost area and simply chuck in a few handfuls from time to time.

- ✔ **Garden soil:** Adding a little soil for every 30–45-centimetre layer of compost introduces plenty of bacteria.

- ✔ **Manure:** Natural nitrogen-rich materials speed up decomposition, which makes fresh manure an excellent natural activator.

  Keen organic gardeners keep a bucket and trowel handy in their car, to scoop up fresh horse droppings from the road.

Of course, humans are efficient producers of a wonderful compost activator – urine. In the days before inside toilets, most households had a chamber pot for night-time use (affectionately known as a 'gazunder' because it 'gazunder the bed'). If your compost bin is in a private place, try to persuade the men of the household (sorry ladies, it's a bit tricky for you) to do their bit and actually wee on the heap – but only if there's no likelihood of being reported to the police for indecent exposure! Unless you invest in a composting toilet though (yes, they really do exist) adding any other type of human waste isn't safe. Enough said.

Loving leafmould

Composted leaves, known as *leafmould*, are one of the best soil conditioners, giving outstanding results in comparative trials run at the Garden Organic headquarters. Organic gardeners shudder to see people burning or binning their leaves, knowing just how valuable they can be as compost.

Best of all, leafmould is dead easy to make. Because leaves are dry and fibrous, they rot down more slowly that most types of waste and so they're best composted separately. In contrast to compost bins, the best types of container for making leafmould are open, wire-mesh types (see Figure 6-2) and, conveniently, they're the cheapest and easiest bins to construct:

1. **Take a roll of 1-metre-high stout wire mesh or plastic-covered wire.** Form a cylinder secured by a single post hammered into the ground or wrap the wire around four posts to form an open-topped box.

2. **Fill your container with leaves, squashing them down as each load is added.** Don't cover, and allow the contents to rot down for a year – sometimes up to two years in the case of large, tough leaves.

3. **Check occasionally to see whether the leaves are sufficiently moist.** A white fungal growth often appears if conditions are too dry – and so water if necessary.

An alternative to building a bin is to use strong plastic sacks; spear the bottom with a fork first to allow excess moisture to drain out and allow air in.

If you've enough space in your composting area, consider gathering leaves from elsewhere too, such as local parks or other people's gardens. Ask the owners for permission first though, and check whether chemicals have been applied to the area – as an organic gardener you don't want to import unfamiliar chemicals to your own plot.

Working with wiggly wormeries

Worm composting – or worm farming – is a fantastic small-space solution, and also an excellent way to compost food waste that can't go on the garden compost heap. Keeping a wormery is an example of nature working for you at its best – the worms gobble up waste and convert it into *worm casts*, a rich material that's enormously beneficial to all soils and plants. The resulting compost is best described as a cross between a fertiliser and a soil improver. A wormery also produces waste liquid that can be diluted and used as a plant food (somewhat smelly, but plants don't mind the pong).

Children find wormeries fascinating, and they're great ways to demonstrate all about composting and recycling on a small scale.

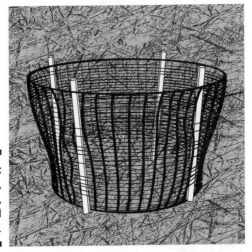

Figure 6-2:
A open, wire-mesh, leafmould container.

You can buy ready-made wormeries by mail order and from garden centres, or you can make your own from a container such as a small plastic dustbin or lidded storage bin (see Figure 6-3).

A wormery must have drainage, and a secure, fastened lid to keep out raiding animals if you plan to compost food waste.

Worms are living creatures, of course, and amply repay you for good living conditions. They like to be cool and damp – but not cold or wet. If the temperature drops too low, their activity levels (and hence the compost they produce) drop too. Conversely, they dislike being too hot! Therefore, the ideal arrangement is an outside location that's shaded from summer midday or afternoon sun, and a container that you can move into a shed or garage for the winter.

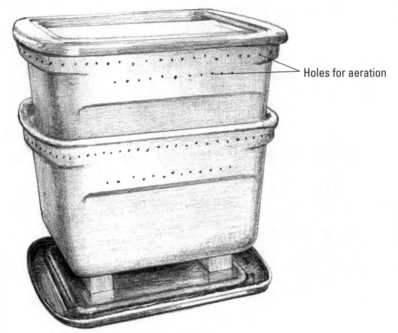

Holes for aeration

Figure 6-3:
A home-
made
wormery.

Here's how to construct your own wormery:

1. **Start your wormery with a layer of bedding such as leafmould, shredded cardboard or newspaper, or a layer of compost from an outdoor heap.**

2. **Moisten it thoroughly – a useful line to remember is 'worms die if they're dry'.**

3. **Introduce your worms along with a couple of handfuls of food waste, and let them settle in for a few days.**

4. **Add waste little and often. The equivalent of 2–4 handfuls of waste a day is ideal.**

For the most efficient use of your wormery, separate uncooked waste to go on the compost heap and put in only cooked food, meat, fish scraps and so on.

Avoid putting in a lot of citrus peels that create very acid conditions that worms dislike.

Although wormeries take many weeks to fill with rich compost, don't forget to drain off the liquid regularly or the worms can drown in soggy material. This liquid can be diluted with one part to ten parts of water and used as a plant food.

Using a doggy poo loo!

Believe it or not, a wormery is now designed specifically to process dog poo and turn it into compost. Just how brave are those worms! Manufacturers advise that the finished compost isn't to be used in food growing areas or where children play, just in case any harmful parasites do survive the process, but this compost is safe to use on ornamental borders. Don't mix food waste and dog poo in the same wormery though, but have separate ones.

If your wormery is designed with several separate tiers fitting together, lifting out the lowest level full of compost is a comparatively easy task, because the worms migrate upwards to busily munch their fresh food supplies. If you've one big container, just remove the top layers of worms and waste until you're down to the good stuff. Enjoy!

Handling Problematic Materials

Unfortunately you can't simply throw everything and anything onto your compost heap. This section guides you through a few of the more awkward composting issues.

Composting food waste . . . safely

Even the most economical cook generates a variety of food waste that can't go on a standard garden compost heap. Cooked food, meat scraps, bread and fish are a gourmet banquet to all sorts of creatures that you really don't want partying in your garden: rats, foxes and neighbourhood cats would soon be piling in for a free feast. Although some local councils collect food waste separately to compost safely in vast containers, in many areas your scraps simply add to the landfill problem. Fortunately, food waste can become a real asset to your garden (see the earlier section 'Working with wiggly wormeries').

One answer is to use the Bokashi system, which employs fermentation and effective micro-organisms (EM) to, in effect, 'pickle' your waste so that it can be safely added to your compost heap or buried in the garden. A Bokashi bucket has a snug-fitting lid and a tap at the bottom where you can drain off liquids. As layers of waste are added, bran impregnated with EM is sprinkled on and the waste firmly pressed down. When full, the bucket is left to stand for a couple of weeks before using – so a Bokashi set comprises two buckets, one to be filling while the other one 'pickles'. A starter kit costs around £65 and is widely available from mail order suppliers.

On a larger scale, secure 'in-vessel' compost units such as the Jora system exist, but they're expensive at around several hundred pounds and generally used in larger places such as schools. If several keen composting households or allotment holders are located close together, however, this option is worth considering. You can buy these units directly from composting and organic product suppliers.

Recycling woody prunings

The problem with woody stems and branches is that they take much longer to rot down than most garden waste.

Adding woody stems to a compost heap on the 'out of sight, out of mind' basis is sure to come back to haunt you when digging out your finished compost. Believe us, after wasting loads of time picking twigs out of your otherwise beautifully dark crumbly compost, you'll vow to separate them out next time.

Also, don't resort to a bonfire and send all those valuable nutrients up in smoke (not to mention annoying the neighbours). Here are a few better ways to handle woody stems and branches:

- ✔ **Ventilating your compost bin:** A 'mattress' of woody prunings at the base helps get plenty of air into your heap (turn to the earlier section "Cooking' your compost heap' for more details).

- ✔ **Shredding 'em up:** A mechanical shredder makes short work of prunings. Add them to the compost heap for six months and use as a weed-suppressing mulch on borders. (If spread directly on the soil, the fresh chippings rob nitrogen from the soil as they decompose).

  Buying a shredder is only worthwhile if you've a lot of prunings. Why not hire one, or share a shredder with gardening friends.

- ✔ **Making a habitat pile:** Dead wood is an important part of the ecosystem and home to many bugs – which, in turn, are food for other creatures that are helpful to the gardener. At the back of borders, at the base of hedges or anywhere out of the way, make piles of twigs and branches.

- ✔ **Taking to the tip:** Most household waste sites now collect 'green waste'. Okay, so you have to use petrol or diesel to get the stuff there, but that's better than burning it. Well, unless your nearest tip is a long, long way away.

Dealing with non-compostables

Even the most enthusiastic compost maker ends up with a bit of waste that can't be composted, such as diseased plant material, weed seeds or the roots of perennial weeds. Unless you're prepared to mix and tend your compost heap so that the temperature gets sufficiently high to kill seeds, roots and diseases (we describe this hard work in the earlier section "Cooking' your compost heap'), keep these items separate – or you're storing up a whole lot of future trouble for yourself.

All this waste can, however, go to the green waste section at your local council tip (or 'recycling centre' as they now like to be known). If you're lucky, your council may already operate a doorstep collection of green waste, in which case, problem solved. The huge quantities of gathered waste is composted in massive rows called *windrows* and regularly turned by machine, hence reaching high temperatures. The one big exception is Japanese knotweed, a noxious and invasive weed that spreads rapidly and is incredibly difficult to eradicate. Contact your council for information on disposing of this weed, and for more information jump to Chapter 21.

Another way to dispose of perennial weed roots and seeds is to put them in a light-excluding watertight sack (old compost bags are ideal), top up with water, tie up the top and leave for at least a year. The resulting sludge smells foul when emptied out, but at least the weeds are dead.

Chapter 7

Enriching the Earth with Organic Fertilisers

In This Chapter

▶ Understanding fertilisers and their contents

▶ Choosing and using the right kind of fertiliser

▶ Securing sources of organic fertiliser

*P*lants need nutrients to grow and flourish, and in order to fend off pests, diseases and environmental stresses. Providing them with the necessary nutrients is vital to successful organic gardening. Adding compost and organic matter to create healthy soil (as we describe in Chapters 5 and 6) goes a long way towards providing essential nutrients for plant growth, but they may still need additional nutrients to grow to their full potential. In this chapter, we provide the low-down on *organic fertilisers* – ones derived from natural plant, animal and mineral sources – and how to use them effectively.

Becoming Familiar with Fertilisers

In contrast to organic matter and soil conditioners that improve the overall soil environment (flip to Chapters 4, 5 and 6 for more details), fertilisers are formulated to provide specific plant nutrients in specific amounts.

Although manufacturers may have you believe that you need to feed all your plants on a regular basis, you certainly don't if you garden organically and follow our guidelines on improving your soil. Many plants growing in healthy soil – with the proper pH and given regular applications of organic matter – thrive just fine without supplemental feeding. Trees, shrubs and perennials especially adapt well to slow, steady growth. Indeed, holding back on the fertiliser can sometimes be the better option because the fast growth stimulated by heavy fertilising can result in weak, succulent plant tissue that's more susceptible to attack by insects and diseases and to damage from severe weather.

Certain plants, however, are described as 'hungry' and do benefit from fertilising, including vegetables, short-lived flowers and plants (for example, roses) that bloom over a long period. Gardeners expect vegetables to put on fast growth and produce abundantly, and when you harvest, you remove nutrient-rich plant material, and so need to replace those nutrients in the soil.

Most fruit crops need feeding too, in order to produce a good crop. Annual flowers thrive with supplemental feeding: the continuous flowering you expect from your petunias and impatiens requires a reliable supply of nutrients. And, although most long-lived woody plants do fine without extra nosh, a dressing of fertiliser – especially in the spring – boosts performance. Finally, anything growing in a container needs supplemental feeding, because the roots can't reach out into the earth in search of nutrients.

Garden centres, DIY stores and mail order suppliers offer fertilisers in so many forms that you can get confused about which ones to choose. Make your decision based on the cost of the actual nutrients, the ease of application and how quickly you want the nutrients to become available to the plants. Also, buy the right fertiliser for the time of year. Always read the small print – nearly every product comes with detailed instructions.

Debating organic versus synthetic fertilisers

Organic fertilisers generally come from plants, animals or minerals. Most of these fertilisers contain a broad range of nutrients, including important trace elements; a few types also add organic matter to the soil and enhance the soil ecosystem. By contrast, synthetic fertilisers have specific chemical formulations and often contain only three nutrients: nitrogen, phosphorous and potassium.

Not only do synthetic products not enhance soil life, but also in some cases they damage soil organisms and repress bacterial action, which is why organic gardeners avoid them in favour of natural products.

Organic fertilisers have other benefits over synthetic fertilisers for soil and plants:

- ✔ They release their nutrients more slowly in the soil, when the plants need them, and so they last longer.
- ✔ They contain the nutrients in complex molecules that don't leach away with the first rain.

✔ They're less likely to burn the young roots of seedlings: synthetic fertilisers are made from mineral salts that can kill roots as well as soil microbes if applied improperly.

✔ They enhance soil health by nurturing the soil microbes that help make soil nutrients available to plants.

In general, organic fertilisers are a kinder, gentler way to give plants the nutrients they need, and are often more sustainable in their manufacture, too.

Choosing between fast-release and slow-release fertilisers

Applying nutrients in a form that plants can use immediately may seem logical, but often that strategy isn't the best one. The nutrients in fast-release, or highly soluble, fertilisers are ready to use as soon as you apply them. The problem is that plants may not be able to use all the nutrients right away, and so any excess nutrients can leach away or runoff, possibly leading to stream or groundwater pollution and causing the proliferation of harmful algae. Later, when the plant is ready to use the nutrients, they're gone.

Most organic fertilisers provide a slow, steady supply of nutrients. Often, the nutrients are bound in organic molecules that require the ongoing action of soil microbes to release them. This process gives plants a limited but steady supply of nutrients, mimicking nature's processes.

Some organic fertilisers, however, are relatively fast-release, particularly liquid and foliar feeds that contain a supply of readily available nutrients dissolved in water so that they're right there, ready for the plant to take up. Slow-release organic fertilisers such as rock powders, on the other hand, break down slowly in the soil environment, releasing their nutrients over months or years.

Be sure to distinguish between fertilisers that contain a broad range of nutrients, and *growth boosters* or plant tonics, such as microbial treatments containing beneficial bacteria and soil fungi. You can use both products together, but a plant tonic on its own doesn't provide nutrients that hungry crops need.

Before adding fertiliser, we recommend that you discover your soil pH. Your plants may be showing signs of a nutrient deficiency because your soil needs a pH adjustment (as we describe in Chapter 5) rather than the addition of fertiliser. Also note that some plants have special pH and nutrient requirements: check the plant descriptions in Part III to find out more.

You can use a home test kit to find out your soil pH and establish the levels of the three major nutrients in your soil (read on to the next section, 'Considering the big three nutrients'); or if you've a problem with no obvious cause, send a sample to a laboratory for testing (Chapter 5 contains more info on using home kits and lab testing).

Considering the big three nutrients

Nitrogen, phosphorous and potassium are the three nutrients that plants need in the largest quantities; they're sometimes referred to as the *primary* nutrients. They each play a critical role in plant growth and development. Healthy, fertile soil naturally contains these three elements, and plants can easily take them up. But if your soil is deficient or you're growing vegetables, fruits or other demanding crops, you may want to supplement the soil's nutrients with fertilisers.

A plant disorder caused by a lack of nutrients is known as a *deficiency* – not to be confused with a plant disease or pest problem. The symptoms vary a lot depending on the type of nutrient that's lacking, and can include stunted growth, discoloured leaves, mottling, distorted growth and poor development. Deficiency symptoms tend to appear first on shoot tips and young leaves.

Complete or *balanced fertilisers* contain nitrogen (N), phosphorous (P) and potassium (K), but don't let the term 'complete' mislead you. It doesn't mean that the fertiliser has all the nutrients that plants need – just that it contains three of the major ones.

You need to know the percentages of nutrients in a bag of fertiliser in order to apply at the right time. For example, plants use a lot of nitrogen during the growing season, and so don't apply a high-nitrogen fertiliser in the autumn when most of the nutrients simply wash away. Fortunately, manufacturers usually give detailed advice on application times on the packet!

At the risk of stating the obvious, always follow the instructions and never to tempted to over-apply fertiliser, thinking that double the amount does twice as much good – overfeeding can do more harm than none at all.

Nitrogen (N)

Nitrogen is responsible for the healthy green foliage of plants, as well as protein and chlorophyll development. (*Chlorophyll* is the pigment that makes plants green and is a vital component of photosynthesis.) Nitrogen moves easily in the soil and leaches out rapidly, especially from sandy soils and in high-rainfall areas or irrigated gardens.

Plants use lots of nitrogen during the growing season, and so nitrogen is commonly the most deficient element. If you add too much nitrogen, however, plants have dark green, leafy growth but less root development and delayed flowering or fruiting. Also, pests may target the overly vigorous growth stimulated by excess nitrogen. Symptoms of nitrogen deficiency include slow growth and yellowing leaves, tinted with red in extreme cases, especially in older foliage.

Phosphorus (P)

Plants need phosphorus for the following reasons:

- ✔ Strong root growth
- ✔ Fruit, stem and seed development
- ✔ Disease resistance
- ✔ General plant vigour

Phosphorus doesn't move in the soil as easily as nitrogen, and so you don't have to add it as frequently.

Depending on where you live, your soil may have plenty of phosphorus, but that nutrient may be unavailable to plants. Phosphorus availability depends on soil temperatures, pH range and the soil levels of other nutrients (such as calcium and potassium). Maintain the soil pH between 5 and 7 to keep phosphorus available. Work phosphorus-rich fertilisers into the soil around the root zone at planting time to make the nutrient readily accessible to plant roots. Deficiency symptoms include stunted plants with dark green foliage, reddish-purple stems or leaves as well as fruits that drop early.

Potassium (K)

Potassium, commonly called *potash*, is essential for vigorous growth, disease resistance, fruit and vegetable flavour and development, and general plant function.

Potassium breaks down slowly, and so you don't need to add it often. Annual applications of organic matter may supply enough potassium, but a soil test is the surest way to determine need. Avoid adding too much potassium fertiliser because it can make other nutrients (such as magnesium) unavailable.

Deficiency symptoms include yellow areas along the leaf veins and leaf edges, crinkled and rolled-up leaves, and dead twigs. Fruit trees growing in potassium-deficient soils may have poorly developed or bland-tasting fruit. In conifers, the needles on the tree become dark blue-green and then turn yellow to reddish brown. (Note that some conifers, mainly pines, normally shed older, yellow needles.)

Providing secondary nutrients

Calcium, magnesium and sulphur are called *secondary* elements. They're essential not only for plant growth, but also for adjusting and maintaining soil pH – the measure of acidity and alkalinity of the soil (flip to Chapter 5 for all about pH). These three nutrients are also vital to plant functioning, and excessive or deficient levels can upset plants' ability to use other nutrients in the soil.

Home garden soils are rarely deficient in these nutrients, but keep your eye out for the following deficiency symptoms:

- **Calcium:** Calcium-deficient plants may have twisted, dark green new leaves and leaf-tip burn. Flowers may have weak stems, and fruit may develop rotten spots on the bottom (opposite the stem end).

- **Magnesium:** Magnesium-deficient plants have curled leaf edges and dis-coloured older leaves. Yellowing between the veins is another classic symptom.

- **Sulphur:** Sulphur-deficient plants display slow growth and are small and spindly.

Limestone, which contains calcium, and dolomitic limestone, which contains calcium and magnesium, are used to raise the pH of acidic soils towards neu-tral, where most plants grow best. In alkaline soils, sulphur helps lower the pH to the optimum level.

Avoiding trace element deficiency

The essential nutrients that plants need in the smallest quantities are called *trace elements* or *micronutrients*, and they include iron, manganese, boron, copper, zinc, molybdenum, chlorine and nickel. Fortunately, organic matter usually supplies adequate amounts of these nutrients, because adding too much of any one of these micronutrients can cause more problems than adding none at all.

Trace element deficiency is often hard to spot because plants vary in their specific needs and symptoms. Too little iron, for example, can cause the leaves of acid-loving plants to turn yellow between the veins; too little boron can cause black spots on beetroots.

If your plants have a trace element deficiency, the best solution may be to adjust the pH to the level that those specific plants prefer (as we describe in Chapter 5) instead of applying a specialist fertiliser.

Some fertilisers contain *chelated* micronutrients. In the process of chelation, the nutrients are chemically bound to other molecules so that the plants can absorb them more easily. Usually, chelated micronutrient fertilisers are used to provide a quick, short-term fix for mineral deficiencies.

Plants can only take up nutrients *in solution* (dissolved in water), and so before rushing out to buy all sorts of fertilisers, just make sure that your plant isn't simply suffering from drought.

Applying fertilisers

Apply fertilisers by spraying, spreading or sprinkling. Here's how to apply some of the common types:

- **Granular:** Granular fertilisers are the most common and easily applied forms, as well as being among the most economical. Sprinkle by hand around plants or broadcast them with a lawn spreader over the lawn. For easy distribution around plants, use two small plastic plant pots of the same size, placed one inside the other with drainage holes just offset to leave small gaps. Shake the pot to distribute fertiliser evenly. Take care to apply at the recommended rate by weighing the amount per metre on kitchen scales, and then marking a small container (such as a clean, dry, yoghurt pot) with the recommended rate.

- **Liquid:** Liquid fertilisers give plants a quick nutrient boost. Common types include seaweed extract, comfrey fertiliser and compost tea, as well as homemade 'teas' and liquid feeds. Liquid fertilisers can be good candidates for *foliar feeding*; that is, being applied directly to plant leaves.

- **Powder:** Some fertilisers, such as limestone and rock powders, are so finely ground that they readily blow in the wind. When applying them in your garden, choose a windless day, and wear a dust mask as well as gloves. As an alternative, look for pelletised forms of these fertilisers.

Granular and powder fertilisers take time to break down and release their contents to the soil and plants, and so apply them a few weeks before planting vegetables and flowers, and use them as long-term sources of nutrients for trees, shrubs, lawns and perennials. Generally, the smaller the particles, the more quickly the fertiliser becomes available to plant roots.

To apply nutrients during the growing season, *top-dress* plants by applying granular or liquid fertiliser to the soil around the plant, but avoid the stems themselves. For even faster results, apply liquid fertilisers directly to plant leaves (called foliar feeding). Mix foliar fertilisers with water with neutral pH (7.0), and apply on a dry but sunless day (the sun's rays can cause leaf scorch). A single top-dressing early in the growing season (March–April) is plenty for most garden vegetables and flowers.

Well-cared-for soil in an organic garden may not need any extra feeding, but container-grown plants depend on you for all their needs and benefit from regular feeding throughout the growing season: the frequency of feeding depends on your choice of fertiliser. Granular types usually last for a number of weeks; liquid feeding is normally done at least fortnightly, depending on the crop.

Getting to Grips with Types of Organic Fertiliser

An extensive range of organic fertilisers is available, from garden centres and large stores and through mail order from specialist suppliers. This section describes a few of the options available to you.

Commercially formulated fertilisers list specific nutrient levels on the package, but bulk products, such as compost and manure, have widely variable contents. The nutrient levels we mention in this section are approximate, because levels vary depending on the product and supplier.

Before applying fertiliser, remember that some sources of bulky organic matter used to condition or improve the soil, such as garden compost and well-rotted manure, already contain a reasonable amount of nutrients. If you've already applied one of these materials, take care not to overdo the feeding.

Buying organic fertilisers

Most organic fertilisers are indeed emblazoned with the word 'organic', which makes distinguishing between these products and synthetic ones easy. A good proportion of these organic fertilisers are for 'general' use and so can be used on all plants – pelleted chicken manure is a popular example. Fertilisers sold for specific plants – such as tomato fertiliser – are formulated for the needs of that crop, but they can be used on other plants other than tomatoes. The labelling simply means that the fertiliser is high in nutrients that boost fruit production, so is ideal for most fruiting crops. Similarly, rose fertiliser is designed to boost flowering, and can be used on other plants to encourage more blooms. Always read the small print on the packet, though.

Organic fertilisers are derived from natural materials and may be derived from plants, animals or minerals. For 'best practice' in terms of an overall organic approach, however, consider the source and use plant, worm or sustainably sourced mineral products in preference to animal ones, unless the source is guaranteed organic too. Examples of popular products include:

✔ **Blood, fish and bone:** This fertilizer is a mixture of dried blood, fish meal from fish waste products, and bone meal, giving a balanced produce combining both slow and faster release of nutrients.

✔ **Bonemeal:** A popular source of phosphorous (11 per cent) and calcium (22 per cent), bonemeal is derived from animal or fish bones and is commonly used in powdered form on root crops and bulbs. This product also contains 2 per cent nitrogen and many micronutrients. Bonemeal targets root growth and so is a popular fertiliser to add to the soil when planting. It can attract dogs and possibly rodents, however, and so place in the bottom of the planting hole.

✔ **Dried blood:** Somewhat gruesomely, blood meal is the powdered blood of slaughtered animals. It contains about 14 per cent nitrogen and many micronutrients. Leafy, nitrogen-loving plants such as lettuce grow well with this fertiliser. Reportedly, blood meal also repels deer (but may attract dogs and cats).

✔ **Pelleted chicken manure:** This product is a concentrated form of chicken manure supplying a balance of nutrients. Supplied in pelleted form to enhance its slow-release qualities and make it easy to handle (though it smells rather strong when you open the carton!).

✔ **Plant-based fertilisers:** A number of plant waste products are used in fertiliser, including alfalfa, cocoa shell and neem. Composted bracken is naturally high in potash, and is usually sold mixed with other material: for example, farmyard manure to use as a soil conditioner or composted wool for use as a potting compost.

✔ **Seaweed:** Check out the later section 'Boosting your soil' for all about seaweed-based fertilisers.

✔ **Wormcast or 'Vermicompost' fertiliser:** As per its name, this product is based on the casts produced by worms, which are rich in a range of nutrients and are extremely good at boosting the soil ecosystem.

Rocking-on with mineral-based fertilisers

Most rock fertilisers decompose slowly into soil, releasing minerals gradually over a period of years. Organic gardeners use many different minerals to increase the fertility of their soils, but fertilising with minerals is a long-term proposition. One application may last a long time because some of these products take months or years to break down fully into useable forms for plants. Epsom salts, gypsum, limestone, nitrate of soda, rock dusts, rock phosphate and sulphur all have their uses.

Boosting your soil

As soil scientists discover more about the ecosystem beneath your feet, they're finding out that improving the soil is far more than just throwing on a selection of nutrients. Products such as those based on seaweed, biochar and wormcasts not only add nutrients, but also have the hugely beneficial effect of boosting soil life and plant growth – not unlike humans taking probiotics to improve digestion. Therefore, these products are of keen interest to organic gardeners.

Biochar

This carbon-rich product is obtained when plant material is heated in a closed container (similar to how charcoal is produced). Looking at the big picture, biochar combats global warming because it can stabilise carbon and store it in the soil. From the gardeners' point of view, biochar is excellent for boosting soil fertility as well as enhancing its structure, improving the soil's water retention ability. Biochar also increases the productivity of most soils. It has a highly porous structure, and thus retains moisture and reduces leaching of nutrients from the soil. The porous structure provides a protective environment for the beneficial soil fungi and bacteria that help plant roots extend their reach, so resulting in greater plant growth and better crops.

EM (Effective micro-organisms)

Becoming increasingly well known as the essential ingredient of the Bokashi composting system, EM is also available as an ingredient in granular and liquid fertilisers. The main strains (which are cultivated using specific technical methods) are lactic acid, which suppresses diseases; phototrophic EM, which boosts regeneration; beneficial fungi, which protect the root zone and stimulate root growth; biosubstances including enzymes and antioxidants; and actinomycetes, which are beneficial soil organisms.

Seaweed

Raw seaweed was a traditional fertiliser in coastal areas where soils are poor, and used to be gathered in cartloads to improve the ground. Although low in the three major nutrients, nitrogen, phosphorous and potassium (check out the earlier section 'Considering the big three nutrients'), seaweed is particularly rich in trace elements and plant hormones, and is hence extremely effective at boosting natural activity within the soil. Seaweed also contains alginates that bind soil particles together, improving drainage.

The use of seaweed has a very positive effect on crop yield and quality. If you live near the coast, you can gather seaweed from the beach after storms – but don't remove from rocks or any place where the seaweed is attached and growing! Seaweed contains salt, and so before adding to the compost heap, rinse in clean water, or stack and leave out in the rain for several weeks.

Don't gather seaweed from any coasts possibly contaminated with radioactivity.

Seaweed-based fertilisers and plant tonics are widely available to buy, in liquid form and as seaweed meal.

Microbial treatments

These products work by stimulating healthy plant growth, enabling nutrients to be absorbed more efficiently and stimulating natural defence mechanisms. Two main types are available to purchase:

- ✔ Beneficial bacteria (*Bacillus subtilis*) can be watered on to help prevent the onset on fungal attacks.

- ✔ Beneficial soil fungi (*mycorrhiza*) can be added to the planting hole when putting in new plants, as a one-off treatment. (*Mycorrhiza* colonise the root system and boost growth, resulting in larger and more efficient roots that absorb nutrients well, helping in plant establishment and withstanding drought.)

Producing your own liquid fertilisers

Although you can buy plenty of suitable organic liquid feeds, something is immensely satisfying (and money-saving) about making your own. Well-rotted compost and manure can be used to make nutritious 'tea' and liquid drained from wormeries and Bokashi buckets can be diluted and used as a plant food.

Growing your own plant food is another fantastic way to get really good grub to your crops. The top plant for this purpose is comfrey (*Symphytum officinale*), a native plant of Europe and Asia. The potash-rich leaves are a wonderful source of plant food. Comfrey leaves can be placed in planting trenches and plant pots to introduce nutrients, or mixed into the compost heap. We suggest that you cultivate a comfrey patch, which forms dense mats of large leaves in sun or semi-shade, in any reasonable soil. Plant in autumn or spring, allowing at least 60 centimetres (24 inches) between individual plants. All types of comfrey are rich in nutrients, but the most outstanding variety that many organic gardeners use is 'Bocking 14'.

To make comfrey fertiliser, place a large quantity of freshly cut leaves into a plastic container such as a water butt (6 kilograms of leaves to 90 litres of water; roughly 13 pounds of leaves to 20 UK gallons of water, or scaled-down as appropriate). Don't use a metal container, though, because rust can contaminate your plant food. Put in the leaves first, add water and then cover with a lid. After about a month, drain off the liquid from the bottom and use directly as a plant feed.

An alternative is to make a concentrated feed by packing a container (with a hole in the base) with cut comfrey, weighed down with a paving slab or large stone. After several weeks, a black liquid starts to drain out: strain and then dilute using 1 part to 40 parts water.

Comfrey smells vile because it's rich in protein, which stinks as it breaks down. But your plants don't mind, even if you do!

Growing green manures and cover crops

Another great way to get organic matter into your garden is to grow your own. *Green manures* are plants that you grow specifically to dig into the soil to add organic matter and nutrients.

Although the terms are sometimes used interchangeably, in fact they've slightly different meanings:

- ✔ *Green manure* usually refers to crops that are planted during the regular growing season specifically to add organic matter and nutrients.

- ✔ *Cover crops* refer to plants grown to help prevent erosion, loosen compacted soil and control weeds, as well as to add organic matter.

Cover crops are most commonly used over winter, when the ground is more likely to be left bare. For more on cover crops as a form of weed control, flip to Chapter 21.

In addition to providing these benefits, green manures and cover crops also:

- ✔ **Attract beneficial insects:** Some green manures and cover crops, such as clover and phacelia, have flowers that beneficial insects love. These insects help with pollination and pest control in your garden. (However, bear in mind that if you plan to dig in a green manure crop, do so *before* flowering. The alternative is to let the crop mature, cut it down and add the clippings to the compost heap.)

- ✔ **Bring up nutrients:** Some green manure crops send long taproots deep into the soil, and therefore draw up nutrients to a level that can be used by garden plants and crops.

- ✔ **Build up nitrogen levels:** Legumes 'fix' nitrogen from the atmosphere and hence are especially good for light, free-draining soils where nitrogen is readily washed out by rain. Leguminous green manures include clover, trefoil and field beans.

- ✔ **Maintain high levels of soil micro-organisms:** When the plants are incorporated into the soil, they feed the essential microbes that make nutrients available to plants. The plant residues also provide surfaces on which the microbes can live.

The best type of plant for your green manure or cover crop depends on what you're trying to accomplish, your soil and the planting time. Although the majority of green manures thrive on a range of soils, alfalfa and winter tares dislike acidic soil.

Mail-order catalogues offer the widest selection of green manures and cover crops, but even small garden centres may sell the most common ones. Consult the package or catalogue description for the amount of seed you need to sow per square metre.

Planting green manures

Using green manures is an ideal way to prepare the soil in new garden beds or borders that you intend to leave fallow (unplanted) for a period of time. Rotovate or dig the area, broadcast the seed, rake in lightly and let the green manure crop grow. Before the plants go to seed, dig over the area or rotovate to incorporate the material into the soil. Don't let the plants produce mature seed if you want to prevent plants from returning next season. The garden is ready for planting straight away. The amount of time between sowing and digging in the crop varies according to the type of plant. Mustard and buckwheat, for example, are among the fastest growers and can be dug in 8–10 weeks after sowing.

Cultivating cover crops

Plant your cover crops after the harvest when garden beds are otherwise bare. Seeds need several weeks of mild weather in order to germinate and start growing strongly, and so early to mid-autumn is the ideal sowing period. When temperatures moderate, the plants grow again.

A few weeks before planting, mow the cover crop if it has become tall, dig or rotovate it into the soil, and leave for several weeks to allow the plant matter to begin decomposing.

Finding a Sustainable Source of Fertiliser

Organic gardening is all about looking at the big picture as well as what happens down at the grass roots, as it were, which means taking into account the sources of the materials you use in your gardens. Soil conditioners, in particular, are bulky and heavy, and some are shipped hundreds or thousands of miles to reach garden centres: consider the amount of nonrenewable petroleum needed to transport these products.

Also look closely at the material itself, which despite being labelled as 'natural' may come from a nonorganic source. Although less of a problem with, say, farm manure, the issue is important with a product such as spent mushroom compost, which is likely to contain chemical residues (unless produced by an organic mushroom grower, of course!).

Start your search for fertilisers in your own neighborhood. You may be able to satisfy all your plants' nutrient needs by using green manures (read the earlier section 'Growing green manures and cover crops' for details) and homemade compost, and by finding sources of fertiliser close to home: coffee grounds from local coffee shops, for example, and waste from various manufacturing processes such as breweries and dairy processors. If you live near the coast, seaweed (rinsed of salt) may be an option.

You can find most of the fertilisers discussed in this chapter in local garden centres and DIY stores. If you can't find what you want, here are a few good online mail-order companies:

- **The Organic Gardening Catalogue:** www.organiccatalog.com
- **Tamar Organics:** www.tamarorganics.co.uk
- **EcoCharlie:** www.ecocharlie.co.uk

Part III

Growing Organically in Your Garden

'He said he was specialising in herbs but he didn't tell me what sort they were.'

In this part . . .

Knowing which plants to choose, what conditions they prefer and where to grow them is a key part of being a successful organic gardener. Chapter 8 leads you into the wonderful world of plants, the sheer magic of growing from seed and how to get your plants off to a flying start in life. Chapter 9 gives you an overview on growing your own chemical-free, healthy feasts, regardless of whether you have a patio, a small garden, an allotment or an extensive plot.

If you're fired up to reduce your food miles, stroll on to producing veggies in Chapter 10. Or check out herbs and edible flowers in Chapter 11 and berries, fruits and nuts in Chapters 12 and 13. If you fancy a frolic with all kinds of flowers – prance over to Chapter 14. And follow our tips on growing and maintaining trees and shrubs in Chapter 15 and lawns in Chapter 16 to make your garden the envy of the neighbourhood.

Chapter 8

Settling in Plants and Keeping Them Happy

. . . .

In This Chapter

▶ Knowing your perennials from your biennials

▶ Sowing seeds outside or starting indoors

▶ Picking promising plants

▶ Making them feel at home

. . . .

Whether you're planting vegetables, fruits, herbs, or trees and shrubs, you need to know a little something about each plant's preferences, such as when to plant it and how it grows. This chapter gives you an overview of the various types of plants and describes planting techniques, whether you're sowing from seed or putting in pre-grown plants. Take a look at Chapters 14 and 15 for more specific information on all sorts of different garden plant species.

Planting Knowledge: Getting to Know Plant Types

Garden and crop plants are divided into categories based on their life cycles – annuals, biennials and perennials – as we describe in this section.

Despite not being specifically organic, the general plant knowledge that this section provides is a huge help when gardening without harmful products.

Appearing here only once: Annual plants

Annuals complete their life cycle in one growing season and need to be replanted each year. Most vegetables and some flowers and herbs are annuals.

You plant annual crops in spring, and harvest in summer and autumn; and then the plants die. The following spring, you start again with new plants. Tomatoes, peppers, sweetcorn and beans fall into this category, as do some herbs (such as dill and basil) and flowers (including sunflowers and zinnias).

Not all annuals behave equally, however. *Hardy annuals* tolerate frost to varying degrees and *half hardy* annuals don't. (Although these terms are used mostly in connection with flowers, exactly the same applies to vegetables and herbs.) Examples of hardy types are nigella or love-in-a-mist, lettuce and carrot, while half hardy ones include busy lizzies, marigolds, beans, cucumbers and pumpkin. People sometimes refer to half hardy plants as *tender* or *frost-tender*.

Hardy annuals are easier to start from seed than half hardy ones; check out the 'Starting from Seed' section later in this chapter.

Checking them out every two years: Biennial plants

Biennials complete their life cycles in two years. Because they flower in their second year, planting biennials every year ensures that you always have some in bloom.

You can grow biennials that you produce for their leaves, such as parsley, as annuals and replant them each spring.

Counting on them every spring: Herbaceous perennials

Herbaceous perennials are plants that live for a number of years. Each autumn the above-ground parts die back. If a perennial is hardy in your region, the roots remain alive and re-sprout the following spring. Many flowers and herbs are herbaceous perennials, as are a few familiar vegetables and fruits, such as asparagus, horseradish and rhubarb. Perennial herbs include thyme, oregano and sage. The thousands of perennial flowers include coneflower, black-eyed Susan and peony.

Although you can start perennial plants from seed, you need to allow a year or so to get good-sized plants. For this reason, they're more commonly sold growing in containers. *Bare-root plants* are sold during their dormant season and are packaged without soil around their roots. Instead, the roots are packed in moist material such as newspaper or sawdust. Asparagus and strawberries are commonly sold in bare-root condition.

Why bare your roots?

If properly stored and shipped, bare-root plants grow as well as, or better than, container-grown plants. Bare-root plants are often less expensive, and you may find a greater selection of varieties when you buy over the Internet or through the post from mail-order nurseries.

These plants must be kept cool so that they don't break dormancy until they're planted. If you purchase plants through the post, be sure to unpack them on arrival and plant them within

a day or two. If a delay is unavoidable, *heel in* outside, which means digging a hole or a trench to put them in (all together if you've a bundle of plants) and quickly covering the roots with soil. The aim is to keep the roots moist and healthy until you can properly plant them.

Avoid buying bare-root plants that have been sitting on store shelves and have begun to sprout. They're no longer dormant and are sure to struggle to get established in your garden.

Persisting year on year: Woody perennials

Woody perennials are plants whose above-ground parts endure throughout the winter and are more commonly called trees and shrubs. Most landscapes include trees and shrubs, which are usually grown for their ornamental properties. Landscape designers sometimes describe these woody plants as forming the *bones* of the landscape. They provide a year-round framework and backdrop for other garden plants.

Woody perennials are sold growing in containers, bare-rooted or balled and burlapped. *Balled and burlapped* plants are dug from the field with a ball of soil around their roots; this ball of soil is then wrapped in burlap or plastic.

Starting from Seed

You can start many plants from seed, but annual flowers and vegetables are the most common types. Starting your own plants from seed has the following benefits:

- ✔ **You can obtain seeds in much greater variety than plants.** A garden centre may offer a dozen or so varieties of tomato plants, for example, but hundreds of tomato varieties as seed. The same is true of many flowers.

- ✔ **You can save money.** Growing from seed is almost always a lot cheaper than buying plants, particularly if you want quite a few.

- ✔ **You can control what's sprayed on plants.** Growers and garden centres are likely to use chemicals; if you start from seed, you can manage your plants organically.

✔ **You can have more success.** Some plants grow best from seed and although you can purchase, for example, carrot, squash and nasturtium as starter plants, these varieties grow so quickly from seed that seed-grown plants often outperform transplanted ones, which need time to acclimatise after planting.

✔ **You can have more fun!** Perhaps this reason is the best one of all.

You can grow plants from seed in two different ways: direct sowing and starting plants in containers. We discuss both methods in this section.

Sowing seeds directly in your garden

Most hardy annual plants grow best when their seed is sown directly into the garden. Direct sowing is the most efficient method for plants that grow quickly and for where seedling roots are so sensitive that they don't like to be disturbed.

Radishes, peas, carrots, Californian poppies and sunflowers all grow best when you plant their seeds directly in the garden.

Preparing the soil

Well-prepared soil is the key to successful seed growing, especially with seeds that you sow directly in the garden. Remove golf-ball-size or larger rocks and clods of soil; and rake the bed flat. For more about preparing your soil, flip to Chapter 5.

Sowing the seeds

Whether you're planting flower or vegetable seeds, the general rule is to plant seeds twice as deep as the seeds are wide. For big seeds, such as beans, that means about around 2 centimetres (1 inch) deep; plant small seeds, such as lettuce, only around 5 millimetres (0.25 inch) deep. Heed the planting depth guidelines on seed packets, because seeds planted too deeply may not grow.

Seed packets also provide specific planting information. Some seeds require light to germinate, for example, and need to be pressed into the soil surface rather than buried.

Always label the area you seed, noting the plant type and planting date, so that if, say, your lettuces fail to appear in several weeks' time, you know that something has gone amiss and you need to sow more.

Tending the soil and the seedlings

After planting your seeds, keep the soil evenly moist, especially the soil surface. If the surface dries out, it can form a crust that prevents seedlings from emerging. In hot weather, a daily light watering in the morning and evening may be necessary.

Sorting out seed types

When choosing varieties of seeds to plant, you may come across the terms *open pollinated*, *heirloom*, *F1 hybrid* and *genetically modified*. The first three types are important for home gardeners; the fourth is a new type that, to date, applies mainly to commercial farmers:

- *Open-pollinated* varieties produce offspring that are similar to the parents. The flowers are pollinated naturally instead of in a plant-breeding lab. Some genetic variability occurs among the plants, and so when growers save seed from their best-performing plants, those traits are passed to the offspring. Many open-pollinated varieties are locally adapted and have unusual colours, shapes and flavours. Gardeners have relied on these varieties for generations because they can save the seeds for replanting.

- *Heirloom* seeds are varieties that have been planted for several generations – perhaps 50 years or more, although no specific longevity is required to qualify as an heirloom.

- *F1 hybrid varieties* have been around since the 1920s. Researchers found that breeding different varieties together resulted in offspring with better traits than either parent, and they grew more vigorously and uniformly. Many hybrid varieties also exhibit improved disease resistance. Hybrid seeds are a result of controlled cross-pollination of specific parent plants. For this reason, plants grown from seed collected from hybrid plants may not resemble the parent plant closely. If you plant seeds from a hybrid tomato, for example, you get a tomato plant but its fruit may not taste nearly as good as the parent plant's.

- *Genetically modified* plants (sometimes called *genetically modified organisms*, or GMOs) are created through gene splicing, wherein genetic material from unrelated plants or even other organisms is inserted into a plant. These varieties generally are available only to commercial farmers. Genetically modified plants may offer benefits, but many questions still exist about the long-term health risks and environmental safety of manipulating the gene pool so dramatically and quickly. GMOs are not allowed in organic growing.

The type of seeds that you plant is up to you, and your decision doesn't have to be all or nothing. Many organic growers plant hybrids; others opt for open-pollinated varieties so that they can save seeds for replanting. If you know that tomatoes commonly suffer from *Fusarium* in your area, for example, go ahead and plant tasty but susceptible heirloom Brandywine tomatoes – but include a few *Fusarium*-resistant hybrid plants too, just in case the disease is especially bad this year and your Brandywines succumb. The key is to experiment in your garden with a range of varieties to find the ones that grow, produce and taste best.

Usually, you see signs of life within a few days for quick sprouters or in two weeks or more for slow growers. Be patient – as long as you use fresh seed, the plants should come up. In unusually wet and cold, or hot and dry soil, however, seeds may rot or fail to sprout. Keep track of the days to germination, and if that period passes with no signs of sprouting, replant when the weather improves.

Starting seeds indoors

For many frost-tender plants, the growing season is too short to grow slow-maturing plants from seed sown in the garden. Tomatoes, peppers, tobacco plants, petunias and pansies are examples of plants that you need to start indoors on the windowsill or in a heated greenhouse. By the time the weather warms up, the plants are several centimetres tall and have a good head start.

Starting seeds indoors is a great way to beat the winter blues as well as to get a flying start on the gardening season. Sow slow-maturing plants, such as tobacco plant, in February–March and fast-growing ones, such as beans, in April.

Ensuring that you have everything you need

To start seeds indoors successfully, you require specific equipment:

- ✔ **Containers:** Any small vessel with drainage holes is sufficient, such as clean yoghurt pots or margarine tubs, although most gardeners use reusable plastic pots or modular trays.

- ✔ **Light source:** A sunny windowsill can raise a good quantity of seedlings, although for large numbers of plants you need a heated greenhouse for better success.

- ✔ **Potting compost:** This compost has the proper balance of drainage and water-holding capacity and is sterile to minimise disease problems.

  Avoid using garden soil to start seeds indoors; it often drains poorly and may harbour organisms that can damage germinating seeds.

- ✔ **Propagator:** Most tender plant seeds require a minimum temperature of 18 degrees Celsius (65 degrees Fahrenheit) in order to germinate successfully. The most reliable way to provide this warmth is to use an electrically heated *propagator* – a tray with a heated base and a clear plastic top, that creates an ideal growing environment for seeds and cuttings.

Planting your seeds

Here's how to go about planting your seeds in containers:

1. **Fill each container with potting compost, firming it gently.**

2. **Water well and allow it to drain.**

3. **Sow seeds at the depth recommended on the seed packet, and cover if necessary.**

4. **Label containers with the type of seed, the planting date and the days to germination; and then set the containers in a warm place.**

5. **Check the containers daily, and as soon as you see the first seedling appear, move them to a well-lit position.**

Caring for the emerging plants

Here's a little advice on how to care for your growing plants:

- ✔ **Watering:** Plants growing in small containers may need watering daily. Strive to keep the soil evenly moist – think wrung-out sponge. Too much moisture can lead to root rot; too little moisture wilts the plants. The best way to water seedlings is from below, placing containers in a sink or tray of water for half an hour or so. Doing so minimises the risk of *damping-off disease.* (See Chapter 19.)

- ✔ **Transplanting:** Depending on the type of plant, the size of the container and the length of time until you set the plants out in the garden, you may need to transplant seedlings into larger containers. Do the transplanting when the roots are starting to fill out the container but before they begin to wrap around the perimeter and grow out the drainage holes.

Keep seed packets so that you can refer to them during the season for information such as spacing guidelines. Also, if a crop performs especially well or a flower is particularly beautiful, having the packet allows you to track the source of the seeds.

Buying as Plants

Few gardeners grow all their plants from seed; most buy at least some plants. Loads of retailers sell plants, from the traditional greenhouse/nursery to the supermarket, and you can also order plants from catalogues or through the Internet.

Wherever you purchase them, buying the best-quality plants that you can afford pays off, which in general means visiting specialist businesses that raise plants for a living.

Knowing your sources

Here are a few pros and cons of different plant sources:

- ✔ **DIY stores:** Garden centres attached to home improvement and mass-market department stores may well have cheap prices and vast quantities of merchandise, but watch out for neglected plants. For the best-quality plants, show up when the delivery trucks do (often just before the busy weekend and bank holidays). Be sure that the perennials, trees and shrubs that you buy are truly hardy in your climate. The staff may or may not have a clue.

✔ **Garden centres and nurseries:** These businesses usually offer the best varieties for your area and can give you advice on growing them. They may even grow the plants on-site to avoid them being subjected to shipping stress – and this style of production is the most eco-friendly too. Usually, the size-to-price ratio is excellent. Although the selection may not be as large as a mail-order catalogue offers, usually you find a good blend of favourite 'bread-and-butter' varieties and newer, more exotic offerings.

✔ **Mail-order catalogues and websites:** The glossy pictures look perfect and enticing, and the descriptions sound like dreams come true. Due to shipping costs, however, usually the plants are smaller and more expensive than locally grown specimens. The plants also have to undergo the rigours of hot or cold and bumpy travel, although good suppliers package their plants well and dispatch quickly. Catalogues do, however, expand the universe of available plant varieties and offer a cornucopia for the specialist and connoisseur.

Whatever your retail source, choose vigorous, healthy specimens. When you buy your plants by mail, you're at the mercy of the supplier, and so when you do find a reliable source, you may want to stick with it instead of repeatedly looking around for the best deal.

Picking winners

While you're out shopping for plants locally, knowing what qualities to look for is crucial. Here's how to pick the winners from the losers:

✔ **Look for disease-free foliage.** Avoid plants with yellow, brown or black spots or with wilted, yellow or mottled leaves.

✔ **Check for pests.** Pass your hand gently over a bed of seedlings. If a cloud of whiteflies or tiny gnats swirls up out of the foliage, move on by. Peek under leaves for aphids, thrips and spider mites, and check stems for scale insects. (Chapter 18 contains details on specific pests.)

✔ **Watch for mechanical damage.** Look for broken stems or bruised leaves, which can indicate rough handling.

✔ **Choose plants whose compact growth is in proportion to pot size.** If the top of the plant appears to be too big for the pot, the roots may be squished and/or the plant has been pushed into vigorous growth with lots of fertiliser. Both conditions compromise the plant's health and its ability to adapt to life in the garden.

✔ **Small is beautiful.** Large plants make a more immediate impact in your garden, but they cost more and recover from transplanting more slowly than smaller ones. Small perennials and annuals often catch up in growth to larger plants within a few weeks and may even surpass them by season's end. And although they're tempting, avoid flowers that are already in full bloom; instead, look for compact plants with healthy foliage.

Taking short cuts with tender plants

You can short-cut the seed-sowing process in a couple of ways, which is ideal if your thumbs are less than green or you don't have the necessary covered space to sow seed from scratch. Although more expensive than using seed, growing plants in the two following ways is cheaper than buying garden-ready plants in late spring – plus you still have the satisfaction of raising the plant through at least some of its young life (and you're pretty much guaranteed results):

Ready-grown seedlings are available in garden centres and nurseries in late winter and early spring. These seedlings are all ready to be transplanted (a process known in the horticultural world as *pricking out*) into small pots or trays, and grown under cover.

Starter plants, which are also known as plugs, tots or baby plants, are young plants that need to be potted straight away into 8-centimetre (3-inch) pots or similar.

Obviously, never buy wilted plants. They need water to survive, and even a short drought when they're small and growing rapidly can affect how they perform in your garden in the coming months. If you see widespread wilting in the nursery, take your business elsewhere.

When you transport your plants from the store to your planting site, protect them from wind, heat and cold. Never carry them uncovered in the back of a truck – conditions in the bed of a moving truck are the equivalent of a hurricane – and don't leave them to cook in a closed vehicle or to shiver in winter.

Preparing and Planting

After you get your plants home from the nursery (as we discuss in the preceding section 'Buying as Plants'), or when you decide that those you planted from seed have grown enough (as the earlier section 'Starting from Seed' describes), you can pop them straight in the ground, right? Not so fast. Plants have a better chance of survival if you follow this advice first:

✔ **Check the calendar and the weather forecast.** Be sure that the temperatures are warm enough for the type of plant. If frost is a threat, you may be waving goodbye to your tender plants.

✔ **Prepare plants for outdoor life.** If you're planting indoor- or greenhouse-grown plants, you need to give them time to toughen up gradually so they can adjust to the natural wind and sun conditions in your garden. Introduce them to the great outdoors on cloudy, calm days, and bring them inside at night. Gradually allow them more direct sun and wind over a period of 7 to 10 days. Allow the soil to dry between waterings, but don't let the plants wilt. This process is called *hardening off*. When the plants can tolerate full sun and wind, they're ready for planting in the garden. (Be sure to cover tender plants if late frost threatens.)

✔ **Time your planting to coincide with seasonably cool and damp weather.** Transplanting invariably damages some roots, and so plants may not be able to take up water fast enough to endure hot, sunny conditions. If you must plant in hot weather, provide shade and keep plants well watered until they can survive on their own. The best times for putting in hardy plants is autumn first and foremost, when the soil's moist yet warm, and plants can concentrate on root growth. In most areas, you can plant through winter in favourable spells, so long as the soil isn't wet. Early spring is another good planting time.

✔ **Prepare the soil:** The perfect garden soil is weed-free, well drained, loosened and fertile. Read Chapter 5 for much more info on soil.

When the weather's co-operative, the ground's ready and your plants are hardened off, you're ready to plant. The following three sections tell you what to do.

Putting in container-grown perennials, annuals and vegetables

Whether your plants are purchased or homegrown, the act of putting plants in the ground is pretty straightforward, and most plants are quite forgiving. Water the plants a few hours before planting and then follow these simple steps to get your potted plants off to a good start:

1. **Dig a hole that's twice as wide as the pot.**

   Use a shovel or trowel, and make the hole deep enough to keep the plant at the same soil level that it occupies in its container.

2. **Gently remove the plant from the pot.**

   Cup your hand around the stem of the plant and tip the pot gently, supporting the soil with your fingers and the heel of your hand, and protecting the stem and leaves from bruising. Push or tap on the bottom of the pot if the plant resists, but don't pull on the stem.

   If the plant is large, lay the container on its side on the ground and slide the plant out. Squeeze or roll the pot if necessary to dislodge the pot full of roots, or *root ball*; if you can't loosen it, cut the pot away.

3. Put the plant into the hole.

In most cases, the *crown* of the plant – where the roots meet the top of the plant, which is usually the soil level in the pot – needs to be at or slightly above ground level. (A few exceptions that benefit from deep planting do exist, however (such as clematis), and so check the instructions that come with the plant.) Add soil to or remove soil from the hole so that the plant sits at the proper height.

4. Backfill with soil.

Gently fill around the roots, firming the soil around the roots while keeping the crown at the proper level.

5. Water the plant.

Saturate the soil gently, being careful not to displace the soil. Add more soil to the hole if needed.

If water appears to be running off rather than soaking in, create a raised rim of soil in a circle around the plant to create a shallow basin (as Figure 8-1 shows). Fill the basin with water, and allow it to soak in. To prevent stem rot, remove the raised area during prolonged wet weather and after the plant is established.

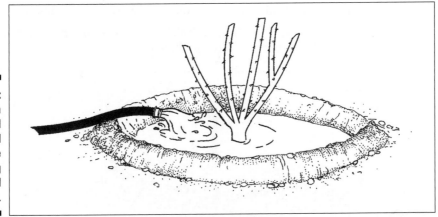

Figure 8-1:
Make a raised ring of soil around the planting hole, and fill with water.

Settling in bare-root plants

Plant your bare-root hardy plants (such as roses, fruit bushes, trees or shrubs) as soon as possible after purchasing or receiving them through the mail. Immediately unwrap the plants from the packaging, and make sure that the packing material – usually sawdust or shredded paper – is moist. If you must delay planting for a few days, dig a hole outside, place the complete bundle of plants in the hole and cover the roots with soil. If the ground's frozen, just take off the outer packaging and ensure that the roots stay moist.

Don't store bare-root plants with any ripening fruit, such as in a refrigerator or root cellar, because the fruit gives off ethylene, which harms growing plants.

Here's how to get your bare-root plants off to a good start:

1. **Prune any damaged or dead roots and stems.**

   Also prune back extra-long roots so that they're even with the others.

2. **Soak the root system.**

   Place the roots in a bucket of tepid water for about an hour before planting.

3. **Dig a planting hole that's twice as wide as your plant's root spread.**

   Follow the instructions that come with the plant to determine how deep to dig the hole. In many cases, the plant's crown needs to sit at the soil level, but the level varies depending on the type of plant.

4. **Make a mound of soil in the bottom of the hole.**

   Set the plant on top of this mound, spreading the roots evenly around it (see Figure 18-2).

5. **Fill the planting hole half way.**

   Add water to settle and moisten the soil around the roots.

6. **Finish backfilling and then water the plant thoroughly.**

   If necessary, create a rim of soil in a circle around the plant to keep water from running off (as we illustrate in Figure 8-1).

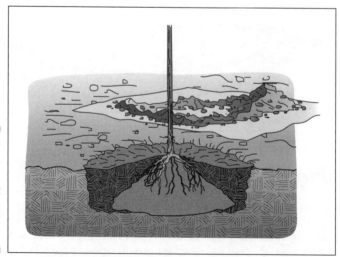

Figure 8-2:
Spread the roots of a bare-root plant around a central cone of soil.

Planting trees and shrubs

Trees and shrubs are often expensive, so take special care when planting them.

Be sure that the soil's moist, but not sopping wet, at planting time to make handling easier. Prune any damaged, dead or broken stems before planting.

When you talk with people who plant trees for a living, you discover that a proper way exists to prepare a hole. What's the big deal, you may ask? Well, if you plant trees and shrubs too deep or too high, or crowd the roots into a small hole, they fail to thrive. Experts have also discovered that adding compost or soil conditioner just to the planting hole isn't only unnecessary, but also can contribute to trouble in the long run: roots tend to stay where the soil is most fertile and may not venture outside the walls of the original hole. The resulting plants have small root systems, are more prone to drought stress and likely to blow over in a strong wind.

The ideal soil for planting has been cultivated, improved with organic matter, plus fertiliser if necessary, and then allowed to settle for several weeks.

Here's the right way to plant a container-grown tree or shrub (flip back to 'Settling in bare-root plants' for details of how to plant bare-rooted ones):

1. **Dig a hole slightly larger than the plant's container.**

   The width of the hole should be able to accommodate the roots, without being at all coiled or bent, when spread out. You may need to widen it further once you remove the pot (in step 3).

2. **Check the planting depth.**

   Test the depth by setting the plant in the hole. The *trunk flare* – where the trunk widens near the base – needs to be at the soil surface or slightly above it. Plant shrubs at or slightly above the soil depth at which they previously grew.

3. **Prepare the roots.**

   Lift the plant out of the hole and slip it out of its pot or remove the wrapping. Prune broken roots and gently unwind tangled roots, preserving as many roots as possible.

4. **Put the plant back in the hole and backfill with soil until about half full.**

   Fill the hole with the soil you removed from the hole, working it gently around the roots and holding the tree in position.

5. **Firm in the plant.**

   This process is often called 'heeling in', because you literally use your heel to firm down the soil. Firming is essential to avoid air pockets around the roots that stop them from coming into contact with the soil.

6. **Finish filling the hole with soil and add water.**

   Using a watering can, or a gentle trickle from a hose, thoroughly soak the roots and surrounding soil.

7. **Make a watering basin (spring/summer only).**

   Build a low ring of soil around the perimeter of the planting hole to hold water for the first few months (refer to Figure 8-1). Knock the ring down when the tree begins growing actively.

8. **Mulch and water again.**

   Spread a 5-centimetre (2-inch) thick layer of bark or shredded leaf mulch over the planting area. Ensure that the mulch isn't actually in contact with the trunk, however, as it can potentially cause rotting. Then water the tree again.

Feeding, Watering and Maintenance

All too often gardeners put poor plants in the ground and simply leave them to get on with growing – and then wonder why they don't do well. If you provide plants with just a bit of nurturing in the initial months after planting, as in the following list, they amply repay your care with lots of strong growth, beautiful blooms and handsome foliage.

- ✔ **Watering:** The first few weeks after planting are crucial, and if the plant's in active growth it hasn't yet put down enough roots to support itself. Therefore, planting during the dormant period (autumn and winter), or in early spring when growth is slow, is the best idea, because plants can concentrate on settling in and putting down roots, instead of making top growth as well.

   If you're able to plant during the ideal seasons, nature's most likely to provide plenty of refreshing showers while your plant settles in to its new home. Otherwise, you need to keep the roots moist during the critical establishment period. If the weather's dry, give the roots a good soaking two or three times a week, making sure that you provide enough water to penetrate right down through the root ball. This amount varies depending on the size of plant, but can be up to a bucketful at a time for a small tree, for example. Early morning or in the evening are the best times to water.

   Mulching the surface with compost, chipped bark or any mulch material is an excellent idea (we describe mulching in Chapter 21); it reduces extremes of temperature and slows water loss by evaporation.

- ✔ **Feeding:** If you plant in well-prepared soil and include a slow-release fertiliser, you don't need to add more food for several months. (Flip to Chapter 7 for the low-down on fertilisers.) Thereafter, feed only early in the growing season (spring or early summer); any later and you encourage too much soft growth that's susceptible to pest infestation or damage from frost.

✔ **Annual maintenance:** When your plants are fully at home, your job's nearly done – and for most of the time you can sit back and enjoy them. Do keep weeds at bay, though, or they compete with your plants for water and nutrients (check out Chapter 21 for loads of weeding tips).

After spells of severe weather, particularly frost and wind, do a quick check round your plants. The roots may have lifted a bit in the cold and require a quick firm-in with your boot; a large plant may have swayed in the wind and opened up a gap around the stem – again a bit of firming is all that's required; or tree ties may loosen and start rubbing the bark. A few minutes attention can save a lot of problems.

Understanding what's at stake

All but the smallest trees are likely to need support for a year or two until they put down enough roots. Using a short stake (about a third of the tree's height is a good guide), place in the ground at an angle of 45 degrees and secure using a wide plastic tree tie. (If you can't find a proper tie, old nylon tights or stockings make excellent plant ties because they stretch gently as the plant grows.) Avoid using tall stakes because the tree comes to depend on the support and doesn't develop enough of a root system to support itself.

Chapter 9

Enjoying Home-grown Feasts

• •

In This Chapter
▶ Choosing edible crops and planning your garden
▶ Knowing what your plants need for success
▶ Growing veg successfully in small spaces
▶ Using covers to extend the harvesting season

• •

*F*or most people, growing chemical-free food is what organic gardening is all about. As news continues to emerge about the dangers of chemicals used on crops and the adverse impact on the environment of shipping food for thousands of miles, more people are choosing to grow their own food – and finding that homegrown vegetables are fresher and taste better than the shop-bought kind.

In this chapter, we look at designing and starting your edible garden, and give you tips to make your gardening more productive – including growing under cover to extend the harvest season, thereby creating havens for your plants and, on a larger scale, you! We also describe how to deal with particular situations: small-space gardening, raising crops in containers and even harvesting a small feast from your windowsill.

Going Your Own Way: Good Reasons for Growing Your Own Grub

For many gardeners, growing organically is all about producing healthy food – fresh from the garden, full of vitamins and most importantly free from harmful chemicals. After decades of people becoming divorced from the food they eat, a quiet revolution is going on. People are becoming increasingly aware of the quality of their food and its source: witness the upsurge of interest in farmer's markets, organic produce and, of course, 'grow-your-own'. Recently, sales of vegetable seeds outstripped flowers, something that would have been unheard of a decade or two ago. 'You are what you eat', as the saying goes.

Although chemical-free crops are the prime appeal for most organic gardeners, don't forget the following other big benefits:

- **Choice:** The home gardener has access to hundreds of different varieties of fruit and vegetables, whereas in the shops your choice is usually limited to several of each variety. Gardeners can concentrate on choosing varieties for flavour, whereas commercial growers are restricted to those that pick, travel and store well. You can also grow some of the old and unusual *heirloom* or *heritage* varieties with fascinating looks and wonderful flavours. Many of these old-fashioned varieties have been saved from the brink of extinction by the charity Garden Organic, which now has over 800 varieties of vegetable in its Heritage Seed Library.

- **Environmental benefits:** Most people nowadays are familiar with the concept of *food miles* – the environmental impact caused by the distance crops have travelled. Browse any supermarket to see that produce is freighted in literally from around the world, consuming vast quantities of fuel in the process. Grow your own, and the food mileage is zero!

- **Health:** Quite apart from the nutritional benefits of eating nutrient-rich, chemical-free crops, the gardening process itself improves your health. Being out in the fresh air is good for you not just physically (gardening is jokingly called 'visiting the green gym') but also therapeutically – getting back to hands-on contact with nature is wonderful for mental health. Research carried out by the horticultural charity Thrive found that gardening had such an impact on health, relaxation and well-being that it should be considered on a par with other types of therapy.

- **Price:** A lot of fruit, veg and herbs cost more to buy than to grow yourself. Some of these plants are really quick and easy to grow too, especially salads including Lollo Rosso lettuce, rocket, mizuna and mixed baby leaves.

- **Quality and freshness:** Many shop-bought veg is cold-stored, treated with preservatives and otherwise prepared to last a long time; those glossy apples may have left their tree months ago!

- **Taste:** Quite simply, a world of difference exists between tired fruit and veggies that have sat on the shelf for days and crisp, fresh-picked home-grown produce. Tomatoes and fragrant strawberries still warm from the sun create a real taste explosion, and sweetcorn straight from the plant is mouth-wateringly delicious.

Deciding What Plants are Suitable for Your Patch

Choosing edible crops that you like – and which like your garden – is a key starting point. A browse through a handful of seed and fruit catalogues reveals a mouthwatering treasure chest of potential crops – but how do you decide what to grow first? Available space certainly has a strong influence; obviously, if you've a pocket-handkerchief plot, large characters such as orchard trees are straight off the list. If your growing room is limited, skip to the later section 'Succeeding in Small Spaces'.

Also, you need to consider your local climate – wind, frost, rainfall – in conjunction with your own growing space. A key point with any aspect of gardening is to work with nature, rather than against it, because you achieve much more rewarding results and harvest better crops.

Avoid low-lying areas where cold air collects (known as a *frost pockets*) that can damage early fruit blossom and delicate young foliage. Generally, inland and upland areas are cooler than land near the coast or estuaries, because the sea has a tempering effect on ground temperature.

Bear in mind that the growing season in the north of the UK is shorter than in the south.

You may dream of a big garden filled with all types of fresh and inviting produce, but getting to that stage takes experience and preparation. For the first-timer, small is beautiful; take time to get it right on a small scale before launching a market-garden-size project. Keep the following ideas in mind to save yourself a lot of work and frustration later in the season:

- ✔ **Start small.** Little plants and seeds turn into a big commitment as they grow. A 3 x 6-metre (10 x 20-foot) garden gives enough space to cultivate a variety of vegetables, such as lettuce, beans, carrots, tomatoes and peppers. If you want to grow space hogs such as marrows or pumpkins, you can expand this area to 6 x 9 metres (20 x 30 feet). Planting too large a space to keep well tended is the number-one cause of gardener frustration and burnout.

    If you've taken on a large area, such as an allotment, cover part of it with landscape fabric to stop weed growth, or sow a cover crop (as we discuss in Chapter 21) to keep your land in order until you're ready to expand.

- ✔ **Keep things convenient and inviting.** For crops that you want to harvest little and often, such as herbs and salads, place the garden in a location where you can see it daily.

- ✔ **Grow a mix of crops.** Planting a variety of crops ensures that something produces. Also, diversity in the garden encourages good insects and helps reduce problems from harmful insects.

Selecting the Best Varieties

Plant choice widens dramatically every year, which means hard decisions for you. Don't just focus on your current favourite crops, but zoom in further to discover plants that give you the best results:

✔ **Look for pest and disease resistance.** For organic gardeners, choosing varieties with natural resistance is of paramount importance. Fortunately, as manufacturers withdraw increasing numbers of chemicals, all gardeners have to look at alternative approaches. The result is that plant breeders are concentrating even harder on producing resistant varieties.

✔ **Note days to maturity.** If you live where summers are short or plan to grow a succession of crops, look for relatively fast-maturing varieties.

✔ **Grow the unusual.** Consider planting unusual crops or varieties – those that aren't readily available in markets. Regular white potatoes are easy to find and inexpensive, but you may have difficulty finding Pink Fir and blue potatoes in shops, and when you do they're often expensive.

✔ **Consider plant size and appearance.** If your garden space is at a premium, look for varieties described as 'compact', or choose those that look so good they merit a ringside seat in your patio containers, raised beds or flower borders.

✔ **Buy Award of Garden Merit (AGM) varieties.** This Royal Horticultural Society award highlights varieties that are outstanding performers in the garden, and so always home in on AGM varieties whenever you're facing a choice. The AGM categorisation applies to both ornamental and productive crops.

Understanding What Crops Need

To grow a great harvest, your fruits and vegetables have essential requirements, from the environment above them to the soil beneath. This section guides you through the plant necessities.

Supplying soil, sun and shelter

Successful organic gardening is based on good soil, and so flip to Chapters 4 and 5 to read all about becoming familiar with your ground and what you can do to improve it. Measuring your soil pH (and amending if necessary) is important: most crops grow best in a slightly acid soil with a pH value of 6.5, although members of the cabbage family, or *brassicas*, prefer a pH of 7–7.5. Altering your soil pH can take up to a year, and so don't delay checking this aspect.

Going for an allotment

If your garden is small or you want to grow a lot of produce, an allotment is well worth considering. With the massive surge of interest in 'grow-your-own', getting a plot may require a wait, or a bit of searching. Start with your district or parish council (likely to have a waiting list, and so check how long it is). Private allotments, land-share schemes and community gardens (including with the National Trust and some garden centres) are springing up nationwide: your local library may have details, and also look at Google Earth (www.google.co.uk/earth) to find the nearest site. Close to your home is always best because you'll be making lots of trips to care for and harvest your crops. If you can find absolutely nothing, write to your council; they're obliged to investigate obtaining land if six of more people request an allotment. Or take matters into your own hands: any group of people can form an association to rent land and sublet it as allotments: contact the National Society of Allotment and Leisure

Gardeners (NSALG: www.nsalg.org.uk) or Scottish Allotments and Gardens Society (www.sags.org.uk/) for advice.

When you obtain an allotment, ask about site rules with regard to vehicle access, permitted buildings, livestock and any problems such as major pests, theft or vandalism. The nearer you are to the tap, the better, because regular hosepipe use may not be allowed. Consider sharing a plot too, because a whole one is well over 100 square metres (more than 1,000 square feet). A recently cultivated plot has more instant appeal than an overgrown one, but do assess impartially because another may be in a better spot or have well-established fruit trees or bushes.

The website www.landshare.net matches landowners with people wanting a plot. Sven Wombwell's excellent *Allotment Gardening For Dummies* (Wiley) can tell you even more about the subject.

Nearly all crops thrive on soil that has been recently improved with plenty of well-rotted organic matter such as manure or compost. Root crops, however, (such as carrots) do best on soil that was manured a year or so before, or you end up with forked roots that chase after clumps of nutrient-rich manure! If your soil is heavy and poorly drained, mound up the soil to make raised beds.

A reasonable amount of sun is vital: the sunnier the site, the better. If your site doesn't get at least six hours of sun each day – don't even try to grow food crops there; get an allotment instead! (See the sidebar 'Going for an allotment'.)

You need to tackle windy, exposed sites. Wind causes physical damage to crops, slows growth and discourages pollinating insects. Consider planting hedges to develop into natural windbreaks, or put up artificial netting or mesh windbreaks in the short term. Crop covers help on a small scale, or on a larger scale, put up a greenhouse or polytunnel. (Check out the later section 'Extending the Season: Growing Early, Late and Exotic Crops' for more info.)

Watering and feeding

All plants need water in varying degrees, of course, but if you're limited with regard to access to water supply (such as on an allotment) give serious consideration to what you grow. Some crops are more hungry and thirsty than others: large-fruited ones such as marrows, courgettes and pumpkins need a highly fertile ground and plenty of water. Tomatoes aren't as thirsty but still need a steady supply of moisture, because fluctuations in supply cause the fruit to split. Deep-rooted perennial plants such as artichokes, tree fruits, briar fruits and bushes, are all good choices because their roots can quest downwards in search of moisture.

As an organic gardener, you provide most of the food for your plants by thorough soil preparation, but fertilising as well helps you to get heavier, better crops. Turn to Chapter 7 for more information on organic fertilisers.

Succeeding in Small Spaces

Small garden owners, even patio and balcony gardeners, take heart: a wealth of wonderful and available gardening solutions ensures that even the tiniest spaces can grow a feast of scrumptious fresh produce. You can now pack many vegetables, herbs, fruits and even trees into pots. Plant breeders are responding to demand with new veg varieties that look good enough to merit pride of place on your patio, and having plants conveniently close means that you're much more likely to grab a salad for lunch, or pep up a dish with a handful of garden-fresh herbs.

Cultivating crops in containers

When you're choosing containers, don't be fooled into thinking that you have to spend a fortune on smart pots. You can use anything that holds soil and make drainage holes in the base for growing great crops. Don't skimp on the soil though: buy good-quality potting compost (in bulk is cheaper if you need a lot).

Drainage is essential; check that pots have sufficient holes and stand just off the ground so that any excess drains freely.

Regular watering is vital, especially for fruit-producing crops such as tomatoes, cucumbers and courgettes where fluctuations cause problems including fruit split. Many different watering systems are on sale if you want to ease the workload, from computer-controlled automatic ones to simple bottle-top watering spikes that turn old drinks bottles into handy mini-irrigation devices. All crops benefit from feeding too, with an occasional dose of slow release fertiliser (which releases the nutrients over a period of time) or with regular liquid feeds.

Producing fruit pots

Advances in fruit tree production have resulted in space-saving trees that enable the smallest backyards and balconies to become mini-orchards. You can grow blueberry bushes in large containers of lime-free (*ericaceous*) compost, and adaptable strawberries thrive in growing bags, tall strawberry tubs and even hanging baskets.

Some fruit trees are naturally dwarf, others are produced by the 'grafting' of a named variety onto a root system or *rootstock* that influences the trees' size. (Chapter 13 contains more on this subject.) If you've room for a couple of trees, choose two different varieties (of the same fruit) that bloom together and pollinate each other, so that you get a good crop. If you've space for only a single tree, it must be *self-fertile* (meaning that pollinates itself) or a *family* type with several different varieties all on one tree – how cool is that!

Grow your trees in a good-sized container (30–40 centimetres/12–14 inches high and wide) that holds about 30 litres (6.6 gallons) of compost. Carry out planting at any time of year, unless your trees are supplied bare rooted and need planting while dormant. If the tub is lightweight, put a couple of bricks in first so your tree doesn't blow over. Use loam-based potting compost, water regularly, feed during spring and summer – and enjoy a wonderful harvest.

Going up: Growing plants vertically

Take a tip from city planners: when you're stuck for space – grow up! Nearly everyone has outdoor space with lots of verticals – walls, fences, window-sills; throw in garden dividers such as trellis or posts, and you've incredible potential for a grow-it-yourself a feast. The only must-have for crops is at least a few hours per day of sun. You can take on vertical growing in one of two ways:

- ✔ Using suspended containers, and planting crops to train upwards.
- ✔ Growing flat against a wall or fence.

Containers have undergone a radical revamp: these days you can buy portable pouches and hanging containers, often made from recycled materials; and small-scale modular versions of the 'green walls' that are popping up in cities such as VertiGarden and Easiwall – great for herbs, salads and strawberries. Most of these containers incorporate integral watering systems and hence are easy to care for.

If you prefer the look of traditional hanging baskets or window boxes, opt for designs that are *self-watering*, with built-in reservoirs that cut watering frequency from daily to a couple of times a week. Tiered growing frames and 'ladder allotment' solutions also make the most of limited ground space.

Climbing or tall-growing vegetables are fantastic space-savers. Instead of sticking to old favourites such as tomatoes or runner beans, consider cucumbers, tall maincrop peas, French beans, sweetcorn, aubergines, sugarsnap or 'mangetout' peas and squash. Bear in mind that tall veg need deep containers and plenty of support.

Trained fruit is fabulous for small gardens too. Fruit trees can be grown in fan shapes, as *espalier* (or horizontally trained) and in single or double-stemmed *cordons* (grown at a 45-degree angle). (Check out Chapter 13 for more on these techniques.) You can train soft fruit on supports too – such as rambling blackberries and loganberries (though do choose thornless varieties for restricted spaces, for obvious reasons) – and grow gooseberries, red and white currants as cordons. Hop to Chapter 12 for much more on soft fruits.

Using frames and supports

Tall cropping plants need substantial supports on which to climb. Never underestimate the weight and wind resistance of mature plants loaded with fruit, especially now that strong summer gales are becoming a more frequent occurrence. Make-your-own options include stout, straight branches saved from winter pruning (hazel and ash are ideal) and frameworks of bamboo canes held together by bought connectors. Use synthetic string when making frames, because natural twine may start to rot before the end of the growing season. Some bought planters and raised beds have integral cane supports, which is worth bearing in mind when buying. If making your own beds, build in lengths of narrow plastic pipe at the construction stage.

You can buy many different designs of tailor-made frame, in materials including wood, plastic and metal. Frames for growing bags are available, too.

Raising windowsill crops

You can use even small indoor spaces to give fantastic crops of healthy food, right through the year, by growing windowsill salads and sprouting seeds.

A sunny windowsill of crops can look great as well as being highly productive. Lettuce and other salad leaves look attractive and are well worth growing for the convenience of having your own fresh leaves to hand. What's better than harvesting your own crisp, fresh leaves to eat at once, full of flavour and vitamins, instead of having tired shop-bought produce that was picked days ago? Simply make regular sowings of seed every 2–3 weeks from late winter through to autumn, to produce a steady supply of leaves.

Relatively new on the scene is the concept of *microgreens*, which is an expanded take on the old favourite crop of mustard-and-cress and uses a range of vegetables such as broccoli and salad onions to sow thickly in trays and harvest when young.

Growing salads within reach

Here are a few suggestions on salad ingredients that grow well on windowsills:

- **Cress:** Grow pots of compost or on trays of moist kitchen paper, to mature in just a few days. Greek cress has a hotter, spicy flavour.

- **Lettuce:** Loose leaf or 'cut-and-come-again' varieties look attractive, which is useful because you can harvest only a few leaves at a time over several weeks. 'Frillice' has bright green, finely divided leaves; 'Bijou' is a handsome glossy red with frilly-edged and crinkled leaves; 'Lollo Rossa' is deeply frilled, green in the centre and crimson-edged; and 'Salad Bowl' is a mix of red and green oak-leaved shaped leaves.

- **Mizuna:** An Oriental salad vegetable with attractive, finely divided, bright green leaves that have a mild spicy flavour.

- **Salad leaf mixtures:** A mixture of different vegetables including lettuce, endive, mustard, rocket and chicory that gives an attractively flavoured and good-looking blend of baby salad leaves. Look for different types such as spicy, stir-fry, Oriental and Mediterranean.

Sprouting seeds

Crammed with vitamins and minerals, sprouting seeds are incredibly easy and quick to grow and are perfect to add to salads, sandwiches and stir-fries. You don't even need a windowsill – just a spot in reasonable light that can accommodate a large jar or a special sprouter. Salad sprouts are most popular in winter when crops are in short supply, but you can produce them all year round too, with the minimum of work.

You can purchase a range of tailor-made seed sprouters, although a large glass jar with muslin secured over the neck is adequate to produce a small, steady supply. Simply fill the jar about a quarter full of seed, and then cover with tepid water and soak for 2–8 hours, depending on the size of seed – less for small seeds, and more for larger ones. Drain off the water and stand the jar in a warm, well-lit spot. Then, just remember to rinse and drain twice daily. Watching the sprouts develop is fascinating and they're available for use in just a few days. Small sprouts such as alfalfa and radish are ready in 2–3 days and all types mature in less than a week.

Here are a few types of sprouting seeds:

- ✔ **Alfalfa:** These small sprouts have one of the highest nutritional values and are ready in 3–4 days. Eat raw.

- ✔ **Chickpeas:** These crunchy sprouts mature in 3–5 days. Eat raw or lightly stir-fried.

- ✔ **Green lentils:** These sprouts are ready in 2–4 days and best eaten raw.

- ✔ **Fenugreek:** These spouts feature a spicy flavour that's strongest when young. Eat raw or cooked. Ready in 3–5 days.

- ✔ **Mung beans:** These popular bean sprouts produce large, crunchy sprouts in 3–5 days. Eat raw or stir-fried.

- ✔ **Radish:** These crisp sprouts have a hot, tangy flavor and are ready in 2–4 days. Eat raw.

Extending the Season: Growing Early, Late and Exotic Crops

The outside growing season is limited to spring through to autumn, with a few hardy winter crops, even if you garden in the mildest areas. In the coldest regions, your season is much shorter. But as we describe in this section, you can employ lots of canny tricks to stretch out the growing period, at either end of the year: from simply raising seedlings on a sunny windowsill to erecting a greenhouse or polytunnel. Just decide how much time – and money – you want to spend.

Starting early

Sowing seeds indoors gets you a flying start on the growing season, compared to sowing directly outside. You can start off hardy crops, such as lettuce, salad leaves, beetroot, carrots, parsley and chives, early in late winter, and *harden off* (gradually acclimatise to the outside world) and plant outside in mid-spring. You can also sow tender veg in early spring, to plant out when all danger of frost is past. And try buying starter plants that are all ready to pot up and carry on growing. (Turn to Chapter 10 for more details.)

You need to harden off plants growing under cover for a couple of weeks before planting out. Here a *cold frame* pays dividends: these small-lidded structures are made of glass or clear plastic. You open the lid during the day and close at night to begin with, and then leave it open by increasing degrees unless frost threatens.

Warming the soil

At the end of winter, the ground is cold and inhospitable to seeds or young plants. However, you can get started 2–4 weeks early by covering and warming the soil, using polythene (clear or black). After a week or two of warming, sow the seed and keep covered – but check regularly and remove the polythene as soon as growth begins.

Using cloches and crop covers

Keeping off the worst of the weather creates wonderful little microclimates, so that you get earlier, heavier and better quality harvests. From simple home-made cloches to bed covers and entire plant houses, the gardener is spoilt for choice.

To make mini-cloches for individual plants, cut the base off large clear plastic drinks bottles and remove the lid.

You can purchase larger, rigid plastic cloches that are suitable for small groups of plants. Cover entire raised beds or rows of crops with a tunnel cloche or cover of fleece or polythene, supported on a framework of hoops, which is integral with some bed designs. Plastic plant houses are economical to buy, some with shelves to grow small plants, or some that go over a container of tall plants such as tomatoes in a growing bag.

Among the latest innovations is the pop up 'greenhouse', which springs up to give a handy 1.8 x 2.4-metre (6 x 8-foot) structure, and an insulated one with double walls.

Growing in a greenhouse

A walk-in structure is heaven for the gardener, creating a little haven from the elements at any time of year. Even a tiny greenhouse means that you can grow quantities of young plants and ultra-early crops such as strawberries, new potatoes and tomatoes. A good greenhouse is costly: but even so, buy the biggest you can afford. When budgeting, take into account essential extras such as benches and a little heater (not to mention the running cost of the heater).

Putting polytunnels into service

If you're a keen gardener who wants to raise lots of crops – and you've the space – go for a *polytunnel*, a structure of metal hoops covered with polythene.

Although not as snug as a greenhouse (polythene isn't as good at retaining heat as glass), the protected environment allows you to harvest veg and herbs year-round, to grow exotic crops such as melons and to get delicious out-of-season harvests of strawberries.

Polytunnels come in a wide range of sizes, but bear in mind that you get what you pay for (like most things in life) and the cheaper, free-standing tunnels aren't likely to last anywhere near as long as a rigid, professional-quality structure.

Chapter 10

Raising Organic Vegetables

. . . .

In This Chapter

▶ Getting in a whirl with crop rotation

▶ Growing veg in beds

▶ Sowing and caring for vegetable plants

▶ Reviewing vegetable varieties

. . . .

*Y*ou can produce harvests of delicious, healthy and chemical-free veggies in a garden of any size, from courtyard tubs and raised beds to large vegetable plots or allotments. Use the organic practice of mixing different plants by placing crops in with your ornamental plants in borders, so long as they get enough sun, air, food and water. Veggies like to be pampered in order to come up with the goods, and prefer a sheltered, sunny site on fertile soil.

In this chapter we provide loads of useful info on easy ways to produce organic crops, including growing on a bed system and rotating your crops from year to year to avoid pest and disease problems. In addition, we give a rundown on the most popular crops, how to grow them and some varieties that are particularly suited to organic gardening. So, what are you waiting for . . . get planting so you can start eating!

Planning Your Vegetable Garden

You can be as creative or traditional as you like in your vegetable-garden design. Plant everything in straight rows or create imaginative curved raised beds (we discuss beds in the later section 'Gardening the Easy Way: No-Dig Beds'). If you've an oddly shaped garden, don't worry – just make rounded and triangular beds; whatever fits. Or go truly creative and make, for example, a heart-shaped raised bed planted with red-leaf lettuce and carrots!

If you want to take an organised approach, draw your garden plan on graph paper, laying out rows and raised beds with a ruler and pencil. To figure out how many plants fit into a row or bed, follow the guidelines on the seed packets and make little dots or circles to indicate the larger veggies, such as broccoli, tomatoes and squash. Flip to Chapter 3 for lots more on garden planning.

When you plan your vegetable garden, leave room for walking paths at least 45 centimetres (18 inches) wide so that you can harvest and work the beds easily. And don't be afraid to mix in herbs and flowers. The more colour and variety a garden has, the more beautiful it is, and the more likely you are to strike an ecological balance with birds and beneficial insects that help keep harmful pests in check.

For organic garden success, keep the following techniques in mind. They may help you grow better and more vegetables, too.

- ✔ **Spread the wealth.** Don't plant all the same type of vegetables in one spot. Instead, say, plant two small patches of beans in different places in the garden, so that even if animals or insects destroy one patch, they may not find the other.

- ✔ **Rotate crops every planting season, if possible.** Crop rotation is an important part of vegetable gardening, both for organic and nonorganic gardeners, as a way of avoiding pests and diseases. Turn to the following section, 'Rotating Crops: Problem Avoidance in Action', for much more.

- ✔ **Use succession planting.** Some crops, such as lettuce and radish, mature quickly, and so you can plant them several times throughout the growing season for a constant supply of tender new vegetables. This technique works best when you plant small patches of each vegetable every two weeks. In this way you don't have a glut of lettuce, and you can extend the growing season.

- ✔ **Use intercropping or catch cropping.** To make the most of available space, grow small and quick-growing crops with or in between larger ones. Try sowing radish (fast) in the same row as parsnip (slow) and lettuces or mixed salad leaves between onions or sweetcorn.

Rotating Crops: Problem Avoidance in Action

Organic gardeners focus on prevention rather than cure, and crop rotation is a major part of growing healthy and productive vegetables. *Crop rotation* means that you avoid growing the same crop in the same spot for several years in a row, primarily because some diseases and pests are particular to a certain plant, or group of plants.

If you grow the same crop in one place for years, not only do pests and diseases particular to the plant build up in the soil and surrounding vegetation, but also the soil gets depleted of any nutrients associated with that crop. Adding fertilisers may not help, because most likely the trace elements are depleted as well as the major nutrients.

For this reason, gardeners use crop rotation to help keep their plots in good shape. The simplest crop rotation rule is not to grow plants from the same family in the same spot for more than a couple of years, but not doing so for three or four years is even better. Farmers have been practising crop rotation for thousands of years, but it was Jethro Tull, inventor of the seed drill and 'father' of the Agricultural Revolution, who some 300 years ago came up with the four-year rotation method that's still widely used today.

Crops are divided into the following four groups, which have common likes and dislikes and are liable to various problems from pests or diseases:

- ✔ **Brassicas:** cabbage, cauliflower, radish, swede and turnip
- ✔ **Carrot and tomato family:** carrot, celery, parsnips, peppers, potato and tomato
- ✔ **Legumes:** all peas and beans
- ✔ **Onion family:** garlic, leeks, onions and shallots

You don't need to worry about building all crops into a rotation: long-lived perennial ones such as asparagus and artichokes obviously stay put, whereas a number of annual ones aren't subject to much in the way of pests or diseases and can be fitted in wherever suits. Just avoid growing such easy-going ones (including courgettes, lettuce, marrows, salads and sweetcorn) in the same spot for years.

Figure 10-1 shows how to go about implementing crop rotation on your plot.

Add lime to the brassica crop plot in the autumn before planting to counter the possibility of clubroot. In this rotation system, lime benefits the brassica crop but has less effect for the following legume crop, which also likes lime. The system has less effect still for the onions, which aren't too fussy and least of all for the potato crop, which dislikes lime. You can then add lime again in the autumn of that year, ready for the brassicas.

Year 1

Plot 1	Plot 2	Plot 3	Plot 4
Legumes (peas & beans)	Alliums (onions, garlic, leeks, shallots)	Root vegetables & tomatoes. Do not add manure before planting.	Brassicas (cabbage, cauliflower, broccoli, kale, and so on). Add lime before planting.

Year 2

Plot 1	Plot 2	Plot 3	Plot 4
Brassicas	Legumes	Alliums	Root vegetables & tomatoes

Year 3

Plot 1	Plot 2	Plot 3	Plot 4
Root vegetables & tomatoes	Brassicas	Legumes	Alliums

Figure 10-1: Using four roughly equal plots for a four-year crop rotation.

Year 4

Plot 1	Plot 2	Plot 3	Plot 4
Alliums	Root vegetables & tomatoes	Brassicas	Legumes

...and then the cycle starts again.

Gardening the Easy Way: No-Dig Beds

The ultimate easy way to grow crops in the ground is in 'no-dig' beds – brilliantly simple, yet effective. Most gardeners love the chance to cut down on work, too! The basic principle of no-dig beds (which can be raised or at ground level separated by paths) is to cultivate the soil thoroughly and then avoid treading on it again. If foot traffic hasn't compacted the ground, you don't even need to dig.

To add organic matter over the years, you can revitalise the soil by spreading a layer of compost or manure on the surface and letting nature take the strain. Soil organisms do the rest, gradually drawing down this new material into the soil.

Grasping the benefits of 'going to beds'

Although you don't have to grow your veggies on a bed system – whether at ground level or raised – doing so provides a tidy and organised method and dramatically reduces the amount of annual maintenance.

For ground-level beds, you can simply separate them with paths: neat and paved if you've the materials and budget or want your garden to look smart; chipped bark or garden shreddings, on their own or laid over landscaping fabric to prevent weed growth, if you're happy with something more functional and cheaper.

Raised beds, however, have some benefits over ground-level ones and are a good low-maintenance way to grow your own veg (low maintenance, that is, after the initial hard work of building and filling). Soil drains well and warms faster, and so you win at both ends of the season with earlier and later harvests. You can buy a wide range of ready-made raised beds, assembled or in kit form.

Raised beds are naturally well drained and so you need to have a source of water close by. Install water butts if your beds are close to buildings, to collect and store rainwater (particularly handy if you're on a water meter!).

If your soil is poor in terms of drainage or quality, raised beds enable you to increase the depth of fertile soil. They're also a more manageable size for newer gardeners to tackle, and are great for children. Many schools use raised beds in their playgrounds, to allow pupils to garden without getting totally covered in dirt (even though children are generally 'mud magnets'!).

Protecting crops against pests is also more straightforward with raised beds. Buy or make raised bed covers using horticultural fleece or ultra-fine insect mesh. Such snug-fitting materials protect crops from many pests including snails, caterpillars, aphids and birds.

Gardeners with bad backs or any mobility problems are sure to welcome the canny innovation of tall wooden raised beds, solid ones or 'on legs' – almost like a table with a bed on top – which do away with the need for bending. One additional advantage not obvious at first glance is pest protection. The legs can be wrapped with copper tape to repel slugs and snails and with non-setting insect glue to trap voracious vine weevils.

Sizing and shaping up

Whether you plan raised or ground-level beds, make sure that you can reach the middle of the bed from both sides, without treading on and compacting the soil. Therefore, you need a total bed width of 1.2 metres (4 feet), though obviously this size can be varied a little depending on your height – and arm length! Make paths between beds around 45 centimetres (18 inches) wide. This space looks a lot when you mark out a new bed system, but don't be tempted to compromise and shrink the width; in the growing season your burgeoning beds of crops are going to tumble out over the paths.

If you do have to tread on the soil in your bed, use a plank or something similar to spread your weight and avoid compacting the soil.

Make your raised beds at least 15 centimetres (6 inches) above soil level, preferably 30 centimetres (12 inches) high to grow a good range of crops, and 38–45 centimetres (15–18 inches) to grow hungry, deep-rooted veg such as beans, marrows, potatoes and pumpkins.

Preparing the ground properly

The key to successful ground-level bed growing is not skimping on the initial cultivation. If you find yourself sweating and cursing at this stage, just remind yourself of all the years ahead when you don't need to dig at all!

Double dig the ground to two spades' depth (as we describe in Chapter 5) and add plenty of organic matter such as well rotted manure or garden compost: a minimum of a barrowful per square metre (10 square feet). Freshly dug soil is looser and therefore higher than before: don't worry if the soil mounds up a little, it soon settles back down.

Raised beds need to be filled with soil, but before you do so (for beds that are standing on soil) check that the ground beneath has reasonable drainage by forking it deeply in several places. Although you can take soil for your raised beds from the garden, do make sure that it's reasonable quality, and mix in plenty of organic matter as above. If you need to buy in soil to fill your beds, save money by purchasing in bulk (loose, or in cubic metre 'dumpy bags') – doing so also uses less packaging than buying bagged topsoil or compost.

If you can, buy a blend of topsoil and compost – though check the quality because some of these blends use recycled municipal compost that's high in woody material. If insufficiently rotted, this compost can 'rob' your plants of nitrogen for the first few months.

Choosing crops for raised beds

Selecting what to plant for ground-level veg growing is no different to conventional grown vegetables. For raised beds, however, especially in higher-profile spots in the garden, you do need to adopt a slightly different approach. After all, looks *do* matter when you're looking at your beds every day.

Luckily, many vegetables now look as good as they taste and make gorgeous patio displays alongside colourful summer flowers. Browse through the seed catalogues and discover red-leaved lettuce, frilly Oriental mizuna, golden courgettes, purple beans, bush or trailing tomatoes bearing yellow or red fruits, and red, orange, green or yellow peppers bushes. Of the leafy vegetables, Swiss chard wins hands down for sheer good looks with vivid red, yellow or orange midribs – 'Bright Lights' is a mix of colours and 'Charlotte' is scarlet. Carrots are top candidates, because they can develop long, juicy roots in good quality, stone-free soil.

Although we advise avoiding space-hungry brassicas, you can buy mini varieties such as 'Cauliflower Nemo F1' and 'Cabbage Samantha F1'. Some flowers make great partners for vegetables too: grow those with edible flowers such as violets, marigolds, nasturtiums and pinks, to make a gorgeous and unusual garnish to salads and other dishes.

Determining What Veg to Plant . . . and When

Although you've hundreds of options when choosing what veggies to grow, nearly all vegetables are *annual plants* that die after one season of growth and fall into overall two groups:

- ✔ **Frost-tender vegetables** – such as courgettes, cucumbers, peppers, sweetcorn and tomatoes – grow best in hot weather and don't tolerate any frost. Although you can sow them after the last frosts, the growing season rarely gives enough time for them to mature to harvest. For this reason, gardeners start these plants indoors, in early to mid-spring, and then plant out after the frosts (or buy ready-grown plants from the nursery or garden centre, of course).

  Alternatively, you can grow these crops under cover: in greenhouses, polytunnels or portable plant houses. (Skip to Chapter 9 for more information.) Have a word with your local nursery or garden centre, or a gardening neighbour, to determine your average last spring frost date, if you're not sure when it usually occurs.

- ✔ **Hardy vegetables** – including broccoli, carrots, lettuce, onions, salads and spinach – tolerate frost. Usually you can sow them in the garden from mid-spring onwards. These crops not only tolerate cool weather, but also need it in order to grow and mature properly. You can keep sowing many crops through the summer to provide a late summer and autumn harvest, and the hardiest ones such as leeks and most brassicas can be grown for a winter harvest.

You can start vegetable plants in your garden in several ways. You sow many crops – broad beans, carrots, peas and radish – directly in the garden soil, where they grow. Other plants that take a long time to mature their crops – such as cabbage, leeks, peppers and tomatoes – grow best if they're transplanted. These plants need an early start in a greenhouse or in your house four to six weeks before you set them in their permanent garden location. This head start is critical in cold areas with short summers. (Find out more about starting seeds indoors in Chapter 8.) Base your choice of veg on how much time you have and on whether your favourite varieties are more readily available as plants or seeds.

Growing methods are changing with the wider availability of ready-grown and new types of veg. Gone are the days when your only option was growing from seed – which can be satisfying, but frustrating when bad weather or pests take their toll. Nowadays you can buy ready-grown seedlings or baby plants in spring to pop in pots to grow under cover until the frosts are over, or garden-ready plants that can go straight into the ground at planting time. The best candidates to buy in this way are frost-tender crops such as tomatoes, cucumbers, peppers and aubergines, which can be troublesome or time-consuming to grow from seed – and can't go outside until late spring or early summer.

The latest development is 'grafted' vegetables: real 'Formula One' thoroughbreds that are grown on specially selected root systems for fantastic crops and disease resistance. Not surprisingly, they come with a higher price tag but are well worth considering if you're limited to having just a few plants.

Determining a planting date

The easiest way to organise your vegetable planting schedule is to make a calendar, which is a wonderful mid-winter job to do beside a roaring fire, surrounded by seed catalogues full of the promise of delicious crops!

Although catalogues often include a sowing, planting and harvest calendar, making your own is useful so that you fill in only the crops you want to grow. Begin by marking your average last spring frost date, and then fill in the planting dates for different crops. You can write 'Plant peas' two weeks before the last frost date, for example. If you do most of your gardening on weekends, fill in the nearest weekend date. Use your calendar to guide your indoor seed-starting, too. If you plan to grow your peppers indoors for eight weeks, and you intend to plant them in the garden a week after the last frost date, count back seven weeks from the last frost date and write 'Start peppers indoors'.

Such calendars simplify your planting and ensure that you don't forget anything.

Sowing, Planting and Caring for Your Veg

When you've planned your site and dug and prepared your soil, you can get down to the sowing and planting.

Sowing seeds and setting out plants

The general rule for planting seeds is to plant them twice as deep as the seeds are wide, but your best bet is to follow the guidelines on the seed packet. Keep the soil evenly moist after planting. Always plant seeds in rows so that later you can differentiate and remove weed seedlings between and within the rows.

If you're transplanting plants that were started indoors or in a greenhouse, give them at least a fortnight to *harden off* (acclimatise to harsher outdoor conditions) before planting them outside. Use your planting calendar (like the one we describe in the earlier sidebar 'Determining a planting date') to help you time your planting. Find out more about sowing seeds and growing your own transplants, hardening off and planting techniques in Chapter 8.

When you plant young vegetable plants in the garden, you can set some types deeper in the soil than they grew in their pots. For example, plant peppers, tomatoes and cabbage-type plants right up to their first set of *true leaves* (the ones that look like miniature adult leaves). Planting more deeply gives plants stability, and some plants form roots along the buried stem.

Fertilising: Feed me, feed me!

Many vegetables are hungry plants and benefit from fertiliser applied to the soil in advance of planting. (See Chapter 7 for more on organic fertilisers.) *Heavy-feeding* vegetables – courgettes, marrows, sweetcorn and tomatoes – may need monthly doses of fertiliser to perform their best, whereas *light feeders* – beans, peas and radishes – need little or no additional fertiliser.

Apply fertiliser according to the label instructions. Sprinkle granular fertiliser 15 centimetres (6 inches) from plant stems, and rake or hoe gently to incorporate it into the soil. Water the soil to dissolve and disperse the fertiliser. Use a watering can to apply liquid fertiliser around the bases of the plants.

If you've healthy soil, you may not need to fertilise. Even organic fertilisers can accumulate in the soil, causing a harmful salt build-up that damages plant roots. Also, excess fertiliser can run off into streams, causing water pollution.

If you give your plants too much nitrogen at the wrong time, you may even prevent some vegetables from forming fruit. Courgettes, peppers and tomatoes, for example, may grow loads of lush foliage but few flowers or fruit.

Weeding and watering

As soon as you see signs of vegetables germinating – or even before – you're likely to see weeds too. Become familiar with what your chosen vegetables look like when they're small so that you don't pull them out instead of the weeds. Planting in rows and marking seedlings carefully helps you distinguish crop from weed.

The best way to control weeds is to hand-pull or slice them off with a hoe when they're young; you disturb less soil that way, and the weeds are easier to pull up than when they're more mature. When you finish weeding, mulch around the vegetables to conserve moisture and help control weeds. (Head to Chapter 21 for loads more on weeding and mulching.)

Watering is critical during the early stages of plant growth, but it's also essential when the plants are forming and ripening fruits. Mulching is an excellent way to conserve soil moisture, but you may need to do supplemental watering, depending on the weather and where you live. Instead of watering with overhead sprinklers or your garden hose, use soaker hoses to apply water directly to the soil: you minimise disease problems and waste less water.

Harvesting time

Reaping the rewards of your labours is one of most gardeners' favourite activity, second only to eating. The temptation is to go out and harvest as soon as you see veg growing, and you'll be glad to know that some crops taste best when they're harvested young, including beans, cucumbers, lettuce, peas and summer squash. The more you pick of these crops, the more they produce! In fact, if you allow vegetables to become too mature on these plants, they may stop producing altogether because the plant feels as if it's 'done its job' in producing seed and doesn't need to bear more flowers and fruits.

For many other veg crops, however, you have to be patient. Beets, carrots, peppers and tomatoes taste best when they're allowed to ripen and grow to maturity in the soil or on the plant. When in doubt, take a bite (after washing the fruit, of course, which is particularly important with organic crops growing on well-manured soil). If the flavour doesn't suit your taste, wait a few days before you try again.

Most vegetables taste sweetest and are most tender when they're freshly picked. Start the water boiling on the stove before heading outside to harvest the sweetcorn for supper. Peas, summer squash, and runner and French beans are also sweet and juicy when they're picked just before eating. Other vegetables, such as most varieties of winter squash, need a week or two to cure after harvest to develop their full flavour, whereas Brussels sprouts taste much sweeter after the first frosts.

Vegging Out With Veg Varieties

Seed catalogues have so many delicious veggies to choose from that you may have a tough time knowing where to start – and stop! If you're growing your first garden, plant just a few of your favourite vegetables, and stick to one variety of each. As you gain experience, add more kinds and experiment with one or two new crops each year. If something doesn't work out the way you expect it to, try a different variety or growing method, or abandon it and give the garden space to another crop. That's one of the beautiful things about vegetable gardens – you start with a clean slate each year and get the chance to improve and change your garden based on last year's experiences.

In the following descriptions of vegetables, we include some choice varieties, planting and care recommendations, harvest tips and specific pests to watch out for (also check out Chapters 17 and 18 for more information on managing pests).

 Many organic gardeners prefer to buy seeds and young plants that are produced organically. More and more seed companies offer organic seeds, and some specialise in them. Support your local organic growers by buying vegetable plants from them if possible.

Alliums: Onions, shallots, garlic and leeks

Garlic, leeks, onions and shallots belong to a group of pungent plants called *alliums*, which generally form bulbs or enlarged below-ground stems. After potatoes, onions are surely the most valuable and adaptable of all vegetables. Useful as both flavouring and a vegetable, onions are ready for use straight after harvest. (You may also come across spring or salad onions that are completely different because they're harvested to eat fresh, and raw.) Shallots have a sweeter, milder flavour than onions and produce smaller bulbs. Garlic is also an easy crop, so long as your soil is well drained. All these plants form bulbs that keep well, for use throughout winter and into spring. Leeks are large, extremely hardy and an excellent standby winter vegetable.

Don't confuse edible alliums with the many members of the allium family that make lovely additions to the flower garden.

Choose onion varieties according to the time of year you sow or plant: 'Troy' or 'Senshyu Yellow' for autumn planting, 'Sturon' or 'Giant Stuttgart' for spring. As well as the usual 'brown' onions, you can grow red or white varieties such as 'Red Baron' and 'Snowball' that look attractive in many different dishes. Salad onion varieties include 'Guardsman' and 'White Lisbon'. Garlic comes in two types: soft-neck and hard-neck. *Soft-neck* kinds produce 12–18 small cloves and are best for long-term storage. *Hard-neck* types produce 6–12 large cloves and don't keep as long in storage. Garlic 'Vallelado' is specially selected for Northern European conditions. You may also come across *elephant garlic* – in fact more closely related to leeks – which produces huge bulbs with a much milder flavour than true garlic. Good leek varieties for organic growing include 'Ardea' and 'Roxton'.

- ✔ **Planting:** Alliums like well-drained, fertile soil and appreciate raised beds if drainage is poor. Sow onion and leek seeds indoors 8–10 weeks before transplanting the plants into the garden. Keep the tops trimmed to about 7.5 centimetres (3 inches) high until transplant time. Leeks are also available as ready-grown young plants.

  If your soil is well drained and you live in a reasonably mild part of the country, sow or plant onions in autumn for a summer harvest. Sow salad onions from early spring through to late summer. Plant cloves of garlic in autumn or early winter, even in cold climates, to overwinter and mature the following summer. Separate a bulb of garlic into individual cloves, and plant so that the tip is just at soil level.

- ✔ **Care:** Keep your alliums weed free, well watered and fertilised with a high-phosphorus fertiliser (such as bonemeal) to promote large bulb growth.

- ✔ **Harvesting:** When the tops begin to yellow and topple over, onions, garlic and shallots are ready for harvest. After pulling them out of the ground, use them fresh or allow them to dry thoroughly in the sun for several days before storing in a cool shed or garage.

  Pull leeks as needed in autumn and winter. Before temperatures drop so low that the ground freezes, mulch leeks with a blanket of straw, pulling it aside to harvest into winter.

- ✔ **Pests and diseases:** Onion fly and white rot are the worst problems of allium-family crops. Always practise crop rotation with all these crops (check out the earlier section 'Rotating Crops: Problem Avoidance in Action'). Remove and destroy infected plants immediately to prevent further spread of pests or diseases.

Don't plant regular supermarket garlic; the variety may have come from abroad and not be suitable for growing in the UK's cool climate.

Ready, set, onions!

You can also grow onions from *sets* (small, immature onions), which are easier to grow, less prone to onion fly and more reliable than onions from seed in areas with short, cool summers. However, you've less choice of variety among sets, and they're more prone to bolting than onions from seed (although heat-treated sets usually give better results) and more expensive than seed. Plant shallot and onion sets in the spring for a late-summer harvest.

Asparagus

Asparagus plants are female or male, and the best varieties are dubbed *all-male*. The female plants produce seeds, which reduces the amount of energy they put into producing spears. The males don't produce seeds and, therefore, produce more edible-size spears. Good all-male varieties include 'Cito', 'Jersey Knight' and 'Gijnlim'.

✔ **Planting:** Asparagus is a perennial vegetable that can live for 20 years, so take special care to create a proper planting bed. Choose a sunny location with well-drained soil. Dig a 30-centimetre (1-foot) deep trench and add 15 centimetres (6 inches) of compost or well-rotted manure. Form 20-centimetre (8-inch) high mounds 45 centimetres (18 inches) apart in the trench, and lay the spiderlike asparagus roots over the mounds, as shown in Figure 10-2.

The crowns (where the roots meet the stems) need to be about 15 centimetres (6 inches) below the soil surface. Cover them with 5 centimetres (2 inches) of soil and gradually backfill the trench, a few centimetres at a time over the course of several weeks as the asparagus spears grow, until the trench is level with the surrounding soil.

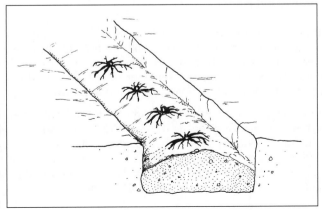

Figure 10-2:
Planting
asparagus
in trenches.

✔ **Care:** Fertilise the bed each spring with compost and a complete fertiliser. Keep the bed weed free and well watered.

✔ **Harvesting:** Don't harvest any asparagus spears for the first year after planting. Let the crowns build up strength. The second year, harvest in spring only those spears larger than a pencil diameter, when about 20 centimetres (8 inches) high, for 3–4 weeks. Cut just below the soil level, using a sharp knife. In subsequent years, harvest spears for up to two months. Then allow the remaining spears to grow to rejuvenate the crown.

✔ **Pests and diseases:** Asparagus beetle is a hard-to-kill pest of asparagus. The adults damage the spears, and larvae eat the fern-like leaves. Handpick and squash to control, and remove the ferns in late autumn. Foraging hens can also help keep the pest in check.

Brassicas: Broccoli, cauliflower, cabbage and company

These closely related plants have the same growing requirements, diseases and pests. All these vegetables thrive in winter, spring and autumn weather, making them indispensable winter standbys. Check days to maturity, which can vary widely among varieties.

Cauliflowers not only come in traditional white-curded forms, but also new coloured varieties such as 'Purple Cape' or 'Orange Sunset', which contain more vitamins and antioxidants than regular white varieties. Cabbages divide into spring, summer/autumn and autumn/winter varieties; the grouping refers to the time of harvest. Some new cabbage varieties such as 'Golden Acre' produce smaller heads that are easier to use and store. Consider including savoy, red and Chinese cabbages too. Kale is considered to be one of the most nutritious vegetables, and so be sure to include a few varieties. Other brassica crops to try include broccoli, brokali (no, not poor spelling, but a cross between European and Chinese broccoli or kailan), calabrese, Brussels sprouts and kohlrabi.

✔ **Planting:** Sow seeds directly into the ground in a seedbed, or start indoors in modular trays, 4–6 weeks before transplanting outside. Brassicas aren't sown direct where they're to grow because of the amount of space they take up. Ready-grown plants are widely available, and can be the best option if you only want a few brassicas.

✔ **Care:** Brassica crops need a moderate amount of fertiliser and water throughout the growing season to grow well; they also like well-drained soil with an alkaline pH (which helps prevent club root disease). Fertilise the soil before planting and again one month later with a complete fertiliser. Place organic mulch such as straw around plants after transplanting to help keep the soil cool and moist.

✔ **Harvesting:** Harvest broccoli when the heads (clusters of flowers) are tightly packed and still green, cutting just below the head. In most cases, new but smaller broccoli heads grow farther down the stem. If the yellow flowers begin to open, the taste becomes bitter, and the plant stops producing more heads.

Harvest cabbage when it's firm to the squeeze. Cut the plants as described for broccoli. To harvest white or *blanched* cauliflower, wrap the upper plant leaves around the developing heads. Harvest within 4–10 days. Harvest Brussels sprouts after the first frosts in autumn when the sprouts are still firm by twisting them off the stem. Pick kale leaves as needed.

✔ **Pests and diseases:** Cabbage white caterpillars are a common pest: the larvae feed on the leaves, decimating the plant quickly. Handpick the caterpillars, or cover the entire crop with fine insect mesh. Cabbage root fly attacks the roots: placing 15-centimetre (6-inch) diameter mats around the base of each plant prevents the flies from laying. Practise crop rotation, and lime the soil if necessary, to avoid club root disease.

Legumes: Peas and beans

This varied group of vegetables is immensely varied and easy to grow. Beans divide into hardy broad beans and frost-tender ones such as French or runner beans. Bean plants grow by forming low bushy plants or climbing up a pole or trellis. In some cases, you can find climbing and bush versions of the same type. Most beans are eaten fresh, but you can also grow types where the pods mature for dry beans used in cooking.

Peas tolerate some frost and can be sown as soon as the soil is sufficiently warm, in spring. Pea varieties fall into two camps: those with edible pods (*mangetout* – a French word that literally translates as 'eat all') and those grown just for the fresh peas inside. Peas with edible pods have flat pods (snow peas) or fat, juicy pods (called snap or sugar peas).

You've a wide choice of legume varieties including 'Broad Bean Sutton' and 'Super Aquadulce' for autumn sowing and 'Hangdown Green' and 'Witkeim' for spring. Climbing beans include 'French Cobra' and 'Helda', and runner beans 'Moonlight' and 'Enorma'. Bush beans include 'Tendergreen', 'Speedy' and 'Hestia'. Peas are grouped by the time taken to mature: early varieties take around 12 weeks, second earlies 13–14 weeks and maincrops 15–16 weeks. Height varies, so do match the variety to your planting spot.

✔ **Planting:** Legumes are easy to grow because the seeds are so large and easy to plant. Sow hardy types (broad beans and peas) directly in well-drained soil. You can sow broad beans in autumn, if your soil is well drained, or early spring. Sow runner and French beans directly where they're to grow, in mid- to late spring, or under cover in mid-spring to get an early start on the season. Harden off before planting out in early summer. Sow peas from mid-spring onwards.

✔ **Care:** After they're growing, climbing French and runner beans need poles for support, whereas tall pea varieties need a screen of netting to climb on. Keep the beds well weeded and watered. Legumes generally don't need supplemental fertiliser because they've the unique ability to make their own nitrogen fertiliser through a relationship with soil-dwelling bacteria called *rhizobia*.

✔ **Harvesting:** Harvest beans when the pods are sufficiently large, but don't leave them on the plant so long that they become stringy. Harvest beans regularly, or they think that they've done their job for the year and stop producing.

Harvest peas when the pods fill and are firm to the squeeze. Keep checking and tasting when the pods begin to size up to be sure that you harvest at the peak of sweetness. Harvest snow peas at any point after the pods form.

✔ **Pests and diseases:** Slugs and snails love the tender foliage of young beans, and mice often eat pea seeds.

Lettuce and leafy salad friends

These quick-growing leaf crops are ideal to start with if you've never grown any veg before. As well as good old lettuce (which comes in loads of different varieties, and types such as crisphead, cos and loose-leaf), you can grow many other leafy plants year-round. Although most are suited to the main growing season, such as rocket and mizuna, others are useful winter crops such as lamb's lettuce and winter purslane. These plants and others are combined in *mixed salad leaves*, which come in mixes such as spicy, Mediterranean and stir-fry.

✔ **Planting:** Sow these seeds little and often to avoid gluts and ensure a continuous supply. Many leafy crops are suitable for container and windowsill growing too, for an early-season or winter harvest. Sow seed thinly, in modular trays under cover to get an early start or direct where you plan to grow, from mid-spring onwards.

✔ **Care:** These easy-to-grow crops just need to be kept moist to produce good crops of succulent leaves.

✔ **Harvest:** Simply pick leaves as required. With some lettuces you pick the whole plant together, whereas others are 'cut-and-come-again' crops in which you harvest a few leaves at a time. This type is best for containers and high-profile spots because the plant looks good for weeks. When plants start to bolt, or run to seed, the flavour becomes bitter, and that's the time to pull up plants and consign them to the compost heap.

✔ **Pests and diseases:** Slugs and snails adore these tasty leaves, particularly when young, and so protect as soon as seeds go in the ground. Turn to Chapter 18 to find out how to respond to these slimy pests. Flea beetle may attack rocket: cover the whole crop with fleece or fine insect mesh right from the seedling stage. Grey mould can be a problem in cool, damp conditions: space plants well apart to allow good air movement.

Peppers and their aubergine cousins

Aubergines and peppers are frost-tender crops that come in a rainbow of colours. Aubergine, which is often called eggplant, most commonly have purple fruit, in a variety of shapes. Peppers are generally are grouped according to their taste: chilli, hot or sweet.

Capsaicin gives hot peppers their heat. Take care when handling hot peppers; don't rub your eyes or an open wound, because the capsaicin can cause painful burning. (Researchers are also studying capsaicin's antimicrobial properties, its ability to relieve pain and its potential to prevent cancer.)

Both aubergines and peppers are great for container growing because the fruits are colourful and ornamental. Different colours include Aubergine 'Rosa de Bianca' (pink and white), Pepper 'Gourmet' (orange), 'Gypsy' (red) and 'Sprinter' (green and red).

✔ **Planting:** Start seeds indoors in mid-spring and harden off before setting plants outside in early summer. Plants love a warm, sheltered, sunny spot and thrive under cover in a greenhouse or polytunnel.

✔ **Care:** These crops need fertile soil and plenty of water to grow well. Fertilise monthly with a complete fertiliser, and add Epsom salts to the water to help growth. Don't over-fertilise with nitrogen fertiliser, though; you get more foliage than flowers and fruits.

✔ **Harvesting:** Pepper fruits turn a rainbow of colours, depending on the variety, as they mature. The beautiful part about peppers is that you can pick them at the green stage or allow them to mature, when they reach their sweetest flavour. You can harvest hot peppers at any stage, but the flavour is hotter and better developed when you allow the peppers to mature. Pick aubergines when the fruit is sufficiently large but before the skin looks dull.

✔ **Pests and diseases:** Red spider mite can be a problem under cover on peppers, and aphids may infest the young shoots. Give good ventilation to crops growing under cover to avoid the fruits rotting. Verticillium wilt disease is the main problem for aubergines. This soil-borne disease causes the entire plant to wilt and die in summer. The easiest solution is planting in containers filled with sterilised potting soil.

Potatoes

Look for early-, second early- and maincrop potato varieties to stretch out your harvest. You plant early potatoes first and they're the quickest to mature – perfect for summer potato salads. If you're limited for space, go for this type. Second earlies are ready in mid- to late summer, whereas maincrops mature during autumn. The later varieties keep longer in storage. Remember that potatoes are frost-tender.

Potatoes also come in baking and salad varieties. Baking potatoes have drier, more mealy-textured flesh; salad potatoes are moist and waxy, and keep their shape when cooked. A huge selection of varieties exists, though of course disease-resistant ones are best for organic gardeners. The new 'Sarpo' varieties have exceptionally good resistance, or try 'Colleen', 'Orla', 'Toluca', 'Remarka' and 'Robinta'.

✔ **Planting:** Potatoes are grown from 'seed', but not seed like most other crops. *Seed potatoes* are small tubers, grown in areas that are generally free from the main potato problems. Potatoes aren't hardy and so gardeners make the most of the growing season by chitting seed potatoes to allow them to develop short, sturdy shoots before they're planted in the ground. *Chitting* is a process that makes tubers produce short stems that have many sideshoots underground so that, in theory, they produce more potatoes.

To chittle, identify the end of the seed with 'eyes' or tiny shoots in depressions. Take egg boxes, shallow trays or seed trays and place the potatoes, 'eye'-end up in the tray, in a light, cool, frost-free place. Chitting generally takes about a month, depending on the temperature. Don't worry if the tubers shrivel – that's quite normal and doesn't affect growth.

You can plant the potatoes when the shoots grow to about 1 centimetre (half an inch) long. If the shoots get too long they're more likely to break off when you plant them. For crops of big tubers, thin the number of shoots on each tuber, leaving the three biggest and strongest.

Always buy certified, virus-free seed potatoes for planting. Never just plant old potatoes from the shops that have sprouted. They may produce a good crop but may also be harbouring pests or diseases that are difficult to eradicate from your plot.

Potatoes grow best in recently cultivated soil that hasn't been amended with fertiliser. Too much nitrogen fertiliser in particular can lead to poor tuber formation.

Plant them 8–15 centimetres (4–6 inches) deep and 30 centimetres (12 inches) apart for earlies, 40 centimetres (16 inches) apart for second earlies and maincrops. Make rows 40–50 centimetres (16–20 inches) apart for earlies, 60–70 centimetres (24–28 inches) for maincrops. As the plants sprout and grow, cover them with soil, mounding or earthing up around the tops of the plants with soil, as shown in Figure 10-3. This method allows the roots to form more potatoes, kills weeds and protects the tubers from the light. Tubers exposed to light turn green and become toxic – never eat green potatoes, even if you cut out the green bits!

Figure 10-3:
Earth up soil around young potato plants.

- ✔ **Care:** Keep the soil moist by watering or applying organic mulches such as hay or straw.

- ✔ **Harvesting:** When the potato tops turn yellow and begin to die back, dig up the tubers. Choose a dry, sunny day to harvest, and with a shovel or fork, carefully dig around the potato plants, and lift up the tubers. Spread them out to dry for several hours, and then store them in a cool, dark, frost-free place in paper sacks. Eat any damaged potatoes immediately; don't put them in to store because they may rot and spoil a whole bag.

  Never store potatoes and apples near one another. Apples give off ethylene gas, which causes potatoes and other vegetables to spoil.

- ✔ **Pests and diseases:** Wireworms tunnel into potato tubers, causing them to rot. These worms are a problem mostly in new gardens created from lawns. Slugs also tunnel into tubers; combat them with a biological control, in the form of a nematode. In both cases, dig up tubers as soon as they're ready, to limit damage.

Fungal diseases, such as potato scab and blight, can ruin a crop. Your first defence is to buy resistant varieties. Control potato scab by lowering the soil pH to below 6 (we describe pH values in Chapter 5). Tackle blight by planting your potato crop in a new place every year, buying certified disease-free tubers, mulching and keeping weeds under control.

Root crops: Carrots, parsnips, beetroots and radishes

Root crops provide good eating through the growing season and well into the autumn and winter, and they're easy to grow so long as you can provide loose, fertile, stone-free soil. If your ground isn't ideal, raised beds provide just the right environment. Radish is one of the quickest and easiest vegetables to grow, and home-grown carrots and beetroot are far sweeter and more succulent than tired shop-bought ones. Parsnip is a useful vegetable for autumn and winter harvest. If you've space, consider turnips and swedes too, because they're also good winter vegetables.

In addition to the usual orange carrots, consider growing white, yellow and purple varieties. If your soil is heavy or stony, try round-rooted varieties such as 'Berlicum' and 'Paris Market Baron'. Some varieties, including 'Resistafly', have some resistance to the troublesome carrot root fly. Beets come in a range of colours in addition to the common dark red (for example, 'Boltardy') including yellow 'Golden Detroit' and pink-and-white 'Barbietola di Chioggia'. Always opt for disease-resistant parsnip varieties such as 'Javelin' and 'Gladiator'. Radishes, such as 'Scarlet Globe' and 'French Breakfast', mature quickly, but winter radish and mooli or Oriental radish are slower growing, for summer and autumn harvest.

- **Planting:** Directly sow root crop seeds a few weeks before the last frost date for your area. Sow the seeds thinly. Radishes germinate within a few days; beetroot and carrots may take two weeks, and parsnips can take several weeks.

- **Care:** Root crops need well-cultivated soil (improved the previous year with compost or manure), weed-free growing conditions and consistently moist soil to thrive. Thin the seedlings so that the eventual spacing is about 5–10 centimetres (2–4 inches) apart, depending on the crop. If you don't thin root crops when they're young, they don't get large enough to eat (you can eat the thinned beet greens). However, try to sow carrots thinly to minimise the need for thinning, because the smell of the disturbed foliage attracts carrot root fly.

- **Harvesting:** Pull up radishes when the roots get large enough to eat. You can harvest carrots and beets as 'baby' vegetables or leave them in the ground to harvest as needed. By all means harvest parsnips from early autumn onwards, but they taste sweeter after the first frosts because the cold turns the starch content into sugar.

✔ **Pests and diseases:** The biggest pest of carrots is carrot root fly. The adult fly lays an egg near the carrot, and the small larvae tunnel into the carrot root (see Chapter 18 for more information). Flea beetle can attack radishes; combat by covering the crop with fleece or insect mesh.

Sweetcorn

One of the most delicious crops to grow at home, sweetcorn is a frost-tender vegetable that's a form of maize with succulent, sweet cobs. Children love sweetcorn and it's easy to grow so long as you can provide a sunny, sheltered site. *Supersweet* varieties such as 'Landmark' and 'Swift' have the sweetest taste and most tender kernels.

Don't grow these types close to any older varieties that aren't 'supersweet' (such as 'Golden Bantam' or 'True Gold') because they're likely to cross-pollinate and develop starchy kernels.

✔ **Planting:** For the most reliable crops, start off seed under cover in small (9-centimetre/4-inch) pots or modular trays. Sow the seed in early to mid-spring, and plant outside after the frosts and after hardening off the young plants. Sweetcorn is also readily available as young plants. Sweetcorn is unusual in that the flowers are wind-pollinated rather than insect pollinated, and so you need to set out the plants out in blocks rather than rows.

✔ **Care:** Sweetcorn needs well-drained, highly fertile soil and warm weather to grow well. Hoe soil up around the plants when they're 20 centimetres (8 inches) tall to support them during windy days and to destroy young weeds that compete with the corn plants. Apply a general fertiliser before planting and water during dry spells.

✔ **Harvesting:** Start checking for maturity when the corn cobs feel full and the silks are brown. You can take a peek under the husks at the corn ear tip to see whether the kernels have matured. Pick the cobs on the young side for the sweetest flavour.

✔ **Pests and diseases:** Although sweetcorn is easy to grow, the sweet cobs are attractive to various creatures, particularly badgers. Turn to Chapter 20 for more on battling badgers.

Swiss chard and spinach

These leafy greens are easy crops to grow because you don't have to wait for the flowers or fruits, as you do with cucumbers or tomatoes – you just eat the leaves, as and when you want!

Swiss chard, spinach and leaf beet or perpetual spinach are vegetable garden staples. Some Swiss chard varieties are ornamental and edible, such as red-stemmed 'Ruby' and multicoloured 'Bright Lights'. Spinach varieties with good disease resistance include 'Bombini' and 'Renegade'. In regions where temperatures warm quickly in spring, look for spinach varieties described as 'slow to bolt', such as 'Palco'.

✔ **Planting:** Get a flying start on the season by sowing the first seeds under cover in modular trays, during early spring, setting one seed per module to avoid root disturbance when transplanting outside in late spring. Or sow outdoors in spring (earlier in mild areas, later in cold ones). Spinach is prone to bolting so make several sowings during the course of the growing season. Make a final sowing in late summer to provide a crop that stays in the ground over winter to harvest in early spring.

✔ **Care:** Leafy greens need nitrogen first and foremost. Improve the soil with compost or manure before planting, and add a nitrogen-rich fertiliser in summer on free-draining soil. Mulch the plants after they establish to keep the soil cool and moist and to prevent soil from splashing onto leaves.

✔ **Harvesting:** Simply harvest greens when you're hungry and whenever leaves are big enough to eat. Pick off the lower leaves first so that new, younger leaves continue to grow from the centre of the plant. When plants *bolt* (send up a flower stalk), the leaves are probably too bitter for most tastes; pull up and compost these plants.

✔ **Pests and diseases:** Snails and slugs can devour a patch in no time. You can trap them; set up barriers; bait them; and, of course, handpick them to keep the populations low. Leaf-miner insects, especially on spinach, can ruin individual leaves. Just pick them off and destroy the damaged leaves, and the plant is fine. Spinach can suffer from mildew, and so choose resistant varieties.

Tomatoes

Easily the most popular garden vegetable, the tomato is frost-tender and comes in a variety of sizes, shapes and colours. The plants, however, fall into two categories. Bush or *determinate* varieties stop growing taller when they reach a certain height and need minimal support, making them ideal for containers (also look for trailing types suitable for hanging baskets or window boxes). Tall or *indeterminate* varieties just keep on growing taller and taller, like Jack's beanstalk! Indeterminate tomatoes require support and training but yield more fruit per square metre/foot of garden space.

Decide on where you're going to grow your tomatoes before choosing varieties, because most types prefer growing under cover in a greenhouse or polytunnel, or outside. Some varieties such as 'Roma' are easy-going and grow in either site. Tomatoes can suffer from blight, and so choose disease-resistant varieties such as 'Shirley', 'Koralik' and 'Diplom'.

Consider what type of tomato you like: little cherry or baby plum tomatoes for salads, larger ones for slicing and eating raw, or something primarily for cooking. All kinds of wonderful varieties are available!

✔ **Planting:** You can sow tomato seeds under cover from late winter onwards, or buy as young plantlets (to pot on and grow yourself) or as ready-grown plants. They need warm growing conditions and so don't put outside until all danger of frost is past. Plant tall and leggy tomato plants to within 10 centimetres (4 inches) of their tops in a deep hole, or place them on their side in a trench (see Figure 10-4); the stems then root. Put supports in place at planting time. Tie or wind indeterminate varieties around their supports as they grow, and snap off extra side shoots to keep the plant from getting too bushy.

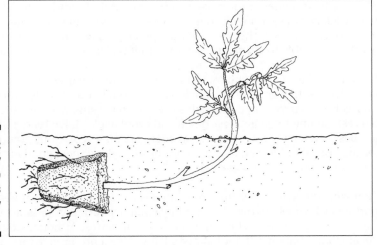

Figure 10-4:
Plant leggy
tomato
transplants
horizontally
in a trench.

✔ **Care:** Mulching with black landscape fabric in cool areas helps speed the growth of tomato plants. Tomatoes need fertile soil, so compost before planting, add a general fertiliser and then feed fortnightly with a liquid fertiliser that's high in potash. Keep the plants mulched and well watered to prevent *blossom-end rot* (discoloration and decay on the end opposite the stem) as fruits mature. Keep soil evenly moist, because fluctuations in supply can cause fruit split.

✔ **Harvesting:** Allow the fruits to turn red (or yellow, gold or whatever their mature colour). The longer you leave them on the vine, the deeper the colour and the sweeter and fuller the fruit flavour. Even if you pick too early, however, fruits continue ripening when you place in a warm, airy room.

✔ **Pests and diseases:** Leaf blight diseases often start as small spots on leaves and then expand to yellow areas, killing leaves and the plant if unchecked. To control, clean up crop debris at the end of the growing season, rotate crops and mulch to prevent the disease spores from splashing onto leaves during rains. Wilt diseases, such as verticillium and fusarium, can cause plants to wilt and die in mid-season. Purchase disease-resistant plants (usually indicated in the variety description), and remove and destroy infected plants as soon as you can to prevent the disease from spreading.

Vining crops: Cucumbers, squash, pumpkins, courgettes and marrows

All these frost-tender crops have the common trait of growing their fruits on long, trailing vines, although some varieties now grow in more compact bush-like patterns. Many of these species can pollinate one another, too, making it nearly impossible to get seeds that grow fruit resembling the original varieties.

Gardeners classify cucumbers as indoor or outdoor varieties, according to where they grow best, and squash as summer and winter varieties. Courgettes, marrows and pumpkins are grown for summer and autumn harvest. Summer squash – pattypan and crookneck – have tender skin and are best eaten soon after harvest. Winter squash – acorn, buttercup and butternut – develop hard skins and dense flesh, making them good for storing through the autumn and early winter.

Pumpkins range in dimension from apple-size to something that needs transporting in a wheelbarrow. You can buy compact varieties suitable for small gardens or containers. The same goes for courgettes. Although courgettes do develop into marrows if not harvested, if you've a preference for one or the other, choose a variety that's named as such.

✔ **Planting:** Sow these vegetables under cover in mid-spring, individually in 9-centimetre (3.5-inch) pots of seed compost. Sow the large seeds on their sides, so that the seed coat slips off cleanly as the seedling emerges. Harden off before planting out after the frosts. You can also sow seed outside, directly where plants are to grow, but obviously the harvest season is shorter. All these crops that produce large, fleshy fruits are hungry ones and need a deep, fertile soil with plenty of extra organic matter. Pumpkins and marrows also grow well on top of a compost heap: simply dig a hole in the top to fill with a bucketload of soil, plant and be amazed.

Even though many bush varieties are available, most squash-family plants need room to spread their vines, and so space them according to seed-packet instructions.

✔ **Care:** Keep the plants well watered, especially when fruits are forming. Protect all squash-family plants and fruits from frost.

Plant bee-attracting flowers around the garden to ensure fruit pollination. If fruits form but rot and drop off before enlarging, poor pollination is probably the cause. For large-fruited marrows and pumpkins, place the swelling fruit on a piece of wood to avoid direct contact with the soil, which can cause localised rotting.

✔ **Harvesting:** Pick cucumbers when they're 10–15 centimetres (4–6 inches) long, before the seeds enlarge. For best flavour, and to keep the plants producing well, harvest summer squash when small and while flowers are still attached. Harvest winter squash and pumpkins when the varieties turn the desired colour and your thumbnail can't puncture the skin.

✔ **Pests and diseases:** Mosaic virus can affect certain plants, and so always go for disease-resistant varieties.

Going beyond the ordinary

Looking for something different? Try these varieties in your vegetable garden:

✔ **Artichokes:** Perennial and easy to grow, but take up a fair bit of space.

✔ **Celeriac** (also called *celery root*): A gnarly, potato-like root vegetable that tastes like celery.

✔ **Celery:** Can be difficult to grow and so choose the easiest type: self blanching.

✔ **Florence fennel** (also called *finocchio*): Its basal leaves form a bulb with a refreshing aniseed flavour.

✔ **Okra:** Also known as lady's fingers for its long, edible pods, okra is a frost-tender vegetable for the greenhouse or polytunnel.

✔ **Oriental vegetables:** A variety of leafy veg – including Chinese amaranth, Chinese cabbage, green-in-the-snow and pak choi – which are excellent for harvesting later in the season and into winter.

Chapter 11

Growing Herbs for the Home and Garden

. . . .

In This Chapter

▶ Planting and using the most common herbs

▶ Surveying some popular herbs

. . . .

Defining herbs is no easy feat when you consider that this group includes plants from every continent and climate. In this chapter we use the term *herbs* to mean plants that people use in some way, from shrubs and trees to short-lived annuals and tough-as-nails perennials.

Throughout history, herbs have served as foods, medicines, fragrances, ornaments and even as magical ingredients. In the days before refrigeration, people used strongly flavoured basil, chives, mint, rosemary, sage, savory and thyme to help preserve and flavour meats. Today, aromatic herbs with scented flowers and leaves bring pleasant fragrances to homes and still help protect woollen and linen fabrics from insect damage. Some medicines consist primarily of herbal preparations. Indeed, people are still discovering the many useful properties of herbs.

In this chapter, we focus on plants commonly grown to flavour foods, to add colour and fragrance to the garden and to make helpful companions for other crops. However, we stress that this chapter covers only a relatively small selection of the many hundreds of herbs that exist.

Growing Herbs

How and where you choose to grow herbs is limited only by your imagination and, of course, by the needs and characteristics of the plants themselves. Most herb plants, however, aren't too fussy about the soil they grow in but it does need to be well drained.

If you're growing herbs simply for their ornamental flowers or foliage, give them fertile garden soil. Herbs grown for fragrance and flavour, however, are more pungent when they're grown in less fertile soil, so go easy on the fertiliser and manure.

Fitting herbs into your garden

You can fit herbs into your garden in myriad ways. Many so called ornamental garden plants are in fact herbs, so tuck them into your flower garden, plant them among your vegetables or give them a special garden of their own. Take advantage of their flowers or leaves to add spark to container gardens and window boxes. Use creeping kinds between paving stones or allow them to trail over retaining walls. Even if you're challenged for space, you can still grow some herbs on a sunny windowsill as houseplants.

If you need a few ideas on how and where to grow herbs, here's a list for inspiration:

- **Attraction for natural predators:** Many herbs have flowers that entice beneficial insects such as hoverflies and lacewings. Even if you're not bothered about a herby harvest, grow a few herbs such as fennel to solve garden pest problems.

- **Container garden:** Treat them as ornamental plants or bring your culinary herbs closer to the kitchen by planting them in pots, tubs or baskets. Choose the most decorative varieties for this purpose (such as gold or purple sage instead of plain old green). In cold climates, grow herbs on the borderline of hardiness such as rosemary and bay in pots that you can bring indoors for the winter.

- **Flower garden:** Many herbs have beautiful flowers or foliage that add colour and texture to flower borders. As a bonus, some of these plants attract butterflies and provide food for their larvae. Good additions to your flower garden include borage, catmint, chamomile, lavender and oregano.

- **Ground cover:** Creeping herbs such as thyme can cover large areas quickly or fill the gaps between stones in a path. Allow them to trail over a wall to add colour and soften the effect of the stone.

- **Herb garden:** Take a herbs-only approach and design an intricately patterned garden. A typical arrangement consists of a geometric border of tidy, compact plants such as hyssop or lavender surrounding groups of herbs with contrasting foliage colours and textures.

- **Vegetable garden:** Some herbs make natural companions for vegetable plants. Basil, for example, is said to improve tomatoes, whereas dill and cabbage complement each other. The flowers of many herbs are attractive to bees and other pollinating insects, which helps to ensure good crops.

Using herbs

Most herbs have fragrant or pungently fla-voured leaves or flowers that make them useful for cooking, crafts, natural remedies, potpourri and more. Consider the following ways to use your harvested herbs:

✔ **Cosmetic:** Many aromatic herbs can be used in ointments, massage oils, face steams, hair rinses and baths.

✔ **Crafts:** Herbs give colour, structure and fragrance to dried wreaths, arrangements and other crafts. Some herbs can be used to dye fabrics.

✔ **Food and drink:** Herbal teas offer alterna-tives to stronger brews. Home-grown fresh or dried herbs can be used in a multitude of ways in sandwiches, soups and salads, meats and vegetables.

✔ **Fragrance:** In the days before frequent bath-ing, vacuum cleaners and indoor plumbing, herbs played a large role in odour control. Today, *aromatherapy*, the art and science of affecting mood with scent, makes liberal use of dried herbs in little pillows and bowls of potpourri.

✔ **Medicine:** People have used herbs to treat just about every known ailment: colds, depression, general aches and pains, headaches and so on. Check out *Herbal Remedies For Dummies* by Christopher Hobbs (Wiley) for ways to use herbs as medicine. Always check that the herb is safe to use, particularly if taking internally: just because a herb's a plant doesn't mean it's safe to consume!

Watching for invaders

Some herbs have a bad habit: they just don't know when to stop growing. These so-called *invasive herbs* travel in the following ways:

✔ **Rhizomes and stolons:** Some herbs take off cross-country, growing horizontal stems from their crowns that creep over or under the soil, forming new plants along the way. (*Rhizomes* grow under and *stolons* on top of the soil.) These plants are useful for covering large areas or filling gaps between paving stones, but rapidly become a nuisance in other locations. Mint is the chief offender: plant in a sunken or raised container to keep its growth within bounds. Pull up escapees as soon as they appear.

✔ **Roots:** With some herbs, such as comfrey and horseradish, your eradica-tion efforts may lead to an even larger patch of the confounded plant. Any bit of root left in the soil may grow into a new plant. Think carefully about getting the site just right before you plant.

✔ **Seeds:** Some plants produce way more seeds than you need. Their little seedlings pop up everywhere, like weeds. Examples of prolific herbs include marjoram and fennel. Keep them in check by removing the flow-ers before they disperse seeds.

Taking a Look at Some Common Herbs

Useful herbs number in the hundreds – at least. In this section, we highlight a few of the most commonly grown herbs. For information about more herbs, as well as in-depth discussions, pick up a copy of *Herb Gardening For Dummies* by Karan Davis Cutler, Kathleen Fisher and the National Gardening Association (Wiley).

Basil

Easily one of the most popular culinary herbs grown, basil *(Ocimum basilicum)* is a tender annual that comes in dozens of varieties, which include both ornamental and tasty forms. For plenty of pesto, grow sweet basil. Or try varieties with unusual foliage, such as purple-leafed 'Dark Opal' and 'Purple Ruffles' or frilly 'Green Ruffles'. To spice up a patio planter, grow compact, small-leafed varieties such as 'Bush Basil' or 'Greek Basil'. For an alternative taste sensation, grow lemon, anise, cinnamon and Thai basil varieties.

- ✔ **Planting and care:** Sow seeds directly in the garden in late spring or early summer, or start indoors by sowing seeds on a sunny windowsill in mid-spring. Give basil moist, fertile, well-drained soil, and space plants about 30 centimetres (1 foot) apart in full sun. Water them in dry weather, and pinch off young flower buds to prevent bloom and encourage more leaves. Protect basil from frost, which kills it.

- ✔ **Special uses:** Use dried or fresh leaves to flavour a wide range of dishes. Basil is a natural insect repellent: grow in pots on the windowsill to repel flies; crush and rub a few leaves on your skin to repel midges and mosquitos.

Calendula

The beautiful flowers alone make planting calendula or pot marigold *(Calendula officinalis)* worthwhile. Add the fact that the flowers are edible and can be used in healing salves, and calendula becomes a must-have in the herb garden. An easily grown hardy annual, calendula is an old favourite cottage garden flower.

- ✔ **Planting and care:** Sow seeds directly in the garden in full sun, in spring or autumn. The plants can tolerate light frosts. If flowers are allowed to form seeds, the plant self-sows.

- ✔ **Special uses:** The yellow, gold or orange flowers have a tangy and peppery taste; they can be used in dyes and added to salves, soaps and lotions, and make a pretty garnish to salads.

Caraway

Caraway *(Carum carvi)* is a member of the carrot family, a biennial that produces aromatic seeds in its second growing season, although some plants may bloom the first year. The plants have fine, lacy foliage topped by umbels of tiny white flowers.

✔ **Planting and care:** Sow seeds directly in the garden during spring in full sun, where they can remain for two growing seasons. In hot locations, give caraway partial shade. Seeds germinate slowly and have deep taproots, which bring minerals to the surface and loosen the soil. Plants grow 30–60 centimetres (1–2 feet) tall, although tend to be shorter in their first year.

✔ **Special uses:** Add the leaves to salads or soups. Use the distinctively flavoured seeds in breads, stews and other foods. The flowers attract many beneficial insects.

Chamomile

Chamomile *(Chamaemelum nobile)* is a low-growing perennial with lacy, aromatic, apple-scented foliage and small, daisy-like flowers.

✔ **Planting and care:** Although chamomile can be grown from seed, buying ready-grown plants is the easiest option. Double-flowered chamomile and the vigorous variety 'Treneague' can only be propagated by cuttings. Small 'plug' plants are a cheaper option to pots if you need a large number of plants. Chamomile can tolerate some drought and appreciates full sun and well-drained soil. Harvest the flowers when fully open, and dry them on screens in an airy place.

✔ **Special uses:** The dried flowers make a popular tea for relieving stress and heartburn. They're also used in many cosmetics and toiletries: chamomile makes an excellent rinse to brighten fair hair. Chamomile is a good ground cover plant and can even be used to make a small lawn, as long as it receives only light use. Plant 10–15 centimetres (4–6 inches) apart for a lawn.

Chives

Their grassy, onion-flavoured foliage makes chives *(Allium schoenoprasum)* popular in the culinary arts, but this perennial plant makes a handsome addition to the ornamental and vegetable garden, too. Use the neat 30-centimetre (1-foot) high plants at border edges. The dense tufts of mauve flowers bloom in early summer. A related species, garlic chives, has starry white flowers in late summer to early autumn. Both species may self-sow freely.

- **Planting and care:** Grow from seed, or buy a large pot-grown plant and divide it up into smaller clumps of the slender bulbs and plant in any well-drained garden soil. Chives prefer full sun but aren't fussy. If you sow from seed, do so in spring, cover the seeds lightly with soil, keep the soil moist and be patient; the seeds may take 2 to 3 weeks to sprout. Keep weeds away to make harvesting easier. Harvest by snipping the leaves close to the ground.

- **Special uses:** The pungent foliage reportedly repels some injurious pests, especially around roses, tomatoes, carrots, grapes and apples. Chives can also help prevent blackspot disease on roses. The flowers attract beneficial insects. Use chives in cooking, or serve fresh in salads, dips and sauces. The flowers can be used as a garnish.

Coriander

This frost-tender annual herb (*Coriandrum sativum*) is immensely versatile. The flat, parsley-like leaves add pungency to Latin American and Asian dishes. The seeds play a major role in curry and other Middle Eastern fare. Ancient Mediterranean peoples prescribed this herb for many medical ailments.

- **Planting and care:** Sow directly in fertile garden soil, where seeds sprout in a couple of weeks. Plant every 2 to 3 weeks for a continuous harvest, because the plants tend to set seed quickly (especially in hot weather) and stop producing new foliage. Sowing can start in early spring under cover (late spring outside) and continue to autumn. Gather young tender leaves before plants send up flower stalks. Harvest seeds when the seed heads turn brown but before they scatter, and dry thoroughly before using for the best flavour.

- **Special uses:** Use leaves and seeds in cooking. Plant near aphid-prone crops to help repel pests. The flowers also attract beneficial insects.

Dill

Dill (*Anethum graveolens*) is another member of the aromatic carrot family. The seeds are an excellent ingredient in pickles, breads and other savoury dishes. The fine, thread-like foliage is rich in vitamins and flavour for fish, sauces and dips. The tall, narrow plants of this annual herb grow 60–90 centimetres (2–3 feet) tall.

ECO-SMART

Buddying up: Herbs for companion planting

The idea of growing certain plants in close proximity for mutual benefit is well rooted in folklore, and yet scientists are only just starting to explore this aspect of gardening. One way that plants help one another is by providing habitat for insects and other creatures that prey on damaging pests.

Many herbs excel in this role because they've small, nectar-rich flowers and aromatic leaves. Herbs in the carrot family (especially dill, caraway, tansy, fennel and parsley) attract beneficial insects such as lacewings and hoverflies.

Some plants help repel certain pests and even diseases: those with a pungent smell, for example, can keep pests away. Planting annual French or African marigolds keeps whitefly out of the greenhouse; members of the allium or onion family mask the smell of carrots that attracts carrot root fly; coriander helps repel aphids. These examples are just a few popular ones and whole books have been written on companion planting. Organic gardeners take full advantage of getting a helping hand from nature.

✔ **Planting and care:** Sow seeds directly in fertile, sunny garden soil from mid-spring to early summer. Barely cover the seeds and sow again every few weeks for continuous harvest. Thin to 20 centimetres (8 inches) apart. Protect from strong winds. For an early crop, sow under cover in early spring, but use pots or deep modular trays to minimise root disturbance when planting out, because dill develops long tap roots.

✔ **Special uses:** The flowers attract beneficial insects. Dill reputedly makes a good companion for cabbage crops and can be planted with low-growing lettuce and cucumbers. Use the seeds and leaves in cooking.

Fennel

Useful in cooking and as an ornamental plant in the garden, and growing up to 2.4 metres (8 feet) high, fennel *(Foeniniculum vulgare)* is a hardy perennial with attractive feathery foliage and flat heads of yellow flowers. It has a tropical look and resembles giant dill plants. Fennel, however, usually self-sows and can become a nuisance weed, although you can avoid this problem by removing the faded flower heads before the seed ripens. Try the bronze-red-leafed variety 'Purpureum' as an ornamental plant. Don't confuse this herb with Florence fennel, the bulb-like vegetable plant.

✔ **Planting and care:** Sow directly in fertile, sunny soil where you want it to grow, in spring or summer, or buy ready-grown plants. Its long tap-root makes transplanting difficult, except when very young. Protect from strong wind.

✔ **Special uses:** You can use all parts of fennel, from the bulblike root to the leaves, stalks and seeds. Harvest seeds when they turn brown; snip leaves and stems as needed, and use fresh or cooked lightly in soups and sauces. The flowers attract many beneficial insects, particularly hoverflies.

Horseradish

Take care where you plant the tenacious hardy perennial horseradish *(Armoracia rusticana)*; its pungent roots extend deep into the soil, and the smallest piece can sprout into a new plant. The wavy 30–90-centimetre (1–3-foot) long leaves are attractive, however, and small white flowers add to the plant's appeal.

✔ **Planting and care:** Plant the roots in light, deeply dug fertile soil in full sun. To keep horseradish from taking over your garden, plant with the roots restricted – such as in a bottomless bucket sunk into the ground. Wait a year or so before harvesting the roots at any time as required.

✔ **Special uses:** The roots are sharply pungent and valued for the zip they give sauces and tomato drinks. The young spring leaves are edible when they're cooked like spinach. Try a little horseradish to open your sinuses the next time you've a head cold. Some biodynamic farmers (see Chapter 2) believe that horseradish is beneficial in fruit orchards and around potatoes.

Lavender

One of the most recognised and popular scents for cosmetics, toiletries and aromatherapy, lavender *(Lavandula)* is a hardy shrub that also adds colour and fragrance to your flower garden. A number of species and varieties exist, and they all have slender greyish foliage and spikes of flowers. The English lavender varieties, such as purple 'Hidcote' and 'Munstead', grow up to 60 centimetres (2 feet) high. Pink-flowering varieties include 'Hidcote Pink' and 'Miss Katherine'. Other species are less hardy but equally appealing, including French lavender *(L. stoechas)*.

✔ **Planting and care:** Buy young plants or take cuttings in midsummer, because seeds may not give you plants of uniform quality. Plant in spring in compost-enriched, well-drained, even gravelly soil, in full sun. Space plants approximately 45 centimetres (18 inches) apart for a low hedge or mass planting. Shear off the faded blooms after flowering, lightly trimming the shoot tips at the same time, and trim the whole plant in spring to encourage bushy growth. Don't cut back into old wood.

  ✔ **Special uses:** Harvest flowers as they begin to open, and dry them in bundles hung upside down in an airy place. Both flowers and leaves have many uses in the home, such as scenting linen, as potpourri and to perfume a hot bath. The flowers attract bees and beneficial insects.

Mint

With hundreds of varieties to choose from, no doubt you can find a mint *(Mentha)* to suit your taste. Peppermint and spearmint are the most popular, but fruit-flavoured varieties also exist. Some plants have variegated foliage, including the pineapple mint Varieagata. Some mints, such as Corsican mint, creep along low to the ground; others grow 60–90 centimetres (2–3 feet) tall. Mint is a hardy perennial and many varieties have the potential to become invasive, so plant with care.

  ✔ **Planting and care:** Buy young plants or dig up rooted stems of the varieties you want, to make sure that you get the flavour or scent you expect. Plant just below the soil surface and keep the soil moist until the plants begin to grow. Mints can be invasive, and so contain them by planting within a bottomless bucket sunk in the ground (so that the rim is just above the soil surface, which prevents the runners spreading), or plant them where you don't mind having a carpet of fragrant foliage.

  ✔ **Special uses:** Harvest the fresh leaves and add them to many dishes, soups, vegetables and beverages. Mint flowers attract beneficial insects. Also, the fragrant plants reportedly repel certain damaging insects and improve the health and flavour of nearby cabbages and tomatoes.

Oregano

Small fragrant leaves on sprawling 30–60-centimetre (1–2-foot) stems topped by loose spikes of white to pink flowers give oregano *(Origanum vulgare)* a casual appeal for planting in vegetable and flower gardens or trailing over a wall or basket. Oregano is a hardy perennial. Many cooks prefer Greek oregano over the readily available common oregano. Before buying plants, pinch a leaf to test flavour and pungency. Some varieties, such as *Origanum laevigatum* 'Herrenhausen' and 'Kent Beauty,' are more ornamental than edible; *Origanum vulgare* 'Aureum' has attractive golden foliage and combines good looks with culinary use.

  ✔ **Planting and care:** Buy ready-grown plants or start new plants from stem cuttings to guarantee the best flavour. Seed-grown plants may lack their parents' pungent flavour. Any good, well-drained soil in full sun is sufficient. Harvest leaves as needed, or cut whole stems and hang the sprigs to dry.

✔ **Special uses:** The tiny flower clusters attract bees, butterflies and other beneficial insects. The fresh and dried leaves add classic flavour to many Latin American and Mediterranean dishes. Plant ornamental varieties in hanging baskets, patio containers and flower gardens.

Parsley

A common garnish on restaurant plates, parsley *(Petroselinum crispum)* is probably the most recognised herb. The leaves are rich in vitamins A and C, and help sweeten bad breath. Although both varieties are edible, the flat-leafed variety has a stronger flavour, whereas the curly-leafed kind is more commonly used as garnish.

The plants are biennial and hardy; they bloom and run to seed only in their second year. The 30-centimetre (1-foot) tall plants form tidy, bright green mounds of ornamental foliage. Plant in vegetable and flower gardens or in container gardens.

✔ **Planting and care:** Sow seed directly in the garden in spring and summer; germination is likely to be slow, but be sure to keep the ground moist at all times. If you start seeds indoors, plant them in pots or modular trays so that you don't have to disturb their taproots when transplanting them later. Give the plants fertile garden soil and a cool, slightly shady spot for summer crops. Snip fresh leaves as needed, or harvest whole stems and dry the leaves on a screen.

✔ **Special uses:** Use for cooking, especially in Greek and Middle Eastern dishes. Curled parsley makes an attractive ornamental garden plant for edging and containers.

Rosemary

Two types of this perennial evergreen shrub exist – upright and prostrate – and both are fragrant and edible. The short, needle-like foliage of rosemary *(Rosmarinus officinalis)* gives off a heady, distinctive aroma when lightly bruised. Ornamental varieties include those with golden or variegated leaves, pink or bright blue flowers and especially sprawling or upright forms.

✔ **Planting and care:** Start with ready-grown plants or raise from rooted stem cuttings, and plant in well-drained garden soil. Rosemary doesn't tolerate soggy soil or complete drought. The herb is susceptible to frost damage in cold areas, where it needs to be planted in a sheltered site against a sunny south or west-facing wall.

✔ **Special uses:** As an ornamental, rosemary excels in the shrub border or trailing over a low wall. Its aromatic foliage is said to repel flying insects from cabbages and other vegetables. Use fresh sprigs in meat stews; employ dried rosemary for culinary use or to scent rooms and linens. Rosemary can be used to make a conditioning rinse for dark hair.

Sage

Sage *(Salvia officinalis)* is a perennial that grows into a shrubby mound of fragrant leaves. It can grow up to 60 centimetres (2 feet) tall. The 5–8-centimetre (2–3-inch) long leaves are fuzzy and oval, ranging in colour from silver-green, purple and golden to mixed white, green and pink, depending on the variety. Sage is equally at home in the herb garden and among the ornamentals in a container or flower border. In summer, sage produces spikes of blue or white flowers.

✔ **Planting and care:** Buy ready-grown plants, or start sage from stem cuttings, although sage can grow slowly from seeds. Plant in organically rich, well-drained garden soil, and give it full sun. Avoid soggy soil. Prune to keep the growth compact.

✔ **Special uses:** The spiky flowers attract bees and other beneficial insects, and look great in the garden. Use sage to scent dresser drawers and to help prevent damaging clothing moths. Use the leaves, fresh or dried, in poultry and meat dishes.

Sweet marjoram

Similar to oregano, sweet marjoram or Greek marjoram *(Origanum majorana)* is tender and has to be grown as an annual. It tends to sprawl and is best confined in a container or planted in a herb garden.

✔ **Planting and care:** Start from seed in late spring indoors, or buy ready-grown young plants. The plant prefers full sun and fertile garden soil. Remove the flowers to encourage more leaves. Harvest and dry the leaves for year-round culinary use.

✔ **Special uses:** The light-purple flower clusters attract many beneficial insects. The leaves are used extensively in cooking, especially in vegetable and egg dishes. Sweet marjoram has an excellent flavour and you need to make sure that you use this herb in any recipes that ask for marjoram. Because oregano is closely related, sometimes people mistakenly use this instead of marjoram.

Tarragon

A staple in French cooking, tarragon *(Artemisia dracunculus)* is used to flavour a variety of foods, especially chicken, fish and egg dishes. French tarragon – the preferred variety for cooking – can be propagated only from cuttings and divisions. If you see tarragon seeds, they're likely to be Russian tarragon, a hardy but less flavourful plant.

- **Planting and care:** Plant tarragon in full sun and well-drained soil, and water sparingly. Consider growing the herb in clay pots to ensure the excellent drainage it requires to thrive. Move into a sheltered spot for the winter.

- **Special uses:** Use tarragon fresh or dried in just about any savoury dish or sauce.

Thymes

Hundreds of thyme *(Thymus)* species and varieties are available, ranging from creeping 2.5-centimetre (1-inch) high mats to 30-centimetre (12-inch) shrubs. All varieties have tiny oval leaves, in colours ranging from woolly grey to smooth green to golden to white-edged. Even the fragrance varies from mild to pungent, and includes lemon, caraway and coconut.

Creeping thyme makes a fragrant, attractive ground cover plant and is particularly useful to set between paving stones; shrubby types make useful miniature hedges. Clusters of tiny white, pink or crimson flowers bloom in summer, sometimes covering the plants. Creeping thymes are the hardiest kind.

- **Planting and care:** Start with rooted stem cuttings to guarantee the flavour and appearance of your thyme. Plant in well-drained soil in full sun. Divide the plants every few years, and trim bushy types regularly to encourage dense growth.

- **Special uses:** The flowers attract bees and many beneficial insects. Much folklore exists on the use of thyme as a helpful companion plant for roses and vegetables. Use the herb between patio and stepping stones, or plant it as a ground cover to replace lawn in small areas. The trailing kinds look good in hanging baskets and planters. Harvest the leaves and young stems for cooking.

Chapter 12

Picking from the Berry Patch

In This Chapter

▶ Planning your soft fruit planting

▶ Choosing the best fruits for your garden

*F*ew plants give you more bang for your buck than berries. Homegrown blackberries, raspberries, strawberries and currants (often collectively referred to as *soft fruits*) take little space and return months of mouthwatering fruit salads, pies, pancakes and fresh-eating goodness. And don't forget if you live in a milder part of the country, grapes are within your grasp. Even if all you have is a patio plot, you can still grow a mini fruit garden in containers or raised beds, with crops such as succulent strawberries and nutrient-rich blueberries.

Any fruit crop is well worth growing: because berries are perishable and the soft fruits are difficult to package and ship, supermarket berries are expensive and often past their prime. Conventionally grown fruit may be heavily sprayed, making growing your own organic harvests an even more attractive prospect.

With the right preparation, siting and planting, you can grow most of these fruits organically without too much trouble. New disease-resistant varieties appear on the market every year, which makes producing your own healthful, pesticide-free berries straightforward.

Bearing Fruit: Berry Basics

Thorough preparation is vital to producing a good crop of soft fruits. The varieties you choose, where you plant them and how you prepare and maintain the soil all determine whether your berry patch produces bumper crops or becomes a disappointing chore.

Choosing where to grow your fruits

Site selection is more critical for growing soft fruit than for most food crops, because most of these plants stay in place for years. You need to consider a number of factors, including how to protect them.

Birds love to feast on soft fruit just as much as people do, and so you certainly require some form of bird protection to achieve a decent harvest. The ideal environment (if you've the space) is a *fruit cage*, which consists of a metal framework covered with netting, with a door for access. If you're growing smaller numbers of plants, why not make your own framework for netting. You can stretch netting over strawberries, or use cloches. Whatever you do, ensure that the netting is stretched tightly or birds can become entangled.

As you make decisions about where to plant your fruit crops, keep the following requirements in mind:

- ✔ **Air circulation and drainage:** Moving air helps to prevent disease spores from settling on vulnerable fruits and leaves; choose a fairly open site, if possible. High winds cause damage, however, so protect crops with a windbreak if necessary.

   Cold air settles at the bottom of slopes (you may hear this situation referred to as a *frost pocket*), where it can damage early-blooming flowers in the spring. Plant your fruits on the slope of a hill instead of at the bottom.

- ✔ **Locally adapted varieties:** Some plant varieties grow better in particular situations than other varieties. Ask at nurseries or garden centres in your area for recommendations, or check out what's on sale at local farmers' markets.

- ✔ **Soil conditioners and fertility:** Fruiting plants need fertile, moist, richly organic soil to produce the best crops. Improve the soil with compost or composted manure at around a barrow per square metre, and add any pH amendments and nutrients before planting. Check out Chapter 5 for more on soil and drainage.

- ✔ **Soil moisture and drainage:** All soft fruits need well-drained soil. Soggy soil encourages root diseases, which are among the most serious problems for fruits. If your soil drains poorly, however, you can still grow fruits in raised beds. Make beds 15–45 centimetres (6–18 inches) high (depending on the type of crop you want to grow) and 1.2 metres (4 feet) wide, and use with plenty of organic matter.

- ✔ **Sun:** All fruits need at least six hours – preferably more – of full sun each day to produce large, flavourful crops.

TIP

If you're limited for space, look into growing 'high-rise' fruits. You can grow most berry fruits on walls, fences or a post-and-wire framework; blueberries are happy in large pots; and strawberries are fine in tall 'towerpots'. Grow a grape vine over a sunny framework to sit under, such as an arbour or a pergola, to create a dappled shady spot reminiscent of Mediterranean holidays.

Controlling weeds

Controlling weeds is important to grow soft fruit successfully. Many fruits have shallow roots, which can't compete with more aggressive weeds for water and nutrients. Weeds also harbour insect pests that feed on your plants and spread nasty virus diseases. Perennial weeds often cause the most trouble because their roots persist from year to year and often sprout if even a small piece remains in the soil. Annual weeds come in the form of seeds blown by the wind or are carried by people, pets, birds and rain.

Weeding a mature berry patch is a strenuous chore, because most of these plants have shallow roots that don't allow cultivation or that grow in such a way that hand-pulling each weed is the only solution. Weeding thorny brambles is an especially onerous job, and so prevention is key. Flip to Chapter 21 for loads of information and tips on controlling weeds.

Buying plants

Most soft fruits are liable to suffer problems with pests and diseases, and prevention rather than cure is definitely the way to go with this group of plants. For organic success, be sure to choose varieties with good disease resistance and purchase the best-quality, virus-free fruit plants that you can find from a reputable supplier. Doing so pays off in the long run!

If you're fortunate enough to have a local nursery that grows its own fruit plants, by all means pay it a visit. Local nurseries usually offer the best varieties for your area and can give you valuable advice on growing them in your particular situation.

In many parts of the country, however, speciality mail-order nurseries are often the best sources of virus-free, disease-resistant fruits. Organic suppliers usually offer a good range of varieties that are particularly suited to chemical-free gardening. Also look for varieties that have the letters 'AGM' after their names; this abbreviation stands for Award of Garden Merit, and is awarded by the Royal Horticultural Society to plants that give outstanding performance.

Don't put in more plants than you've time to harvest and maintain. Getting overexcited about all the promising fruits you can grow is all too easy, and you can end up buying more plants than you need. Luckily, small fruits freeze very well, but you still have to weed and pick them.

Discovering the Delights of Soft Fruits

Growing berries is one of the most rewarding gardening activities. The season begins with gooseberries and strawberries, and then currants, blueberries, raspberries and blackberries ripen in succession through the summer and early autumn. Pick your own favourites from this section, and get growing!

Beautiful blueberries

Blueberries have shot to popularity as a superfood, rich in vitamins and anti-oxidants. Blueberry has ornamental value as well as edible appeal: it offers small white flowers in spring, glossy green leaves in summer and spectacular crimson foliage in autumn. As an edible fruit, it can't be beaten for fresh eating, pies, pancakes, dessert sauce and jam.

Blueberries are fussy about their soil requirements. They're acid-loving plants with very specific soil needs, including lots of decomposed organic matter and an acidic pH of 4.5 to 5.2. They grow where azaleas and rhododendrons naturally thrive, but if your soil is borderline with regard to pH, you can also alter your soil using sulphur to accommodate their needs. You need to allow at least a year for sulphur to lower soil pH significantly, so plan well ahead, and test the soil before planting. (See Chapter 5 for more on soil amendments and pH.) If your soil isn't at all suitable for blueberries (such as thin soils overlaying chalk or limestone, for example) plants can still be grown in large containers, such as wooden half-barrels, using lime-free (sold as *ericaceous*) compost mixed with equal parts by volume of sand or coarse grit.

All blueberries have shallow roots and need moisture-retentive yet well-drained soil. Provide plenty of leafmould into the soil at planting time. Cover the soil around the shrubs with organic mulch – such as pine needles, shredded oak leaves or chipped bark – to maintain the soil moisture and prevent weeds. Keep the soil moist throughout the growing season, preferably using rainwater (which is free of lime), but if that isn't available use tap water rather than allowing plants to dry out. Avoid deep cultivation, which can damage the shrubs' roots.

Plant blueberry bushes 1.2–1.5 metres (4–5 feet) apart. Don't allow them to fruit for the first two years, to let plants concentrate their energy into developing a good strong plant. Do so by rubbing off the flower buds as they form.

Plant two different blueberry varieties to be sure of a good crop, because they need to pollinate each other. Although some varieties are self-fertile (and set a reasonable crop with their own pollen), such as 'Sunshine Blue' and 'Top Hat', you still get a better crop with two plants.

Ramblin' brambles: Blackberries and friends

If you love fresh berries, you'll be glad to know how easily you can grow them. These delicate and perishable fruits are expensive in the shops, but you can plant your own small patch and produce enough for fresh eating and freezing, too. As well as cultivated varieties of blackberry, which are bred to bear heavy crops of succulent, large and delicious fruits, you can also use related plants such as loganberry, tayberry and Japanese wineberry, all of which you grow in the same way. Collectively, you may find them referred to as *briar fruits*.

Blackberries and related berries are great for making the most of your space, because they grow vertically: train against walls, fences, trellis or a post-and-wire framework. Grow them on boundaries or as garden dividers. However, you must train them as they grow, or they quickly develop into a mass of growth. They also do well on poorer soil where fussier fruits don't thrive. Taking weed-control precautions before you plant is important, because most briar fruits sport lots of thorns – which make weeding the mature plants difficult – and shallow roots that are easily damaged by hoes.

Although these briar fruits do grow well on soils that are less than ideal, you get a better crop on well-prepared ground – deeply dug, with plenty of organic matter mixed in. The ideal time to plant is autumn or during mild spells in winter. If you're putting in more than one plant, allow 1.8–2.4 metres (6–8 feet) between each one. The exception is with 'giant' varieties such as 'Fantastia' and 'Silvan', which need a whopping 5 metres (16 feet) of space! Immediately after planting, cut all the stems back to 30 centimetres (12 inches) from the ground, to encourage strong new shoots. (Next summer, remember to remove the remains of these original stems to stop the plant flowering in its first year – your plant needs to concentrate on growing rather than fruiting.)

Briars fruit on 2-year old stems needs to be pruned out anytime from the end of harvest to the following winter, but you can make life easier by training your plant from its early days (rather like having dogs or children, really). You can train your fruits in one of two ways. Train fruiting stems to one side only, and new growth to the other, or train the fruiting stems both ways in a wide fan with the new shoots coming up in the middle (see Figure 12-1). To train them in this way, put up wire supports and fix them to an existing wall, fence or free-standing post-and-wire framework using *vine eyes* (galvanised screws with an 'eye' through which to run the wire). Make the supporting posts at each end of 10-centimetre (4-inches) square timber.

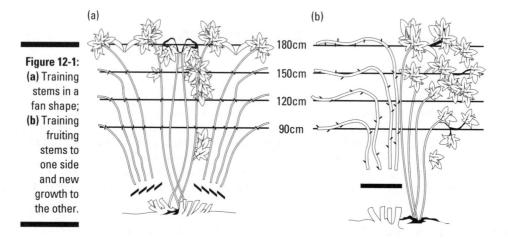

Figure 12-1:
(a) Training stems in a fan shape; **(b)** Training fruiting stems to one side and new growth to the other.

Potential briar fruit pest and disease problems include leaf distortion caused by aphids, cane spot and raspberry beetle maggots in the fruit. Grow flowers to attract natural predators of aphids, prune out dead or diseased growth and use pheromone traps to control raspberry beetle.

Quite a few briar fruit varieties are viciously thorny, which is fine if you've enough space for them to grow without causing trouble, but less so if your space is limited and people may pass close by. If so, seek out those varieties with few prickles or even none at all, such as 'Blackberry Oregon Thornless', 'Waldo' and 'Apache'.

Keeping current with currants and gooseberries

Currants of various colours (black, white and red) and gooseberries (all from the *Ribes* species) make excellent jams, jellies and dessert berries. As well as planting in your productive garden, use currants and gooseberries as ornamental garden shrubs. They bear attractive flowers and fruit, have maple-shaped leaves and remain 1–1.2 metres (3–4 feet) high. Almost all gooseberries do have thorns, however, and so choose their planting locations carefully. Full sun is best for all this group of plants.

When planning your fruit garden, remember that gooseberries and redcurrants and white currants have similar requirements and need to be grouped together: all three can also be grown in space-saving shapes such as *cordons* (on single stems) and *standards* (bushy plants with a clear stem, rather like a mini-tree). (See Chapter 9 for more info on small-space success.) In contrast, blackcurrants can only be grown as bushes. The most commonly grown *Ribes* fall into two major groups for cultivation purposes:

- ✔ **Currants** don't have spines and bear 1-centimetre (about a third-of-an-inch) fruit in clusters that look like miniature bunches of grapes. Redcurrants and white currants have a mild flavour, whereas blackcurrants have a stronger taste. Varieties with good disease resistance include: blackcurrant 'Ben Connan' and 'Ben Sarek' (which are compact and suitable for small gardens) and the larger Foxendown; white currant Rovada; and redcurrant Junifer.

- ✔ **Gooseberries** have a spine at the base of each leaf. They're the earliest cropping of all the soft fruits. The fruit is larger than that of currants, varies in colour from greenish white to red and is borne singly or in small clusters. Varieties with good disease resistance include 'Greenfinch', 'Invicta', 'Pax' and 'Rokula'.

Jostaberries are a comparatively new fruit that's a cross between blackcurrant and gooseberry. It has red or black fruits that are larger than currants, is vigorous and has excellent disease resistance. You grow them the same way as blackcurrants.

Currants, gooseberries and jostaberries can pollinate themselves and don't need another variety to produce fruit.

Blackcurrants like a rich soil with plenty of organic matter, and fertiliser that's high in nitrogen: space bushes 1.2–1.5 metres (4–5 feet) apart, depending on the variety size. Immediately after planting, cut the whole bush back to 5 centimetres (2 inches) from the ground – which sounds drastic but is the foundation for future healthy growth. When fully grown, annual pruning consists of thinning out several of the oldest branches.

Gooseberries, redcurrants and white currants like a well-drained, fertile soil, and fertiliser that's high in potash: space bushes 1.5–1.8 metres apart. Cordons (single stems) need to be grown up a cane against two horizontal wires, the lowest 60 centimetres (2 feet) from the ground and the higher one at 1.2 metres (4 feet). Plants can also be grown as half standards, on a clear stem. Prune bushes and half standards to encourage a vase-shaped plant so that plenty of light and air can circulate. Do so by shortening stems by a third at bud burst and completely removing stems in the centre. On mature bushes, prune by shortening side shoots in summer to 8 centimetres (3 inches), and in winter shorten the main shoots by about half, as well as removing crossing, dead or damaged branches.

Choosing resistant varieties is particularly important with gooseberries because American gooseberry mildew is a major disease problem. Swollen buds on blackcurrants are a sign of blackcurrant gall mite: prune out and destroy infected shoots.

Going ape for grapes

Growing organic grapes (*Vitis* species) successfully depends on your climate, cultural strategies and the varieties you choose. Dry climates provoke fewer diseases than damp, humid climates. Grapes tolerate a wide range of soil conditions; well-drained soil in the pH range of 5.5 to 7.0 is best. What they must have is full sun and very good air circulation to hamper diseases.

Grapes divide into two broad categories: table or dessert grapes and wine or juice grapes. Table grapes have tender skins suitable for fresh eating and may contain seeds or be seedless. Wine and juice grapes may have tougher skins but plenty of sweet juice for liquid consumption or making into jelly. Ripe fruit colours range from green to pink and red to deep purplish black. You can grow grapes for wine or juice in even quite cold areas in the southern half of the UK, but dessert grapes need a mild location and a sheltered site (or a large conservatory, greenhouse or polytunnel!).

Before planting young grapes, prepare the soil thoroughly as described in the earlier section 'Choosing where to grow your fruits'. Install a sturdy support consisting of two or three heavy wires strung 60 centimetres (24 inches) apart on sturdy posts. Brace the end posts.

Several pruning and training systems exist, but the basic idea of them all is to establish one or two main trunks per vine. Each trunk grows horizontal lateral branches that you attach to the wires. The flowers and fruit appear on wood that grows in the current year from the laterals that grew in the previous year. Plant in November/December, and cut the young vine by two thirds of its size, cutting back to a bud. Starting in winter after the first growing season, begin the pruning and training as follows:

1. **In the first winter, choose two healthy, vigorous canes to keep, and remove the rest.**

   Prune these main trunks back to three or four buds each.

2. **In the next summer, select the most vigorous shoot from each trunk, and remove competing shoots.**

   Train the shoots on a string until they reach the top wire, and then pinch them to encourage lateral branching, as shown in Figure 12-2.

3. **In the second winter, remove all growth from the trunk and lateral branches.**

Cut laterals back to ten buds. Let vines grow unpruned through the summer.

4. **In the third winter and subsequent years, choose the laterals for the current year, as well as replacement laterals for the next year.**

   Leave ten buds on the current-year laterals and two buds on the replacements. (Remember that grapes grow fruit on wood that grows in the current year from last season's laterals.) Prune off all other wood, removing as much 90 per cent of the previous year's growth.

Grapes are subject to a number of pests and diseases, and so concentrate on giving your plants the best possible growing conditions. Under cover, watch out for red spider mite, which you can combat with a biological control.

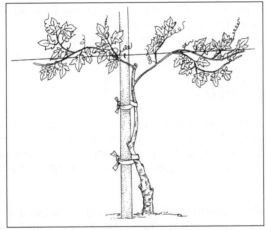

Figure 12-2:
Train grapes
on a trellis,
and prune to
a main stem
with lateral
branches.

Robust raspberries

Easy to grow, reliably performing raspberries are excellent garden fruits, producing heavy crops of delicious berries to eat fresh or use in desserts or preserves. If you've room to plant several different varieties, you can harvest from midsummer right through the autumn.

Raspberries are tolerant of a wide range of sites and conditions, although they do best on well-drained soil that has plenty of organic matter. On poorly drained soils, lift up the soil in rows and plant raspberries on top of the mound, so that the roots don't become waterlogged. Summer fruiting varieties need support, which is best provided with a post-and-wire framework that's 1.8 metres (6 feet) high with the wires spaced 45 centimetres (18 inches) apart. Autumn fruiting raspberries are shorter and sturdier, and usually don't need support unless your site is windy.

Buy and plant raspberries, which are known as *canes*, in autumn or winter when dormant. Plants are usually sold in bundles of five or ten canes. Plant each one 45 centimetres (18 inches) apart with 1.8 metres (6 feet) between rows. Beware of planting too deeply; the uppermost roots shouldn't be more than 5 centimetres (2 inches) below soil level. Cut back canes to 15–20 centimetres (6–9 inches) immediately before or after planting, to encourage the production of plenty of strong shoots. Tie in growth as it develops. Each year, thin out the number of canes in early summer to seven per plant. Prune after fruiting has finished for summer-cropping types: cut out the old canes and tie the new ones in place. Prune autumn-fruiting raspberries in late winter.

Raspberry varieties with good disease resistance include (in order of ripening): 'Malling Jewel', 'Redsetter', 'Glen Ample', 'Tulameen' and 'Octavia'.

Raspberries can suffer from a number of pests or diseases. Ensure that your plants are correctly spaced, trained and thinned, to encourage good air movement, and buy resistant varieties from a reputable supplier.

Rhubarb rhubarb

Although rhubarb is, strictly speaking, a vegetable, most people consider it a fruit because the long pink or red sticks are used as a dessert, and so we popped it into this chapter. Rhubarb is perennial and forms a clump that can reach a considerable size over the years; plant it somewhere where it can develop undisturbed.

You can buy and plant the dormant plants or crowns from autumn to late winter, but put in pot-grown plants anytime. Prepare the ground with plenty of organic matter, and allow the plant to establish for a year before harvesting. You can *force* rhubarb (that is, encourage it into growth early) by covering the clump with a light-excluding container. You can buy handsome (and costly) terracotta rhubarb forcers, but an old dustbin does exactly the same job!

Sublime strawberries

Succulent fruit still warm from the sun is an amazing taste sensation. Almost everyone adores strawberries, and their small plant size and suitability for containers means that every garden can house a few plants, even if just on the patio. Growing your own means being able to choose the delicious varieties that the supermarkets ignore, because they're too tender to pack, transport and sit on the shelf – not a problem for the home gardener though!

A selection of varieties can give you a harvest from early summer right through the autumn. Most varieties fruit during a six to eight-week period in June and July, whereas *perpetual* varieties produce a smaller crop but over a much longer period, from June through to autumn. You can also grow strawberries in containers to move under cover in spring to produce an early crop.

Strawberries are easy-going plants that thrive on a range of soils, but on heavy, poorly drained ones grow in raised beds to ensure a decent crop. The ideal pH is slightly acid at 6.5. Strawberries like ground prepared with organic matter such as manure, but go easy on the fertiliser or they're likely to produce leafy growth rather than fruiting. They also do well in containers – use ordinary pots or tall towerpots, or buy special frames for strawberries in growing bags – and so you can have a feast even from your patio.

Avoid growing strawberries in ground previously used for potatoes, which can pass on disease.

The best times for planting young strawberries or *runners* are October to April (weather permitting) for bare-rooted runners that have been freshly lifted, or April–July using cold-stored runners. Unpack and plant immediately, and soak in water for just a few minutes before planting. Space plants 30–40 centimetres (12–16 inches) apart with 75–90 centimetres (30–36 inches) between rows. Set the plants so that soil covers the roots but the crown remains above the soil, as shown in Figure 12-3. Keep the soil moist but not saturated. If plants look healthy and are growing strongly, allow them to fruit in their first year: otherwise, pinch off all flowers for the first season to encourage strong root and top growth.

In early summer as the fruit is forming, spread straw or lay polythene between the rows and tuck under the fruits, to keep your crop clean. As soon as possible after harvest, cut off all the old leaves (taking care not to damage the crowns) and remove the leaves, straw and any weeds. Don't cut back perpetual varieties, but remove old leaves in late winter.

Strawberry plants send out runners that take root and develop new in mid- to late summer. They root with little or no help from you, but space the runners evenly around the parents to give each plant plenty of space to grow. Plan to replace your strawberry planting every three to five years; harvest declines significantly after this period.

Mouldy old problems

Many fruits, including strawberries, can suffer from *grey mould* or *botrytis*, which when discovered during harvesting is often referred to simply as 'yuk' (put your fingers in squidgy berries, and you soon see why). The disease is most prevalent in damp, cool, still weather, when fruit remains damp for long periods of time. During the harvest period, check your plants thoroughly every day or so, removing and binning infected fruit to prevent it infecting many others.

Strawberries can suffer from a number of pests or diseases (see the 'Mouldy old problems' sidebar). Although most have no organic control and rely on good growing conditions to avoid the problem, you can combat pests such as vine weevil, chafer grubs and leatherjackets with biological controls.

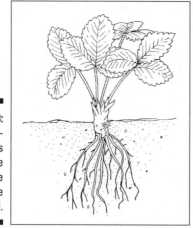

Figure 12-3: Plant strawberry plants so that the crowns are just above the soil.

Chapter 13

Cultivating Fruits and Nuts for Your Organic Orchard

. . . .

In This Chapter

▶ Focusing on fruit tree make-up

▶ Planting, pruning and preventing pests

▶ Selecting the right fruit trees for you

▶ Deciding on nut trees

. . . .

*F*reshly picked fruit from your own trees and shrubs is juicy joy – and easier to grow than you may think. Certain fruit and nut trees need more loving attention than many other plants, but the harvest is worth the effort. Growing your own fruit has two huge advantages: many fruit varieties that you grow at home taste far better than shop-bought fruit, and you can ensure that the fruit you and your family eat isn't sprayed with pesticides and fungicides.

Even if you've nothing more than a large patio planter, you can grow your own fruit; in a good-sized garden, you can plant a miniature orchard. When you're considering how to fit fruit trees into your garden, remember that many are also ornamental, especially when they're blooming.

In this chapter, we introduce you to the delights of growing fruit and nut trees in your garden. Producing fruit and nuts trees successfully is a huge subject, however, so this chapter can cover only the basics. For more detailed information on cultivating, fertilising, pruning and so on, consult any of the excellent books devoted entirely to this fascinating pursuit, such as *The Complete Guide to Fruit Growing* by Peter Blackburne-Maze, or one of the Royal Horticultural Society (RHS) guides.

Getting to the Roots of Fruit Tree Anatomy

Fruit and nut trees resemble other trees in most ways but differ in one important aspect: unlike ornamental plants, people grow fruit and nut trees primarily to produce food. To make these fruit factories more and more efficient, plant breeders continue to develop special techniques, such as reducing the size of the trees, making trees produce at an earlier age and yielding more fruit from each one. That's good news for home gardeners.

Accepting that size (and shape) does matter

Trees are easier to harvest and maintain when you can reach all the branches. Although traditional orchard trees were standards that grew a few metres/several feet high, these days nurseries graft trees onto the roots of smaller-growing varieties. (See the sidebar 'The whys and wherefores of grafting' for the technical details.)

Rootstocks are chosen for several reasons: for their influence on the size of the tree, for resistance to diseases and pests and to produce a good root system. We list the rootstocks for each type of fruit that we describe in the 'Coming Over all Fruity: Choosing Fruit Trees for Your Garden' section, later in this chapter.

Fruit trees come in different forms, some influenced by the rootstock, others trained to a certain shape (see Figure 13-1). Trained trees in particular are fantastic small-space solutions:

- ✔ **Bush:** This term is rather misleading in this context as it refers to a small free-standing tree, but the term is used to distinguish it from *standards* and *half standards* used in traditional orchards rather than gardens. (These have a clear stem of 1.2–1.8 metres (4–6 feet) and grow into large trees). A bush tree has a clear stem of around 1 metre (3 feet), and then develops a head of branches up to 2.4–4.5 metres (8–15 feet) depending on the variety and rootstock. This type of fruit tree is generally pruned to grow to a vase shape with an open centre, to allow you to harvest the food easily and to let plenty of light and air through the tree (preventing disease problems).

- ✔ **Cordon:** You usually grow these single-stemmed trees at an angle of 45 degrees, supported against a wall, fence or post-and-wire framework. Plant them 75–90 centimetres (30–36 inches) apart.

✔ **Espalier:** Also known as horizontally trained trees, you grow them against a wall or fence. The branches are trained out in 'tiers' from a central vertical stem. Apples and pears are the most common espaliers.

✔ **Fan:** As the name suggests, branches are trained in a fan shape, to go against a wall or fence. This pattern is not only space-saving, but also a great way to produce fruit in cold areas because south or west-facing walls have a storage-heater effect. You can buy plums, cherries, nectarines, peaches and apricots, among others, as fans.

✔ **Minarette:** These columnar-trained apples and pears produce fruit on short spurs on one main stem. You can plant them as close as 1 metre (3 feet) apart.

✔ **Stepover:** These dinky little fruit trees are edible edging, no less. As the name suggests, they're low enough to step over and can be used at the front of a border or around a lawn.

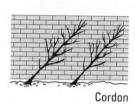

Cordon

Standard

Half-standard

Bush

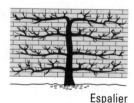

Espalier

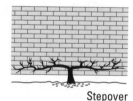

Stepover

Figure 13-1:
You can train fruit trees in a variety of ways to suit your needs and your garden.

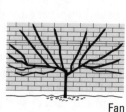

Fan

Minarette

The whys and wherefores of grafting

Here's the low-down on grafting. Tree nurseries slip a bud, called a *scion*, from a named fruit variety, such as 'Cox's Orange Pippin', under the bark of a dwarfing rootstock variety in early spring. The two grow together, and when the scion bud starts growing vigorously, the nursery prunes off the dwarfing rootstock's top growth to just above the bud. The place where the two parts meet is called the *bud union*, which usually shows up as a bulge, bend or scar.

Plant breeders and tree nurseries graft fruit and nut trees for a variety of reasons:

✔ **Reproduce exact copies of desirable trees:** Nurseries can make as many trees as they

need by grafting buds of a desirable variety onto uniform rootstocks.

✔ **Influence the mature size of the tree:** Reducing the tree size has many advantages, especially for home gardeners.

✔ **Encourage fruit bearing at an earlier age:** Some standard-size apple trees can take up to ten years to begin bearing fruit, whereas a dwarf bears fruit in two years.

✔ **Increase disease and pest resistance:** Some rootstocks resist soil-borne diseases and harmful pests better than others.

✔ **Adapt to different soils:** Some trees grow better in clay soils; others prefer loam.

In cold areas, the best way to get a reliable harvest is to opt for wall-trained fruit if your garden permits. Otherwise, frost can damage the blossom or pollinating insects may not brave chilly or windy conditions.

Cross-pollinating: Sex and the single tree

Many tree fruits – such as most apples, pears and plums – require *cross-pollination* to bear fruit, which means that you need two different but compatible varieties planted near each other so that the pollen of one species fertilises the flowers of the other.

The trees must be of the same type and bloom at the same time for cross-pollination to occur. Other fruit and nut species are *self-fertile*, which means that they can pollinate their own flowers, but even those species often produce larger crops when they mix pollen with a friend. Reputable nurseries and garden centres, good mail order catalogues and Internet sites can tell you which varieties can pollinate each other.

Low winter temperatures and the timing of spring frosts play important roles in your selection of fruit species and varieties for your organic orchard. Local nurseries generally sell plants that are best suited to your local climate and mail-order nurseries can steer you toward appropriate varieties.

Budding genius

Fruit trees grow different kinds of buds, and being able to recognise the various types is useful. The *terminal bud* grows at the end of branches, and that's where new branches and twigs grow from each spring. When the terminal buds expand, they leave *bud scars*, which look like slightly raised rings around the twig. You can measure how much a tree grows each year by looking at the distance between bud scars. *Leaf buds* appear along the twigs and expand into leaves. *Flower buds* are usually fatter than leaf buds and swell first in the spring.

Some trees – such as most apple, pear, cherry, plum and apricot – produce their fruit on *spurs*, which are short, modified twigs. Spurs usually live and produce flower buds for several years or longer before becoming unproductive. Figure 13-2 shows examples of these bud types.

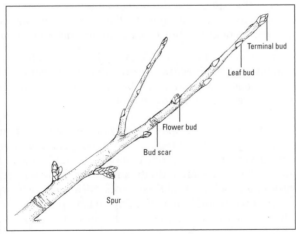

Figure 13-2:
Fruit and nut trees have several kinds of buds.

For the best-quality apples and pears, leave only one fruit on each spur, and pinch off the others in early summer. Spurs and flower buds develop best on limbs that are angled slightly above horizontal. Branches that grow upright and those that dangle below horizontal produce little, if any, fruit.

Looking After Your Fruit Trees

As part of establishing your successful, low-maintenance organic orchard, you have to plant your fruit trees where they can thrive, give them the fertile soil they need, prune them for health and maximum production, and deal with the inevitable pests and diseases.

Planting for success

All fruits need moisture-retentive but well-drained soil. (Flip to Chapter 5 for more on soil testing and drainage.) Soggy sites spell doom for these species. Adequate water is also critical, especially when the fruit is developing and expanding.

Professional fruit growers also consider air movement when they plan their orchard placement and layout. Air affects tree fruits in several ways:

- ✔ **Circulation:** Constantly but lightly moving air helps prevent disease organisms from getting a foothold on your trees. Many fungus diseases that infect leaves need water and moisture to spread and grow, and so keeping the leaves dry is important.

- ✔ **Frost pockets:** Cold air flows downhill and collects at the bottom of a slope. Trees that bloom in early spring are especially vulnerable to cold temperatures at that time, and the flowers may be severely damaged if they're planted where cold air collects. Plant fruit trees and shrubs on the slope instead of near the bottom, but avoid the windy top of a slope.

- ✔ **Wind:** Too much wind can keep pollinating insects, such as bees, from flying and pollinating the flowers at critical times. It also knocks fruit off the tree and damages the branches. Plant a windbreak if necessary, or put the trees where a building shields them.

If you buy your plants locally, they may already be growing in a container. These trees can be bought and planted at any time of year. If you order them from a mail-order nursery, however, they can only be sent while in a *dormant* (non-active growth) state between mid/late autumn and late winter, and *bare root* – that is, without any soil around their roots. Be sure to plant bare-root trees right away, or unwrap and heel in if doing so isn't possible. Refer to Chapter 8 for information on how to plant container-grown and bare-root plants.

After planting, establish a wide ring of organic mulch around your trees to conserve soil moisture, to prevent grass and weeds from competing with the tree roots and to reduce insect pests. See Chapter 21 for the low-down on mulch and its benefits.

Producing heavy crops of fruit stresses trees and shrubs, and so fruit- and nut-bearing species are likely to need additional nutrients; organic gardeners in particular need to pay attention to cultivation, because stressed plants are more susceptible to pests and diseases. See Chapter 5 for details on soil testing and Chapter 7 for more on fertilisers.

Pruning fruit trees

Producing bushels of high-quality fruit and developing a sturdy tree that can support the crop are the twin goals of pruning and training fruit trees. If you end up with an attractive garden specimen too, that's a bonus! Although you use the same basic pruning techniques on all fruit trees, each kind of fruit tree has unique timing and method requirements for reaching your goals.

You need to prune fruit trees regularly for several reasons:

- ✔ **To remove dead, damaged and diseased wood:** Do so before any other pruning and whenever is necessary.

- ✔ **To control tree and shrub size:** Keep fruit down where you can harvest and care for it without a ladder.

- ✔ **To provide air circulation:** Circulation helps ward off pests and diseases. Crowded limbs invite fungus diseases and provide habitat for damaging insects.

- ✔ **To increase exposure to sunlight:** Fruit that's exposed to direct sunlight tastes better than fruit shaded by leaves and branches.

- ✔ **To increase the quality and quantity of fruit:** Branches trained to 60-degree angles where they meet the trunk develop the most flower buds. Spacing the limbs up and down and around the trunk provides the best conditions for the fruit to mature.

Professional fruit growers use several pruning and training methods, depending on the type of fruit they grow. For example, free-standing bush trees are usually trained to have an open centre (sometimes also called a 'vase' shape). In this style, you select four or five well-placed main branches and then prune out the central leader. This method limits the height of the tree and creates a spreading crown.

Although you can train your own fruit trees to the shapes we describe in the earlier section 'Accepting that size (and shape) does matter', most gardeners – and especially newer ones – find that buying ready-grown trees is a more than worthwhile investment.

Preventing pests and diseases

Humans aren't the only beings who love fruit; insects, birds, diseases and other creatures appreciate these trees and shrubs, too. Some insects damage the fruits; others concentrate their efforts on the foliage and wood. Insects take a toll, but you can control them without resorting to pesticides. Turn a blind eye to less-than-perfect fruit, and let your tastebuds relish the flavour instead.

Sticky *pheromone* traps, baited with hormones that the bugs find sexy, capture apple codling moths and plum moths. Other insects can be trickier to deal with, but luckily, you can fool many pests with traps and barriers. See Chapter 18 for more information on organic controls and purchasing sources.

Plant breeders have developed many modern fruit varieties that resist or at least tolerate some of the most troublesome diseases. Certain varieties are stronger growers too and resist pests more effectively than others. Another bonus with some newer varieties is that they're self-fertile (setting a crop with their own pollen) so that you don't have to worry about buying two different trees. As an organic gardener, scan the latest catalogues and home in on the newest and best tree varieties.

When growing fruit organically, good hygiene is the name of the game. In fruit-growing terms this means being vigilant and removing any diseased or infected fruit as soon as possible, in order to break the life cycle of the pest or disease. For example, young pear fruitlets infected with pear midge fall to the ground, where the pest carries on its happy life; mummified plums or apples infected with brown rot continue spreading the disease. Remember to put diseased fruit in your green waste collection or dustbin, not on the compost heap.

Coming Over all Fruity: Choosing Fruit Trees for Your Garden

If you're new to gardening, start with apples, pears or plums (so long as you like them, of course). You can also grow cherries with relative ease, but keeping birds off your harvest is much more a challenge because they adore the succulent red fruits. Peaches, apricots and nectarines are much trickier and so only attempt these fruits if you live in one of the mildest areas of the UK.

Adding apples to your plot

Apples *(Malus domestica)* are among the most popular and easiest fruit trees to grow, producing good harvests of crisp, crunchy, juicy fruit with relative ease. Most apples require cross-pollination, with the exception of some newer self-fertile varieties; you can also use ornamental crabapples to pollinate apple trees. When choosing an apple-tree variety, consider these factors:

✔ **Culinary or dessert:** Apples fall into two main groups: dessert varieties that can be eaten straight from the tree, and culinary varieties that are ideal for cooking. Of course, a bit of crossover exists between the two – some 'cookers', as they're known, can be eaten fresh if you like a tart, acid fruit, and dessert apples can be used in cooking, although they don't retain their taste and texture in the same way.

✔ **Size:** As apple trees increase in size, they become harder to prune and spray, and so choose trees on semi-dwarfing and dwarf rootstocks that reach only 2.5–3.75 metres (8–12 feet) tall. In order of size, from small to taller, these rootstocks are M27, M9 and M26. If your growing conditions are less than ideal (poor soil or cold site, for example), go for a more vigorous rootstock to offset this factor. You can also use pruning techniques to control tree height. Prune apple trees in late winter, while they're dormant, and follow up in midsummer to remove overly vigorous sprouts.

✔ **Pollination:** Apple varieties are divided into pollination groups according to when they flower. Choose two varieties from the same group, or varieties that are in adjacent groups, because sufficient overlap usually exists in flowering time for the bees to do their stuff.

✔ **Cold tolerance:** Some varieties are better at standing up to spring frosts than others ('Fiesta', for example), which is worth bearing in mind if you live in a cold area.

✔ **Disease resistance:** This aspect is key when you're choosing apple varieties for organic orchards, because apple scab and powdery mildew can be a real problem. New varieties with good resistance include 'Falstaff', 'Red Devil' and 'Red Windsor'. You're also likely to come across a few *triploid* varieties, which means that they produce sterile pollen. This group includes the ever-popular cooker 'Bramley's Seedling'.

Another really clever idea from the plant breeders is to graft several varieties on to one tree: they pollinate each other, and you get a selection of different delicious fruits (check out the sidebar 'The whys and wherefores of grafting'). They really understand the need to keep things in the family! Family apple trees are most widely available, though you can also find other family fruit trees such as pears, too.

Cheering up your garden with cherries

Cherries *(Prunus)* are glorious in their spring bloom, and sweet cherries eaten straight from the tree are divine. Cherries ripen from June into July, providing the first tree fruit of the season. Cherries belong to the same genus as peaches, almonds and plums.

Cherries come in sweet and sour (or acid) types, which although similar in many respects do differ in significant ways:

- ✔ **Pollination:** Sweet cherries need cross-pollination, except for the variety 'Stella', and so you need two compatible varieties. Acid cherries, also called pie cherries, are self-pollinating ('Morello' is most widely grown). Sour cherries can pollinate sweet cherries but may not bloom at the same time. (The trees must bloom at the same time for the varieties to cross-pollinate.)

- ✔ **Hardiness:** Sweet-cherry trees do best in milder regions in areas of low rainfall, while acid cherries tolerate cooler conditions.

- ✔ **Culinary use:** Sweet cherries, common in supermarkets in early summer, are best when eaten fresh. Sour cherries make the best pies and jams, but you have to grow your own; markets rarely offer them. Some varieties are sweet enough to eat fresh, too.

When choosing cherries, consider rootstocks, shape and pollination. The modern rootstocks Gisela and Tabel (don't confuse rootstock name with the variety, by the way) produce compact trees to around 1.8–2.4 metres (6–8 ft) high, while Colt rootstock produces taller trees. Newer varieties are self-fertile, such as 'Celeste', 'Cherokee', 'Newstar' and 'Stella'. Often the easiest way to grow cherries is in a fan shape against a wall or fence.

Birds are certain to take a portion of your crop, if not the whole thing, unless you cover the ripening fruit with a net (which is where fan trees really score). Birds tend to bother acid cherries less than sweet cherries, but better to be safe than sorry. The fruits of some varieties tend to crack in the rain as they ripen, but others resist this bad habit.

Of the diseases that affect all *Prunus* species, bacterial canker and leaf spot are the most serious. Practise good sanitation by raking up foliage and dropped fruit, and prune out any infected wood immediately.

For best flavour, let sweet and sour cherries ripen fully on the tree before picking, but keep them covered to prevent bird theft!

Picking peaches and nectarines

Peaches and nectarines *(Prunus persica)* are actually the same species, but peaches are fuzzy and nectarines are smooth-skinned. If you live in a mild part of the UK and have a sheltered, south-facing wall, one of these exotic fruits may be for you. If not, don't even consider a garden tree! The only alternative is to grow a dwarf variety such as 'Diamond' in a tub that can be brought under cover for the winter – but the few fruit you get isn't exactly a large harvest. Peaches and nectarines are self-pollinating, and so you need only one tree. Most peaches are grown on St Julien A rootstock, although the newer Montclare rootstock has shown promising results.

The most serious of problems is peach leaf curl – a fungus disease – which causes leaves and fruit to drop prematurely. The spores are spread by rain-splash, and so covering the whole tree with clear polythene during the infection period of late winter to mid-spring significantly reduces infection. The downside is that the cover stops pollinating insects from reaching the flowers, and so you need to use a soft paintbrush to transfer pollen from one bloom to another. A new variety, 'Avalon', has so far shown good resistance to the disease.

Peering into the world of pears

Pears (*Pyrus* species) share many characteristics with apples, and they grow in similar conditions. Like apples, pears are usually sold as grafted trees and require similar pruning and training, and come in many of the same shapes. With their glossy dark green foliage, pears make especially good garden specimens in addition to providing delicious fruit. However, pears do flower slightly earlier than apples, and so if you can offer them the shelter of a sunny wall, you're likely to be harvesting better crops. Consider these points when choosing pears:

- **Pollination:** In the same way as apples, pears are divided into pollination groups, so choose two varieties from the same group or adjacent ones. Just to complicate things a bit further, some varieties aren't compatible; check before buying.

- **Rootstocks:** Pears are grafted onto 'quince' rootstocks. Quince C is ideal for most gardens, producing small trees of around 3 metres (10 feet) in height, and also for trained trees. If you've poor soil, opt for the slightly more vigorous Quince A.

- **Disease resistance:** Some varieties are particularly susceptible to scab disease: those with a reasonable level of resistance include 'Louise Bonne of Jersey'.

- **Cold tolerance:** Some pears grow well in cooler areas, such as 'Conference', others such as 'Doyenne du Comice' need a mild climate.

Pears taste best when you pick them while they're still hard and allow them to ripen at room temperature or in the refrigerator. Fruit that over-ripens on the tree develops hard, gritty spots in the flesh and may turn brown and mushy near the core. Pears can keep well in the refrigerator if they're picked just before ripeness.

Plumping for plums, damsons, gages and prunes

These closely related stone fruits are fairly easy to grow and can produce good crops of fruit in summer. Most varieties are dessert ones, wonderful for eating straight from the tree, and you can use damsons for cooking.

Although all these stone fruits are similar in their needs to apples (check out the earlier section 'Adding apples to your plot'), finding the right spot is especially important because these trees bloom early in spring. Frost doesn't usually damage the flower buds, but it can damage the flowers themselves – or if the spring weather is wet and miserable, bees (understandably!) prefer to stay in their cosy hives rather than come out to gather pollen. If you garden in a cold area, grow fan-trained trees against a sheltered, sunny wall or fence.

You can grow plums and their relations as free-standing bush trees, minarettes or fans. Two rootstocks are available: Pixy is the most dwarf type, producing a tree around 2.4 metres (8 feet) high, whereas St Julian A is semi-dwarfing and gives a tree of around 3–3.5 metres (10–12 feet) high. Use this latter one on poor soils.

Plums are self-fertile. Good varieties include the ever-popular 'Victoria', 'Blue Tit', 'Denniston's Superb' and 'Prune Damson'.

 Never prune plums or cherries in winter: they're susceptible to silverleaf disease, which enters through open wounds. Prune these fruits only when really necessary, and in midsummer when cuts heal faster.

Going Crazy for Nuts

When you plant these ornamental trees, you get to enjoy the nut harvest as an added treat. In this section we introduce you briefly to a few nut trees that can enhance your garden. Most nut trees need only a little care but can be messy when the fruit and foliage drop. Plant the large-nut species, such as walnuts, where you can enjoy their beauty without worrying about falling nuts. Use smaller species, such as filberts, as hedges or small garden trees.

Angling for almonds

Almonds *(Prunus amygdalus)* are related to plums and require similar grow-ing conditions (check out the earlier section 'Plumping for plums, damsons, gages and prunes'). However, almonds are susceptible to a disease known as peach leaf curl, which is exacerbated by damp conditions, so only try growing almonds as a crop in drier and milder regions of the country. Warm spring weather followed by a cold snap ruins their lovely pink flowers and damages their developing fruits. A grafted variety such as 'Robijn' gives most reliable results.

Craving cobnuts and filberts

Also known as hazelnuts (*Corylus* species), these delicious nuts grow on orna-mental trees or large shrubs up to .5 metres (15 feet) high. These nut trees prefer moist, well-drained soil and climates in which late-spring frosts don't damage their flower buds. They require cross-pollination to set fruit, which is ready to harvest in late summer. The flowers are wind-pollinated, so ensure that you plant close together. Cobnuts and filberts can pollinate each other, which means that the varieties 'Cosford' and 'Kentish Cob' are compatible.

Collect the nuts as they fall from the trees; dry them in the sun until the ker-nels snap when bitten; and store them in a cool, dry place.

Squirrels are the most serious pests so avoid trying to grow these trees for crops if grey squirrels are regular visitors to your plot.

Waiting for walnuts

Definitely a long-term proposition, these stately tall trees take at least several years to begin producing nuts. They do make handsome garden trees though, growing to over 7.5 metres (24 feet) high with large, glossy leaves that are aromatic when crushed. Walnuts thrive on any reasonable soil so long as well drained. Choose a site that isn't prone to frosts, which can kill the spring flowers. Although the species *Juglans regia* is widely available, if nut produc-tion is your main aim, look for a variety bred for this specific purpose, such as 'Broadview'.

Chapter 14

Saying It With Flowers

· ·

In This Chapter

▶ Selecting healthy flowering plants

▶ Picking the best varieties

▶ Choosing and caring for roses

· ·

The best gardens contain an inspiring mixture of plants. Trees and shrubs (which we cover in Chapter 15) provide your garden with structure, and vegetables (see Chapters 9 and 10) and fruits (see Chapters 12 and 13) put food on the table. In contrast, flowers are pure fun, bringing your garden to life and adding colour, vibrancy, drama and romance. Daffodils, tulips and other spring bulbs cheerfully greet the end of winter; annuals flower their socks off right through summer and into autumn; and a careful selection of perennial flowering plants put on a constantly changing and colourful show throughout each season. Thread a little foliage through your flower borders and you have it made, ornamentally speaking.

Flowers are among the easiest crops to grow organically. Yes, insects and diseases do bother some of them, but provided that you create mixed plant-ings and don't have huge patches of just one plant, your flowers are unlikely to suffer any major problems. Keeping them well fed isn't hard, either. This chapter covers all the basics you need to grow happy flowers year-round, and goes into detail on one of the most popular of all flowers: romantic roses.

Mixing It Up with Flowers: The Basics

Flowers are diverse, resilient and compatible with one another. You can mix them up any way you like, and as long as you give them their basic food and preferred soil, water and sun (or shade) requirements, you can reasonably expect loads of blooms or attractive foliage. Even if a plant dies or gets eaten by bugs, it usually costs little to replace. In the case of annuals, which live only until the frosts anyway, you can always try again next year.

Annuals complete their life cycle in a single year, whereas *perennials* grow from one year to the next, usually sprouting from their overwintering roots. *Bulbs* (the sort that light up your garden and not your house!) are perennial plants that store food in special swollen stems or roots. We describe growing these different types in more detail in the later section 'Selecting and Growing Flowers of all Types'.

Promoting diversity in any garden or border planting is a crucial part of organic gardening, and doing so is easy in a flower garden. Except for large formal plantings or commercial-cut flower fields, the best organic approach is to grow only a few plants of each flower species or variety and mix them up. Here are a few good reasons to continue that practice:

 ✔ **You can encourage beneficial insects and other organisms.** These beneficials fight harmful pests and diseases and thrive in diverse environments.

 ✔ **You can have season-long colour.** Doing so is easy to manage when you plant perennials, annuals and bulbs that bloom at different times throughout the year. You can mix and match colour schemes, too.

 ✔ **You can save garden space.** Plant ornamental vegetables and herbs in your flower beds or flowers in your vegetable or herb garden. You can plant bulbs right under the root zones of annuals and perennials to extend the season of colour.

 ✔ **You can fool pests.** Do so by planting only a few plants of each species in spots around the garden or landscape. The critters may find some – but not all – of your tobacco plants or lilies!

Before you fill out the catalogue order form or go to the garden centre to buy every flower that tickles your fancy, take time to plan your garden for success and prepare your soil, as the following sections discuss. (For more info on garden planning and soil preparation, go to Chapters 3 and 5, respectively.)

Creating mixed borders

Flowers come in a rainbow of colours and a vast array of shapes and sizes. For many gardeners, mixing and matching them with creative flair is the best part of gardening. The traditional 'old-style' garden often had single-plant beds – of just roses or annuals, for example – but this approach was both labour- and chemical-intensive. Pests not only came to dine, but had a mass party and gorged themselves! From both an ornamental and an organic point of view, by far the best style of planting is to create *mixed borders* that are a blend of different plant types. In this way, pests rarely become a problem, your border is home to all kinds of garden-friendly wildlife and you get colour and interest throughout the seasons.

The year kicks off in late winter with the first of the spring bulbs – snowdrops and winter aconites – progressing through the spring with narcissi, crocus and grape hyacinths, leading into early summer with tulips and alliums. Annuals fall into two groups: _hardy_ (frost-tolerant) and _half-hardy_ (frost-tender). Stalwart perennials can be found in flower in every season, although you experience a greater bounty in summer and autumn. Although ornamental grasses are often grouped alongside perennials, and their 'flowers' have considerable beauty, their decorative foliage from spring to autumn – sometimes all year – is what gives long-lasting appeal. When you come to winter, seed heads and even dead foliage create great effects, as well as providing important hibernation sites for beneficial insects.

When you design your flower garden, keep in mind that plants have a greater impact when you plant them in groups of the same kind. A single cosmos plant looks lost in a 5-metre (16-foot) long border, for example, but six cosmos of the same colour make a bold statement. The same goes for perennials; always plant at least three and preferably five or more of each kind, especially the smaller varieties. With bulbs, think large! Even in the smallest gardens, you can pack in large numbers: consider a dozen the bare minimum for tulips and daffodils and two dozen for crocus and small bulbs.

Whether you choose annuals, perennials, bulbs or combinations, consider the whole year when planning your border. A good mixed border also contains a 'skeleton' of permanent plants, which we discuss in Chapter 15.

Preparing your soil

Annual flowers grow rapidly from seedling to mature flowering plant in just a few short weeks, and so they need plenty of good nutrition in the form of organic matter added to the soil, and a general fertiliser mixed in before planting. Perennials, too, need to put down roots and develop leafy tops to make food for their roots, which live from one year to the next. Adequate soil fertility, moisture and organic matter keep your flowers growing robustly, producing more and larger blooms, and fending off pests and diseases.

Bulbs, however, call for slightly different treatment. Because they carry their own store of energy to start with, and may suffer from rotting if they sit in moisture for any length of time, you can kill them with kindness, so to speak. The ideal soil for bulbs is free-draining and with plenty of fibrous organic matter such as leafmould. If your soil is heavy and slow to drain, incorporate a couple of shovelfuls of coarse grit before planting. Like all plants, keep them in good health to avoid problems.

Make sure that your soil is free from perennial weeds before you plant, or you're storing up ten times the amount of work for later.

When you're done preparing your soil, make a list of plant combinations that suit your site; and then boldly go forth to make your selections. For information on choosing the healthiest specimens and proper planting techniques, refer to Chapter 8.

Planting and aftercare

Consistent maintenance throughout the growing season guarantees plenty of flowers and lush, healthy plants. Perennials and bulbs, which live for more than a year, are better prepared for winter when they've had adequate nutrition and water during the summer and autumn.

Keeping your garden looking good and growing strong doesn't have to be a lengthy chore if you take a few minutes each day or on the weekend. Here's what you can do to keep your flowers looking their best:

- ✔ **Deadhead:** Removing spent flowers – or *deadheading* – before they go to seed keeps annuals and some perennials blooming longer. Snip or pinch the dead flower off, making the cut just above a bud or a leaf.

- ✔ **Fertilise:** Plants need plenty of fuel to pump out the flowers. Supplement your fertile soil with a mulch of compost or manure in the spring, and feed again in midsummer with a complete fertiliser, such as pelleted chicken manure. Chapter 7 contains the low-down on organic fertilisers.

- ✔ **Pinch:** Flowers that get tall and floppy, especially perennial asters and chrysanthemums, stay more compact if you pinch back their early-summer stems to encourage them to grow shorter and more numerous shoots. When the plants reach around 30 centimetres (1 foot) high in spring, snip off the top 8–10 centimetres (3–4 inches).

- ✔ **Scout for problems:** As you walk through the garden, keep a sharp eye out for anything unusual, such as holes in flowers or leaves, wilting, insects or off-colour foliage. Catch a problem early, and you've a better chance of solving it without taking drastic action.

- ✔ **Support:** Some tall, floppy flowers, such as delphiniums and peonies, need a little help to stay upright. Use bamboo stakes to tie up individual delphinium or lily stems. Surround peony clumps with purchased circular wire or homemade hazel stick or stake-and-twine supports. If you've a large garden, consider growing a couple of hazel bushes to harvest for this purpose. Another option is to use branches left over from tree and shrub pruning to support plants.

✔ **Water:** If Mother Nature provides regular, gentle rainfall from spring through autumn, you've got it made. More than likely, though, you have to lend a hand. Established perennials are usually happy without extra watering, so long as you match the right plant to your soil, but annual flowers benefit from an occasional long drink (a good soaking a couple of times a week). Shallow watering that wets only the top several centimetres (top few inches) encourages roots to grow close to the surface, where they're more vulnerable to drought.

 ✔ **Weed:** No, weeding isn't fun, but it is necessary. Pull up or hoe small weeds as soon as they appear, disturbing the soil as little as possible. Chipped bark or cocoa shell mulch prevents weed seeds from sprouting. Replace or add more mulch as needed to smother weeds, but keep the mulch a few centimetres away from plant stems. Check out Chapter 21 for much more info on dealing with wicked weeds.

If you grow flowers in borders surrounded by lawn, you face the additional chore of edging. *Edging* means separating the lawn and the flowers with a barrier. Use a half-moon edging tool to cut away a slice of lawn around the entire perimeter of the border in the spring and again in autumn. To use the tool, push the blade straight down into the turf (it makes a lovely, satisfying, crunch) about 10 centimetres (4 inches) or so, and pull the handle back toward yourself to pop out the wedge (which can then go on the compost heap).

Permanent edging options do away with the edging chore: you can use flexible plastic or metal edging (available at garden centres) or bricks, landscape timber or stones. If you use these materials, bury them so that they're flush with the ground, which makes mowing easier.

Selecting and Growing Flowers of all Types

In Chapter 8 we describe how plants are divided into categories based on their life cycles. As regards flowers, annuals and perennials are the important types (and we define them in the earlier section 'Mixing It Up with Flowers: The Basics'). Here we discuss these two types plus a third: bulbs. We also cover adding garden *foliage* – green leaves – to enhance whatever flowers you plant.

Enjoying annual events

Annual plants live short but spectacular lives because they have to accomplish their entire life's purpose – perpetuating the species – in only one growing season. They bloom for varying periods, from a few weeks in the case of hardy annuals to several months through summer to autumn in the case of half-hardy ones. The third of this short-lived trio is biennials, which bloom in late spring and early summer, and which you can use in the same ways as annuals. The secret to keeping annuals blooming all summer is preventing the plants from forming seeds by deadheading them (which we describe in 'Planting and aftercare', earlier in this chapter). Some plants that you may consider to be annuals – such as pelargoniums, fuchsias and begonias – are in fact perennials in mild climates. Count yourself lucky if you can enjoy these plants year-round (or dig them up and bring indoors for the winter).

Use versatile annuals anywhere you want non-stop colour. Plant them in mixed gardens with perennials to provide a burst of summer bloom, create a cut-flower garden for bouquets or use hanging baskets and patio planters for portable colour. The beauty of annuals is that you can change the look of your garden from one year to the next to suit your current taste and whim.

You can purchase hundreds of different annual flowering plants in every shape, form, colour and size imaginable, and we don't have enough space to describe them all. Best for the organic garden are the ones that produce nectar for bees and butterflies such as scabious, candytuft and poppy, plus those such as phacelia and poached egg flower that attract other pollinating or beneficial insects. Mix flowers in with your productive garden to entice these gardeners' friends. Some annuals even help repel pests, such as annual French and African marigolds that keep off whitefly.

You can easily start hardy annuals yourself from seed, especially those with large seeds, in the garden or in the house before transplanting. Flip to Chapter 8 for information on starting from seed. The easiest flowers to grow from seed include calendula, nasturtium, sunflower and sweet pea. Half-hardy annuals with tiny seeds – such as begonia, petunia and impatiens – are tough to start and need several months of pampering before they're ready for the garden.

If you're new to gardening, half-hardy annuals are good candidates to buy as seedlings or young 'plug' plants in mid-spring for growing on, instead of trying to start right from scratch with seed.

Planting perennial favourites

Perennial plants live from year to year, but *herbaceous perennials* die to the ground in the autumn and sprout from their roots again in the spring. Happy perennials increase in size and in the amount of blooms produced with each growing season that passes. Most perennials are easy-care and require little in the way of maintenance, apart from staking or supporting taller varieties, and cutting back dead growth in early spring. After a few years, though, perennials develop into large clumps that can become congested, and flowering declines, which means digging up and dividing your plants.

Being able to divide one plant into more is a great feature of perennials. The best plants for dividing form clumps of stems and have fibrous roots. Easy plants to divide include bee balm (*Monarda* species), daylilies, hosta, ornamental grasses, Siberian iris and almost anything else that creeps over the ground, rooting as it grows. A few varieties dislike being disturbed and are best left alone, such as peonies and hellebores.

The best time to divide perennials depends partly on their season of flowering. Divide late-summer-flowering plants, such as asters, in early to mid-spring as soon as they start growing. Spring and early-summer bloomers, such as dicentra, recover better if you divide them in autumn. Divide iris (the sort that forms large, fleshy roots known as rhizomes) immediately after flowering. Here's the basic method for dividing perennials with fibrous roots:

1. **Dig up the whole clump, and drag it onto a tarp.** Check it over and look for groups of rooted stems that can form new, self-supporting plants. Blast the clump with water from the hose to wash away soil that obscures the crown, or soak the whole clump to make root separation easier.

2. **Pry, tease, cut or pull apart the clump.** Some perennials come apart easily; others may require a sharp knife or other drastic measures. For large tough grasses, Siberian irises and daylilies, push two garden forks into the clump back to back, and pry the handles apart to divide the clump in two, as shown in Figure 14-1. Repeat as needed to reduce the clump to manageable pieces.

Discard the dead and less vigorous pieces, and replant the rest as soon as possible. (Chapter 12 has loads of planting advice.)

You can choose from thousands of perennial plants. Look for these attributes:

- **Butterfly- and bee-attracting plants:** Butterflies and moths glide from flower to flower looking for energy-rich nectar. Some of their favourites include bee balm, *Centaurea*, coneflowers, goldenrod, penstemon, salvia, scabious and verbena.

- **Deer-resistant perennials:** Although you may think that deer eat anything, they're repelled by plants with strong scents or flavours and by some toxic plants. Resistant plants include alliums, artemisia, black-eyed Susan, catmint, hellebore, tansy and yarrow.

- **Hard-to-kill perennials:** If you're just starting or need low-maintenance plants, give these tough customers a try. Perennials that can survive in well-drained soil almost anywhere include artemisia, blanket flower, catmint, *Euphorbia*, feverfew, *Heliopsis*, Oriental poppy, sedum, tickseed (*Coreopsis* species) and yarrow. If your soil tends to run on the damp side, try bee balm, daylily, mint and Siberian iris.

✔ **Shade-loving perennials:** Shade is a relative concept, ranging from dense to dappled. Most of these perennials prefer a few hours of direct sunlight each day, but can survive in all but the deepest shade. For your shady nook, try *Bergenia*, comfrey, *Euphorbia robbiae*, lily-of-the-valley, lungwort and Solomon's seal.

Figure 14-1:
Using garden forks to divide perennial clumps.

Blooming bulbs

Some plants form swollen underground roots or stems, which people tend to lump together and call *bulbs*. Not all these fleshy appendages are the same, however, and the differences affect how you plant and use them, as we explain in this section.

To simplify bulbs and bulblike plants, we divide them into two groups:

✔ **Spring-blooming bulbs** include bluebells, crocus, fritillary, glory of the snow (*Chionodoxa* species), hyacinths, *Narcissus* (daffodils), snowdrops, tulips and winter aconite. Plant most bulbs in early autumn to allow them time to root before winter; most survive in the ground and bloom when the soil warms in the spring. Tulips are a little more fussy, so leave in the ground only if your soil is well-drained; otherwise, lift when the foliage dies back, store for the summer and replant in late autumn.

✔ **Summer-blooming bulbs** include alliums, amaryllis, canna, crocosmia, dahlia, gladiola, lilies and tuberous begonia. Many of these bulbs are frost-tender. Dig them up at the end of the growing season and store them in a frost-free place, covered with coir fibre that's kept barely moist. Lilies, alliums and crocosmia, however, are frost-tolerant.

When you shop for bulbs, look for firm, heavy, unblemished specimens. Avoid any with gouges or signs of withering, softness or decay. Bulbs vary in size from one species and variety to the next. In general, you want *top-size* bulbs, which usually are the largest bulbs available for the particular variety.

After you get your bulbs home, plant them as soon as possible. If you must store them – even briefly – keep them dry and cool (10–18 degrees Celsius/50–65 degrees Fahrenheit). Don't store them with apples or other fruit, however, because ripening fruit gives off ethylene gas, which is deadly to dormant flower buds inside the bulbs.

Bulbs like the same loose, fertile, well-drained garden soil that other plants enjoy. If you're planting bulbs in an existing, well-maintained garden, you need only add a bit of fertiliser to the hole at planting time; otherwise, turn to Chapter 5 for more on soil preparation. Slow-release, complete, granular fertiliser works best at planting time. Mix it into the soil at the bottom of the hole, covering it with a thin layer of soil before setting in the bulbs.

How deeply you plant your bulbs depends on whether you have true bulbs, corms, tubers or rhizomes (check out the earlier sidebar 'Discovering bulbs and bulblike plants'). You handle each type a little differently. As a general rule, plant bulbs with three times their height in soil from the top of the bulb. Rhizomes and tubers vary: check packaging for details.

Determining which end goes down and which points up is easy for bulbs with a pointed top or roots clinging to the bottom. If, however, you have shrivelled, featureless anemone tubers and can't tell which side is up, plant the bulbs on their sides; the plants can figure things out.

Squirrels and mice often come to dine on newly planted bulbs in autumn. Keep them at bay organically by adding a sprinkling of chilli powder to the planting holes. If this method fails, lay wire netting over small bulbs and cover with a thin layer of soil: the bulb shoots will grow through.

Fancying fantastic foliage

Flowers are fabulous, but you can have too much of a good thing; or rather, not enough of another – namely, foliage. Just as a meal of rich food is overwhelming without plain bread or vegetables, a border made up of all flowers and no foliage can look unsatisfactory. Perennials and ornamental grasses with attractive foliage give an untiring display of form and colour from when the leaves unfurl in spring, or all year in the case of evergreens.

Discovering bulbs and bulb-like plants

True bulbs – including onions, lilies, tulips and daffodils – have pointed tops and flat bottoms called *basal plates*, from which roots grow. If you cut one open, you see that a bulb consists of rings or layers with developing leaves, flowers or stems in the centre. The bulb itself lives from year to year and develops new bulbs from its base.

Other bulb-like plants form corms, tubers or rhizomes. *Corms* – such as colchicum, crocus, crocosmia and gladiola – resemble bulbs, but their flesh isn't layered when cut open. Each corm lives for a single year, but it produces *offsets* (new corms) around its basal plate. *Tubers* – such as tuberous begonias – don't have a basal plate and sprout from several *eyes* (growing points). They just grow larger and form more eyes each year but don't produce offsets. *Rhizomes*, such as bearded iris and canna, are simply swollen, creeping stems. They grow from the tip, which may branch and root, forming new plants.

Even in autumn, when most plants die back, you can leave on the dead leaves of most varieties to create an enchanting picture when silvered with frost (with the exception of fleshy-leaved perennials like hosta and sedum, which collapse in a heap). Leaving the leaves on provides more than just ornamental value, however. Many beneficial insects and other creatures need shelter for the winter, and even though your border doubtless harbours some pests too, don't forget that these creatures provide a valuable supply of food for birds.

Running for the Roses

Roses have a strange image: they're the traditional romantic gift given by men while also being seen as temperamental, demanding and prone to pests (roses, not men!). This prickly reputation may make you think that you need to use toxic chemicals to grow roses successfully. Yet the keys to growing roses organically are really quite simple:

- Choose strong, disease-resistant varieties that are happy to mix with other plants.
- Get the plants off to a strong start by thorough ground preparation, and remember their annual care.
- Catch and treat pest problems early, and encourage natural predators.

You can find details on performing all these tasks successfully in this section.

Making the right rose choice

Over the years, rose breeders have developed many categories of roses, such as ground cover, patio, hybrid tea and modern shrub roses. Although they share the name *rose*, each category has unique features and garden merit, and some types are more suited to organic growing than others. The types suited to organic growing include many shrub roses both old and new (though some of the beautiful old varieties are prone to disease so check plant descriptions), patio and ground cover types, climbers and ramblers.

As we describe in Chapter 17 on pest control, the best way to minimise problems is to mix plants together to 'dilute' their attraction to pests and diseases, and to use other plants to entice natural predators of pests. Some types of rose are antisocial, however, and don't grow well when rubbing shoulders with other plants. For this reason, avoid these potential trouble-causers: single-flowered and cluster-flowered bush types (often still referred to by their old titles of Hybrid Tea and Floribunda).

Choosing disease-resistant roses

Quite a few older varieties of rose (such as shrub roses or ramblers) are weak growers and prone to diseases, so search out strong growing variet-ies with good natural resistance. If you're starting a new garden with roses or want to replace your disease- and pest-prone varieties, you've plenty of naturally disease-resistant varieties to choose from. (If you're *replacing* roses, watch out for 'rose sickness' – see the sidebar 'Avoiding rose sickness'.)

Order catalogues from several rose specialists and look for descriptions like 'healthy', 'vigorous', 'tough', 'reliable' and 'disease-resistant'. Breeders pro-duce many newer roses specifically with disease resistance in mind but still retaining the charming appearance and fragrance of the typical 'old' varieties (such as English shrub roses, a large and diverse group of beautiful roses). You can buy loads of different shapes and sizes of roses, from dainty minia-tures suitable for tubs, spreading ground cover roses for hanging baskets, banks and borders, to large bushes and vigorous, giant climbers.

Avoiding rose sickness

Never plant roses in the same spot where roses have been growing previously, because they're likely to suffer from *rose sickness* (or *replant disorder*). The cause isn't known, but is likely to be due to a build-up of pests in the soil that can transmit virus diseases, and may be related to a lack of certain nutrients. If you're desper-ate to replace one rose with another, dig out a cube of soil measuring at least 45 centimetres (18 inches) and replace with fresh garden soil from elsewhere.

Buying roses

Everybody sells roses – from grocers to DIY shops to mail-order nurseries. Grabbing a cheap rose with a pretty picture on the wrapper, however, doesn't guarantee you value. Different nurseries often sell the same rose varieties, but the difference is in how they handle the plants. Buy from plant outlets that take good care of their roses. Don't buy plants that have shrivelled stems, wilted leaves or dusty dry packing material around their bare roots.

For the widest choice of varieties, buy from a rose specialist. Doing so usually means buying by mail order because plants are dispatched bare-rooted, which means you can only get roses during the dormant period (autumn–late winter). If you've a rose nursery or an excellent garden centre just down the road, you can buy container grown roses at any time of year.

Bare-root roses grow vigorously after planting as long as they remain cool and moist before you buy them.

Planting roses

Nearly all roses are made of two parts grafted together. The top part, called the *scion*, is the desirable flowering rose. The *rootstock*, on the bottom, adds hardiness and tolerance to a wide range of soil types. Where the two parts meet is called the *bud union*, as shown in Figure 14-2.

Growing problem-free, beautiful roses begins with putting them in the right place and planting them properly. In this section, we show you how to get your new roses off to the best possible start.

Picking an ideal time and place

Roses establish faster, and resist pests and diseases better, when you plant them in an ideal location. They require at least six hours of direct sunlight each day for good flowering and growth, but avoid overly hot spots that bake in the midday sun. A site that also gets morning sun, to dry the foliage quickly and keep it disease-free, is ideal. Choose a planting location away from shady buildings or trees, and avoid trees, shrubs and nearby large hedges with roots that compete with the roses for moisture and nutrients.

Make sure that the site is open to allow the summer breezes to blow through; good ventilation helps keep leaf diseases to a minimum. However, too windy and it can cause damage to the leaves and flowers. Also choose a location from which water drains promptly. Roses don't grow well where soil stays wet or where water puddles on the surface.

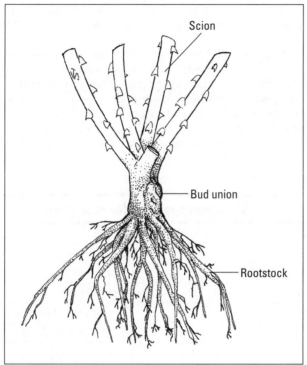

Figure 14-2:
The scion
and root-
stock join at
the knobby
bud union.

Scion

Bud union

Rootstock

You can plant roses any time of year, but certain times are better than others (depending on how your plants are packaged). Bare-root roses can only be planted while dormant. Container roses establish best when planted in autumn or early spring, when plants can concentrate on putting down roots instead of making lots of top growth at the same time.

Preparing the planting site

Roses thrive in loamy, well-drained garden soil with an optimum pH of 6.5 (see Chapter 5 for all about pH values) and do particularly well on clay, so long as the drainage is adequate. Begin with a soil test to determine pH and nutrient levels so that you can make corrections, if necessary, while you prepare the soil.

Most soils, whether clay or sandy, benefit from the addition of organic matter, which improves drainage, aeration and nutrient-holding capacity. Double-dig the soil and work in organic matter – such as compost, rotted manure, shredded leaves or finely ground potting bark – at the rate of approximately one barrow per square metre (10.8 square feet). Incorporate a phosphorus-rich fertiliser before planting; if using a general fertiliser, avoid one high in nitrogen that encourages soft, sappy, disease-prone growth.

Rose roots form strong associations with mycorrhizal fungi, so adding one of these products is well worth the extra cost. (Check out Chapter 7 for more.)

Plant spacing varies according to the growth habit of the rose variety. Plants that grow too close together are tall and spindly, and produce only a few small flowers. For a guide to plant spacing by rose type, see Table 14-1. (The spacings are the absolute minimum for organic rose growing; where possible, allow more room between your roses to give plenty of air movement and to allow space for other flowers that create diversity.) The plant description in the catalogue or on the plant tag tells you what type of rose you have and also recommends the proper spacing.

Table 14-1	Minimum spacings for rose plants
Type of Rose	*Spacing*
Climbing roses	2.5–3.8 metres (8 to 12 feet)
Floribunda	1.2 metres (4 feet)
Ground-cover roses	1 metre (3 feet)
Miniature roses	45 centimetres (18 inches)
Shrub roses	1.5–1.8 metres (5–6 feet feet)
Single flowered bush (Hybrid tea)	1.2 metres (4 feet)

Planting a bare-root rose

Plant bare-root roses as soon as possible after purchasing or receiving them through the post. Unwrap plants from the packaging and soak the root system in a bucket of tepid water for about an hour before planting. If you must delay planting for a few days, keep the plants moist and in a cool, dark location, or place them in a temporary soil trench in a shaded location.

Don't store rose plants with any ripening fruit, such as in a refrigerator or root cellar, because the fruit gives off ethylene, which harms growing plants.

See the section on settling in bare-root plants in Chapter 8 for step-by-step instructions on how to plant your bare-root rose.

Planting a container-grown rose

Keep container-grown plants watered and in a sunny location until they can be planted in the garden. Make sure that the soil in the pot is moist but not sopping wet at planting time to make handling the plant easier. Prune out any damaged, dead or broken stems before planting. Refer to Chapter 8 for details on planting container-grown plants.

Fertilising and mulching for roses

Roses need plenty of nutrients and regular watering to grow vigorously and flower profusely. You don't need synthetic chemical rose fertilisers, though; many organic options are available.

Soil improvers – such as compost, leafmould and well-rotted manure – contribute nutrients to soils, but their most important role is to provide organic matter that has positive, long-term benefits. Mulch bare soil around roses every year, in late winter or early spring, applying the mulch in a layer at least 5 centimetres (2 inches) thick. Avoid the mulch touching the stems.

Roses also benefit from a dressing of organic fertiliser in early spring and again in early summer. Choose a product high in potash to boost flower production, but low in nitrogen, which would encourage soft leafy growth at the expense of flowers.

Products based on seaweed appear to be beneficial to organic rose growing.

Watering your roses

During the first few months after planting, watering your new rose is important if the weather is dry while the plant is actively growing. Watering during the winter months is very rarely necessary. When your plants are established, extra water is only required during dry spells of more than a couple of weeks. If you've prepared the ground thoroughly, the organic matter acts like a sponge and holds on to the moisture.

When you water, soak the entire root zone and then wait until the soil is dry 5–10 centimetres (2–4 inches) down before watering again. You can check the water penetration in the soil by digging out a shovel-length wedge of soil, but try not to damage the plant roots in the process.

If you live in a very dry area, don't grow roses in the first place! Regular water use is rather environmentally unfriendly.

Solving common rose troubles

If you follow the advice in this chapter, your organic roses have a great chance of thriving and fighting off the many diseases and pests that beset roses. However, being aware of potential problems and 'nipping them in the bud', so to speak, is what organic gardening is all about.

Check your plants regularly for signs of diseases (such as blackspot and mildew), remove and bin infected leaves, snip off dead flowers and make sure that you pick up and dispose of (not compost) fallen foliage at the end of the season. Watch out for infestations of pests such as aphids and leaf-rolling sawfly and deal with promptly. Surround your roses with wildlife-friendly plants to encourage predatory insects, and encourage birds too. For more on how to combat pests and diseases without chemicals, read Chapters 17–19.

Don't assume that any insect you spot in the garden is the perpetrator of damage: nothing's further from the truth. Most of the insects you see in your garden are harmless; only a few cause damage. Some actually help!

Chapter 15

Managing Garden Trees and Shrubs

In This Chapter

▶ Achieving tree and shrub success

▶ Planting trees and shrubs effectively

▶ Caring for long-lived garden plants

▶ Finding the right trees and shrubs for your garden

*T*rees and shrubs lend structure to your plot; they form the framework around which you plant your flowers and productive gardens. As these long-lived plants mature, they become like old friends. Losing one to accident or disease leaves a hole in your garden – a gap in the hedge, so to speak.

As we describe in this chapter, taking care of these irreplaceable assets and using them to your best advantage starts with choosing the right plants in the first place, planting them correctly and caring for them to keep them thriving.

Planning for Long-Term Success

When you're setting out into unfamiliar territory, you need a map. Knowing the lay of the land – what to expect around the next bend in the road – saves missteps, as well as valuable time and energy. A plan of your garden is just as helpful when you're choosing and planting the best trees and shrubs. Miss a turn, and you may not get where you intend to go. In Chapter 3, you can find out how to assess your growing conditions and make a plan. That chapter is a good reference as you read through this one.

Putting everything in its place

Happy trees and shrubs live for a long time and suffer few problems. Note the essential word 'happy', though. Plants from nurseries and garden centres originate from all around the world, and so obviously a plant from a cool, damp, Himalayan valley doesn't thrive in the same conditions as a sun-lover from the Med. So before you begin shopping for these long-term garden investments, assess the conditions of your planting site and use this information to narrow the list of potential plants to those that thrive in your particular location and situation.

One aspect that many people fail to consider when placing trees and shrubs in their gardens is the plants' mature size. Most of these woody plants grow so slowly that you can easily forget that the spindly twig you plant by the front gate is going to grow wide enough to divert traffic within a few years.

Play safe by spacing trees where they can grow to full size without overhanging buildings and roads, growing into utility wires or crowding the house. Choose shrubs that don't cover the windows or pavements.

 Inevitably, allowing enough essential room for future growth means that the space between your small, newly planted shrubs and trees looks bleak and barren to begin with. Tackle this problem in the most attractive way, by infilling with smaller shrubs and ground cover plants, groups of perennials and grasses, colourful bulbs or annual flowers, until the larger trees and shrubs fill in.

Avoiding troublemakers

Buying trees and hedging plants is like entering into any long-term relationship: the characteristics that attract you in the first place may lose their appeal in time if the bad habits outweigh the good ones. When you choose trees and shrubs for your organic garden, consider the attributes that you want your plants to have. Try not to focus only on fast growth, colour, texture, shape and flowers, but keep other factors in mind too. If you want a tree to plant in the lawn, look for deeply rooted, long-lived species where you've space to mow beneath. No time for raking? Stay away from trees that drop copious twigs and leaves. Be aware of the following particular potential problems:

  ✔ **Invasive roots:** These wreak havoc in drains, and trees planted too close to your house can even damage foundations. Remember that the root systems of most trees grow as wide as they do high. Thirsty weeping willow trees (Salix) are notorious. Always match the mature tree size to that of your garden.

✔ **Messy trees:** These drop leaves, sap, fruits, nuts and twigs frequently, adding to garden maintenance. Avoid planting trees such as crab apples and hawthorn where the branches overhang paths or patios, because the trodden fruit is messy and can cause the paving to become dangerously slippery.

✔ **Over-vigorous hedges:** Leyland cypress has caused many ferocious neighbourhood disputes. Although people buy this tree as the fastest-growing hedging plant, it keeps on growing many metres high unless pruned regularly – up to three times a year.

Research is essential to avoiding such problems. Find out as much as you can about a species before you buy, and for your organic garden, opt for trees and shrubs that are naturally healthy, easy to grow and ideally have a benefit to wildlife too, so that you can entice plenty of natural predators and pollinators into your garden. If you can't resist varieties that are liable to pests or diseases, search out those that offer disease resistance, if available.

Giving Your New Trees and Shrubs the Best Start

The way in which you plant your tree or shrub determines whether it thrives, merely survives or dies. Simple mistakes, such as planting too deeply or too shallow, can make all the difference. Good soil preparation is vital for these long-lived plants, as is the short-term aftercare during the first months of their lives as they settle in to your garden. Read the following sections to get your plants off to the best possible start.

Selecting the right season

The best time of year to plant trees, shrubs and hedging depends on your climate and the type of plant you're installing. In addition, you need to be able to care for the plants properly in those crucial first few weeks when they depend on you for water. (Check out the later section 'Getting short-term care right'.) Don't plant in summer and then go away on holiday for a fortnight!

The ideal time to plant all _hardy_ (frost-tolerant) plants is in autumn, while the soil is warm, usually moist, and when the plant can concentrate on root rather than top growth. Planting can continue through winter, as long as conditions aren't freezing, and into early spring.

The nearer to the growing season you plant, the more likely you are to have to spend at least some time watering your new tree or shrub.

Plant evergreens (and any plants that aren't reliably frost-hardy) in spring, so that they've a whole growing season to establish before the cold weather arrives.

Nurseries and garden centres sell woody plants in three ways: in containers, bare-root and *root balled* (sometimes referred to as *balled and burlapped*, the latter being the wrapping). Flip to Chapter 8 for details on installing plants in these different forms. Although you can buy nearly all plants in containers and hence year-round, trees and hedging usually offer better value for money, and better plants, if bought bare-rooted or root balled during autumn and winter.

Picking out healthy plants

One of the first steps to low-maintenance, problem-free, organically cultivated trees and shrubs is selecting healthy specimens. Refer to Chapter 8 for tips on choosing healthy plants in general. Here are a couple of tips specific to trees:

- ✔ **Mechanical damage:** A few broken twigs usually aren't reasons to reject a plant, but avoid those with gashes on the trunk and main limbs, as well as any with torn limbs. Balled and burlapped plants need to have a solid, unbroken root ball, which indicates intact roots.

- ✔ **Branch and trunk structure:** Look for trees with straight, evenly tapered trunks and evenly distributed limbs. Unless the tree is supposed to have several trunks or large main branches, such as ornamental cherries and crab apples, choose trees with a single main trunk that doesn't fork. Avoid trees with crowded or lopsided branches. Trees (such as birches) that are sold in clumps ideally have similar-size trunks that don't rub against one another; the trees become larger and more crowded as they grow. Figure 15-1 compares trees with good and poor structure.

Shrubs vary considerably from species to species; desirable structure in one may be undesirable in another. In general, choose shrubs with symmetrical branches that don't rub against one another. Avoid shrubs with roots growing on the surface or out of the drainage holes of their pots.

Getting short-term care right

Trees and shrubs are extremely low-maintenance plants in the long term, but to get them off to a long and healthy life requires TLC for the first few months of their lives:

- ✔ Watering during dry spells in the growing season is vital, until the plant establishes a good root system.

- ✔ Mulching is extremely beneficial because it retains moisture in the soil and modulates the soil temperature around the roots.

- ✔ Staking is usually essential for trees and tall shrubs.

Figure 15-1:
Healthy
structure
(left); poor
structure
(right).

Good tree structure   Poor tree structure

After a windy spell, check your new plants in case the root ball has loosened and needs a quick re-firm with your boot, or whether a tree has swayed in the wind and created a gap in the soil around the base of the trunk. Such gaps can fill with water, freeze and cause damage.

Chapter 8 contains all the information you need on plant aftercare and maintenance.

Taking the Long View for Trees and Shrubs

While the earlier section 'Giving Your New Trees and Shrubs the Best Start' details the initial attention that your new trees and shrubs need, this section provides the gen on longer-term care. The good news is that established trees and shrubs need less attention than just about any other landscape plants. Except in unusual circumstances, they rarely need watering and they need little fertiliser. All they request is your observation for potential problems, an annual mulch of organic matter to keep the soil in good heart and occasional pruning to keep them healthy and respectable-looking.

Fertilising follies

Unless your soil is unusually infertile or free-draining, you don't need to fertilise trees and shrubs more than once or twice a year. When preparing the site for planting, incorporate a fertiliser that's high in phosphorus to boost root growth. In future years, apply a general fertiliser in early to mid-spring, and again in early summer over the root zones of flowering shrubs (the *root zone*, where the roots grow, usually is at least twice as wide as the branch spread). See Chapter 7 for more on using organic fertilisers.

Practising pruning

You need a good reason to prune a twig or remove a limb from a tree or shrub; every time you cut into a plant, you open a wound that's vulnerable to disease. Keep your overall goal in mind to guide you towards making the right cuts and minimise the size and number of cuts you need to make.

Two basic pruning cuts are all you need to maintain your trees, shrubs and flowering plants: thinning and heading:

- ✔ **Thinning cut:** A *thinning cut* removes a branch back to its origin, as shown on the left in Figure 15-2. Use thinning cuts to maintain your plants' natural appearance while decreasing their height, width or branching density.

- ✔ **Heading cut:** A *heading cut*, shown on the right in Figure 15-2, removes shoots or branches back to buds. Plants usually respond to heading cuts by sprouting new shoots near the pruning site, resulting in denser growth.

When you make a thinning cut, make sure that you cut at the right place. If you look closely where a branch joins the trunk or a larger limb, you should see a series of raised ridges, called the *branch collar*. That's where the scar tissue begins to form when the limb dies or is removed. Make your cut just outside that collar without leaving a stub. Stubs invite infection that may lead to the death of the tree. Never cut a limb flush with the trunk, and always support the limb you're removing to avoid tearing the bark on the trunk.

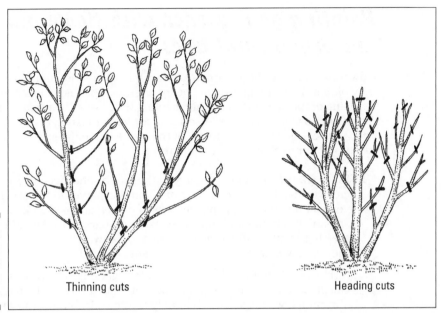

Figure 15-2:
Thinning
cuts (left);
heading
cuts (right).

Thinning cuts   Heading cuts

Choosing the Perfect Trees and Shrubs

When you choose new trees and shrubs, think about the roles you want them
to fulfil in your garden. Do you need shade or shelter from the wind? Does a
corner of the garden need a spark of colour? Consider all the seasons of the
year when you make your decision; the best shrubs and trees have practical
or decorative value in several seasons, not just one.

For the organic gardener, though, permanent plants have uses that go way
beyond these considerations. Large plants play an important life-support role
for pest-controlling wildlife and pollinating insects, and so the varieties we recommend in this section have benefit to wildlife to a lesser or greater extent.

If you want to know more about trees, shrubs and conifers, and how to care
for them, pick up a copy of *Gardening For Dummies* by Sue Fisher, Michael
MacCaskey and Bill Marken (Wiley). The book also lists many of the most
attractive and disease- and pest-resistant varieties of each tree and shrub.

Painting your garden with flowering and ornamental trees

Flowering trees give your garden a colourful exclamation point whenever they bloom. The anticipation of cherry or crab apple blossoms marks the changing of the seasons, often highlighting the start of 'gardening time'. Although blossom is wonderful, do look for longer-lasting features so that your tree 'earns its keep' in terms of the space it occupies, such as attractive foliage, coloured stems and autumn fruits.

- **Birch (*Betula* species):** When you think of birches, you likely picture a clump of white-barked trees. Not all birches have white bark, however; you can buy pinks, creams, browns and even almost black. Birches are splendidly ornamental trees because their bark looks beautiful all year, they bear catkins in spring that are popular with seed-eating birds and they give wonderful autumn leaf colour.

  Birches cast light shade and hence make good garden trees because you can grow a wide range of plants beneath. Most birches thrive in reasonably moist, well-drained, preferably acidic soils, but try river birch in damp soil. If you have to prune (but do try not to), do so in late spring to early summer after the leaves have fully emerged. If pruned too early or late in the season, birches bleed sap excessively. Also, avoid disturbing the soil around their shallow roots.

- **Flowering crab apple (*Malus* species):** These excellent small-garden trees offer two seasons of interest: masses of spring apple blossom followed in autumn by persistent and colourful fruit popular with birds and small mammals. Crab apple fruit can be used in preserves and jellies, and if that isn't useful enough, they can also serve as pollinators for the good old domestic apple. Hundreds of varieties are available, and many of the newest ones have built-in disease resistance. Plant them in nearly any well-drained, moderately fertile soil and full sun. If necessary, prune while dormant, in late winter to early spring.

  Select for flower colour (white to deep pink and purple), height and growth shape (weeping, vase-shaped, columnar, to wide and low), leaf colour (green to reddish) and fruit size and colour (red to yellow).

- **Hawthorn (*Crataegus* species):** This group of trees offers clouds of spring bloom on neat, well-shaped trees, followed by bright orange to red autumn fruits that birds just love. Most common are varieties of *Crataegus laevigata*, although the less usual *C.* x *lavalleei* 'Carrierei' is more decorative.

- **Serviceberry (*Amelanchier* species):** These trees grow about 4–5 metres (13–16 feet) high and often form multiple-trunked trees (known as *multistems*). In spring, they produce clouds of white flowers, which ripen to edible deep red to black fruits similar to blueberries by early summer. Their glossy, deep green, oval foliage turns brilliant yellow to orange in the autumn. Although serviceberry thrives in most soils, you achieve the best autumn leaf colour in moist, acidic soils.

✔ **Sorbus (*Sorbus* species):** This extensive group of excellent garden trees includes rowan or mountain ash. Most sorbus form compact trees with spring flowers, attractive foliage and autumn berries – mostly in shades of orange or red, but white and even pink-berried forms do exist.

Filling your garden with flowering and foliage shrubs

The seasonal stars of the show, flowering shrubs light up your garden with displays of flowers. The best shrubs, however, offer long periods of bloom along with other attributes such as fragrance, attractive foliage, coloured bark or stems, and autumn fruits. Handsome foliage shrubs also contribute a great deal to the garden, with evergreen leaves that look good all year or coloured deciduous foliage from spring to autumn. Evergreen shrubs, or those with prickly predator-repelling stems, make particularly good nest sites for birds.

✔ **Barberry (*Berberis* species):** Prickly-stemmed and easy to grow in sun or shade, on all but the poorest of soils, *berberis* come in a wide range of varieties and sizes, including both evergreen and deciduous. Those with an upright habit, such as *B. darwinii* and *B. thunbergii*, make excellent hedges as well as good border plants. Deciduous varieties include 'Rose Glow' and 'Red Chief' that have attractive colourful leaves.

✔ **Butterfly bush (*Buddleja davidii*):** As the name suggests, this shrub is a real magnet for butterflies, which flock to the clusters of nectar-rich blooms in colours that include white, blue, pink and purple. Butterfly bush is fast and easy to grow, thriving on any well-drained soil and preferring sun. To keep this shrub within bounds, you can prune it hard in late winter or early spring.

✔ **Cotoneaster (*Cotoneaster* species):** Deciduous members of this group have small leaves and in the case of *Cotoneaster horizontalis* distinctive, herringbone-patterned branches. Many species and varieties are evergreen. Size varies considerably, from ground-covering plants to tall shrubs that grow 4–5 metres (13–16 feet) high. Most cotoneasters have nectar-rich flowers that are particularly attractive to bees, and colourful autumn fruits (birds love the red and orange fruits although yellow ones appear less desirable and often remain on the plant all winter). Cotoneasters are easy to grow and thrive in any reasonable soil, in sun or shade.

- ✔ **Firethorn (*Pyracantha* species):** A wildlife favourite, firethorn is a tall, thorny shrub smothered in nectar-rich clusters of tiny flowers in early summer, followed by autumn berries in red or orange that birds love. You can get yellow-fruiting species, though these are obviously less palatable as birds tend to leave them till the end of the winter, or sometimes don't eat them at all. Firethorn's dense growth is good for nesting. Grow firethorn as a free-standing shrub or as a hedge, or train against a wall or fence (in which case you need to prune it after flowering to keep in shape). Firethorn is happy in any reasonable soil, in sun or shade. Some pyracanthas are susceptible to scab disease; although well-grown plants have good resistance. You can buy resistant varieties such as the Saphyr types.

- ✔ **Holly (*Ilex* species):** This huge group of mostly evergreen trees and shrubs includes everything from the classic English holly *(I. aquifolium)* to the less-well-known inkberry *(I. glabra)* and hundreds of species and varieties in between. Most hollies produce large crops of attractive berries (which birds love and so often don't last long), but most species bear male and female flowers on separate plants. Plant at least one of each species if you want berries, or check if any other hollies are growing close by in your neighbours' gardens as you may already have a plant of the opposite sex close by, so you need only buy one. The plant names aren't always reliable as regards clues about the sex of the shrub, though: 'Golden Queen', for example, is a male variety.

  In general, holly enjoys moisture retentive but well-drained soil and full sun or part shade. Holly also makes an excellent hedge; plant 45–60 centimetres (18–24 inches) apart.

- ✔ **Hydrangea (*Hydrangea* species):** Popular for its huge balls of white, pink and blue flowers, this group of shrubs is extremely useful for sites in part or even full shade. Moisture-retentive and neutral to acid soil is preferred, and so avoid planting hydrangeas where you may have to water.

- ✔ **Lilac (*Syringa* species):** If you give your lilac any reasonably fertile soil and full sun, you can expect it to live for many years. Prune it to remove spent flowers and weak growth. The common lilac *(S. vulgaris)* offers the widest range of flower colours, from white to pink and blue to deep purple. Some varieties have double flowers or extra fragrance. Meyer lilac *(S. meyeri)* and Manchurian lilac *(S. patula)* 'Miss Kim' stay smaller than the common species.

- ✔ **Spirea (*Spirea* species):** These easygoing shrubs are useful for informal hedges and mixed shrub borders. Most have flat clusters of little white to pink flowers; some, such as 'Magic Carpet' and 'Goldflame', even offer three seasons of interest with their brilliant yellow foliage, floral display and autumn colour. Plant in any well-drained soil, and give them full sun.

  After flowering, cut the weakest or oldest one-fourth of the shoots to the ground each year to keep shrubs vigorous and tidy.

✔ **Viburnum (*Viburnum* species):** This diverse group shares the attribute of profuse flowering; some, such as *Viburnum carlesii* and *V. x carlcephalum*, have intoxicatingly fragrant flowers. Birds appreciate fruit-bearing native species such as *V. opulus* for food. Most viburnums bloom in spring or summer, although the useful laurustinus *(V. tinus)* flowers in winter, and has evergreen foliage too. Most of these shrubs grow in any well-drained but moisture-retentive soil. Some prefer acidic soil; others are less fussy. Full sun to part shade suits them fine, depending on the species and climate.

Considering conifers

Needle- and cone-bearing trees and shrubs, called *conifers*, provide the back-drop for colourful shrubs and flowers and serve as hedges, screens and wind-breaks. Their imposing size and stiff formality make many evergreen trees difficult to integrate into small home gardens. Think twice before planting a potentially 16-metre (50-foot) tall blue cedar in your front garden! In larger settings, where the trees can attain full size, evergreen trees add grandeur. Conifers provide excellent refuges for wildlife, particularly large specimen trees or hedges.

Dwarf and compact conifers are invaluable for the year-round colour and texture they add to the garden. Some creep over the ground and drape over walls; others grow into neat cones, pyramids and rounded cushions. Foliage colours range from gold through a wide range of greens to silver and even purplish. Some plants appear fuzzy and soft; others are stiff and bristly.

Although you can shape certain conifers into geometric and fanciful forms, a process known as *topiary*, most don't require pruning at all except to remove dead, diseased or damaged limbs and undesirable growth that detracts from the plant's appearance. In fact, pine, spruce and fir trees that grow in *whorls* (with layers of branches around the trunk) don't sprout new limbs in response to pruning. To control their growth, pinch or prune their new, soft growth in late spring before it hardens, cutting into only the new tissue.

A few conifers, notably yew, do tolerate more pruning and usually sprout new growth to replace what you remove. Conifers that usually grow into a pyramid shape with one central trunk sometimes develop additional *leaders* (competing main trunks) at the top of the tree. Remove all but one leader to retain the tree shape.

Conifers grown for hedging, on the other hand, do need regular pruning. In the case of the ultra quick-growing Leyland cypress, you may have to prune up to three times a year in order to keep it within bounds. Consider your choice of conifers – and your like (or dislike!) of pruning – carefully, if you plan to plant a hedge.

✔ **Cypress and false cypress (*Cuprocyparis* and *Chamaecyparis* species):** These two closely related groups share many features but differ in their preferred growing conditions. The cypress group *Chamaecyparis* prefers cool, moist, humid conditions; another group of cypress (*Cupressus*) enjoys the heat and drier soil found in Mediterranean-type climates. The hybrid between the two groups, Leyland cypress (x *Cuprocyparis leylandii*) tolerates a wider range of soils and climates than either of its parents. Cypresses have flat, scale-like foliage that's compressed against the twigs, giving the branches stringy or fanlike textures.

Hundreds of varieties are available, from dwarf and low-growing forms to stately trees. Leyland cypress is used widely for hedges because it grows up to 1 metre (3.2 feet) per year and tolerates most reasonable soils. Hinoki *(C. obtusa)* and threadleaf *(C. pisifera)* false cypresses have many popular varieties used in home and commercial landscapes. Cypresses require no pruning except to shape the plant or remove damaged limbs, with the exception of those grown for hedging. Trim in early spring before the birds nest, and again in late summer after the last fledglings have flown.

✔ **Juniper (*Juniperus* species):** Versatile and tough as nails, junipers are justifiably among the most popular landscape shrubs. They tolerate poor, dry soil, as well as urban and roadside conditions; they come in a seemingly infinite number of shapes, sizes, colours and textures. Depending on the species and variety, you can find a juniper to grow in any climate. Ground-hugging forms make excellent carpets for slopes and lawn substitutes. Taller varieties serve as shrubs for hedges and planting around buildings.

Among the many species, look for Chinese *(Juniperus chinensis, J.* x *media)*, creeping *(J. horizontalis)*, savin *(J. sabina)* and Rocky Mountain *(J. scopulorum)* juniper varieties. Shore juniper *(J. conferta)* enjoys drier and coastal conditions.

Avoid wet, poorly drained soils, which makes junipers prone to root rot.

✔ **Pine (*Pinus* species):** Some pines grow into large, picturesque, forest trees, making good specimens and windbreaks, but a few dwarf varieties stay small enough to serve in home gardens. For these pines, seek out Japanese red pine *(Pinus densiflora)* 'Umbraculifera', Japanese white pine *(P. parviflora)* Glauca Group, Japanese black pine *(P. thunbergii)* and mugo pine *(P. mugo)*.

Pines have long needles that give them a softer texture than most other conifers. The needles occur in bundles of two, three or five. Pines with the same number of needles in a bundle often have other common characteristics, such as growth habits and cultural requirements. *Two-needled pines*, such as Scots pine *(P. sylvestris)* for example, tolerate drier soil and more heat than the *five-needled species*, such as white pine *(P. strobus)*.

✔ **Spruce (*Picea* species):** Give spruce trees plenty of room if you plant them in your garden, because they tend to spread widely at the base as they mature. Most spruce have a stiff, formal pyramid shape, which looks best in large gardens or when the trees grow in groups. Use for windbreaks or large screens.

You can buy a few dwarf varieties that grow into small mounds or weeping specimens suitable for planting in small gardens. For dwarf varieties, look for Norway *(Picea abies)*, 'Little Gem', 'Pumila Nigra', 'Nidiformis' or Bird's Nest Spruce; black *(P. mariana)* 'Nana'; or white spruce *(P. glauca)* 'Conica', also known as Dwarf Alberta Spruce.

Spruces prefer cool climates and well-drained but moderately moist soil. Avoid planting them in dry soil and polluted urban locations.

✔ **Western red cedar (*Thuja plicata* 'Atrovirens'):** Increasingly popular as an alternative to Leyland cypress for hedging, this conifer has lustrous green foliage, responds well to clipping and grows at a reasonable speed of around 45 centimetres (18 inches) a year. You need to space hedging plants 60 centimetres (2 feet) apart. A number of other thujas are compact in shape, which is ideal for the mixed border, and come in many shapes, including globe, cone, column, pyramid and weeping.

✔ **Yew (*Taxus* species):** Yews, among the most widely grown conifers for hedges and shearing into topiary shapes, respond to pruning by sprouting ever-denser growth. Keep in mind that most yews grow into approximately 10–20-metre (30–60-foot) trees if allowed to do so, although regular trimming can keep them to a fraction of this size. They grow best in well-drained, fertile, moist soil and full sun to part shade, and prefer a site sheltered from cold winter winds.

Chapter 16

Creating and Caring for Your Organic Lawn

In This Chapter

▶ Selecting easy-to-care-for grasses

▶ Starting your lawn correctly

▶ Maintaining your lawn organically

▶ Considering lawn alternatives

Many people think that to have an attractive lawn, they have to douse it with herbicides, insecticides and fungicides. That, of course, is a fallacy, unless you desire a flawless 'bowling green' sward. Growing a great-looking lawn organically is possible and even easy, although an organic lawn-care programme does require an attitude adjustment.

The secret is to think of your lawn as a mixed garden of grass and other compatible, low-growing plants that tolerate mowing.

As in any other kind of gardening, your success depends on how well you lay the groundwork by preparing the soil, choosing the right seed or turf, and giving the plants what they need. This chapter explains your lawn's growth habits, fertiliser needs, and pests and diseases. You can also find out about 'alternative' lawns here; that is, taking a truly wildlife-friendly approach by having long grass or a managed wildflower meadow.

Getting Down to Grassroots

If you dig out a wedge of turf and soil and look at it, you see several layers. At the top is the mostly flat grass blade, which in healthy grass is bright green; that's the part of the plant you mow every week. At the next-lower level, you see rounder grass stems and then the *crown*, where the roots meet the stems. The new grass growth emerges at the ground-hugging plant crown.

Under the soil, you find masses of roots for each grass plant. Then, of course, you have the soil. Although gardeners – organic or otherwise – usually give lots of tender loving care to the soil that nourishes plants, they often neglect the poor lawn even though it takes the most punishment in the garden.

Choosing the Right Grass

Organic lawn care gets a lot easier if you grow the right grass for your site, sun and soil conditions. You can discover grasses that thrive under nearly every combination of lawn conditions. Finding the right grass variety for your lawn is easier than ever because plant breeders work hard to produce grasses that thrive under different conditions.

One particular variety of grass can't do everything that you require. For that reason, most grass seed and turf is sold as combinations of grasses that complement one another. The labels on grass seed packages list the percentage of each seed by weight.

Preparing the Soil

When you're planting a new lawn, you've only one chance to get it right. After you plant the grass, you can't easily improve the soil or add soil conditioners, as you can with your vegetable gardens or borders. Here are the essentials to preparing your soil:

- ✔ **Test for pH.** Ideally, the soil needs to be neutral to slightly acidic; pH 6–7 is best. Amend the pH if conditions are extreme (see Chapter 5).

- ✔ **Correct any potential drainage problems.** Look for wet or poorly drained spots where grass can't thrive, and search out the cause. The problem may be compaction beneath the ground so that water can't drain freely, or perhaps drain pipes from your roof are emptying into the garden. If all the ground is wet for long periods, you may need to consult a landscaper about installing land drains.

- ✔ **Cultivate the ground.** Dig or rotovate the soil to a spade's depth (but not before clearing perennial weeds: check out Chapter 21).

- ✔ **Clear the ground of weeds.** You get only one shot at this task when creating a lawn, so make a thorough job of it. Be especially careful to clear all perennial weed roots. Adopt the 'stale seed bed' technique that professional growers use: allow the prepared soil to rest for a week or two (to allow weeds and weed seeds to sprout) and then use a hoe to slice them off just under the soil.

> ✔ **Add organic matter.** Spread a 5–8-centimetre (2–3-inch) layer of well-rotted manure or compost, and rotovate or dig in.
>
> ✔ **Rake the soil smooth and level.** Hollows, ruts and dips cause uneven turf growth, and result in wet or dry patches that encourage disease and attract insect pests. Rake once, tread or roll the soil to firm it, and then rake again. Remove large stones or lumps of debris.

For more about improving your soil, changing pH and adding organic matter and other conditioners, flip to Chapter 5.

Planting the Lawn

Whether you're planting seed or laying turf, do so during the best times of year if at all possible: autumn or early-mid spring. At these times, the soil is sufficiently warm for growth to begin without delay, and enough rain is usually around to avoid having to water much.

The unusual weather patterns of recent years, however, mean that this guideline for rainfall is far from certain – so watch the weather and use your common sense before picking up the phone and ordering a truckload of turf.

You can lay turf or sow seed right through summer, but you're far more likely to end up with a large water bill (water is a precious resource, and so using it as sparingly as possible is the wisest course).

Going for turf

Most people assume that starting a lawn from turf is easier, faster and more reliable than seeding. Well, as Meatloaf sang, 'two out of three ain't bad'! Using turf is faster and more reliable, because doing so is like laying a carpet in your garden and you can have a great-looking lawn in one day. But the process is no easier; *turfing* (installing turf) requires as much soil preparation work as seeding and even more aftercare. If you plant turf properly, however, and nurse it through the establishment period, your lawn starts out entirely free of undesirable weedy plants, such as dandelions and thistle.

Bear in mind that turf costs far, far more than a box of seed. (Flip to the later section 'Creating a lawn from seed' for all about sowing grass seed.)

Choosing your turf

Much of the turf available to buy is described as 'cultivated meadow turf', which is fine for creating good-quality and hard-wearing lawns.

Check the quality before ordering or buying. Make sure that the turf looks healthy, fresh and green, and is evenly moist. Don't purchase turf from a retail outlet if it may have been standing around for several days.

If you want anything more than a small amount of turf, go direct to a turf supplier who can deliver to your door when you require. Specialist-grown turf is available – at a higher price, of course – but may be worth considering if you want a top-quality lawn to manage organically. Rhizomatous Tall Fescue (RTF) turf, for example, has been specially bred to cope with dry conditions.

Laying your turf

For the best results when turfing, get the soil thoroughly moist and work quickly. In addition, make the ground as level as possible and ensure that the soil is good to go before the turf arrives. You don't want the turf to sit and dry out in a heap.

Turf is made up of living plants that need light, air and water: left rolled up, it quickly yellows and dies.

If for some reason you can't install the turf for a day or so, cover it lightly with a tarpaulin to keep it moist. Mist with water, if necessary, but don't soak it, because wet turf is heavy to work with and may fall apart.

If work is delayed for longer than a couple of days, unroll the turf – ideally on top of weed control fabric (also known as 'landscaping fabric' or 'geotextile', and which is widely available from garden centres and DIY stores) laid over soil (otherwise the grass starts to root immediately into soil), and keep it moist. We know that doing so is a lot of work, but it saves having to throw the turf away.

Here's how to lay the turf:

1. **Start at a straight edge, such as a driveway or patio.**

2. **Lay the pieces end to end to form the first row, making sure that they butt up against each other tightly, with no bare soil showing.**

3. **Finish one row, and then offset the beginning of the next one so that the starting ends of each row are staggered instead of in a line (just like a wall of bricks).**

As you work, press all over each laid turf with the back of a rake, to bring it into contact with the ground beneath. If you have to stand on freshly laid turf, put down a board first so that it spreads your weight.

Caring for your turf

Even after you've covered the entire area of turf, your work is far from over. Aftercare is critical for lawn success. Follow these steps:

1. **Spread a small amount of sieved topsoil over the turf, and work it into the cracks between strips with a broom.** This technique ensures that the edges quickly root together.

2. **Water – and keep watering!** The turf needs pampering until the roots dig deep into the soil to forage for their own water. Don't let the turf dry out for four weeks. (At the same time, take care not to overwater; yellowing of the older parts of the grass stems is a classic sign. Reduce watering if you notice this sign, but take care not to stop altogether if no rain falls.)

3. **Mow the grass when it starts growing vigorously.** Make the first cut with the mower blades set high.

Creating a lawn from seed

Pros and cons exist if you decide to start your lawn with seed. For example, weeds can and will sprout along with the grass; and yet you've many more improved varieties of seed to choose from compared to starting with turf. Also, seed allows you to add the seeds of other desirable lawn plants as well, such as clover and white yarrow. In addition, seed is much less expensive than turf, but you do need patience. A seed-sown lawn takes months to become established enough to use, and you've the extra hassle of keeping birds away from a free feast.

The amount of seed you need depends on the type of grass you're planting. Use the number on the seed box to figure how much seed is necessary, and buy about 25 per cent more than you think you need.

Manufacturers have considerately packaged their seed according to site and soil type. So, if you've a light and free-draining soil, go for drought-tolerant grass seed that includes grass varieties that are especially deep-rooting. If trees overhang your lawn, opt for a shade-tolerant seed mix.

Prepare the soil as we describe in the earlier section 'Preparing the Soil', and then go over it one more time with a rake to remove all rocks and make the surface as level as possible. Water the area thoroughly (unless the soil is already moist, when it looks dark and is damp to the touch) and allow it to drain for a couple of hours.

Sow the seed with a spreader, unless your lawn area is small enough to sow by hand. In the latter case, instead of just throwing out handfuls of seed, make a simple sowing device with two plastic plant pots (minimum 1 litre/35 fluid ounces in size) placed one inside the other, the holes slightly offset so that only a small amount of seed trickles through.

No matter how you sow, be careful to get uniform coverage. Here's how:

1. **Divide the seed into two equal lots, for example if you need to spread 5 kilograms (11 pounds) of seed, divide into two 2.5-kilogram (5.5-pound) applications.**

2. **Adjust your spreader to deliver seed at half the rate recommended on the seed package.**

3. **Sow the first half of the seed across the lawn in rows.**

4. **Sow the second half of the seed in rows at right angles to the first until the whole lawn is covered.**

5. **Rake very lightly to mix seeds into the top 3–6 millimetres (0.13–0.25 inch) of soil.**

Letting the tender grass seedlings dry out kills them. For complete germination, you need to keep the top layer of soil constantly moist. Unless rain falls in the day or two after sowing, soak the soil down to a depth of 15 centimetres (6 inches). Then water with a sprinkler or a hose fitted with a rose, as often as three to four times daily until the young grass plants have appeared and are growing thickly and strongly (usually around 2–3 weeks).

Allow the young grass to become well established and around 8 centimetres (3 inches) high before mowing. Make the first cut with the mower blades set high, so as to just cut off the tops.

Maintaining Your Organic Lawn

Maintaining a lawn organically, without chemicals, requires you to understand a little bit about the habits of grass and the problems that plague it. Fortunately, proper mowing, watering, fertilising and aerating go a long way toward preventing such problems.

Grasping the full importance of mowing

The lawn mower is your most important turf-maintenance tool. Mowing not only cuts the grass down to size, but also, if done properly, helps grass grow thicker. Mowing can reduce the weed population, too, and even feed the turf. If you collect the grass clippings, they make a fantastic addition to compost heaps, mixed in with dry, carbon-rich materials such as woody weeds and shredded prunings.

One frequently discussed question is what height to set your mower blades. A general rule is never to remove more than one-third of the grass height at any one time; doing so enables the lawn to recover and look good within several days.

For an average hard-wearing lawn that's cut once a week, the grass height needs to be around 18–25 millimetres (0.75–1 inch). Organic gardeners are unlikely to want to cultivate ultra-fine, bowling-green type lawns, but in that event, the height of cut can be as little as 6–12 millimetres (0.25–0.50 inch) – cut two or even three times a week.

Cut the lawn while it's actively growing, that is from spring to autumn, and aim to make a final cut late in autumn so the lawn looks neat throughout the winter.

Don't be tempted to cut the grass very short in one go – something that many gardeners do, thinking that they can then miss out a later cut. Not only does the grass look yellow and bare, but also you're likely to end up with scalped patches that are an open invitation to weeds.

Here's how to get the best cut from your mower:

- ✔ Make sure that the blade is sharp (sharpen it at least twice per season).
- ✔ Vary the mowing direction once a month to avoid soil compaction.
- ✔ Don't mow when the grass is wet.
- ✔ Overlap by about one-third of the width of the mower deck with each pass.
- ✔ Clean the grass off the mower after each mowing.

One of the best things to happen to the organic lawn is the *mulching mower*, which pulverises grass clippings into smaller pieces than a conventional mower does. Grass clippings are probably the best fertiliser your lawn can get because they provide free and natural nitrogen. When chopped into little bits, the clippings begin to break down into useful nitrogen almost as soon as they hit the ground.

Before mowing long grass, such as a meadow or the long fringes of grass around your garden edges, disturb the grass with a broom or stout stick to encourage insects and other creatures to move out. Ideally, cut a large area in stages over a week or two. Useful slowworms, which are fantastic consumers of slugs, are particularly vulnerable to mower and strimmer injury.

Watering your lawn

Water is an increasingly scarce resource, so don't fall into the trap of wanting a vivid green lawn all summer whatever the weather. When established, a general purpose, hard-wearing lawn survives periods of drought. Although the grass may well turn yellow or brown, it recovers with surprising speed after a good fall of rain.

The only time to consider watering a lawn (seeded or turfed) is when new.

Watering your new front lawn in the evening with a hose in hand does more harm than good. First, you'd have to stand for hours and hours to apply an adequate amount of water, and second, shallow sprinkling makes the roots lazy; if they get a little bit of water regularly, they become conditioned to staying near the surface of the soil. If you then stop watering, your lawn dies of drought because the roots haven't grown deep enough to forage for their own water.

In general, high-quality oscillating and impulse sprinklers offer the most uniform coverage and cover the most ground when watering new lawns.

The best time of day to water your new lawn is in the cooler temperatures of early morning. You lose less water to evaporation than at midday, and the grass blades dry quickly, minimising disease problems.

Avoiding lawn problems with cultivation, not chemicals

For all gardeners, employing good lawn management to avoid problems is common sense. For example, feeding your lawn makes the grass stronger and healthier, so giving weeds less chance of a look-in, and aerating the lawn and removing *thatch* (the surface layer of dead grass) not only keeps grass healthy, but also does away with moss, a common lawn problem.

Feeding your lawn

More than any other nutrient, grass needs nitrogen for strong growth; and because it grows almost continuously, it needs a constant supply. Grass clippings themselves provide some natural fertiliser, but you can use several other organic materials to feed your lawn as well.

Natural fertilisers contain nitrogen that doesn't dissolve readily in water but needs a little help from soil micro-organisms to become available for plants. That's good, because as a result the nitrogen is released slowly, and consequently, the lawn grows slowly and steadily. Synthetic chemical lawn fertilisers, on the other hand, tend to release lots of nitrogen at the same time, which makes the lawn grow fast at first, adding to your mowing chores. Also, chemical lawn fertilisers can be a source of water pollution.

Just by leaving the grass clippings on the lawn to decompose, you're adding the equivalent of about 0.5 kilogram of nitrogen per 100 square metres (1 pound per 1,000 square feet).

Many people go on a lawn-feeding frenzy at the first sign of spring, but that's not the best time to feed the grass. The most important time to fertilise is in autumn, followed by spring. Autumn feeding helps the grass grow strong and packs away nutrients for the following year. Helpful fertiliser manufacturers label their products accordingly – 'autumn lawn feed' and so on – with organic products also clearly labelled as such.

If you want to 'green-up' your lawn quickly and naturally, use a hose-end sprayer to apply liquid seaweed. The iron in the seaweed encourages a rich green colour.

Thinking about thatch

As grass plant parts die, they can form a tangled mat of undecomposed or partially decomposed organic matter on the soil surface called *thatch*.

A little thatch is a good thing: less than 6–12 millimetres (0.25–0.50 inch) thick and thatch helps cool and cushion the soil, as well as conserve moisture. Thick thatch may cause problems, however. A layer more than 12 millimetres (0.50 inch) thick keeps water and nutrients from reaching the soil and provides a cozy home for turf-destroying insects and diseases.

If thatch builds up on your lawn, remove it, or *scarify* the lawn. For small areas, you can use a lawn rake to scratch the thatch from the soil. Although great for toning up your muscles, scarifying manually way is backbreaking work, so try this approach only on small lawns. For large areas, rent a *powered scarifier*, which cuts the thatch and lifts it to the surface, where you can easily rake it up.

Aerating your lawn

The soil under a lawn takes a lot of abuse. You walk and run over it, stand on it, run a heavy mower over it regularly and sometimes even drive over it. The result is compaction that slows the growth of the grass (remember that roots need air just as much as top growth). Although you can't turn and condition the soil every year for a lawn, a specialised way does exist to cure lawn compaction and invigorate the soil: aeration.

Aeration is simply the process of creating holes in the turf. Performed correctly, it removes cores of compacted soil, leaving room for air, water and nutrients to penetrate. On small lawns, you can aerate by hand. Just buy a hand aerator that uses foot power to remove cores of soil, or use a garden fork, spearing it into the lawn and working it back and forth to make holes. For large lawns, rent a power aerator from the local tool-hire shop. Steer the aerator over the lawn like a mower and it jams its tines into the turf, removing cores of soil in the process. (You can put these cores on your compost heap.)

Whatever method you choose, afterwards brush sharp sand into the holes to make lots of lovely drainage channels, otherwise they simply close up.

If you use your lawn heavily, aerate once a year.

Top-dressing your lawn

Most lawn owners neglect one very important lawn-care practice: *top-dressing*, which is simply spreading a thin layer of organic matter over the lawn. Top-dressing isn't fertilising as such, but it does improve the soil and can provide nutrients depending on the material used. Top-dressing is the only way to improve the soil from the top down.

Top-dressing is simple to do. In autumn, spread a thin (about 2.5-centimetre or 1-inch deep) layer of organic matter over a freshly mown lawn, rake it out more or less evenly and work it down into the grass with a stiff broom or the back of a rake. The classic mix of organic matter is an equal blend of sieved topsoil, sharp sand and coir, but you can use topsoil, shredded compost or sieved leafmould. The material works its way down through the grass, with the help of earthworms and other creatures, to improve the texture of the soil. You can make the process even more effective by aerating the turf first (check out the preceding section).

Your lawn looks dreadful for a week or two before it settles down – but top-dressing really does a power of good to your lawn.

Weeding your lawn

Most organic gardeners are prepared to overlook a less than perfect lawn, on the basis that if they love the lawn's daisies their garden wildlife love them in return. Regular mowing keeps most so-called weeds within bounds: rake creeping weeds such as buttercup first to bring up the runners to a level where the mower can cut them. If you decide to take a 'relaxed' attitude to lawns, pull off the seed heads of potentially invasive plants such as dandelion before they've a chance to seed.

If you're keen on a weed-free lawn, the best approach is to grow healthy, thick grass. Fertilising, watering and mowing properly all make the grass thicker, which makes it tougher for weeds to get a foothold. You can also use old-fashioned elbow grease. Long-handled speciality weeding tools make a fast and easy job of pulling dandelions, plantain and other lawn weeds.

Perhaps the best way to deal with weeds is to change your definition of them. Take clover, for example. Just because clover isn't a grass plant doesn't mean that it doesn't belong in the lawn. Clover stays green through tough weather, recovers nicely from mowing and is soft and cushiony. Also, unlike grass, it increases the fertility of the soil by taking nitrogen from the air and making it available to plant roots in the soil. Other so-called weeds, such as yarrow and Roman chamomile, attract beneficial insects.

Managing pests

Although a long list of insects munch on grass, only a few pests do serious damage to lawns, and you can buy organic treatments for the problem.

The most damaging turf pests live in the soil: chafer grubs and leatherjackets feast on grass roots and kill the plants in the process. Signs to alert you to an infestation are slow-growing, yellowing or dying patches of lawn, and the attentions of wildlife: flocks of starlings are attracted to leatherjackets, and foxes and badgers dig little craters across your lawn in search of chafer grubs.

To help you identify them, leatherjackets are around 2.5 centimetres (1 inch) long, greyish black, with no legs; chafer grubs are creamy-coloured, about 1.5 millimetres (0.5 inch) long, with legs. Both pests can be combated with organic controls, in the form of nematodes, applied from August to October.

Switching to Lawn Alternatives

Having a lawn isn't compulsory. If you've a good-sized area of grass, don't feel that you need to mow the whole area regularly. Letting some of it develop into a meadow is a fantastic way to encourage biodiversity, as well as saving you time and fuel (unless you cut the whole area with a push mower).

And if getting grass to grow is a problem, remember that lawns don't belong everywhere. Trying to grow grass where it refuses to thrive is a recipe for heartache. For example, grass doesn't like shade, wet roots, too much foot traffic, or hard and dry soil. In such situations, you may do better to find a good-looking substitute. In this section, we look at some of your options.

Growing ground covers

When you're trying to fill a shady spot in which grass doesn't grow, or you want to reduce the size of your lawn, you're likely to look into ground covers. By their very nature, *ground covers* are low-growing plants that spread rapidly to colonise large expanses.

Good ground-cover options for shade include prostrate (ground-hugging) cotoneasters, lesser periwinkle (*Vinca minor* – not to be confused with the thuggish *Vinca major*) and lilyturf (*Liriope*). Many taller perennials also make fine shade garden plants; read Chapter 14 for more ideas.

Converting a lawn to something wilder

The easiest way to create a bit of instant biodiversity is to stop mowing your lawn and see what comes up. The best time to start this experience is early summer, leaving the grass uncut for around six weeks. Chances are that mainly grass grows, but wild-flower seed can stay dormant for many years, and just occasionally you can find a few gems. Even if your lawn doesn't contain much in the way of flowers, long grass is a useful breeding site for insects and moths, and gives a lovely hazy haymeadow look in summer.

To manage this type of 'relaxed' lawn, cut in midsummer when the flowers have set seed, and then mow once in late summer and again in autumn. Remove the clippings, or else they rot down and encourage grass to grow at the expense of flowers. Continue down the route to meadow conversion by sowing or planting yellow rattle (*Rhinanthus*), which is semi-parasitic on grasses, reducing their vigour and allowing flowers more freedom to grow. Take out patches of turf and replace with pot-grown wild flowers and bulbs (Table 16-1 contains a list).

Make your meadow or 'relaxed lawn' look intentional by regularly mowing a crisp edge, and paths through the middle. Otherwise well-meaning neighbours may pop round to offer the loan of a lawnmower, or ask if someone has just died! (And from your point of view, being able to stroll through the heart of your meadow is lovely.)

Making a meadow

Naturally functioning, wild-flower meadows sound too good to be true, and in a way, they are. In contrast to the common belief that making a meadow involves little more than sowing seeds and allowing nature to take its course, meadows require more work than that. Although after a meadow's established it does take less time and labour than a lawn or a flower bed, getting a meadow started properly, from scratch, takes just as much preparation and labour as establishing a lawn.

As with most garden features, the best results take a bit of work in the first place. Most gardens have fertile soil that encourages vigorous grass growth at the expense of flowers, and so you need to remove the turf along with the top few centimetres of nutrient-rich soil (stack it in an out of the way corner to rot down for a year; it makes gorgeous crumbly soil). Sow a meadow seed mix suitable for your site and soil, and add pot-grown plants. Bulbs can be planted in autumn: suitable varieties are described as 'ideal for naturalising'.

To create a meadow, follow these steps:

1. **Cultivate bare soil by digging or rotovating to a depth of 15 centimetres (6 inches).** Remove weeds, especially the roots of perennials such as bindweed, dock and nettle. Allow the ground to settle for a couple of weeks.

2. **Rake the surface of the soil to a fine crumbly texture.** Don't work the soil if the soil is so wet that it sticks to your boots.

3. **Sow seed in autumn or spring, broadcasting by hand to cover the area evenly.** On heavy soil, sow in spring to avoid seed rotting over winter. Rake lightly to cover the seed with soil.

4. **Keep foraging birds off.** Use homemade bird scarers made of foil or CDs strung together.

5. **Water only if a dry spell occurs in spring during the first month or so.** Be careful not to overwater.

6. **Cut the grass during the first year when 10–20 centimetres (4–8 inches) high.** Thereafter, mow once in midsummer and once in autumn, after flowers have set seed.

Table 16-1	Suitable Flowers and Bulbs for Meadows
Flowers	*Bulbs*
Cow parsley	
Cowslip	Snakes-head fritillary
Field scabious	
Harebell	
Knapweed	
Mallow	
Ox-eye daisy	
Red campion	Narcissus: species such as Tenby daffodil (*N. obvallaris*) and Lent lily (*N. pseudonarcissus*)
Yellow rattle	Autumn crocus species

A less labour-intensive way to establish a meadow is to plant within existing turf. Remove patches of turf throughout the lawn, and replace it with wild-flower plants or seeds and bulbs (Table 16-1 contains a few suggestions). Gradually remove more and more of the lawn each year.

Suppliers of wild-flower seeds and plants

Here are places where you can obtain wild-flower seeds and plants:

Emorsgate Seeds: Limes Farm, Tilney All Saints, Kings Lynn, Norfolk PE34 4RT; phone 01553-829028; fax 01553-829803; website www.wildseed.co.uk; email enquiries@emorsgateseeds.com.

The National Wildflower Centre: Court Hey Park, Roby Road, Knowsley, Liverpool L16 3NA; phone 0151-738-1913; fax 0151-737-1820; website www.nwc.org.uk; email info@nwc.org.uk.

The Organic Gardening Catalogue: Riverdene Business Park, Molesey Road, Hersham, Surrey KT12 4RG; phone 01932-253666; fax 01932-525707; website www.organiccatalogue.com.

Pictorial Meadows: Manor Oaks Farmhouse, 389 Manor Lane, Sheffield S2 1UL; phone 0114-267-7635; fax 0114-267-7636; website www.pictorialmeadows.co.uk; email info@greenestate.org.

Part IV
Managing Problems

'Living near a nuclear power station
can be worrying but at least we don't
get any slugs or snails.'

In this part . . .

*J*ust as you expect wasps at a picnic, you can count on weeds in a garden, bugs on the plants and the horti-cultural equivalents of colds and flu – plant diseases. But these problems don't have to spoil your fun or your gardening success. Instead of reaching for a lethal chemical potion, turn to this part for environmentally safe and effective solutions.

For an overview of organic pest and disease control, look to Chapter 17. Discover how to prevent many problems and diagnose those that do arise. When you know what's 'bugging' your garden, read on to find out about the many organic controls – including the 'good' guys that you want on your side.

Chapter 18 fills you in on the 'bad' guys of the insect world to keep at bay. Turn to Chapter 19 to find out about diseases and disorders and to Chapter 20 for information about animal pests. Weeds can be among the biggest headaches for organic gardeners, and so Chapter 21's information on what you need to do to take control is invaluable.

Chapter 17

Creating a Natural Balance: Preventing Pests and Diseases Organically

. . . .

In This Chapter

▶ Developing an organic pest prevention strategy

▶ Identifying and inviting in beneficial organisms

▶ Using organic pesticides safely and responsibly

. . . .

*W*atching slugs ravage through your lettuces and caterpillars chomp your cabbages can be heartbreaking. In such situations, even the most eco-friendly gardener may be tempted to reach for insecticide! But as this chapter describes, organic gardening is essentially about taking steps to prevent pest problems and plant diseases and looking at the garden as a whole; the aim is to create a balance of nature where insects and other creatures keep on top of the problems. When intervention is necessary, organic gardeners choose environmentally friendly methods and nontoxic pest control.

This chapter looks at the subject; turn to Chapter 18 for details on combating specific insect pests, and check out Chapter 19 for more on plant diseases.

Dealing with Pests the Organic Way

Spraying pesticides to get rid of pests may be satisfying in the short term, but the long-term effects are detrimental and include the following:

✔ Poisoning the soil and water

✔ Creating an unhealthy environment for yourself, your family and your pets

✔ Eliminating wildlife and beneficial organisms

✔ Wasting money on unnecessary chemical products

Not surprisingly, therefore, organic gardeners take a different approach, as this section reveals. They strive to maintain a healthy balance of organisms, and they treat problems only when treatment is clearly warranted. The goal is to manage pests, not annihilate them.

Organic gardeners heed several basic tenets as regards pest management:

✔ **Accepting that pesticides are rarely the answer:** Organic gardeners ask themselves whether controlling the pests they find is really necessary. A few aphids on your roses aren't likely to cause any major damage if your garden is a haven for beneficial insects that dine on aphids. As a matter of fact, organic gardeners specifically try not to eliminate every insect pest, because if all the pests disappear, so do the insects, birds and spiders that feed on them. Tolerating a small number of pests means that you can keep their predators around in case your garden has a sudden pest-population explosion.

✔ **Encouraging a balance of nature:** Many creatures, large and small, feed on pests, and by getting to know pests' enemies and actively encouraging them, organic gardeners get nature on their side. Working from the soil up to build a healthy garden ecosystem, organic gardeners make wildlife welcome in a wealth of ways, such as feeding birds, establishing nest boxes, bat boxes and hedgehog homes, and sympathetically managing the garden by encouraging beneficial insects with nectar-rich blooms and places to hibernate.

✔ **Finding eco-friendly solutions:** Legislation caused the withdrawal of many garden chemicals and the result was a huge boost to the organic approach because no other alternatives now exist. Gardeners have to look at a range of solutions, such as traps, barriers and other physical deterrents, and biological controls (which we describe in Chapter 18).

✔ **Believing that not all problems are pest problems:** Organic gardeners refuse to assume that pests cause all problems in the garden. Other factors may be at fault: excessive heat; not enough or too much sun; lack of or too much moisture; weedkiller drift from outside; freezing temperatures; hail, wind, air and water pollution; and mower and strimmer injury. These problems are especially likely in plants growing in unfavourable environments such as shade-loving plants placed in full sun. Plants stressed by these factors are also more vulnerable to insect and disease attack. Eliminating the environmental stress solves the underlying problem, which in turn may make pesticides unnecessary.

✔ **Keeping plants healthy and happy:** Pests can indicate to gardeners when something's wrong, because healthy plants rarely suffer big pest infestations for no reason. Plants may be stressed, or have undergone a shock during transplanting or their settling-in period. Healthy plants and a healthy soil are the foundation for the organic gardening approach.

Choosing pest- and disease-resistant plants

One effective way to help ensure that you have healthy plants is to select pest- and disease-resistant varieties. Plant breeders work constantly to introduce plant selections (*varieties*) with characteristics different from those of the original species. One of the most important factors that breeders look for in a variety is *disease resistance* – the ability of a plant to remain unaffected (or only slightly damaged) by a particular disease.

Many modern plant varieties resist devastating plant diseases, such as the potato blight that led to the Irish famine of the mid-19th century. As increasing numbers of chemicals are withdrawn, plant breeders are working even harder to develop resistant varieties – so do check the seed catalogues that come out each year to see what's new. (Chapter 19 contains more on combating plant diseases.)

Although plants that are resistant to insect pests are less common, they do exist – and so again, keep your eyes peeled for new varieties. For example, the widespread pest of carrot root fly can now be combated by several carrot varieties that have a degree of resistance.

Knowing which diseases and pests are most likely to affect the plants that you want to grow is useful. These potential problems are mentioned in the respective plant descriptions in Part III of this book. Company catalogue write-ups often mention pest resistance, too, because pest resistance is a good selling point.

Making your garden less inviting to pests

Ask yourself whether your garden may be unintentionally rolling out the red carpet for pests. Most pests are opportunists that take advantage of weak or stressed plants and take up residence where the eating is easy. This section provides guidelines so that you can avoid giving pests a helpful hand.

Putting the right plant in the right place

Choose the best location for each plant, taking into account its particular needs for water, sunlight and nutrients. Plants emit a chemical signal when they're weakened, and pests get the message loud and clear.

Although experts debate the degree to which stress affects human health, in the plant kingdom, no such quibbling exists. When plants are in the wrong location and don't get their needs met, they become stressed; the longer the stressful situation continues, the greater the decline in plant health. Of course even correctly located, healthy plants can fall prey to pests, but they're better able to survive the attack than a plant already weakened by stress.

Confusing pests with mixed plantings

Insects have chemical receptors that help them zero in on their favourite foods, making long rows of cabbage or carrot plants look like a giant billboard flashing the message, 'Dinner plants here; come and get 'em!'. Therefore, plant smaller patches of each crop and scatter really pest-prone ones such as carrots throughout the garden.

Combining different types of plants in your garden, instead of planting each crop in large blocks, confuses insects so that they're less likely to find all the plants. Diseases are less likely to spread in mixed plantings, too.

Keeping time on your side

Young plants, with their tender, succulent stems, are easy prey for pests. As plants mature, however, their tissues become more fibrous and less prone to damage. You can use this feature to your advantage by planting a crop so that the plants are growing strongly when the predominant pest insect hatches.

Another technique is to start plants in small pots and plant out when they're well developed and able to withstand a bit of nibbling.

Avoiding open wounds

Like an open skin wound, damaged bark or foliage provides an ideal entry point for diseases and insects. Even torn leaves caused by a thunderstorm provide an opening for invasion. Although you can't lessen the ravages of the weather, though, you can protect plants from mechanical damage caused by strimmers and rotovators. Encircle your trees, shrubs and fruit trees with a wide band of mulch to help keep power equipment away from the plants. Also, ensure that your mower blades are sharp so that they make straight clean cuts instead of leaving ragged edges on grass blades.

Prune only at the best time of year: for example, plums and other *Prunus* trees are susceptible to disease and as such are best pruned in summer when wounds heal fast.

Rotating crops

Moving each vegetable crop to a new location every year can help foil pests. At the end of the season, many insects leave eggs or pupae in the soil near their favourite host plants. If the young emerge in the spring and find their favourite food in the same location, they have a feeding frenzy. If their food is on the other side of the garden, they may starve before they find it.

In addition, diseases can build up in the soil to infect the same crops each year. Crop rotation is easy with annual flowers and vegetables that you replant each year.

Steering clear of over-fertilising

Applying too much fertiliser in the mistaken belief that if a little is good then more is better, is all too easy.

Unfortunately, excess nutrients are just as harmful to plants as nutrient deficiency. Excess nitrogen, for example, causes stems and leaves to grow rapidly, producing juicy growth that's a delicacy for aphids and other pests because they find it easy to puncture and consume.

The simplest way to prevent nutrient imbalances is to provide nutrients in the form of organic matter and organic fertilisers, which make nutrients available gradually. Check out Chapter 7 for all about organic fertilisers.

Cleaning up debris

Fallen leaves, dropped fruit and other debris can harbour insects and diseases, so during the season and at season's end, pick up and destroy fallen fruit. Similarly, turn plant residues into the soil or add them to your compost pile. Dispose of diseased plants in the 'green waste' section at your local tip or doorstep collection (the large quantities of composted waste heat up to a sufficiently high temperature to kill diseased material).

Cultivate the soil to work in debris that may shelter insects through the winter and to expose hiding pests to cold temperatures and predators.

Inviting in beneficial insects and creatures

Spiders, birds, frogs, toads, other creatures and a host of insects prey on garden pests. Make your garden attractive for them, and they'll do much of your pest-control work for you. Find out more about beneficial creatures in the later section 'Welcoming Natural Pest Controllers into Your Garden'.

Identifying culprits and problems

Even the most accomplished and diligent organic gardeners face pest problems from time to time. But don't panic! The first step in managing a specific pest is to identify it.

Just because you see an insect on a plant doesn't mean that this insect is a pest. Ants and spiders, for example, may take up residence on plants, but they're generally harmless. Always take the time to research pests and make a positive ID. Use a field guide to identify insects so that you don't inadvertently destroy beneficial ones.

If you think that a pest is attacking your plant, give the entire plant a once-over. Ask the following questions:

- ✔ Where's the damage?
- ✔ Is the damage all over the plant or confined to one area (young leaves, buds or fruit, for example)?
- ✔ Is discoloration all over the plant or in distinct locations?
- ✔ What type of plant is it?
- ✔ Are nearby plants also affected and if so, what types?

After the once-over, examine the plant more closely:

- ✔ Check the tops and bottoms of leaves, looking for insects, caterpillars and egg masses.
- ✔ Look carefully at the new growth, because this growth is a common gathering place for insect pests.
- ✔ Touch the leaves and watch for scurrying or flying insects.
- ✔ Examine the plants at different times. Try to catch the pests in action.
- ✔ Jot down notes, take photos or collect samples so that you can research possible culprits.

Don't confine your research to the daylight hours, because many pests operate under cover of darkness. Go out well after dark, with a torch, and see what you can find. The garden teems with life at night, and so you're likely to make interesting discoveries of friend and foe.

If you see spots or discoloured areas on the leaves during your close up examination, a disease may be the cause:

- ✔ Note the size, colour and shape of the spots.
- ✔ Look at the spots' margins.
- ✔ Are the edges of the spots distinct or fuzzy?
- ✔ Note whether the lesions are on the top or bottom of leaf surfaces, and whether they're all over the plant or confined to one area.
- ✔ Are the flowers and fruit also affected?

If only the lower leaves on a plant are chewed, you may be dealing with an animal pest. Different animals can reach different heights, and so for clues, measure how high up the plant the damage occurs.

Chapter 18 identifies common garden pests, and so you may find your culprit in this chapter. If not, consult a good illustrated guidebook to garden problems. After you identify the pest, discover as much as possible about when it appears and on which plants, what factors contribute to its abundance, what kind of damage it does, and at what life stage you can control it most easily. Pest controls, such as those we describe in the later section 'Preventing and controlling pests', are more effective if you catch the pest at the most vulnerable part of its life cycle.

Establishing thresholds

One of the most challenging parts of organic gardening is determining whether you really do need to take action to combat a pest. Resist the temptation to react immediately with a pesticide; instead, analyse the situation first. Do you see a few scattered insects or a cast of thousands? After you spot a particular pest or symptoms of its damage, examine similar plants in your garden to determine the extent of the population and its distribution. Is the damage located on the leaves of a plant you may be harvesting in a week or two? Is the damage purely cosmetic? Assessing the situation in this way can mean that you may not need to take action at all.

Small populations of pests may not cause enough damage to warrant any intervention, and they may provide a consistent supply of food for the predators that keep them in check. If you kill all the pests, their predators may well leave too. And when the next population of pests arises, the predators are gone.

Some pests do multiply quickly, however, so keep a close eye on plants so that pests don't get out of hand. Aphids, for example, are remarkably prolific: a single aphid can produce 5.9 billion offspring in 6 weeks. That's a lot of aphids, very quickly! However, early intervention with something as simple as hand-squashing a small infestation can save a big problem later.

Preventing and controlling pests

When you take action against pests, you need to choose your method. Organic gardeners use a variety of techniques to manage pests, starting with prevention, and then moving on to controls that are the least toxic and least disruptive to the garden ecosystem. The following sections provide an overview of the various methods available to organic gardeners. In Chapters 18 to 20, you find more details on controlling specific pests and diseases.

Physical methods

One of the simplest ways to keep pests from attacking plants is to keep the two apart. The following methods involve preventing pests from reaching plants and removing the ones that do take up residence:

- ✔ **Barriers:** Use barriers as your first line of defence against pests. They keep pests away from plants before they can do any damage. Fences are the obvious solution for animal pests such as deer and rabbits. Row covers protect young crops from insect attack. Bird netting keeps birds from eating your berries.

- ✔ **Handpicking:** For some gardeners, removing pests, such as lily beetles and slugs, by hand is a satisfying endeavour, not to mention an easy, nontoxic solution. Dense colonies of aphids can be squashed between finger and thumb.

- ✔ **Hosing off:** Small insects such as aphids and blackfly are easily dislodged by a spray from the hose. Often, washing plants every few days is enough to keep these pests in check.

- ✔ **Repellents:** You can keep pests at bay by using substances that are unappealing to them. Deer, for example, may avoid trees in which bags of human hair or fragrant soaps are hanging, and neem oil is reputed to repel a range of pests. You may need to try several repellents or rotate them to keep pests away.

- ✔ **Scare tactics:** Shiny CDs hung on a string may frighten birds, at least long enough for you to gather your fruit harvest. Motion detector-activated sprinklers can scare off deer and cats.

- ✔ **Trapping:** You can use traps in two ways: set them out to detect the first appearance of a pest so you can start preventive measures, or use them to reduce pest populations. Popular traps include sticky pheromone (insect hormone) traps for apple codling moth and yellow sticky traps for the greenhouse.

Biological controls

Biological controls use the deliberate introduction of living agents to control pests. Some of the biggest innovations in pest control are coming in this field. In light of recent bans on common chemical pesticides, you're likely to see more and more biologically based pesticides introduced. Read all about biological controls in Chapter 18.

Biological control isn't to be confused with simply encouraging beneficial insects in the garden, a subject we cover in the later section 'Welcoming Natural Pest Controllers into Your Garden'.

Other methods

A huge range of pesticide sprays and dusts is available. Organic growers choose products that are the least toxic and most targeted to the pests they want to control. Insecticidal soap and horticultural oil are two mainstays, but do bear in mind that a product can be 'organic' (that is, of natural origin) and yet still harmful to beneficial insects. Look for more detailed information on pest and disease-control products in Chapters 18 to 20.

Welcoming Natural Pest Controllers into Your Garden

Sometimes, the most efficient pest control is right under your nose. Many familiar garden denizens are voracious eaters of the very pests you're trying to control; you just need to invite the right creatures in to dine. This section helps you to sort out the good bugs from the bad and gives you tips for keeping the good guys where you want them: in your garden.

Identifying beneficial insects

Insects that prey on or live off insect pests are known as *natural predators* or *beneficial insects*. You may not be aware of the fact, but you rely on these allies to help keep the insect balance in your garden from tipping too far in the destructive direction. If you familiarise yourself with the good guys, you can encourage their presence in your garden and avoid killing these innocent bystanders just because they happen to be the insects you spy on your favourite dahlias. This section highlights the most visible and common beneficial insects, but is by no means an exhaustive list.

You can boost populations of certain beneficial insects by buying stock from mail-order catalogues. A number of companies that supply biological controls (something we discuss in Chapter 18) also sell beneficial insects such as ladybirds.

The following beneficial insects are worth befriending:

- **Centipedes:** Indoors and out, multi-legged centipedes feed on many insect pests. Most species don't bother humans (unless you count the screech with which they're frequently greeted). You can't do much to encourage their presence, but if you leave them alone to do their job, you've fewer harmful insects around.

- **Ground beetles:** Many beetle species live in or on the soil, where both their larval and adult stages capture and eat harmful insects. They vary in colour (black, green and bronze) and in size. Although most live close to the ground, feeding on aphids, caterpillars, fruit flies, mites and slugs, the 2.5-centimetre (1-inch) long caterpillar hunter beetle climbs trees to feed on gypsy moths and other tree-dwelling caterpillars.

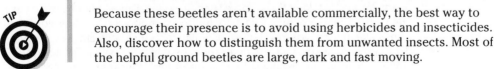

Because these beetles aren't available commercially, the best way to encourage their presence is to avoid using herbicides and insecticides. Also, discover how to distinguish them from unwanted insects. Most of the helpful ground beetles are large, dark and fast moving.

✔ **Hover flies:** These insects get their name from the adults' habit of hovering around flowers. The adults, resembling wasps, are important pollinators; the brownish or greenish caterpillar-like larvae have an appetite for aphids, beetles, caterpillars, sawflies and thrips. If you grow an abundance of flowers, you're likely to see hover flies in your garden.

✔ **Lacewings:** The delicate green or brown bodies and transparent wings of these 12–19-millimetre (0.5–0.75-inch) insects, shown in Figure 17-1, are easy to recognise in the garden. The adults live on nectar and the spindle-shaped, yellowish or brownish larvae feed on a wide variety of soft-bodied pests, such as aphids, scale, thrips, caterpillars and spider mites. Each of the distinctive, pale green, oval eggs sits at the end of its own long, thin stalk on the underside of a leaf.

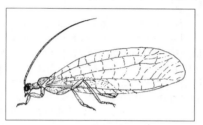

Figure 17-1:
Lacewing.

✔ **Ladybirds:** The familiar red, black-spotted ladybird is what most people think of when they praise ladybirds' appetite for aphids. Both adults and larvae prey on soft-bodied pests, including mealybugs and spider mites. The ladybird larvae look like small, black, segmented woodlice with rows of knobby or hairy projections and four orange spots on their backs. (Take a look at the sidebar 'Beware the harlequin' for details of a newly imported ladybird.)

If you plan to purchase and release ladybirds, prevent them from flying away from your garden by setting out another attractive food source, such as an artificial yeast/sugar or honeydew mixture, which are available from commercial suppliers.

✔ **Spiders:** All spiders are predators, ridding the garden of many common pests. You can provide good habitat for spiders by mulching with hay and straw, which reduces insect damage by 70 per cent due solely to the numbers of resident spiders.

✔ **Wasps:** Although thinking of these annoying insects as beneficial can be difficult, the fact is that they do help rid your garden of flies, caterpillars and many larvae by taking them home to their young. Unfortunately, wasps are also attracted to anything sweet, including your alfresco lunch or coffee-time cake, but try not to kill these useful insects just because they want to share your snack. Instead, deter them by hanging up a clever device called a *waspinator* (available by mail order and from some retailers, priced around £13), which is designed to mimic a wasp's nest in shape – so the real wasps fly elsewhere, thinking the territory is already taken.

Beware the harlequin

The harlequin ladybird (*Harmonia axyridis*) is a foreign ladybird that was unknown in Britain until 2004, but is now spreading rapidly throughout the country. Although not a plant pest, it causes concern because of its reputation for eating native ladybirds and other beneficial insects. Its prey of choice, however, is greenfly and other aphids, and so it has some benefit to gardeners.

Harlequin ladybirds can feed on a wide range of other insects when aphids are in short supply, but whether they're going to reduce the numbers of native beneficial insects is still to be seen. Adult harlequin ladybirds are highly variable in appearance, with many different colour forms and variable numbers of spots and other markings. In the UK, the commonest ones are orange with 15–21 black spots, and black with two or four orange or red spots. The harlequin ladybird survey is asking the British public to record sightings. For details of the survey and much more information (including useful images to help identify harlequins), visit www. harlequin-survey.org.

Attracting beneficial insects

You can take important steps to welcome beneficial insects into your garden and encourage those you purchase to stick around:

- ✔ **Avoid using broad-spectrum insecticides, which kill a wide range of insects, including beneficials.** Even some organic insecticides, such as pyrethrin (which we discuss in Chapter 18), are toxic to beneficial insects. Often, beneficials are even more susceptible to the insecticide than pests, because as predators and parasites, they must move quickly over leaf surfaces and thus come into contact with insecticides more readily. Many insecticides are also toxic to bees.

  If you must use a chemical as a last resort, spray only in the evening, when bees have returned to the hive.

- ✔ **Grow plants that attract beneficial insects.** With a constant supply of nectar, adult beneficial insects can live much longer than they otherwise would. Many of the tiny beneficial insects can access 'shallow' flowers that are cup or saucer-shaped more easily than they can tubular flowers. Goldenrod is a favourite, attracting more than 75 species of beneficial insects. Include this plant and others from the parsley and sunflower families, such as alyssum, aster, coriander, daisy, dill, fennel, gazania, marigold, phacelia, poached egg flower, sunflower, yarrow and zinnia.

- ✔ **Include a diversity of plants in your garden to attract a variety of insects.** Choose a mix of species, including evergreens, and plants of different sizes and shapes. A mixture of trees, shrubs, perennials and annuals in your garden provides a lot of options for food and hiding places. Try to have something in bloom throughout the growing season.

✔ **Provide hibernation and breeding sites.** Although lots of dinky designs of insect homes are on sale, initial research shows that they offer virtually no advantage over sympathetic garden management and a bit of selective untidiness! Winter shelter is most important, so don't cut back and tidy your borders until spring because the dead stems are fantastic hibernation homes. Pile up dead leaves and plant stems – especially hollow ones – in out of the way sites, such as at the back of borders or the bases of hedges.

✔ **Supply a water source for beneficial insects.** Fill a shallow birdbath or bowl with stones and water. Change the water frequently to discourage breeding midges.

Encouraging other natural predators

Many creatures depend on insects for food, and you can enlist them in your pest-control efforts. Birds, bats, frogs, toads, newts, slowworms and even small mammals can eat surprisingly large numbers of insects. Offer them the habitat they enjoy, and let them get to work:

✔ **Amphibians:** Frogs, toads and newts are wonderful allies, consuming quantities of slugs every night during the gardening season. They lay their eggs in water, and so a water garden or pond ensures that you can enjoy future generations. You can easily provide drinking water by setting a low dish or birdbath on the ground near tall plants that offer shelter. These creatures spend a lot of time out of water too, and so give them places to hide, such as stone or log piles, and dry stone walls.

✔ **Bats:** Bats mainly work under cover of darkness, and so all their hard work goes largely unappreciated, although you're likely to see them come out in the twilight. Their steady diet of insects – beetles, moths and midges – makes them fantastic garden visitors. Bats roost and hibernate in roofs, barns and hollow trees, so keep a look out for signs of bat activity if you're carrying out any work in such places. Bear in mind that bats are protected by law and their roosts mustn't be disturbed: even touching or handling a bat without a licence is illegal.

Consider putting up a bat house to help keep bats nearby. Bat houses, which look like birdhouses with entrance slots in the bottom, are available at some garden centres, or by mail order from a number of suppliers. For more information, go to the Bat Conservation Trust website at www.bats.org.uk.

✔ **Birds:** If you've ever watched a mother bird feeding her young, you know that her nestlings are non-stop insect feeders. Granted, birds do snare valuable, soil-enriching earthworms, but they also consume huge numbers of insects. A house wren, for example, can gobble more than 500 beetles, grubs and insect eggs in an afternoon.

Welcome birds into your garden by providing food – such as fruiting trees and shrubs, birdseed, suet, water from birdbaths or ponds – and shelter that includes a diversity of trees and shrubs (including evergreens). Put up birdboxes to encourage feathered friends to raise their families nearby. Loads of styles are available, but do purchase the designs approved by the Royal Society for Protection of Birds (www.rspb.org.uk) or the British Trust for Ornithology (www.bto.org).

Try not to have a pet cat, however much you adore having a moggie around the house; they can't help responding to their natural instincts and catching birds. If you do have a cat, fit a collar with a bell to warn birds of its presence, and try to keep it indoors while young fledglings are learning to fly and are at their most vulnerable.

✔ **Hedgehogs:** Generations brought up on Beatrix Potter books adore these 'Mrs Tiggywinkles', and gardeners welcome them with open arms for the large numbers of slugs and snails they gobble up. You can buy hedgehog homes to put in a quiet corner of the garden, but do leave piles of leaves and twigs, too. Don't dig out a compost heap in winter because your spiny friend may be enjoying its winter sleep there. Leave out dishes of fresh water, and in dry summer weather when insects are hard to find, a dish of dog or cat food may go down a treat.

Don't supply bread and milk though; despite being seen as a favourite, these foods upset hedgehogs' stomachs.

✔ **Slowworms**: Often thought of as snakes, slowworms are in fact legless lizards. They munch many garden pests, and are found in warm places such as compost heaps, under sheet mulches such as cardboard or newspaper, and under stones or slates.

Observing Commonsense Organic Pesticide Use

Many gardeners rely on pesticides to achieve beauty and bounty in their gardens. As an organic gardener, you've already made the commitment to eliminate synthetic chemical pesticides from your garden in favour of organic ones, but you still need to follow all the safety precautions recommended on the labels of organic products. This section outlines important safety information about buying and using organic pesticides.

Many people mistakenly believe that *organic* and *nontoxic* mean the same thing, so we must lay this myth to rest. *Organic* means that the product comes from naturally occurring sources, such as plants, animals and soil minerals. Certain organic pesticides – for example, nicotine – are toxic; they're every bit as dangerous to humans and other animals as to insect pests.

Knowing pesticide types

Pesticide is a general term that describes materials used to kill pests. The three most commonly used pesticides are

- ✔ **Fungicides** to control fungal diseases
- ✔ **Herbicides** to kill weeds
- ✔ **Insecticides** to kill insects

Other pesticides include *bactericides* to control bacterial diseases, *molluscicides* to control slugs and snails, and *miticides* or *acaricides* to kill mites.

At the risk of stating the obvious, make sure that you're applying the right pesticide for the problem. An insecticide isn't going to control fungal diseases or fungicides kill insects. Some pesticides are nontoxic to all but the intended pest, whereas others affect multiple organisms. Pesticides that kill a wide range of insects are called *broad spectrum*; use them only as a last resort, because they kill beneficial organisms as well as harmful ones.

Whether you grow plants organically or not, always use the least toxic pesticides possible.

Protecting yourself, the plants and the environment

Many of the insect, weed and disease controls that organic gardeners use are toxic, especially if improperly used. Broad-spectrum botanical insecticides such as pyrethrins – which many organic growers use and we cover in Chapter 18 – harm beneficial insects and particularly aquatic organisms, and can also injure pets and people, if used improperly. Knowing when, where and how to apply these chemicals is part of responsible gardening.

Personal safety

Before you grab that spray bottle or can off the shelf and head out to the garden, pause to check what you're wearing. No matter how innocuous the pesticide, you must protect yourself from potential harm. Always read the instructions and make sure that you take any necessary precautions.

A dust mask is helpful when you're applying nontoxic dusts to prevent inhalation.

Most chemical injuries occur during mixing, while you're preparing to spray. Put on any necessary protective clothing before you get started. Always mix and pour chemicals, including organic pesticides, in a well-ventilated area where accidental spillage doesn't contaminate or damage food or personal property. Even something as nontoxic as diatomaceous earth can irritate your lungs, and spilled oil can ruin your clothes. Following are other points to keep in mind:

- ✔ Don't use your kitchen measuring cups and spoons; buy a separate set for garden use.
- ✔ Clear all toys and other stuff out of the area you plan to spray, including the areas where the spray may drift (check the wind direction).
- ✔ Don't allow other people or pets into the area while you're spraying, and keep them out for the duration recommended on the product label.
- ✔ Check whether an interval is required between applying the product and harvesting any edible crops.

Plant safety

Read the pesticide label carefully, and apply the chemical only to listed plants. Consider weather and overall plant health, too. Some chemicals more easily injure drought-stressed and insect- or disease-weakened plants. High temperatures or intense sunlight can also increase the chance of plant damage.

Environmental safety

One of the reasons people choose to garden organically is to keep the environment safe for wild creatures and insects, and so remember that some botanical pesticides, such as pyrethrins, are very toxic to fish and beneficial insects.

When you apply any product, follow the label directions very carefully. Never spray or dump chemicals (organic or non-organic) near bodies of water; never pour them into the sink or down the drain. Mix up only as much as you need.

Also check the weather. Don't spray or apply dust in breezy conditions, because the chemical may drift away from the target area and harm nearby plants or animals. If you expect rain, don't bother to apply any products that are going to wash off before doing their job.

Keeping records

Use a calendar with plenty of space on it to write notes and record everything that affects your garden: seed-planting and first-harvest dates; rainfall amounts; unusual temperatures and weather events; the appearance of pests and diseases; and so on – record everything on the calendar. Also note which fertilisers and pesticides you use and on which plants.

After keeping such calendars for a couple of years, you may see patterns emerging that help you anticipate problems and keep them from becoming too troublesome. Good records show you what works and what doesn't, allowing you to make informed changes in your gardening practices.

Keeping records in this ways is one of the easiest and most important organic gardening practices that you can undertake.

Chapter 18

Managing and Controlling Insect Pests

In This Chapter

▶ Getting to know bugs and grubs

▶ Surveying insect control techniques and products

▶ Finding the best controls for each pest

Most of the insects in your garden don't harm your plants, but the ones that do are enough to keep you on your toes. As an organic gardener, you're committed to creating a natural balance in your garden and to protecting the good guys and innocent bystanders from harm while eliminating the bad guys (as we describe in Chapter 17). To do so effectively requires that you target your pest-control approach, which means that you need to know a little about insects and organic insect-control methods.

In this chapter, we describe the major insect pests (as well as nematodes, slugs, snails and spider mites, even though they're not technically insects) and explain what you can do as an organic gardener to protect your plants and manage pests. Use the control approaches we suggest here in conjunction with the general prevention-based techniques from Chapter 17.

Understanding Insects

Each insect has preferred foods and methods of feeding. Some primarily eat certain plants; others are less fussy. Some chew roots or the youngest leaves; others tunnel through stems or pierce holes in their host and suck plant sap.

Insects pass through several life stages, often looking different in each step. Knowing about this development process is important because at different stages the insects live in different places. A beetle, for example, may spend parts of its life in the soil, on tree bark and on leaves. Also, insects are more vulnerable to attack by predators, parasites and traps during certain life stages as compared to others. Being able to identify all the life stages provides you with more ways to control the insect. Here's what to look for at each stage:

- ✔ **Eggs:** Each insect species has unique times, places and methods for laying its eggs. For example, cabbage white butterflies lay clusters of greeny-yellow eggs underneath plant leaves, and apple codling moths and plum moths lay their eggs inside fruit.

- ✔ **Larvae, grubs, nymphs, maggots and caterpillars:** When the eggs hatch, they become immature insects. This immature stage, during which the insect eats and grows rapidly, is often the most plant-destructive period of an insect's life. Plant symptoms include holes or tunnels in leaves, fruits, bark and stems, as well as stunted and deformed growth.

  The name of this life stage depends on the kind of insect you're describing. Immature moths and butterflies are called caterpillars, for example, whereas young beetles are called grubs.

- ✔ **Pupae:** Many insects – including beetles, moths, butterflies and flies – go through a stage between larva and adult when they form a cocoon or hard shell around themselves. They don't eat or cause damage at this stage and don't succumb easily to predators or pesticides. The transformation of a larva into an adult is called *pupating*.

- ✔ **Adults:** Adult insects are ready to mate and lay eggs. Most have wings and are at their most mobile stage. Some adult insects, such as thrips, feed on plants by piercing or rasping holes and sucking or sponging plant juices. Others, such as vine weevil, chew on plant parts. Adult butterflies and moths don't damage plants and in fact help pollinate flowers.

Many insects spend part of the year, usually winter, in plant debris and fallen fruit. Sometimes the easiest way to control these insects is to rake up debris thoroughly and destroy it. Other insects need access to their hosts only during a very short period; using barriers and traps at just the right time may prevent them from doing damage or laying their eggs.

Get to know your pests, and you may find easy ways to control them or stop them from doing any damage.

Managing Insect Pests

Sharing your vegetables, flowers, trees, shrubs and lawn with insects is a balancing act. On one hand, you want a safe, attractive garden and a bountiful, pesticide-free harvest. On the other hand, armies of marauding insects and other pests may seem intent on destroying your dreams. What's an organic gardener to do?

The answer is to manage the whole garden so that your plants are as healthy as possible; get nature on your side so that beneficial insects and creatures feast on troublesome pests; and use eco-friendly control methods where needed. Check out Chapter 17 for an overview of this approach. In the following sections, we outline techniques and products specifically for combating insect pests.

Removing pests manually

Getting rid of insects can be simple. You can incorporate some of the following easy techniques into a stroll around your plot:

- **Handpicking insects:** When you go out to tend your plants, take a can of soapy water – which can become the final resting place for any unwanted bugs you encounter. As an alternative to the catch-can, spread plastic under plants and shake the plants to dislodge pests. Then pour the insects from the plastic into a pail of soapy water. (Do make sure that you're not drowning any of the good bugs, though!)

  Tiny insects are difficult to pick off, but a little judicious pinching between finger and thumb can remove masses of them. Or you can prune, if you aren't removing lots of blooms, because aphids tend to cluster near flower buds and growing tips, and so cutting off those portions helps reduce the population and control damage spread. Pick off leaves that have leaf miners and other insects.

- **Vacuuming the leaves:** Pest insects tend to congregate on the upper portions of plants, whereas beneficial ones frequently hide on the lower leaves and branches. You can use these tendencies to your advantage by vacuuming the upper leaves with a low-suction battery-powered vacuum (you don't want to lose the leaves too) when you see pests accumulating. Next, dispose of the vacuum bag so that insects can't crawl back out.

- **Giving plants a brisk shower:** Simply knocking the insects off with water can greatly reduce their damage, especially if you spray plants every day or two, before the insects have time to make the journey back up onto the plant. This technique can be used on houseplants, too. Avoid spraying leaves in the evening, because wet foliage at night can encourage disease organisms to spread.

An estimated 70 per cent of all insect pests spend part of their life cycle in the soil, which is why birds flock to bare soil looking for food. Whenever you cultivate the soil, you help bring larvae and eggs to the surface, where they can be picked off by birds and other creatures.

Keep in mind that cultivating warms the soil faster in the spring and encourages insects to emerge from the soil sooner. If you have chickens, let them roam free in the garden after the final harvest and after turning the soil in the spring to clean up insects and leftover vegetables.

Barring the way with barriers

Here's a simple yet compelling g piece of logic: insect pests can't damage your plants if they can't get to them. Block their access with effective barriers around your plants, such as those explained in this section.

Particle barriers

Substances made up of sharp material, fine grains or powders can create a physical barrier between plants and pests. Particle barriers include:

- ✔ **Absorbent material:** Particularly useful against slugs and snails, a layer of material can be placed around vulnerable plants or young seedlings. You can buy granules designed to combat slugs, or use bran bought from the supermarket or grocery shop.

- ✔ **Diatomaceous earth:** Called DE for short, this white powder consists of the fossil remains of microscopic water creatures, called *diatoms*, and is mined from areas where ancient oceans or lakes used to exist. The particles pierce an insect's exterior cuticle and cause dehydration. The sharp particles also injure and deter slugs and snails.

  Apply the DE dust to damp foliage to control soft-bodied insects, or spread a 15-centimetre (6-inch) band of DE on the soil around each plant stem to control crawling pests. Some DE products contain nontoxic bait that attracts pests and induces them to eat the dust, which is also fatal. Wood ashes and limestone can have the same effect. These powdery materials work best when dry and need to be reapplied after rain.

  DE kills beneficial as well as harmful insects, and so isn't the best choice in all situations.

Horticultural fleece and insect mesh

These lightweight air- and water-permeable fabrics raise the temperature around plants and extend the growing season. They can also keep plants relatively safe from insect pests, such as cabbage white fly and carrot root fly, and keep birds off ripening fruit – if you spread them over your plants early enough in the season. If you wait too long before covering your plants, the insects have a chance to set up housekeeping in the garden, and then they thrive under the protective covering.

These materials are so lightweight that you can simply drape them loosely over plants on a temporary basis, but if the cover is needed for any length of time, support the fabric on a frame – if homemade, secure the edges in the soil or with boards to keep opportunist insects from slipping in through the sides. You can use light- or medium-weight fleece or mesh covers to form *low tunnels* – row covers supported by hoops.

You can keep the covers on all season long without overheating your plants, unless the weather is unduly warm, in which case you need to remove them. Also, at the appropriate time, remove covers from plants such as strawberries that depend on insects for pollination when the plants bloom.

Collars

Collars are small mats, used around brassica plants to protect from cabbage root fly. This common pest burrows into the soil immediately around the plant stems during the growing season. A 15-centimetre- (6-inch-) wide collar around each plant can prevent this pest from carrying out its dastardly deed. You can buy collars impregnated with copper that also help to repel slugs.

An alternative to buying collars is to make your own from any solid water-resistant material, such as old vinyl flooring. Cut it into squares or circles and make a slit from one side into the middle so that it fits around the plant.

Tree protectors

Caterpillars and other insects crawl up the trunk en route to the leaves, and crawl back down the trunk to rest or pupate in the soil. Catch them during their travels with strips of cardboard, fabric or insect glue that encircles the tree, and form a barrier. Some insects, such as the codling moth, like to hide under corrugated cardboard, especially in the autumn as they prepare for winter. To trap these insect pests, cut old boxes into long strips and wrap the strips around the tree trunk, with the ridges facing the tree. Destroy the infested cardboard strips before spring and replace them with fresh ones.

You can also wrap 45-centimetre- (18-inch-) wide sacking strips, folded in half, around the trunk, with string securing the sacking to the tree at the inside of the fold. Insects become trapped under the fold as they head upward. Even simple wide strips wrapped around the trunk collect caterpillars underneath. These traps are only a temporary detour for most insects, so you need to check the traps frequently and dispose of the insects.

Grease bands or barrier glue can be fixed around the trunks of fruit trees to trap winter moth and ants. Glue can also be applied to the legs of greenhouse benching to stop pests crawling up and onto your plants.

Of course, these materials don't discriminate in which pests they catch, so you may inadvertently kill the good ones.

Copper bands

Copper has the unique ability to repel slugs and snails, whose slimy coatings react chemically with copper, generating a toxic reaction – similar to an electric current – that sends them elsewhere.

You can use copper sheet metal to fashion permanent edging around your garden beds; or why not staple copper-strip (available from garden centres) to the sides of wooden planter beds, or glue it around the tops of containers.

Resisting with repellents

Just as humans dislike certain tastes, many insect pests avoid certain substances, meaning that repellents are a good way to prevent pest problems.

Neem

Neem comes from the Indian neem tree (*Azadirachta indica*), which has been used for centuries to make products such as insect repellants. It doesn't poison insects outright. Instead, when insects eat the active ingredient, neem interrupts their ability to develop and grow to their next life stage, and stops them laying eggs. It also deters insects from feeding and is effective against aphids, thrips, fungus gnats, caterpillars, beetles, leaf miners and others.

Amazingly, plants can absorb neem so that any insects that feed on them may be killed or deterred from feeding. Neem breaks down in the presence of sun and soil within a week or so. To discourage insects from eating your plants, spray neem before you see a large infestation.

Other plant extracts

Many herbs, spices and plants – including tansy, nasturtium, garlic, onion, marigolds, rue, mint, rosemary, sage and geranium – contain ingredients that repel or kill insects. Garlic is one of the best-known and most-effective extracts against thrips and other leaf-eating insects: The strong odour disguises the true identity of the host plant, and so pests pass them by.

Tricking with traps

You can employ traps in two ways: set them out to detect the first appearance of a pest so that you can start preventive measures; or use them to reduce pest populations. This section discusses two common types of traps.

Sticky traps

Usually coming in the form of sticky yellow card, these traps are primarily used in gardening under cover, to trap and kill pests and as an early warning detection method that the pest is about and you need to control it. Sticky cards can also be used outside to trap carrot-root fly.

You can take advantage of insects' colour preferences in making traps. If you have scrap wood, paint it yellow, cover it with a sticky coating and place it in the garden to lure aphids, fungus gnats and several types of flies (including whiteflies). Codling moths prefer white traps. To make cleanup easier, cover the trap with plastic wrap before applying the sticky coating.

Pheromone-baited traps

These traps are baited with a *pheromone* – the scent that a female insect releases to attract a male of the same species. The artificial pheromone in the trap lures male insects, and a sticky coating or the trap's configuration prevents them from leaving. Codling moths and plum moths are some of the insects easily captured in this type of trap.

Controlling pests biologically

The legal withdrawal of many pesticides over recent years, and the rise in popularity of organic gardening, has caused this sector of the garden market to flourish. *Biological control* – the use of a living organism to combat a specific pest (or pests) – is environmentally friendly, safe for children and pets, and easy to use. You can buy a wide range of predatory insects, nematodes (microscopic organisms) and bacteria from mail-order suppliers (see 'Suppliers of biological controls'). For biological controls to be effective, follow the guidelines and apply at the recommended minimum temperature.

Insects

Tiny parasitic wasps, ladybirds and predatory mites are some of the organisms that can be used to kill aphids, spider mite and mealy bug. Although most of these creatures operate best in an undercover environment, principally creatures such as introduced parasitic ladybirds as they can locate their prey effectively in a confined space, other biological controls work well outside.

Nematodes

Not to be confused with pest nematodes, *beneficial nematodes* are microscopic, worm-like organisms that live in moist soil. Naturally occurring, they prey on many soil-dwelling pests by entering through their body openings or by penetrating their coverings. They then release bacteria to stop the pest from feeding and quickly kill it. The nematodes then reproduce inside the dead pest and produce a new generation that hunt down more pests!

This mode of action means that you need to have the pest present for the nematodes to work: you can't use them as a preventative measure.

You can purchase beneficial nematodes from biological control suppliers by mail order. Most controls contain a specific nematode to tackle one pest, although nematode mixes such as Nemasys 'Grow Your Own' can be used to target a broad range of pests.

Beneficial nematodes are living organisms, so you need to store and apply them properly. They're most effective in moist soil and at soil temperatures of 15–32 degrees Celsius (60–90 degrees Fahrenheit). Exposure to the sun kills nematodes, so they're best applied in early evening or on cloudy days when the soil temperature is at least 13 degrees Celsius (55 degrees Fahrenheit).

Cleaning up pests with soaps and oils

Insects breathe through pores in the cuticle that surrounds their bodies. If you plug up the pores, the insects suffocate and die. That's where soaps and horticultural oils enter the picture. Disrupt the cuticle with these sprays, and the insects can't maintain their internal moisture.

Soaps and oils kill a wide range of pest insects but affect beneficial insects, too. Use them with caution to avoid harming the garden-friendly guys.

Horticultural oils

Horticultural oils are made from refined mineral, fish or vegetable oils. Oils effectively kill any insect that they cover – including eggs, larvae, pupae and adults – but they don't differentiate between good and bad bugs.

Some products combine oil with ingredients such as insecticidal soaps or botanical insecticides, which make them even more effective. Oil helps these other ingredients stick to the plant or penetrate the insect's cuticle.

Insecticidal soaps

Insecticidal soaps penetrate and disrupt the cuticle that holds moisture inside insects' bodies. When sprayed with soap, many soft-bodied insect pests, such as aphids, dry out and die. Some pests, especially beetles with hard bodies, remain unaffected, however. To make soaps more effective, some products combine soap with pyrethrins, a botanical insecticide that we describe in the following section, 'Using plant-based insecticides'.

Insecticidal soap is nontoxic to humans and other animals, and breaks down quickly in the environment. If you use a concentrated product, dilute it with soft water before use for the best effect. Hard or mineral-rich water decreases its effectiveness.

Suppliers of biological controls

Agraland Limited: The Old Brickyard, Ashton Keynes, Swindon, Wiltshire SN6 6QR; phone 01285-860015; fax 01285-860056; website `www.agralan.co.uk`.

EcoCharlie: PO Box 77, Petworth, West Sussex GU28 8AW; phone 01485-271977; website `www.eco charlie.co.uk`; email `enquires@eco charlie.co.uk` or `info@ecocharlie.co.uk`.

Green Gardener: Chandlers End, Mill Road, Stokesby, Great Yarmouth, Norfolk NR29 3EY; phone 01493-750061; fax 01493-750098;

website `www.greengardener.co.uk`; email `jon@greengardener.co.uk`.

The Organic Gardening Catalogue: Riverdene Business Park, Molesey Road, Hersham, Surrey KT12 4RG; phone 01932-253666; fax 01932-525707; website `www.organic catalogue.com`.

Tamar Organics: Cartha Martha Farm, Rezare, Launceston, Cornwall PL15 9NX; phone/fax 01579-371182; website `www.tamarorganics.co.uk`; email `sales@tamarorganics.co.uk`.

The downside to insecticidal soap is that it also disrupts the waxy cuticle on some plants, making it toxic to young and thin-leafed plants, especially tomatoes. If you aren't sure of the plant's sensitivity to the product, always test it on a leaf or two, and allow a couple of days to pass before spraying a whole plant. Follow the label directions carefully.

Using plant-based insecticides

Insect and disease killers that come from plant extracts are called *botanical pesticides*. Although derived from natural sources and hence sometimes called 'organic', botanicals aren't necessarily safer or less toxic to non-pest insects, humans and animals than synthetically derived pesticides. In fact, most botanicals are broad-spectrum insecticides, which kill both good and bad bugs indiscriminately. Some botanicals cause allergic reactions in people; others are highly toxic to fish and animals; and some may even cause cancer. After all, nicotine in cigarettes is a natural product too . . .

Use all pesticides, including organic ones, only as a last resort and only after thoroughly reading the label on the package. Chapter 17 contains advice on how to use pesticides safely.

Pyrethrins

These insecticidal compounds occur naturally in the flowers of some species of chrysanthemum plants. The toxins penetrate the insects' nervous system, quickly causing paralysis. In high-enough doses or in combination with other pesticides, the insects die. The compound breaks down rapidly when exposed to sun and air, and becomes less effective if stored for longer than one year. Many commercial products contain pyrethrins.

Powerful synthetic compounds that imitate the natural chrysanthemum compounds are called *pyrethroids*. These products aren't approved for use in organic farms and gardens.

Although relatively harmless to humans, pyrethrins are highly toxic to fish and bees and moderately toxic to birds. They kill both beneficial and pest insects. To keep bees safe, spray pyrethrins in the evening after bees have returned to their hives for the night, and avoid spraying blooming plants.

Seek other pest control methods before resorting to insecticides. Rotenone (derris) used to be a popular organic insecticide, but because of its extreme toxicity to fish has fallen out of favour. No rotenone products are now approved for organic production.

Getting Rid of Common Insect Pests

In this section we provide an alphabetical guide to tackling some of the worst-offending insect pests that prey on vegetables, flowers, trees, shrubs and fruit:

- ✔ **Ants:** Several types of ant are commonly found in gardens. You see black ants on plants where aphids are present: they 'milk' the aphids for sweet sticky honeydew, protecting them from predators and some-times even moving them around. Often ant activity is the first and most visible sign of an aphid infestation. Yellow meadow ant builds nests in lawns, making mounds of earth. Red ants are aggressive and can give a nasty nip if disturbed.

  Ants thrive in dry conditions and you can sometimes combat them suc-cessfully by flooding the nests with water. All ants can be tackled using a biological control in the form of a nematode, best applied during the April–September period when the temperature is above 10 degrees Celsius (50 degrees Fahrenheit). Pennyroyal mint helps to deter ants, so plant it near doorways and other house entry points. Pyrethrum powder also kills ants, but bear in mind that although organic (derived from chrysanthemum leaves) this powder is a non-specific pesticide that also kills beneficial insects.

- ✔ **Aphids:** These pear-shaped pests, shown in Figure 18-1, pierce holes in plant tissue and suck the juices. They range in size up to 3 millimetres (0.12 inch), and their colour varies depending on the species: black, green, red or even translucent. They excrete the waste from the sap they consume as a sticky substance called *honeydew*, which attracts ants. Honeydew on plant stems and leaves may be colonised by *sooty mould*, which although not harmful to the plant is unsightly; wash or wipe sooty mould off the leaves. Aphids proliferate quickly, especially in spring when females can give birth to live young as well as laying eggs, and they tend to congregate on the newest leaves and buds. Gardeners dislike aphids because they also spread viruses, for which no cure exists.

You can control aphids in a number of ways. Initially, prevent attack by covering the plant or crop with very fine mesh. Tackle small infestations by blasting them off with a hose or pinching between finger and thumb. Entice natural predators by planting some of their favourite flowers, or buy and introduce ladybirds and lacewing larvae during the May–early September period. Under cover, use a biological control, the parasitic wasp *Aphidius colemanii*, early in the season when temperatures are above 12 degrees Celsius (53 degrees Fahrenheit). You can also spray aphids with natural insecticides, although these products are non-specific and kill the good guys too. Certain plants have resistance to aphids – particularly varieties of lettuce that are resistant to root aphid – and some plants are also resistant to the virus diseases that aphids can transmit.

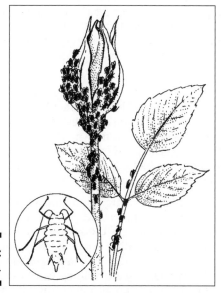

Figure 18-1:
Aphids.

✔ **Cabbage white butterflies:** These pests are widespread destroyers of all brassica crops as well as flowers such as nasturtiums. Protecting brassicas with barriers is the best form of defence, using a fine-gauge netting (such as EcoGreen, which has a tiny mesh size of 0.6 millimetres square). Biological control is available in the form of a nematode, which you can water directly on to the caterpillars in summer from July onwards. This approach attacks all caterpillars, though, so do take care to identify the pest correctly before applying.

✔ **Cabbage whiteflies:** Not to be confused with whiteflies, these common pests of brassicas thrive in greenhouses and other under-cover growing areas. Small, winged, white adults, up to 2 millimetres (around 0.10 inch) long, live under the leaves and fly up in clouds when disturbed. The young whitefly or scales remain on the leaves, excreting honeydew that may in turn be affected by sooty mould. Interrupt their life cycle by digging up and composting winter brassicas as soon as harvest is complete. Inspect under leaves regularly; remove and bin any leaves where eggs have been laid. Encourage natural predatory insects and spray with insecticidal soap only as a last resort.

✔ **Carrot flies:** These common pests mainly affect the roots of carrots, but can also be found on related crops such as parsnip and celery. The first sign is often reddening foliage and stunted growth; pull up and inspect a root for signs of tunnelling. The adults lay eggs in April/May and July/August, and so covering crops with horticultural fleece or fine insect mesh (as we describe in the earlier section 'Barring the way with barriers') during these periods gives good protection. Carrot flies aren't strong fliers and dislike windy sites: surrounding the crop with a low (45-centimetre/18-inch high) fence also deters them. Carrot flies are attracted by the smell of the crop, so cultivate the veg on dry, windless evenings instead of during the day, and plant strong-smelling crops such as onions close by to mask the smell. Lift crops in autumn rather than leaving in the ground to overwinter.

✔ **Chafer grubs:** These creamy-coloured, C-shaped grubs measure about 1.5 centimetres (0.5–0.75 inch) long and have distinct legs. The grubs live in lawn soil and feed on roots, causing patches of grass to yellow and die. While the damage caused to grass may not be severe, badgers may come in search of the juicy grubs and can cause a lot of damage by digging up the lawn. You can use a biological control to combat chafer grubs that should be applied from August to October.

✔ **Codling moths:** These 12-millimetre (0.5-inch) long brown moths lay their eggs on the leaves and twigs of apples and other fruits, starting when the trees' flower petals begin falling in the spring and continuing through the summer. When the small, white, brown-headed caterpillars hatch, they tunnel through the centre of the fruit, as shown in Figure 18-2. Control adult codling moths by trapping and killing them with sticky pheromone-baited traps, hung in the branches in spring. One trap protects up a quarter of a hectare (half an acre) or 16–20 trees.

Immature larvae spend the winter under the loose bark of fruit trees and in fallen apples. You can trap the larvae by wrapping corrugated cardboard around the tree trunks in summer and then destroying it after the insects crawl inside. Monitor and replace every week or two. You can also combat the larvae with a biological control in the form of a nematode, applied in September or October when the temperature is above 14 degrees Celsius (60 degrees Fahrenheit). Apply to the ground beneath the tree and to the tree trunk itself.

Figure 18-2:
Codling
moths.

✔ **Cutworms:** These 2.5–5-centimetre (1–2-inch) long caterpillars (see Figure 18-3) chew through the stems of young plants at night, killing them, and spend the day in the soil nearby. Pick the caterpillars from the soil near decimated seedlings. Spray horticultural oil (see 'Cleaning up pests with soaps and oils') in midsummer to kill the eggs on host plants. Remove plant debris from gardens to prevent overwintering by adults. Wrap the stems of young vegetable plants with 5–7.5-centimetre (2–3-inch) wide strips of newspaper so that half the paper extends below the soil surface; these strips are known as 'cutworm collars'.

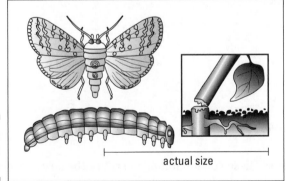

Figure 18-3:
Cutworm
caterpillars.

actual size

✔ **Flea beetles:** These highly mobile, shiny blackish beetles are only about 3 millimetres (0.12 inch) long, but they tend to feed in large groups. Adults emerge in spring and do most of their damage by midsummer. Eggs, laid in the soil, hatch into larvae that eat plant roots until late summer. Brassicas are their prime targets, along with nasturtiums and wallflowers; young seedlings of many plants are particularly vulnerable during dry weather. Most damage happens in April and May.

Control by covering vegetables and susceptible flowering plants with horticultural fleece or insect mesh (see 'Barring the way with barriers' earlier in this chapter), or delaying plantings until the beetles subside. Radish is a particular favourite of flea beetles and growing a row or two of this speedy plant as a 'sacrificial' crop may be worthwhile.

✔ **Leafhoppers:** These small, wedge-shaped adults jump from plant to plant, especially when disturbed. The adults and immature nymphs suck plant juices, distorting plant growth and spreading plant diseases. Many beneficial insects prey on and parasitise the nymphs. You can try spraying plants with blasts of water to dislodge the immature insects.

✔ **Leaf miners and sawflies:** The larvae of tiny sawflies, moths, beetles and flies, these pests tunnel through the leaves of trees, shrubs, flowers and vegetable plants (honeysuckle, tomato, holly, box, birch and lilac), leaving discoloured patches on the foliage. Control by planting vulnerable crops in a new place each year and covering with row-cover fabric in spring (we describe row covers in 'Barring the way with barriers'). Remove and destroy infested leaves (see Figure 18-4), and rake up any that fall in autumn. Leaf-miner damage is mostly cosmetic.

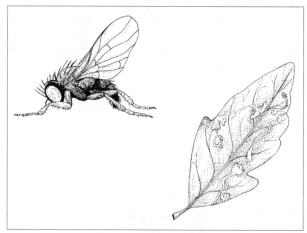

Figure 18-4:
Leaf miners.

✔ **Leatherjackets:** These soil-inhabiting pests are the larvae of crane flies, or 'daddy long-legs'. Measuring up to 5 centimetres (2 inches) long, leatherjackets are brown to grayish black in colour and lack legs or a distinct head. They feed on the roots and stems of young plants, including potatoes, and can cause lawn damage. Affected plants develop yellowing foliage and may wilt and die; lawns develop yellow patches.

Leatherjackets are most likely to be a problem in land that has recently been cultivated that was previously lawn or grass. They're most active in spring but may cause damage at other times of the growing season. If you discover lots of leatherjackets when digging over new ground, wait until the adults have hatched in late summer before planting or sowing crops. Birds feast on these pests so encourage them to the surface of a lawn by thoroughly watering the grass and covering with plastic sheeting or tarpaulin overnight. A biological control in the form of a parasitic nematode can be applied from late August to October.

✔ **Lily beetles:** Lily beetle adults are bright red with black heads, and measure 6–7 millimetres (0.25 inch) long. Most of the damage is done by the reddish brown grubs that cluster along the stems and under the leaves, often covered with slimy black excrement. Hand-picking and squashing them is the only effective means of organic control.

✔ **Nematodes:** Plant-damaging nematodes are microscopic, worm-like creatures that live in the soil. (They're from a different species to the beneficial parasitic nematodes that we discuss in 'Controlling pests biologically'.) They usually attack plant roots, causing abnormal growths and decreasing the plant's ability to take up water and nutrients. Some nematodes also attack stems and leaves. Control by rotating vegetable crops, and avoid planting susceptible crops in the same place each year.

✔ **Raspberry beetles:** These common pests of raspberries also damage other related fruits such as blackberries and loganberries. The beetles are inconspicuous and overwinter in the soil, emerging from April to early June. The best means of control is with a raspberry beetle trap during this period that combines a floral design with a scented attractant, drawing the pests into a funnel-shaped bucket.

✔ **Rose sawflies:** The 12-millimetre (0.5 inch) long sawfly larvae and the adults eat the undersides of rose leaves and related plants in spring and early summer, quickly stripping them to skeletons. Hand-pick small infestations, or spray with insecticidal soap or horticultural oil.

✔ **Scales:** Adult scale insects (see Figure 18-5) can have a hard or soft shell-like exterior that resembles bumps on plant stems and leaves. These pests suck plant sap and can weaken and kill plants if present in large numbers. Many species secrete sticky honeydew that encourages fungus. Control is difficult on large trees and shrubs; your best bet is use a biological control in the form of nematodes. Apply under cover from March to June, when the temperature is over 14 degrees Celsius (57 degrees Fahrenheit), and outside from May to June. Remove and destroy badly infested stems, and spray with horticultural oil. Indoors or on small plants, clear light infestations with a cotton ball soaked in soapy water.

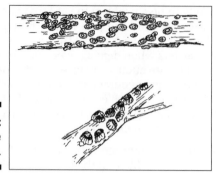

Figure 18-5:
Scale
insects.

✔ **Slugs:** Slugs feed on seedlings and on the tender leaves of many ornamental, fruiting and vegetable plants during the night or in rainy
weather. Some species work underground and tunnel into vegetables,
especially potatoes. Slugs are generally active when plants start growing
and temperatures rise above 5 degrees Celsius (40 degrees Fahrenheit).
Slugs breed all year; the peak egg-laying periods are March–April and
September–October. Sometimes they're hard to spot: you see just their
trails and the holes they chew in leaves and fruit. They proliferate in
damp areas, hiding and breeding under rocks, mulch and garden debris.

You can control slugs organically. Organic-approved slug killers are
available that don't have the persistent harmful effects of slug pellets.
Traps work well if used repeatedly over a period of time: place boards,
cabbage leaves, pieces of old carpet or other hiding places in the
garden. In the early morning, lift the traps and destroy the slugs by placing in salted water, or you can just leave them on the lawn for birds to
feast on (although you run the risk of the slugs doing a runner, or rather
a slither).

Shallow pans of beer also attract and drown these pests. Keeping slugs
off your delicate plants in the first place, using one of the many barrier
methods, is very effective. Surround plants and gardens with copper
barriers – metal strips that seem to shock slugs if they attempt to crawl
across them. Sharp materials are a good deterrent: crushed eggshells
and sharp grit are traditional, now joined by a slug barrier made from
crushed ceramic bathroom-ware – an excellent example of recycling in
action. Barriers such as absorbent granules based on Fullers Earth, bran
and wood ash also deter them but must be refreshed on a regular basis –
every week or two if the weather is very wet – in order to be effective.

You can make individual 'collars' or mini-cloches for susceptible plants
by cutting large plastic bottles into pieces (use the top half and remove
the lid to make a cloche). Biological control, in the form of a nematode,
is effective, particularly against slugs that stay in the ground; apply
during March–October. One application gives around six weeks control.

🗸 **Snails:** These pests attack plants in the same way as slugs and you can combat them with the same methods, with the exception of biological control. Snails tend to hibernate in winter, which is a good opportunity to gather and destroy them. Thrushes love to feast on snails and you may hear a regular 'tap-tapping' in your garden, which is the sound of a thrush breaking open the shell by banging a snail on a stone (known as a 'thrush's anvil'). Placing a few large stones around your garden in quiet spots for this purpose is a good idea. Hand-picking these pests is a good method of control and snails are less yucky to collect by hand than slugs!

🗸 **Spider mites:** These tiny arachnids, shown in Figure 18-6, are almost microscopic, but when they appear in large numbers, you can begin to see the fine webs that they weave. Use a magnifying glass to identify them. They suck plant sap, weakening plants and causing leaf discoloration. They're especially active in dry conditions. Favourite hosts include fruit trees, miniature roses, citrus and houseplants.

Encourage beneficial insects, many of which prey on spider mites. Under cover, use a biological control *Phytoseiulus,* released from April to July when temperatures rise above 10 degrees Celsius (50 degrees Fahrenheit). (Before then, use a soft soap spray, but don't spray when introducing the beneficial predator!) Inspect plants in late summer and if necessary introduce a new generation of predators to prevent the pest overwintering. Clean the greenhouse in autumn, removing plant debris in which pests may overwinter and washing the framework and benching.

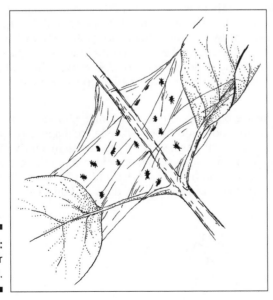

Figure 18-6:
Spider
mites.

✔ **Thrips:** These tiny, slender-bodied flying insects damage all soft parts of ornamental and vegetable plants, including leaves, flowers and roots. Infested flowers and young fruits look distorted. Leaves have silvery or white discoloured patches on them, sometimes speckled with black. Use a magnifying lens to identify them. Encourage or release lacewings and other predatory beneficial insects. Introduce the biological control *Ambleysius* from February to June.

✔ **Vine weevils:** Adults and larvae of this snout-nosed beetle species damage fruit and ornamental plants. Plants growing under cover and in containers are most vulnerable. The 8–9-millimetre (0.3-inch) long black adults emerge from the soil in early summer and lay eggs near the soil on host plants. When the eggs hatch, the larvae burrow into the soil and eat the roots. The legless 'C'-shaped larvae do the most damage because they proliferate unseen until the plant starts to collapse and die. Their favourite plants include fuchsia, primula, begonia, geranium and strawberry. The adults eat crescent-shaped notches in the leaves, and operate under cover of darkness.

To control, knock the adults off the plants onto a drop-cloth in the evening. Use biological controls (such as beneficial nematodes) for the larval and pupal stages: apply during the March–November period when temperatures are above 10 degrees Celsius (50 degrees Fahrenheit).

✔ **Whiteflies:** Resembling tiny, white moths, these insects (see Figure 18-7) are a common pest under cover and congregate on the undersides of leaves, sucking plant sap and spreading plant diseases. Infested plants may release clouds of them when disturbed, so vacuuming up the adults can be very effective. Control whiteflies with insecticidal soap during the winter months, or by trapping them with yellow sticky traps. Be sure to treat leaf undersides, where whiteflies and their larvae reside. In spring, introduce the biological control *Encarsia* at the first sign of the pest, when temperatures are above 10 degrees Celsius (50 degrees Fahrenheit).

✔ **Wireworms:** These 2.5-centimetre (1-inch) long, copper-coloured worms tunnel through plant roots and tubers, causing damage and opening wounds that encourage disease. Control the larvae by cultivating often and destroying exposed insects. Chickens clean up in the garden before planting time, and you can trap worms with bits of cut potato in the soil. Check the potatoes for worms every few days and discard.

Figure 18-7:
Whiteflies.

Chapter 19

Battling Plant Diseases

. . . .

In This Chapter

▶ Figuring out the problem

▶ Preventing plant diseases

▶ Tackling existing diseases

▶ Scouting out environmental problems

. . . .

*P*revention is the best way to protect your plants from diseases, and the most effective way to prevent disease is through thoughtful gardening and crop planning and informed maintenance (as we describe in detail in Chapter 17).

In this chapter, we explain the most ecologically friendly ways to prevent and manage plant diseases. And because disease problems can strike the plants of even the most efficient gardener, we also discuss diagnosing and treating the most common diseases. One of the issues in this area is deciding whether the problem is in fact a disease at all or some other malady, and so we also tell you about some disorders and environmental problems that you may mistake for diseases.

Diagnosing What's Wrong with Your Plant

At first glance, the symptoms of many diseases, environmental stresses, nutrient deficiencies and insect attacks can look similar. Even something as simple as wilting may have several possible causes: for example, too little water, stem or root disease, high temperature or stem-boring insects. Fortunately, most plant problems have more than one symptom, which helps you pinpoint the trouble. So consider all the possibilities before you jump to any conclusions (and check out Chapter 17 for an overview of evaluating plant problems).

To diagnose a disease problem, start by gathering all the facts and looking at the overall conditions:

- ✔ **Compare with healthy plants.** Note specific differences between healthy specimens and sickly ones. Check leaf colour and size, as well as overall plant vigour. Look at the bark and stems for any sign of bark damage (bearing in mind that physical damage stops water and nutrients from going up into the plant), and for any cracking or weeping, which is a sign of disease.

- ✔ **Examine the environment.** Check soil moisture and pH (we cover pH in Chapter 5) and recall any fertilisers or other products you used recently (fertilisers are the focus of Chapter 7). Rule out unusually hot or cold temperatures, consider wet or dry weather, and look for mechanical damage, such as severed roots, leaves torn by high winds or hail, or strimmer injury. We talk more about environmental causes in the later section 'Rooting Out Environmental Problems'.

  Don't forget to look at what's been happening immediately outside your plot as well: for example, someone may have recently applied a herbicide that drifted onto the affected plant, or car wheels may have sprayed road salt onto your hedge.

- ✔ **Investigate insect activity.** Check leaves and stems for obvious pests and sticky residue or droppings. Dig gently around the roots for grub and nematode damage. (Turn to Chapter 18 for descriptions of insect pests and the damage they cause.)

Here are typical symptoms that indicate plant disease:

- ✔ Discoloration and spotting
- ✔ Soft, watery plant tissue
- ✔ Sudden death of stems or twigs

If you suspect that disease is affecting your plant, compare the symptoms with those we discuss in the 'Combating Common Garden Diseases' section, later in this chapter.

Understanding Plant Diseases

Several kinds of organisms cause diseases in plants, just as they do in people:

- ✔ *Bacteria* are nearly impossible to eliminate after the plant is infected.

- ✔ *Fungi* cause most plant diseases, which is fortunate because they're most readily prevented with good garden care and management.

- ✔ *Viruses* are the toughest ones because they're incurable; all you can do is try to prevent them.

In this section, we provide an overview of diseases that fungi, bacteria and viruses cause – and ways you can prevent and control them. We describe specific diseases in the later section 'Combating Common Garden Diseases'.

Plant pathologists (scientists who study plant diseases) use the phrase *disease triangle* to illustrate the fact that plant diseases result from an interaction among three things: a *pathogen* (disease-causing organism), a plant and an environmental condition.

The vast majority of plant diseases can't be treated – only prevented from spreading further.

Finding the fungus among us

Fungi play an important role in garden ecosystems, and the number of species that cause problems is relatively small. 'Good' fungi are responsible for much of the decomposition that takes place in your compost pile. Also, without fungi you'd have no yeast bread (yeast is a fungus) and (yikes!) no beer.

If you study them closely, you find that fungi are fascinating. They range in size from a single cell to the largest known living organism on the planet: a 5.5-kilometre (3.5-mile) wide underground fungus in Oregon that consists of a huge tangled mass of threads called mycelium. Occasionally, the fungus reveals itself in mushrooms at the bases of dead trees.

Like all living organisms, fungi have distinct life cycles that vary from species to species. Most fungi have exacting requirements that allow them to live and spread, and knowing these requirements helps you predict and prevent problems in your garden.

Most fungus species infect a single plant species, called the *host plant*, and most require the presence of water to spread. If you can interrupt any step of the process, you can prevent the spread of disease.

Most plant-disease fungi spread by releasing huge numbers of dust-like spores. The spores are dispersed in many ways: on the wind, in water droplets, in your clothing as you brush by infected plants. If a spore lands on the species' host plant and the environmental conditions are right (which usually means that moisture is present), the spore germinates and begins to grow. Fortunately, you can take many steps to minimise the spread of these fungi in your garden (see Chapter 17).

Battling bacteria and viruses

Disease-causing bacteria, fungi and viruses are all *pathogens* – that is, they can cause disease. Bacteria and fungi form spores that can spread by means of rain, water splash and other methods of physical transference. Viruses differ in that they're parasites and can only exist inside living cells. Viruses are transferred by a *vector* – a living host such as an aphid or another sap-sucking insect, which is why pest control is an important part of gardening.

Bacteria have colonised nearly every habitat on Earth. They're remarkably durable and able to withstand environmental extremes that kill other organisms. Bacteria cause more plant problems in tropical regions than temperate ones because most require warmth and moisture to spread. Bacteria disease symptoms on plants include spotting of leaves, stems or fruits, as well as *soft rots*, which make plant tissues watery or slimy. Although bacterial plant diseases can be controlled by the same types of antibiotics used in animals, this strategy usually isn't practical, and so gardeners need to rely on prevention.

Plant diseases caused by viruses are often named for the symptoms they cause. Cucumber mosaic virus, for example, affects cucumbers and related plants and causes leaves to become mottled.

Protecting Your Plants Against Disease

Some diseases, especially of trees and shrubs, are incurable and so prevention is critical. Fortunately, your gardening methods can go a long way towards keeping diseases out of your vegetable and flower patch, and away from your fruits and crops. (Check out Chapter 17 for more on the essential role in organic gardening of prevention and natural balance.)

Many of the techniques that we discuss in this section involve keeping plant foliage dry, because the presence of moisture is required for most diseases to spread.

Inspect your plants frequently. You've a better chance of preventing a serious outbreak of disease if you catch it early. Look for stem and leaf wounds and damage, off-colour foliage, wilting, leaf spots and insects whenever you work among your crops and garden plants.

Choosing plant varieties wisely

When selecting plants for your garden, choose disease-resistant varieties. Many popular flowers, vegetables, perennials, fruit, trees and shrubs come in varieties that resist common diseases and even some pests; indeed, plant breeders are working harder than ever to produce varieties with natural resistance. Although you can find disease-resistant plants in most catalogues, nurseries and garden centres, the firms that specialise in organics are likely to have the best range of suitable varieties.

Happy plants mean healthy plants, so always make sure that you choose plants that are adapted to your region, soil and site. Struggling, stressed plants are far more likely to succumb to disease. See Chapter 3 for more about designing your garden for success.

Keeping plants dry and mulched

Most of the diseases we describe in this chapter thrive on moist leaves but not on dry foliage. Here are suggestions for keeping leaves dry:

- ✔ **Space and prune plants to provide good air circulation.** Fresh air helps leaves dry quickly and thwarts diseases. Disease spores don't have a chance to settle and infect your plant.

- ✔ **Water the soil, not the plants.** Soaker hoses and drip irrigation are better choices than sprinklers because they apply water directly to the soil. If you must use sprinklers, early-morning watering is best, because the sun evaporates any water on the leaves. Avoid evening watering; the foliage stays wet all night, giving fungus spores a chance to grow and infect plants.

- ✔ **Avoid working with wet plants, because diseases spread easily when the foliage is wet.** Many diseases spread through splashed water. Beans, strawberries, raspberries and other plants are particularly susceptible.

Mulching is another way to keep your plants healthy and prevent disease. A thick layer of organic mulch around your garden plants and shrubs keeps weeds from gaining an upper hand. The mulch also helps maintain consistent soil moisture and temperature, which keeps plant roots healthy and better able to resist disease. Soil- and water-borne diseases, such as blackspot on roses, have a harder time infecting plants when mulch prevents muddy water from splashing onto leaves.

To discourage fungi that attack tree trunks and stems, however, keep mulch a few centimetres/inches away from the actual stems.

Preventing plant disease in other ways

Add the following techniques to your gardening routine and you're well placed to prevent most disease problems:

✔ **Avoid excess nitrogen fertiliser.** Nitrogen makes plants grow fast and juicy. As a result, the outer layers of the leaves and stems that protect the plant are thinner than usual (similar to human skin) and more susceptible to insect damage. Use organic fertilisers that release their nutrients slowly to avoid encouraging insects. Check out Chapter 7 for more fertiliser suggestions.

✔ **Maintain a clean garden.** Dispose of diseased leaves, fruit and wood in the green waste collection (or take to your local tip) and not in the compost heap, which simply provides a cosy environment for them to survive.

✔ **Stay clean under cover.** Any undercover growing environment, such as a greenhouse, polytunnel or cold frame, offers ideal conditions for diseases to proliferate. Make a regular routine of going through your space at least once or twice a week, removing dead leaves, flowers or debris.

✔ **Keep your tools clean.** If you prune diseased plants, clean your pruning shears between cuts by wiping the blades with a cloth dipped in methylated spirits.

✔ **Clean your shoes.** Knock the dirt off your shoes to keep pests and diseases from travelling from one garden to another.

✔ **Practise crop rotation.** Many diseases live in the soil from one year to the next, waiting for their favourite host plants to return. Foil them by planting something different in each spot each year. This method is especially effective for protecting annual vegetables.

✔ **Prune at the correct time.** Certain plants heal much faster if pruned at the right time of year (the time varies according to the plant, just to further confuse the hapless gardener). The quicker a wound heals, the less time infection has to enter. Only prune when necessary, and consult a gardening reference book to ensure that you carry out work at the optimum time for your plant.

✔ **Control insects.** Many insects – including aphids and leafhoppers – can spread diseases between plants. Keep them under control, and you help prevent disease. Pests such as aphids also secrete a sticky substance called honeydew that in turn encourages a harmless but unsightly black fungal growth called sooty mould, which is often mistaken for a disease. Flip to Chapter 18 for all about pest control.

Getting to Grips with Disease-Control Techniques and Products

Preventing plant stress and environmental imbalances are the most important steps in controlling disease. Beneficial microbes, especially in the soil, usually keep the populations of plant-disease-causing organisms in check, but environmental factors can tip the balance in favour of the bad guys. High humidity and soil moisture encourage diseases to spread. Stress from transplanting, pruning and insect infestation can weaken plants and make them more vulnerable to infection from fungi, bacteria and viruses.

In addition, a pesticide you use against one problem can sometimes make another problem worse, and broad-spectrum fungicides kill beneficial fungi as well as harmful ones.

As we explain in the earlier section 'Understanding Plant Diseases', the only plant diseases you can control effectively after the plants become infected are those caused by fungi. The following products are currently acceptable for occasional organic use:

- ✔ **Bacterial fungicide:** This form of *Bacillus subtilis* (sold as a product called Revive) works by boosting the plants' natural immune systems and inhibiting fungal germination and growth: effectively filling the vacuum that harmful fungi would otherwise colonise. This fungicide works best when applied early in the growing season as a preventive measure, before diseases have spread.

- ✔ **Beneficial fungi:** Some of the newest fungicides are fungi themselves. These good guys grow in the soil and into roots, protecting the plants from harmful diseases and improving overall health and vitality. Apply them to the soil on or before planting or water them into lawns and gardens. You can also apply these fungicides to foliage. These products contain viable fungi, and so you need to store them properly and use them according to label instructions for best results. Chapter 7 contains more details on beneficial fungi.

- ✔ **Potassium bicarbonate:** This natural chemical controls powdery mildew, downy mildew and blackspot on a range of crops including roses, courgettes, cucumbers, strawberries and other plants. It also supplies some potassium fertiliser when sprayed on foliage, which strengthens plants' cell walls and makes them harder for pests and diseases to penetrate.

  Follow label directions carefully, spraying all leaf surfaces thoroughly to ensure contact with the fungus. Use to eradicate the disease when present, not as a preventative measure.

- ✔ **Sulphur:** Useful for controlling nearly all fungus diseases on leaves and stems, sulphur is one of the oldest pesticides known. In recent years, the control of industrial emissions has seen reductions in the level of sulphur dioxide in the atmosphere, with a corresponding rise in plant disease.

  You can dust the powder directly on leaves or mix finely ground dust with water and a soapy wetting agent that helps it adhere to leaf surfaces. Sulphur creates an environment in which many diseases are unable to thrive, and is particularly effective on roses. Sulphur candles can be used to fumigate empty greenhouses or polytunnels.

Sources of information

As gardeners demand more organic methods of disease control, alternatives to synthetic, chemical pesticides are becoming more common. To keep up with the latest information, visit the following websites:

✔ www.gardenorganic.org.uk – Garden Organic is the UK's leading organic gardening organisation, dedicated to

research and promoting organic growing for 50 years.

✔ www.rhs.org.uk – The Royal Horticultural Society (RHS) is the UK's largest gardening charity, dedicated to advancing horticulture and promoting good gardening. The advice given is for all gardeners, not just organic ones.

Certain fruits are sensitive to sulphur: don't use on redcurrants or white currants, or on gooseberries, and use with care on other fruit.

Although sulphur is considered acceptable for occasional use by the organic gardener, it's still not recommended for frequent use because of certain adverse effects that it has on the garden's inhabitants.

Copper-based fungicides are no longer recommended for organic use, because copper is much more toxic to humans, mammals, fish and other water creatures than most synthetic chemical fungicides. It also builds up in the soil and harms plants and micro-organisms.

Some gardeners find that repeated sprays of compost teas seem to minimise disease problems, in addition to providing nutrients. Find out more about making and using compost tea in Chapter 7.

Combating Common Garden Diseases

Many names of plant diseases describe the symptoms they cause – for example, powdery mildew, leaf curl and club root. Some diseases attack only one plant part, whereas others can affect the entire plant. The following list details some of the most common diseases of trees, shrubs, vegetables, flowers and fruits:

✔ **Anthracnose:** This group of fungi can attack many plants (beans, vine crops, tomatoes and peppers) and trees (dogwoods, maples, willows and sycamores). Look for small, discolored leaf spots or dead twigs. The disease can spread to kill branches and eventually the whole plant. You can spread it easily by splashing water and walking through wet plants. Many plant varieties are resistant to anthracnose fungi; choose them whenever you can. Prune off affected plant parts, if possible, and dispose of the debris in the green waste or your dustbin, not in the compost pile.

✔ **Apple scab:** This fungus attacks apple and crab-apple trees, producing discolored leaf spots and woody-brown scabs on the fruit. The leaf spots start out olive-coloured, eventually turning brown. You can plant scab-resistant varieties, such as 'Saturn' and 'Sunset': conversely, avoid varieties that are particularly susceptible to disease such as 'Cox's Orange Pippin'. Remove badly infected young fruits in midsummer: rake up and destroy fungus-infected leaves and fallen fruit as soon as possible in autumn, to prevent the fungus from re-infecting the trees in spring. Prune out infected twigs.

✔ **Botrytis or grey mould:** This fungus attacks a wide variety of plants, especially in wet weather and cool conditions. It causes watery-looking, discoloured patches on foliage that eventually turn brown. Infected flowers – especially roses, geraniums, begonias and chrysanthemums – get fuzzy white or grey patches that turn brown, destroying the bloom. Strawberry and raspberry fruits in particular develop light-brown to grey mouldy spots, and the flesh becomes brownish and water soaked. Discourage botrytis by allowing air to circulate freely around susceptible plants, and avoid working with wet plants. Remove and destroy any infected plant parts because the disease spreads rapidly to healthy fruit and growth.

✔ **Brown rot:** A common problem of many tree fruits, you can easily identify the disease by brown patches that quickly spread over each fruit. Affected shoots have blossom that withers and dies, and the twigs take on a mummified appearance in winter. Control by picking off and disposing of infected fruit (not on the compost heap) and pruning out damaged shoots. Boost the tree's health by spraying seaweed fertiliser as a foliar feed in spring and summer.

✔ **Canker:** Cankers appear as oozing, sunken or swollen areas on the bark of susceptible trees, such as peach, apple, maple, spruce and willow. The new shoots turn yellow, wilt and then die back. The disease attacks the woody stems of susceptible plants, forming cankers that can kill infected branches. Use resistant or less-susceptible plants, and keep them growing vigorously. Avoid bark injuries that provide an entrance for infecting fungus. Remove and destroy infected branches, cutting back to healthy wood that doesn't contain any black or brownish streaks. Ensure that pruning is carried out at the correct time, so that wounds heal as fast as possible.

✔ **Club root:** This fungus infects mainly brassica crops (such as cabbage, broccoli and cauliflower) and grows best in acidic soils. Symptoms include stunted growth, wilting, poor development and swollen lumps on the roots. To help combat, practise good garden hygiene by keeping tools clean and picking up plant debris. Add lime to raise the soil pH to 7.2 (Chapter 5 has all the gen on pH), and avoid planting susceptible crops in infected soil for at least 7 years. Some varieties have resistance to the disease. Raising young plants in pots, and planting out when well established, gives them a good enough start in life to grow to maturity with minimal impact from the disease.

✔ **Coral spot:** This disease can affect all woody plants, entering the plants through wounds and dead wood. Bright red or orange spots appear and the damaged part soon dies. Prune out all infected wood, cutting back into healthy growth. Avoid by removing dead, diseased and damaged growth from trees, shrubs and climbers.

✔ **Damping off:** A problem mostly in young plants and seedlings, this fungus rots stems off near the soil line, causing the plant to keel over and die. Prevent damping off by planting seeds and seedlings only in potting compost or your own compost that has been sterilised (micro-waving it for two minutes does the job), and avoid overwatering. Air circulation helps prevent the fungus, too, so take care not to sow seeds thickly in the first place, to avoid ending up with dense clumps of seed-lings. Water seedlings from below, by standing pots or trays in water for around half an hour. If you water from above, do so in the morning so that the foliage dries in the shortest possible time.

✔ **Honey fungus:** Several species of the *Armillaria* fungus cause this dis-ease, which infects and kills the roots and lower trunk of woody plants, primarily trees, shrubs and woody climbers. Symptoms include smaller-than-normal leaves and honey-coloured mushrooms growing near the base of the tree (see Figure 19-1). Affected plants may die suddenly, or decline over a period of months or even years. Honey fungus grows on dead tree stumps and then spreads to infect living plants, so remove stumps by digging them up or having the stumps professionally ground down.

Certain plants are susceptible to honey fungus, including birch, most hedging conifers, forsythia and the *Prunus* species, so avoid growing these plants if infection is identified. Encouraging healthy, vigorous growth by improving the soil, mulching and feeding, helps your plants resist infection. A number of woody plants are known to have good natural resistance: contact organisations such as the Royal Horticultural Society (www.rhs.org.uk) for details.

The honey fungus spreads by means of underground *rhizomes* (stems that creep and spread below ground), said to resemble bootlaces, but neither toadstools nor *rhizomorphs* (thin root-like threads) are defini-tive signs of the fungus. The only sure-fire method of identification is to remove the bark of an affected plant to see whether a sheet of white mycelium beneath that has a strong smell of mushrooms. If you identify honey fungus outside your garden but close by, install a 50–60-centime-tre (20–24-inch) high barrier of material such as butyl rubber, buried vertically in the soil, to prevent infection.

Mycelial plaques

Figure 19-1:
Honey
fungus.

Honey fungus on tree bark

✔ **Leaf spots and blights:** Several fungi show up first as circular spots on the leaves of tomatoes, potatoes, peppers and other vulnerable vegetables, flowers and ornamental plants. The spots increase in size until the leaves die and fall off. The fungi spread easily in damp weather and in gardens where overhead watering wets the foliage, especially late in the day. The best control is to remove all plant debris at the end of the gardening season, clean tools between uses, practise crop rotation, buy disease-resistant varieties and avoid contact with wet plants.

Potato blight is a common problem: if a potato crop is badly infected with around 10 per cent of the foliage dying off, cut back the top growth to ground level (the cuttings can be safely composted) and wait 2–3 weeks before lifting the potatoes – this pause allows the skins to harden. Ensure that all the crop is cleared from the ground, and don't compost any infected tubers.

The same fungus causes tomato blight, with symptoms first seen on the leaves, quickly spreading to the fruits. Space plants widely (so the foliage of one doesn't touch its neighbour) to ensure good air movement, ventilate greenhouses and polytunnels, and water the soil rather than the foliage.

✔ **Mildew (downy and powdery):** These two fungi produce similar symptoms: a white, powdery coating on leaves. They infect a wide variety of plants, including roses, vegetables, fruit trees, strawberries, raspberries and lilacs. A different species of mildew attacks each kind of plant. A mildew that attacks lilacs, for example, doesn't harm roses. The fungi disfigure plants but may not kill them outright. Instead, they weaken their hosts, making them unattractive and susceptible to other problems. Downy mildew attacks during cool, wet weather. Powdery mildew (as shown in Figure 19-2) appears during warm, humid weather and cool nights, especially when the soil is dry.

Many vegetable and flower varieties are resistant to mildew; read package and catalogue descriptions carefully. Remove infected plant debris from the garden, and avoid getting the leaves wet. Use potassium bicarbonate (which we describe in the earlier section 'Getting to Grips with Disease-control Techniques and Products') to treat infected plants.

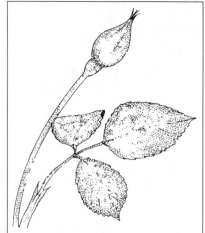

Figure 19-2: Powdery mildew.

✔ **Onion diseases:** The *Allium* family, which includes shallots, garlic and chives as well as onions, is liable to several diseases that can cause severe problems: onion downy mildew, onion neck rot and onion white rot. Avoidance is by far the best course of action, because the spores can last for a number of years. Always buy seed and sets from a reputable source, practise crop rotation and be sure to grow onions in their ideal conditions: for example, in full sun and well-drained soil.

✔ **Root rot:** This broad term covers several fungal root diseases that cause susceptible plants to turn yellow, wilt and sometimes die. Nearly all plants are susceptible under the right conditions, such as excessive soil moisture, poor soil aeration and wounding. The fungi can survive in the soil for many years without a host. Prevent root rot by building healthy, well-drained soil. Microbial fungicides can help foil many root-rot diseases.

✔ **Rose blackspot:** This fungus causes black spots on rose leaves, as shown in Figure 19-3. Yellow rings may surround the spots, and severe infections can cause the shrub to lose all its foliage. The disease spreads easily in splashing water; it overwinters in fallen leaves and mulch around the plant. Therefore, remove old mulch after leaf fall in the autumn, and replace it with fresh mulch. Prevent blackspot by choosing disease-resistant roses and cleaning up and destroying any diseased leaves that fall to the ground. Avoid wetting the foliage when you water. *Underplanting* roses (planting under the main plant's canopy of branches) with chives (*Allium schoenoprasum*) helps roses resist infection.

Fungicide sprays containing sulphur or potassium bicarbonate can also offer some protection against blackspot.

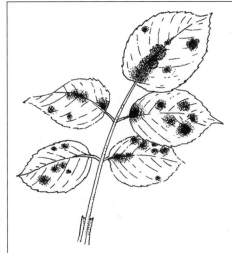

Figure 19-3:
Rose blackspot fungus.

✔ **Rust:** Many fungi cause rust, and the symptoms of this disease vary widely, depending on the kind of plant they infect. Usually, the symptoms include yellow to orange spots on the leaf undersides, with white or yellow spots on the upper leaf surface. Susceptible plants include brambles, hollyhocks, roses, pines, pears and leeks. Each rust species infects a specific plant species, so the rust on roses can't infect beans, for example. Symptoms of this disease include yellow, orange, reddish-brown or black powdery spots or masses on leaves, needles or twigs (see Figure 19-4).

Provide good air circulation to keep foliage as dry as possible, remove and destroy infected parts, and keep your tools clean. Choose to plant disease-resistant varieties.

✔ **Verticillium wilt:** This fungus affects many plants, including tomatoes, aubergines, potatoes, raspberries, strawberries, roses, Japanese maples and cherries. Look for wilting and yellow leaves, especially older ones. In some plants, the leaves curl up before falling off. Prevent future infections by cleaning up all garden debris, cleaning tools thoroughly with disinfectant and avoiding susceptible species. Choose resistant varieties, and practise crop rotation.

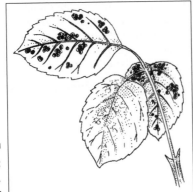

Figure 19-4:
Rust fungus.

✔ **Viruses:** This group of incurable diseases infects vegetables, brambles, strawberries, trees and flowering plants. Usually, the leaves develop mottled yellow, white or light-green patches and may pucker along the veins. Flowers can develop off-colour patches, and fruit ripens unevenly. Aphids, leafhoppers, nematodes and whiteflies (insects that we discuss in Chapter 18) spread the virus as they move from plant to plant. Prevention is the only strategy. Buy only virus-free plants from a reputable source (which means turning down well-meant offers of free fruit plants from friends and neighbours) and keep pests in check. Remove and destroy infected plants as soon as signs of virus become apparent.

Rooting Out Environmental Problems

Plants live intimately with their environment, which means that air, water and soil quality, weather and animals can take their toll. Sometimes the disease culprit is fairly obvious, but at other times plants' responses to environmental damage can mimic diseases caused by micro-organisms or insect pests. Look through this section of probable causes before you start blaming viruses, bacteria and fungi.

Dodging weedkiller damage

Weedkilling sprays can drift on the wind to affect nearby plants. If a section of plant turns brown seemingly overnight, try to determine whether anyone in the area has used a herbicide. You can't fix the damage, but if you prune off damaged foliage, the plant may recover. Some herbicides are systemic and move within the plant to kill it, roots and all, whereas other attacked plants may not be killed, but show distorted or discolored foliage.

Avoiding lawn-mower and strimmer damage

Mechanical damage to the bark and stems of trees and shrubs poses a serious threat to their health. Water and nutrients flow through the stems just under the bark, and breaking the bark interrupts this flow, causing stress, wilting and even death. Even small wounds open the plant to insect and disease invasion.

Maintain a wide weed- and grass-free area around trees, shrubs and gardens so that you don't have to mow or strim close to them. Hard plastic or wire-mesh tree guards also offer protection.

Defending against leaf scorch

When the edges of leaves turn yellow and then brown, as shown in Figure 19-5, suspect environmental damage from drought or heat. Trees in paved areas where heat rises from the pavement are vulnerable, as are any plants in extremely dry soil or unusually hot weather.

Avoid planting susceptible trees, such as Japanese maples, in hot, dry locations. Plants with delicate leaves may also suffer similar symptoms from wind damage.

Figure 19-5:
Leaf scorch.

Fortifying against nutrient deficiency

Although most natural soils contain enough nutrients to support healthy plants, disturbed soil around new homes (where nutrient rich topsoil has been removed and only poor-quality subsoil is left) are likely to have nutrient shortages. Each nutrient causes specific deficiency symptoms, but some symptoms resemble or mimic other problems or diseases. For example, nitrogen-deficient plants have yellow older leaves and stunted growth; lack of potassium causes yellow leaf margins; and phosphorus-deficient leaves usually have purplish streaks or an overall purplish appearance. Iron deficiency, caused by high pH, is especially prevalent in acid-loving plants such as azaleas, blueberries, rhododendrons and camellias. The leaf veins remain dark green, but the rest of the leaf becomes yellow.

In such cases, conduct a soil test (as we describe in Chapter 4). Also, flip to Chapter 7 for more information about specific nutrients and how to use organic fertilisers to address the problem.

Sometimes drought is the culprit: plants can only take up nutrients in solution and problems such as bitter pit on apples, caused by a lack of calcium, are usually down to dry conditions.

Steering clear of salt damage

Salt used to de-ice roads poses a serious threat to perennials, trees and shrubs. As water drains off the roads, salts in the water accumulate in the soil, burning foliage and roots, and killing plants. Salt spray from passing cars can also damage or kill trees and shrubs. Injury appears as stunted growth, brown needles on conifers and wilting.

You can leach road salts out of the soil with heavy irrigation, but a better solution is to avoid planting within 7 metres (20 feet) of a frequently salted road and to divert drainage water from the road away from plants.

If you live in a coastal area where salty air and soil are the norm year-round, choose salt-tolerant plants recommended by your local nurseries.

Fending off frost and winter injury

Cold temperatures, frost, wind and frozen soil combine forces to damage plants in several ways. Late-spring and early-autumn frosts injure tender plants as well as hardy plants that aren't sufficiently dormant to withstand cold temperatures. Young, succulent, actively growing shoots and expanding flower buds are usually the most vulnerable. Injury symptoms include wilted brown leaves, stems and flowers.

Avoid fertilising and pruning plants in late summer, which can promote new growth that doesn't mature before freezing occurs. Protect vulnerable plants when severe frosts are forecast, by covering them with thick horticultural fleece and moving container-grown plants under cover or at least against the wall of a building for shelter.

Low winter temperatures cause the most damage to plants growing in containers, in areas where they're marginally hardy, and in places where winters bring little snow cover (snow insulates the soil and prevents the soil temperature from dropping dangerously low). Here are a few symptoms of injury caused by low temperatures:

- **Dried-out evergreen leaves and needles:** The leaves and needles of evergreens face the challenge of drying out in the winter without being able to replace their lost moisture. When the soil freezes, the roots can no longer take up water to transport to the leaves. Winter sun and wind take their toll, and symptoms include bronze or brown needles and leaves. Wrap vulnerable shrubs with fleece or sacking, plant them in protected places, and remember to water regularly but sparingly during the winter months. Take care not to overwater: many plants can withstand surprisingly low temperatures so long as their roots aren't waterlogged, because the water then freezes and causes permanent damage.

- **Root damage:** Root damage may appear later in the growing season, when plants fail to grow or sprout leaves, or start to grow but die suddenly in late spring. Spread 10–15 centimetres (4–6 inches) of loose mulch over the roots of vulnerable shrubs in autumn.

- **Split trunks and branches:** Snow and ice can accumulate on tree and shrub branches and split them from the trunk. Protect shrubs by wrapping them with sacking and heavy twine to hold the branches together. If you see snow accumulating to such an extent that the plant begins to bend, go out with a broom and knock off the snow. Prune damaged limbs immediately to prevent further damage from bark tearing.

Chapter 20

Outwitting Invading Creatures

In This Chapter

▶ Considering the weapons at your disposal

▶ Fending off larger foes

▶ Repelling rodents

▶ Defending attacks from above and below

---

*N*o discussion of garden pests is complete without considering the various animals that can plague your plants. Although seeing wildlife in the garden is mostly wonderful, certain creatures really seem to take advantage. Insect feeding (which we discuss in Chapters 17 and 18) is subtler and causes incremental damage over time, but larger pesky creatures, such as deer and rabbits, can quickly eliminate an entire plant or row of plants.

Gardeners enjoying the country life are, alas, more likely to be troubled by animal pests than town or city dwellers, though loss of natural habitats means that increasing numbers of creatures are adapting to life in built-up areas. And, although the majority of troublesome creatures are wild ones, domestic pets cause their own share of problems.

This chapter looks at some of the most common animal pests – large and small, living above, on and below ground – and the steps you can take to minimise the damage.

Some of these animals are no fools and do their work under the cover of darkness, which means that you're unlikely to catch them in action. Instead, you need a little detective work: examine the plant and scout for signs that give away the culprit doing the damage. After all, you don't want to waste time and money putting up a rabbit fence that's only 1 metre (3 feet) high when deer are responsible, or installing an expensive 2.5-metre (7.5-foot) deer fence that's no deterrent to squirrels!

Gearing Up For Battle

As an organic gardener, you're keen to live in harmony with your surrounding environment, which can be a bit of a challenge when creatures great or small start to home in on your plot. Fortunately, plenty of chemical-free options are available to help you protect your precious plants.

Depending on which troublesome creature you're tackling – and how much money you have to throw at the problem – try the following methods to help keep animal invaders at bay:

✔ **Barriers:** Small-scale combat works well and costs little, whether you use tree guards to protect saplings from rabbits, netting over your fruit and veggies to repel birds, or wire mesh to prevent squirrels munching your bulbs. Such barriers can be a bit of a fiddle to install, but are worth the effort. Check out the later sections 'Warding off those wascally wabbits', 'Beating the birds' and 'Guarding against grey squirrels' as appropriate.

✔ **Fences:** The only successful way to combat big furry pests – such as deer, rabbits and badgers – is to keep them out completely, as we discuss in 'Combating Larger Animals' in the following section. A suitably designed fence is usually effective but takes a heck of a lot of time and trouble, not to mention cash, to put up. If you've a large garden, a compromise may be the only affordable solution, such as fencing-off an animal-proof area around the house and choosing tough plants or individual plant guards for the rest of the plot.

✔ **Removing temptation:** Otherwise known as not banging your head against a brick wall. For example, if you can't keep rabbits off your veg patch, don't even think of growing lettuces.

✔ **Repellents:** Repellents vary a lot in how well they work, and also depend on just how hungry your invading creatures are and whether they've young to feed. Loads of homespun repellent recipes are available, as well as an ever-increasing range that you can buy. The drawback is that most repellents need frequent re-application, especially after rain. Also worth considering is manure from large predators, such as lions and tigers, which is said to keep off deer and cats in particular. You can buy this 'zoo poo' by mail order and from many retail outlets. Although repellents are worth a try, bear in mind that some people swear by them and others swear about them!

✔ **Scare tactics:** We don't quite mean hiding in the bushes and shouting 'boo' – but almost! From high-tech ultrasonic deterrent devices and motion-detector water squirters to a whole variety of cunning plans involving musical birthday cards, empty bottles, plastic snakes and so on. Results aren't guaranteed but are certainly worth a go. High-powered water pistols can be surprisingly effective (and satisfying) too. If you've the patience to sit and wait, a few direct squirts can sometimes be enough to convince the critters to go elsewhere. Also, a dog with strong territory-protecting instincts is a good bet.

Combating Larger Animals

This section helps you in the battle against your garden's larger enemies, whether they come in from the wild or make themselves at home from a neighbouring house. So, marshal your troops – you've organic produce to protect!

Defending against deer

Deer can be among the most troublesome of garden pests, mainly due to their ability to leap over fences. Rural wooded areas are their homes of choice, but leafy suburbia is their idea of a 'des res' too. Deer are most likely to visit gardens when other food sources are scarce, especially in late winter and early spring. In such times, they eat just about anything. But even in times of plenty, they're tempted into gardens for gourmet treats such as tulip flower heads.

To identify deer damage, look closely at your affected plants. Deer don't have upper front teeth, so when they eat they tear plant tissue rather than cutting it, leaving ragged edges. Deer prefer tender new growth when available, but eat buds and twigs in winter. Although they tend to start by feeding among trees and shrubs – so that they can duck for cover if threatened – when left undisturbed they soon become bolder and may come right up to your house.

Deer can reach as high as 1.8 metres (about 5 feet), so if you see damage at eye level, you're probably dealing with a deer, not a mutant rabbit. Look for telltale hoof prints and piles of deer scat (usually rounded pellets with a dimple on one end, about the size and shape of a chocolate-covered peanut or a small black olive).

Repulsing with repellents

The following repellents may keep deer out of your garden:

- **Hair:** Ask your barber or hairdresser if you can have some hair trimmings and hang in mesh bags about 1 metre (3 feet) off the ground. (Birds are grateful for this top-quality nest material in spring as well.)

- **Soap:** Hang bars of soap from low tree branches or from stakes so that the bars are again about 1 metre off the ground: cheap, highly scented soaps are said to work best.

- **Spray:** Use spray repellents on foliage. Here's one recipe: mix three raw eggs in a gallon of water and spray the mixture on plants; the substance apparently smells worse to the deer than it does to you.

For best results, spray plants before the deer develop their feeding habits and reapply sprays after heavy rain.

If you continually use the same deterrent, the deer get used to it and over time ignore it. So vary your methods, try different products and combine them now and then. You can use lion or tiger manure as we mentioned earlier (which repels by scent) along with a bad-tasting hot pepper spray, for example.

Employing scare tactics

Stringing fishing line between posts scattered through your garden sometimes confuses deer enough that they go elsewhere. Make sure that you tie it tightly, to avoid animals and birds becoming tangled up in it. You also have to remember that the fishing line is present, though, to avoid walking into it yourself. This option is better for less frequently visited gardens than for your vegetable garden.

Using fencing

The only sure-fire way to keep deer out of your garden is to put up a tall fence. Deer have been known to jump fences that are up to 3 metres (9 feet) high, but a 2.5-metre (7.5-foot) fence deters most intruders unless they're hungry.

Deer have quirky tendencies that you can use to help ensure that your fence is successful. Deer are intimidated about jumping when they can't tell how much distance they have to clear. For that reason, they're less likely to jump a fence over a narrow, long garden than a fence that surrounds a large, wide garden. The two long sides appear to be too close together for the deer to see a place to land.

Therefore, you can create the same illusion by installing a fence so that it slants outward away from the garden. This technique can intimidate the deer by making the fence appear wider than it really is.

Also, place a circle of 1.2-metre (4-foot) wire fencing around young trees, especially fruit trees. Make sure that the diameter of the fence is large enough that the deer can't reach over to eat the twigs.

If all else fails, you may need to resort to low-voltage electric fencing, as shown in Figure 20-1. Place an electrified strand 1 metre (3 foot) high and a metre outside your other fence. Although this sort of fencing sounds nasty, it works by giving a mild shock that just scares and repels animals – it doesn't harm or kill them.

Planting deer-resistant plants

Many plants are touted as deer resistant, but if deer are hungry enough, they eat just about anything. Still, if you live in an area where the deer threat is high, including plants with aromatic foliage such as catmint and yarrow, and prickly plants such as berberis, *Genista hispanica* and pyracantha, increases the likelihood that at least something in your garden survives.

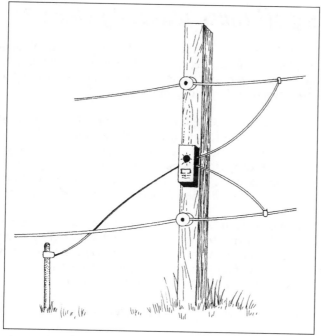

Figure 20-1:
Low-voltage
electric
fencing may
be the only
solution to
foiling deer.

Battling beastly badgers

If you were brought up on the *Wind in the Willows* children books, you may have difficulty seeing these handsome creatures as pests, but occasionally badgers can be destructive in gardens. As powerful diggers, they turn over ground in search of grubs and worms, and their love of sweet things can lead to devastation of fruit bushes or a sweetcorn crop at harvest time.

As with all garden enemies, knowing what they're after can help. If badgers are scraping up your lawn, they're looking for big, juicy, chafer grubs, and so getting rid of the grubs means no food to attract badgers in the first place. You can fight off chafer grubs in an environmentally friendly way by applying a *biological control* (the deliberate introduction of a predatory organism, in this case microscopic nematodes). You can find more on this subject in Chapter 18.

A stout fence around 1 metre (3 foot) high is the best defence against badgers. If you live in the sort of environment where badgers live, chances are that rabbits trouble you, too, so installing a rabbit fence covers all bases.

Warding off those wascally wabbits

Rabbits are one of the most common of garden enemies, nibbling the foliage of almost any plant and returning again and again, day and night, to finish the job. They make their homes out of sight: in natural cavities and under buildings, and in burrows that they dig themselves.

Unlike deer (which we discuss in the earlier section 'Defending against deer'), rabbits have both upper and lower front teeth, so you can identify their damage by a clean, angled cut on the ends of leaves and twigs. If you suspect rabbits, look for their droppings, which are round or slightly flattened, for confirmation; think marbles or chocolate covered peanuts. The individual pellets are smaller and rounder than the more elongated deer scat.

Rabbits tend to eat vegetables and flowers in spring and summer; sprouting tulips are a favourite spring treat. In autumn and winter, they go for twigs and bark and can cause considerable damage to trees and shrubs. They may strip bark off of young trees; if they remove the bark around the entire trunk or stem, which is known as *girdling*, the tree is likely to die.

You can try several techniques to foil rabbit feeding:

✔ **Fencing:** The best way to keep rabbits away from your plants is to fence them out. Because they burrow, a fence must also extend underground. Choose a chicken-wire fence that's 1.2 metres (about 4 foot) high with 2.5-centimetre (1 inch) mesh. Bury the bottom 30 centimetres (1 foot) of the fence, bending the lower half into a right angle facing outward.

✔ **Repellents:** Sometimes rabbits can be repelled with hair gathered from hair salons and dog groomers. I (Sue) sprinkle it around the boundary of a garden and replenish it every few weeks. You can also purchase commercial repellents that are made to spray on the ground or directly on plants.

✔ **Trunk protectors:** Protect tree trunks with a cylinder of wire mesh. Make sure that the material is 10–15 centimetres (4–6 inches) away from the trunk. Plastic 'wraparound' tree guards also work well. (See Figure 20-2.)

Guarding against grey squirrels

Squirrels are usually bold and have capitalised on our love of feeding birds, regularly visiting bird tables and feeders to steal a tasty meal. These agile, fearless creatures can cause quite a problem, especially in newly planted bulb beds; crocus and tulip bulbs are like sweets to them. Squirrels also like to eat fruits, nuts, berries, seedlings and bark, not to mention raiding bird's nests for eggs and even baby birds. Squirrels are visible daytime visitors, so you're likely to see them in action, but look out for telltale part-nibbled bulbs and fruits.

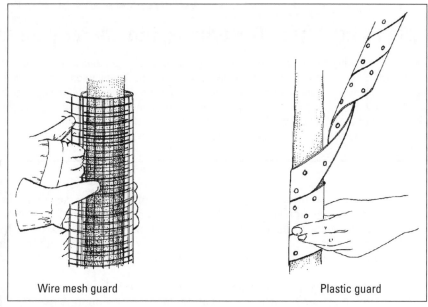

Figure 20-2: Wire or plastic tree guards protect bark from rabbits and gnawing rodents.

Wire mesh guard   Plastic guard

You can't get rid of squirrels permanently. If you evict your current residents, new ones simply come to take their place. The only course of action is to protect vulnerable bulbs and use squirrel-proof bird feeders to avoid boosting populations. If you put up bird boxes, add a metal surround to the entrance hole so that squirrels can't gnaw their way in.

To protect your bulbs in autumn, cover newly planted beds with chicken wire; the bulbs grow right through it in spring. A sprinkling of chilli powder added at planting time can work well, too. Be sure to plant bulbs at the proper depth and take care not to leave any bulb debris (such as pieces of the papery outer covering) on the soil surface to attract squirrels.

Although a more expensive option, motion detector-activated sprinklers can offer short-term help.

Fighting off feline foes

Visiting felines that hop over your fence (or squeeze through impossibly narrow gaps) can be a real pain, particularly if you don't have your own territorial moggy or pooch to scare them off. Of course, the problem is far greater in urban areas where garden space is at a premium, but can be a nuisance even in the country if your neighbour happens to keep half a dozen cats.

Man's best friend? Perhaps, but not for your lawn

Cats aren't the only domestic animals that can cause problems for gardeners: dogs are also a pain, particularly when their wee causes yellow patches on lawns, and when they dig up and lay on your plants. While you can put up fences to keep dogs within a certain area, the yellow patchy lawn problem is less straightforward to deal with. What you can do is to add products available on the market to your canine chum's drinking water that helps neutralise the chemicals in the urine.

The best solution is to prevent them getting into your garden in the first place. Keep a close lookout for the points where cats enter: a broken board in a fence or a worn spot at the base of a hedge can be closed off quickly and easily. Similarly, remove anything that may attract them, such as the perennial catmint (*Nepeta*), which they absolutely adore.

When they do gain access, however, you can at least make life hard for them. Roaming cats enjoy loose soil and mulch, and frequently use gardens and landscaped areas as litter boxes. The fine soil of a seedbed is their top toilet choice, and having your newly sown flower or veggie seeds dug up before they've had a chance to grow is annoying, to say the least. Laying rough-textured or chunky bark mulch or ornamental rocks on the soil may repel them, because these materials are uncomfortable to soft paws, as are prunings from prickly bushes such as pyracantha and holly. If you so desire, you can also lay chicken wire on the soil and cover it with mulch, while strips of 'prickly' plastic (designed for this purpose) can be fixed to the tops of walls and fences.

Cats don't like the smell of dog hair or anise oil, so try spreading these substances on the soil. They also hate the smell of citrus fruits (peeling an orange always ensures that you don't have to share the sofa with a cat) so shredded lemon and grapefruit peel deters them, but does need to be re-applied frequently. Some gardeners find that the plant nicknamed the 'scaredy-cat plant' (*Coleus canina*) is successful. You can also buy commercial deterrents as well as ultrasonic cat scarers: as with all these products, some gardeners report great success while others find the results disappointing.

Cats are intelligent creatures and soon work out where they're not welcome. So if you keep a capacious, high-powered water pistol close to hand and deliver a few good squirts, you don't hurt them but do encourage them to wander elsewhere.

Vanquishing Voles and Mice

Voles and mice look similar. Both are small rodents, but the tail of a vole is much shorter than that of a mouse. Mice are fond of young seedlings and pea seeds, especially those growing in a warm house or greenhouse on a cold winter day; they're omnivores, though, and eat almost anything. Voles, on the other hand, are almost exclusively herbivores, although they become troublesome for gardeners only in years of abundant populations.

Mice and voles can cause damage to plants in the wintertime, when food is scarce, and the bark of your favourite tree makes for an easy meal. Fruit trees are especially at risk. Even during the summer, if you've a thick layer of mulch surrounding the tree right up to the trunk, the rodents can hide in the mulch and feed undetected. Check trees and shrubs on a regular basis and look for small gnawed areas of bark a centimetre or two across (rather than the much larger bites of deer and rabbits). Keep a look out for half-eaten nuts and fruits too, which indicate that these pests may be present.

To guard against giving them sanctuary and to deter feeding, leave a space of 5–10 centimetres (2–4 inches) between the trunk and the mulch. If necessary, remove all the mulch around trees and shrubs in the winter, because the animals don't like to feed out in the open, where predators can find them.

Where voles are a problem, wrap the trunks of young trees with a tree guard made of wire or plastic. Mousetraps can be set in buildings or greenhouses, and you need to decide whether to use humane traps that catch them alive to be released elsewhere or use something more terminal.

The use of traps or poisoned bait outside isn't advisable because you can inadvertently harm birds and other creatures such as hedgehogs.

Resisting rats

Although rats aren't interested in eating your plants, they do carry diseases (such as Weil's disease, which is transmitted in their urine) and so are nearly always unpopular garden guests. A supply of food is likely to entice rats into your garden, and so avoidance is far better than cure. Put out food for birds in feeders and on tables, rather than on the ground. When composting any cooked food waste, particularly meat scraps, always do so in a closed container such as a tumbler, Bokashi bucket or wormery – adding meat to a standard compost heap is asking for trouble. These compost solutions are safe because the waste is secure from pests, in the case of a tumbler; part-composted and made unpalatable in a Bokashi bucket; or processed by worms in a wormery. These solutions are available from many suppliers, including www.wigglywigglers.co.uk. If you do have an infestation of rats, poisoned bait in secure, tamper-proof (and bird-proof) stations is the best solution.

Defending Against Lofty and Low-down Creatures

Your precious veggies and plants are vulnerable to attack from all directions. This section describes how to protect your garden from above your head and below your feet!

Beating the birds

Birds in the garden are usually an asset because they feast on troublesome insects such as aphids. But when pigeons munch your winter greens and blackbirds devour ripe raspberries, they cross the line into nuisance territory. Half-eaten fruits and leaves are classic signs of bird damage – and of course, if you tiptoe quietly up to your crops, you may well see your feathered visitors enjoying a feast.

Scare tactics are one form of defence. Noise, fluttering objects and anything resembling a predator can startle birds away. Try criss-crossing your veg or fruit patch with unwanted CD disks tied to string. The noise and the flashing of the sun on the shiny surfaces can scare birds away. Or instead of string, use a thin nylon line that vibrates and hums in the breeze.

You can also use the modern version of the scarecrow: balloons and kites with images of predators, such as owls and hawks. Place them in the garden to convince birds that their enemy is on guard. Rubber snakes laid among your brassicas are said to keep pigeons off, too.

Birds catch on quickly, and so change your scare tactics regularly.

The truth, however, is that ripe fruit is so tempting to birds that they usually work round any scare tactics. Netting is the only sure-fire solution and the ideal approach is to use a *fruit cage* – a ready-made structure formed by using stout netting stretched over a rigid frame, with a door for entry and high enough to walk in – usually a minimum of 1.8 metres (6 feet) high. Strawberries, however, can be protected with netting on a low frame, and the same applies to winter vegetables such as brassicas.

Do take care to stretch the netting taut and secure the edges, because birds can easily become tangled up and be badly injured.

Maintaining your defences against moles

These creatures are the innocent bystanders (or innocent burrowers) of the garden-pest realm. Unlike voles (check out the earlier section 'Vanquishing Voles and Mice'), moles are carnivores and don't eat plants. They simply love to burrow in search of grubs, earthworms and other insects. In the process, they inadvertently expose plant roots to air or push the plants out of the ground, in both cases killing the plants.

Moles produce two types of tunnels:

- ✔ Tunnels that lie just beneath the surface and appear as raised ridges in your lawn
- ✔ Tunnels that go much deeper, connecting the surface tunnels

When they're digging the deep tunnels, moles create the characteristic round, volcano-like mound of soil that gives away their presence.

Field mice and voles can also use mole tunnels to forage for plant roots and flower bulbs.

Moley deterrents

The following mole deterrents – which are sometimes effective, sometimes not – are worth a try. Whatever their level of success, at least you've an unusual topic of conversation at parties.

- ✔ **Ferret dung:** Place in the mole tunnels (ferrets prey on moles, but first you need to find a ferret-keeper . . .).

- ✔ **Human urine:** Again, place in the tunnels (at least you've a ready supply!).

- ✔ **Mole smokes:** Light and put in the tunnels to give off toxic gases (although the smoke can just scare them off, it may kill if the mole can't escape).

- ✔ **Mole spurge plant (*Euphorbia lathyris*):** Moles dislike the smell (you can buy the plants or grow readily from seed).

- ✔ **Noise:** Inventive ideas include placing empty glass bottles in mole holes so the bottle is half-buried (the wind blowing across creates a 'scary' echoing noise); putting musical birthday cards in the tunnel to play continually; and arranging at least half a dozen children's plastic windmills over the affected area.

- ✔ **Ultrasonic mole deterer:** A costly option that doesn't always work.

The best strategy for controlling moles is to use a deterrent as soon as you see any signs of mole activity, so that you encourage them to travel elsewhere. A weird and wonderful armoury of methods is available (see the sidebar 'Moley deterrents') but if the moles don't shift and the problem is severe, consider calling in professionals who can trap and kill the animals.

Don't use mothballs in the garden. While their use as a mole repellant is sometimes recommended, as organic gardeners, you don't want this potential carcinogen contaminating your soil.

Chapter 21

Weed It and Reap!

. . . .

In This Chapter

▶ Distinguishing weeds from beneficial wild plants

▶ Using techniques to ward off weeds

▶ Tackling weeds with the right tools

▶ Understanding problems that weeds may harbour

. . . .

Controlling weeds is a challenge for all gardeners, but especially so when you're trying to grow organically. Weeds compete with your lawn and garden plants for food, water and sun; they sometimes harbour injurious pests and diseases; and they run amok, making the garden look unkempt. The organic weed-control methods that we describe in this chapter – knowledge, techniques and tools – offer new hope of winning the battle against weeds without poisoning the environment.

Remember that weeds also offer an opportunity. They give observant gardeners clues about the soil in which they grow and provide habitat for helpful insects as well as harmful ones. Some weeds are edible too, or have medicinal properties. And some so-called weeds are valued garden plants: one person's trash is another person's treasure. After all, the oft-quoted definition of a weed is simply 'a plant that's growing in the wrong place'.

Winning the Weed Wars

Almost everyone dislikes the laborious and unglamorous task of weeding, although you can gain a degree of satisfaction when tackling a weedy patch and creating order from it. The truth is, however, that you can't have a garden, or grow crops, without having to control weeds as well. Weeds are immensely successful simply because they've evolved to grow in your locality, and so they nearly always out-perform garden plants.

Although some gardeners reach for the weedkiller, organic gardeners soon discover through experience that the best approach is to prevent weeds from sprouting in the first place.

Use the techniques in the following sections to prevent and control weeds in your garden. Choose the methods that match your needs (and your weeds!), whether you're starting a new garden or maintaining an established planting.

Knowing your enemy

Not all weeds are the same, and the sooner you become familiar with your garden invaders, the quicker you can find out which ones to swoop on so they don't get so much as a toe-hold. In turn, discovering which weeds aren't threatening can save you a lot of work.

Weeds divide into three main groups:

- ✔ *Annuals* complete their life cycle within one growing season, and sprout fresh from seed each spring. Most of these guys are a nuisance rather than a real threat, because a session with a hoe soon sees them off, with one or two exceptions such as sorrel that are hard to shift.

- ✔ *Biennials*, which grow one year, flower the next and then die, are similar to annuals.

- ✔ *Perennials* form bigger and more invasive root systems from one year to the next. They're the neighbourhood yobs, sneaking in and refusing to leave, and can regrow from even tiny pieces of root left behind after a weeding session.

Always clear the ground thoroughly of weeds before you do any permanent planting such as shrubs or herbaceous plants (see the later section 'Clearing overgrown ground to remove weed habitat'). Otherwise, perennial weeds manoeuvre their way through a border and are a nightmare to try and clear.

'One year's seeding is seven years' weeding'. Bear this saying in mind because it's true. One weed plant can produce hundreds of seeds, and although most germinate in the first year or two after seeding, a few continue to pop up in subsequent years. So, even if you haven't had time to deal with the whole plant, we heartily recommend a regular go-round of your garden to pick off seed heads before they ripen and spread. Of course, this approach means that children should blow dandelion clocks when out on walks, not in the garden! Remember that sneaky weeds such as dandelions continue to mature their flowers into seeds even if you pull up the whole plant.

When dealing with weed seeds, bag them up with your garden waste to be collected (if your council does so), take to the tip or put in the bin.

Don't add weed seeds to your compost heap unless you're really confident that the heap's going to heat up sufficiently to kill them.

Facing up to wicked perennial weeds

These weeds are top of any gardener's hate list, so get familiar with these bad guys and don't let them get so much as a toe through the garden gate:

- ✔ **Bindweed:** This climbing, twining perennial with slender stems, arrowhead-shaped leaves and large, white saucer-shaped flowers is a great one for sneaking into your borders and growing into your plants. Therefore, bindweed is hard to eradicate organically. It grows from thick, white, fleshy roots that are brittle and tend to break when you're trying to dig it out, and so use a garden fork and lift gently to ensure that you don't leave any fragments behind.

- ✔ **Couch grass:** This weed differs from annual grasses in that it forms a network of roots with sharp, white, pointed growing tips, spreading out rapidly if left unchecked.

- ✔ **Creeping buttercup:** Although pretty when in flower, don't relax your guard if this con artist gets into your borders or veg plot. It spreads like wildfire by means of runners, which root wherever they touch the ground, and is especially fond of damp conditions. The only place to cut creeping buttercup some slack is in your lawn, because regular mowing simply chops off the young runners.

- ✔ **Dandelion:** Discover how to spot the new, young, rosettes of leaves in spring and whip out these tenacious plants before an incredibly long taproot heads down to the other side of the world! Also look out for tell-tale golden flowers in borders – dandelions tend to hide around and under plants. Dandelions are edible, which is some consolation: the leaves make a piquant addition to salads and flowers can be scattered as a garnish. During the Second World War, the roots were roasted, ground and used as a substitute for coffee.

- ✔ **Dock:** Dock leaves are a traditional remedy for taking the pain out of nettle strings, but these plants are a right pain if allowed to take over in the garden. Unchecked, docks grow over 1 metre (3 feet) high with enormous tap roots.

- ✔ **Ground elder:** Also known as goutweed because people have long used it as a traditional herbal remedy for gout, this low-growing weed spreads incredibly fast and adores shady sites.

- ✔ **Nettle:** This plant is useful for the organic gardener as an excellent compost activator and as an ingredient to make your own liquid plant food. Nettles are also an important butterfly food plant. That aside, however, nettles can also be a tenacious pest, so chop off the tops before they seed and take over.

Having nightmares about Knotweed

Several plants may have a claim to being the worst weed, but Japanese Knotweed (*Polygonum japonicum*) surely must be the most horrendous one that you may have the misfortune to come across. You can see colonies of it near waterways, which provide the ideal means for it to spread, but it can pop up almost anywhere. Japanese Knotweed is covered by two pieces of legislation in the UK: causing it to grow and planting it in the wild are offences, and you must dispose of any at a licensed landfill site because Japanese Knotweed is classed as 'controlled waste'. Your local council should be able to give advice on identification, treatment and disposal. It grows up to 2 metres (6 feet) tall, with arching stems and large oval leaves, and the roots (which are almost impossible to remove) have been known to penetrate tarmac or concrete. Watch out!

Mulching for weed prevention

The old saying of prevention being better than cure is never truer than with weeds. Just like other plants, weeds need soil, air and light to grow, and if you deprive them of these crucial requirements, they die.

When you've created a nice, clean area of soil and your plants are in, put down a mulch to stop weeds sneaking in. *Mulch* is a term used to describe anything that covers the soil for the purpose of preventing weeds, conserving moisture or moderating the soil temperature. Another similar way to combat weeds is to smother them and keep them in the dark, though this approach works only with certain mulching materials.

Many materials make good mulch. The ones you choose really depend on what's locally available, how much you want to spend, the appearance factor, where you plan to put it and whether you want a decomposing or non-decomposing mulch.

Although mulches are excellent for helping your plants to establish, because they stop moisture from evaporating out of the soil, they also stop a certain amount of rain getting through. For this reason, only spread mulch when the soil's already moist.

Decomposing mulches

The best mulch materials for organic gardens also add organic matter to the soil as they decompose, boosting the soil structure and the whole ecosystem. Usually 5–10-centimetre (2–4-inch) layers are sufficient to do the job, depending on the density of the material. Take a look at the following popular mulches and their uses:

✔ **Chipped bark:** Tree bark is the most popular landscape mulch. Available in shreds or chunks of various sizes, bark lasts a long time (depending on the particle size) and gives your borders a finished look, making a handsome colour contrast to your plants.

✔ **Cocoa shell:** This by-product from the chocolate industry makes an excellent mulch and some gardeners say that it also helps deter slugs.

The slightly chocolaty smell can be attractive to dogs and cocoa shells are toxic to them if eaten.

✔ **Garden compost and manure:** These materials are excellent soil conditioners, help conserve soil moisture and suppress weed growth. They're also likely to contain weed seeds, however, garden compost in particular, unless your heap gets hot enough to kill the seeds. (Flip to Chapter 6 for more details on compost.)

✔ **Lawn clippings:** Clippings cost nothing and work best in flower and vegetable gardens, where they decompose quickly. Put on only a thin layer (2–3 centimetres/1 inch) at a time, however, or the clippings may heat up and possibly cause damage. If you don't use a grassbox, allow the clippings to dry on the lawn before raking them up. Fresh clippings may mat down and become slimy as they decompose.

Grass cuttings are likely to contain weed seeds, especially if they come from an organic lawn that's full of flowers. And, if you're getting clippings from a well-meaning friend, be sure that the clippings don't come from a chemically treated lawn.

✔ **Leafmould and pine needles:** These materials are among the best sources of free, attractive and nutrient-rich mulch for flower beds, fruits and vegetables. To find out how to turn your autumn leaves into leafmould, turn to Chapter 6. You can spread newly fallen leaves over the bare soil between plants, but make sure that no smaller plants are beneath or they get smothered and die (as well as the weeds).

Pine needles acidify the soil. Place them freely around acid-loving plants, but monitor the soil pH around less tolerant plants. (Check out Chapter 5 for all about soil pH.)

✔ **Newspaper and cardboard:** Use cardboard or several layers of whole newspaper sheets in pathways, between rows of fruit or vegetables, or around border plants to smother weeds. (Avoid using the coloured glossy pages.) To hide the unsightly material and stop it blowing away, cover with a thick layer of loose mulch, such as bark, shredded leaves or straw. Depending on rainfall, you may have to replace newspaper during the growing season, though it can last a long time. You can simply dig in any mulch that remains at the end of the year to improve the soil structure.

If you've lots of ground to cover, ask a local newspaper printer whether you can have or buy the ends of paper rolls left over from printing. Rolling out a section is easy, and then moisten the paper with a hose and apply as mulch; continue unrolling the paper for the next section.

✔ **Straw and hay:** Although straw and hay are traditional mulches for vegetables and strawberries, beware! Hay contains weed seeds that can add to your problems. Straw from grain crops, such as oats and wheat, contains fewer seeds and is a better choice as a weed-suppressing mulch. Allow the soil to warm up in the spring before putting mulch around tomatoes and other heat-loving crops; otherwise, the straw insulates the soil from the sun's warmth.

✔ **Wood chips, sawdust and shavings:** Although suitable for mulch, these products break down more quickly than bark and compete with your plants for nitrogen as they decompose. Stack these materials for at least six months so the breakdown process gets under way. If you use these substances around crops and border plants, add an additional nitrogen source, such as those we describe in Chapters 6 and 7. Fine materials such as sawdust can compact so tightly that water can't penetrate.

Never use materials from pressure-treated wood. Although the green-hued, CCA (chromated copper arsenate), pressure-treated wood was phased out in 2004, the newer types of pressure-treated wood still contain substances that you don't want in your organic garden.

Some organic mulches can go sour if they get too wet and packed down, and begin to decompose without sufficient air. If your mulch smells like vinegar, ammonia, sulphur or silage, mix and aerate it with a garden fork. Don't apply sour mulch around flowers, vegetables, fruits, or young shrubs and trees; its acidity can damage or kill the plants. Cover unused mulch piles with a tarp.

No matter what kind of organic mulch you use, keep it away from direct contact with plant stems and trunks. Make sure that you leave a gap of at least 5 centimetres (2 inches) around plant stems to prevent moisture building up around the trunks and to deter insects, slugs, rodents and diseases. Be sure to loosen mulch with a rake periodically to allow water to penetrate easily.

Non-decomposing mulches

Organic gardeners favour the mulch materials listed in the preceding section as they rot down and are taken into the soil, improving the structure over time (which is a priority for organic gardening). These other mulch materials don't decompose but have other special uses that make them useful in certain situations – to replace a lawn, or to cut down on weeding, for example:

✔ **Glass:** Coloured glass is a popular mulch in contemporary gardens, and is used as part of a design scheme to create a dramatic contrast with the plants. Different colours are available, and this material is usually made from recycled glass. Glass needs to be laid over landscaping fabric (see third bullet point in this list) to stop weeds growing through from below.

✔ **Gravel and stone:** These chippings can look attractive, contrasting with plants in both colour and texture. They're ideal to use around alpines and exotic plants on the borderline of hardiness, because they help improve drainage around the collar of the plant (which is vulnerable to rotting).

Gravel and stone are good at retaining moisture in the soil, but they do make unfortunately efficient seedbeds for annual weeds! Putting down landscape fabric (which we describe in the next bullet point) under them first helps prevent perennial or deep-rooted weeds, though you're likely to have some annual ones seeding into the surface.

Avoid sand, which attracts cats, ants and weed seeds.

✔ **Landscape fabrics:** These products are made of woven plastic and allow water to pass through, but shade the ground and prevent weeds from coming up. They're good to use around permanent plants where low maintenance is especially desirable. When planting a new border, simply cut an X in the fabric to plant through and tuck the fabric around the base of the plant. The fabric looks unsightly, however, and needs concealing with a material such as chipped bark. Bear in mind that fabric used in this way also prevents organic material from reaching the soil.

Although the synthetic fabric lasts a long time, it may need to be replaced at some point. Use it around trees and shrubs or under decks where you don't want weeds, but avoid using landscape fabrics in gardens where you want to change the planting or develop more natural-looking planting schemes.

✔ **Mulch mats:** These mats are made from a variety of materials, including coir fibre and recycled rubber. Circular mats are designed to be placed around trees; the long strips are for edging beds. Coir is biodegradable and is excellent in schemes where soil may need to be retained only for the first few years, until the plants have established.

✔ **Plastic sheeting:** Commonly used to cover soil under heat-loving crops such as tomatoes and squash, black and coloured plastics heat the soil and white ones keep it cool. Plants growing in plastic mulch need careful and frequent irrigation because rain can't reach the soil.

Don't use plastic sheeting around garden plants, because it prevents water and air from reaching roots.

Some organic gardeners avoid plastic mulches despite their benefits, because as they age they become brittle and break into pieces but never truly biodegrade.

✔ **Rubber:** The vast numbers of used tyres that we generate are becoming increasingly popular as garden mulch, which is a great way of using up a problematic waste material. Rubber 'chippings' (shredded tyres) are dyed to resemble chipped bark, while bright colours are available that make an excellent soft surface for play areas. Rubber doesn't decompose like chipped bark does, which is a plus as it lasts for years.

Pulling and cultivating

Good old-fashioned hand-pulling and hoeing aren't among gardeners' favourite garden chores, but they do work, especially if you follow these basic rules while weeding:

- ✔ **Disturb the soil as little as possible.** This rule is really important, because many weed seeds lie dormant in the darkness just under the soil surface. When you churn up the soil, you expose the seeds to the light and air they need to sprout and attain pest status.

- ✔ **Get them while they're small.** Small weeds with fragile roots and stems take little effort to destroy. Large weeds take more work, disrupt more soil and can contribute to the seed population in your soil if you leave them long enough to go to seed. The longer the weeds live, the more water and nutrients they rob from your food and landscape plants, too.

- ✔ **Weaken perennial weeds.** Hand-digging the whole plant, roots and all, is the way to tackle pesky perennials, but not always practical on a large-scale organic basis. Repeatedly weakening weeds by chopping off their top growth with a hoe, or pulling by hand, deprives the plant of the chance to generate nourishment and can eventually kill it.

Leaning on your weeding techniques

If you intend to pull large weeds by hand, wait a day or so after a good fall of rain. If the weather's dry, moisten the soil first, ideally the day before so that the soil can drain. The weeds are then much easier to pull and you're more likely to get the whole root than in dry soil. You can leave small pulled weed seedlings in the garden to decompose; remove larger ones to the compost pile.

Weed your garden in sections. When you complete a section, immediately cover the soil with a layer of organic mulch to prevent more weeds from invading (the earlier section 'Mulching for weed prevention' covers mulch materials). Any weeds that do manage to grow through the mulch are easier to pull. If you like a neat edging to your lawn to stop the grass from invading your borders, install an edging strip.

Tooling up for weeding

With so many different weeding devices on the market, you may struggle to choose the most effective tools. The kinds of weeds that you're dealing with may influence your tool selection. For plants with long taproots (dandelions and burdock, for example), you need a tool that reaches down into the soil and pulls out the entire root without disturbing your lawn too much.

Most weeds don't require such a specialised tool. The most effective and all-around useful weeding tools are hoes, which disturb little soil as they work. A good hoe is the gardeners' greatest ally in the war against weeds, doing away with masses of seedlings in a few sweeps. Buy the best you can afford and handle before you make your purchase to ensure that the hoe's right for you.

Hoeing is great exercise for upper-body trimming – so you save time and money by not having to visit the gym!

Two popular hoes are used in the UK, both of which slice plants off just below the soil surface (see Figure 21-1):

- ✔ **Dutch hoe:** This tool works with a pushing action, skimming on or just below the surface of the soil to slice off weeds; ideal for light soils.

- ✔ **Swan neck or draw hoe:** The curved head is used to weed with a chopping action, pulling the tool towards you. Good for heavy soils, and also useful as a cultivating tool for such jobs as earthing-up potatoes.

Figure 21-1:
A Dutch hoe (left) and a swan neck or draw hoe (right).

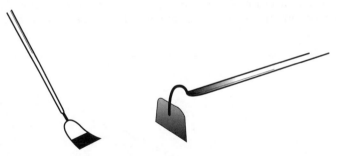

Here are a few tips on using a hoe:

- ✔ **Avoid using a long-handled hoe for close weeding around crops or plants, in case of damage.** Do the fiddly bits by hand, with a trowel, or using a short 'onion' hoe.

- ✔ **Hoe on a dry, breezy day.** Weeds that are sliced off or uprooted then quickly dehydrate and die, but in damp conditions they can re-root and grow again. Working in good conditions allows you to go over an area of ground in the morning, and return in the afternoon to finish off any weeds missed the first time.

- ✔ **Work in short spells.** Take a break between hoeing sessions, to avoid over-working your muscles.

Smaller hand tools and those with shorter handles are available too; they allow you to weed raised beds or weed while sitting or kneeling.

All weeding hoes need occasional touching up with a sharpening stone.

Firing weeds with flame guns

Among the latest weedkilling tools to appear are propane-fuelled flame guns, which make quick work of weeds. These devices don't set plants on fire; they've special nozzles that work by boiling the sap inside plants and bursting their cells. So although the name sounds exciting, the process is rather dull.

The least expensive flame gun is hand-held and costs little more than a high-quality rake. The gear attaches to any standard propane tank, such as the kind used for barbecue grills. The most expensive models allow you to wear the fuel tank as a backpack and include convenient squeeze-control valves. For the most effective control, use your flame gun when weeds are small (see Figure 21-2). Large weeds and tough perennials needed repeat treatments.

 Follow the manufacturer's instructions; Safety precautions depend on the size of the device, but protective gloves and goggles are likely to be a good idea.

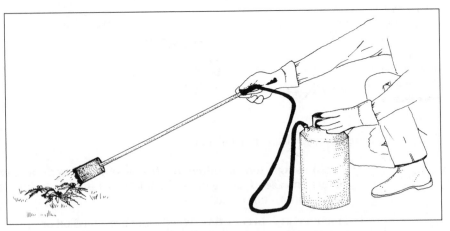

 **Figure 21-2:** Propane-powered flame guns are especially effective against weeds.

 Avoid using flame guns in windy or dry conditions. Keep a hose or other water source handy to douse unexpected flames.

 Flame guns use a nonrenewable resource, propane, to generate the heat. Obviously the propane gas means that using these tools isn't an eco-friendly method of weed control. Therefore, for organic gardeners who work with an eye on sustainability, this method is only to be used when no alternative exists – such as dealing with weeds in awkward corners on path or paving crevices.

Resorting to organic herbicides

When all else fails, gardeners can turn to herbicides to kill weeds. Before you accuse us of blasphemy, check out these organic weed-control chemicals:

✔ **Fatty acids:** Plants have a waxy coating on their leaves that prevents moisture loss. Natural fatty acids extracted from substances like palm oil damage the waxy layer, allowing the plant to dry out and die. This type of herbicide works best on young, tender, actively growing weeds in hot, dry weather, but is less effective on mature plants and perennial weeds.

✔ **Other natural acids:** Plants are sensitive to changes in pH (as we explain in Chapter 5). Some products use acetic acid (derived from vinegar) or pelargonic acid (derived from fruit) as their active ingredient. These acids damage the plants' protective waxy coating, killing the sprayed plant parts in a matter of hours.

Regular kitchen vinegar is only 5 per cent acetic acid; although it may kill weed seedlings, it has little effect on mature plants.

These organic weed-control products are acceptable for spot treatments but don't use them extensively, because they also kill beneficial organisms and lower your soil's pH. New formulations made from a combination of vinegar and citrus, cinnamon and/or clove oils have been introduced recently.

Covering the ground with cover crops

Open ground is an open invitation for weed seeds to take root and for creeping plants to expand their territory. If you plant crops that you can dig into the soil later, you can prevent and smother weeds, protect the soil from erosion and enrich the soil at the same time. Such thickly planted cover crops prevent weed seeds from sprouting and crowd out the ones that do. When the cover crop's job is done, simply rotovate it into the soil where it decomposes and adds organic matter. (Cover crops grown primarily to add nutrients are called *green manures*, which we discuss in Chapter 7.)

Choosing cover crops: Legumes, grasses and buckwheat

Cover crops fall into two broad categories. Within each group, some crops live for a single season and others are perennial, coming back year after year:

✔ **Grasses and buckwheat:** These cover crops grow quickly, allowing you to dig in some of them just a few weeks after planting; others can remain in place for months. They add lots of organic matter to the soil.

✔ **Legumes:** Plants that can convert nitrogen from the air to nitrogen in the soil are called *legumes* (peas and beans belong to the same group, but don't confuse them with cover crop plants). Legumes for cover crops include several types of clover and alfalfa. These plants increase soil fertility while they grow and add rich organic matter when they're dug in. Some of them, especially alfalfa, have deep roots that bring water and nutrients nearer the surface where most plants can use them.

Legumes provide an excellent source of nectar for bees as well as habitat for numerous beneficial insects.

Using cover crops

Cover crops can serve your garden needs in different ways, depending on your goals and time frame. Remember, however, that unlike some other weed-control measures, cover cropping requires you to plan ahead:

✔ **New garden preparation:** The year before you plant a vegetable, fruit or flower garden, turn over the soil and sow a thick cover crop. Depending on the crop and on whether you've time, turn under the first cover crop and grow another before cultivating the soil for food or flowers.

✔ **Between gardening seasons:** If you've harvested the last of your vegetables and removed the crop residue from the garden by early to mid-autumn, sow a cover crop for the winter. If you live in a colder part of the country, choose a fast-growing grass and plant it by early autumn so that it has time to establish. Turn it under in the spring. Be sure to dig in the crop before it seeds; otherwise, it can become a weed itself.

✔ **During the garden season:** Some cover crops, especially clover, are useful as permanent ground covers in orchards and in the aisles between permanent planting beds. Clover encourages beneficial insects and adds nitrogen to the soil while also preventing noxious weeds.

Mail-order catalogues are usually the least expensive sources of cover-crop seed. Read more about cover crops and green manures in Chapter 7.

Clearing overgrown ground

Taking on a plot that resembles a jungle is a prospect that often sends would-be organic gardeners reaching for the weedkiller. But don't despair. Excellent organic methods are available to get your jungle under control.

The best method is the easiest – and your main requirement is patience. Covering the ground with a light-excluding mulch (see the section 'Mulching for weed prevention') and leaving in place for at least a year kills off even the toughest weeds. Even better, when you peel back the covering, the ground's likely to be in a good condition to cultivate with a mechanical rotovator.

Chances are, though, that you need to do some cutting down of vegetation to get to this stage. To start, assess and identify what you're dealing with: is it grass or nettles that you can handle with a strimmer, or do you have to tackle big clumps of brambles that call for a tougher approach? You need to know whether these weeds include something nasty such as Japanese Knotweed.

Inspect the ground in case anything dangerous is lurking within – broken glass or rusty metal, for example.

Mow, scythe or otherwise cut back the vegetation as near to the ground as possible, and dig up the roots of woody weeds such as brambles. Pile the trimmings to one side, and cover and leave to rot down for compost or put through a shredder first. Cover the ground with a light-excluding mulch, taking care to bury the edges, and overlapping any joins.

If you plan to grow vegetables, you can get a reasonable crop in the first year by planting vigorous varieties (such as courgettes, cabbages and potatoes) through holes cut in the mulch. If you plan to do this, first spread a layer of manure or compost before putting the mulch in place.

Spotting Problems that Weeds can Hide

Weeds contribute to the two other major headaches that gardeners face by providing homes for pests and diseases. Don't just destroy the weeds, though, because knowing which insects and diseases they can harbour helps you decide whether to encourage their growth or eradicate them.

Providing homes for insects, good and bad

Wild plants provide habitat for a wide range of insects, but not all bugs are bad bugs. Some insects (such as the beneficial insects we discuss in Chapter 17) help your garden, and many of them depend on wild plants for habitat: that is, places to lay their eggs, forage for food and spend the winter months.

Wild plants with small flowers – especially umbellifers such as yarrow, hog-weed and wild carrots – attract many beneficial insects. In addition, wasps that prey on aphids, caterpillars and other pests also enjoy pollen and nectar-rich flowers, such as dandelions, daisies, clover and nettles. Non-invasive flowers can be welcomed in places such as meadows and lawns, but ensure that you remove the spent flowers of invasive ones such as dandelions before they go to seed and spread beyond their allotted space.

Another way that weeds benefit your garden is by acting as decoys; they attract pests that otherwise discover and damage your crops. In some cases, you can wait until these weeds have attracted a load of pests and then destroy them, taking care of two problems at the same time.

Some wild plants create a haven for damaging insects. For this good reason, make fruit and vegetable gardens no-go zones for weeds – quite apart from the fact that they pinch the water and nutrients.

Harbouring diseases that spread

Wild plants often suffer the same diseases that affect cultivated plants and spread their misery around. Related plants such as those in the nightshade family – including deadly nightshade, potatoes, tomatoes and aubergines – can infect one another with verticillium wilt and other diseases. Wild brambles share viruses with strawberries and cultivated brambles. Insects that feed on these plants often spread diseases as they travel, and the soil remains contaminated even after the diseased weeds are gone. Avoid planting vulnerable plants in the same soil where related species grew within the past few years, and control insects that spread diseases. (See Chapter 19 for more on plant diseases and Chapter 18 for insect control.)

Part V
The Part of Tens

'Edmund's very green-minded – he's obsessed
with feeding the soil whilst protecting our
birdlife.'

In this part . . .

For organic gardening in a nutshell, check out this part, a great place to get started if you want to be an organic gardener but don't know what to do first. Chapter 22 sums up the major principles and techniques of organic gardening in a few short pages and Chapter 23 offers ideas for making your garden, home and indeed your whole lifestyle more sustainable and eco-friendly.

Chapter 22

Ten Best Organic Gardening Practices

In This Chapter
▶ Combining the best strategies
▶ Beating the pests naturally
▶ Promoting plant health

*T*he most successful organic gardeners use a combination of strategies to grow healthy food and ornamental plants. When you're just getting started, though, all these practices can seem a little daunting – even discouraging. But if you add the ten practices that we describe in this chapter to your gardening routine one at a time, you can be gardening organically before you know it!

Enriching Your Soil

Plant health starts with the soil, so putting this organic gardening practice at the top of your list makes perfect sense. Get your soil right, and many other potential problems are likely to be less troublesome. (Turn to Chapters 4 and 5 for much more on soil and how to make yours healthier.)

Soil is composed of various sizes and shapes of mineral particles, which give it texture. You can't do much to alter your soil's texture except bring in loads of sand or topsoil, but you can change the other components: organic matter, air, water and soil organisms. Organic matter, which decomposes into humus, increases soil's ability to hold moisture and drain efficiently, feeds the beneficial organisms and adds important plant nutrients. You can increase the amount of organic matter in your soil by adding compost and using plant-based mulches, like leafmould, chipped bark, well-rotted manure and straw. Make your own compost (see Chapter 6) or buy it from a local nursery.

Avoiding excessive cultivation, compacting the soil as little as possible and adding organic matter enables you to improve the ratio of air and water in your soil.

Mulching Early, Mulching Often

Weeds flourish on open ground, but mulch can slow them – or even stop them in their tracks. Surround your garden plants with chipped bark, pine needles, grass clippings, leafmould, straw and other organic materials to shade the ground and keep weeds from sprouting. Use bought mulches such as biodegradable coir, paper matting or weed control fabric (or make your own from cardboard or whole newspapers) in paths and around trees and shrubs, covering them with loose mulch materials.

You can grow living mulches, too: sow cover crops in empty vegetable garden beds and over the whole garden at the end of the growing season to crowd out weeds. Find out more about mulches and cover crops in Chapter 21.

Choosing Healthy, Disease-Resistant Plants

Your plants don't get sick if they're immune to, or at least tolerant of, the nastiest diseases. Plant breeders work long and hard to develop varieties of your favourite fruits, vegetables, flowers and plants that fight off devastating diseases. Read catalogue descriptions and plant labels to find resistant plants whenever possible, and ensure that you buy and plant only healthy plants. Take time to find the healthiest specimens, as we describe in Chapter 15.

Don't bring home insect-infested plants. If you've doubts about a plant's health, quarantine it in a separate area before adding it to your garden.

Putting Plants in the Right Place

Struggling plants attract diseases and insects, but thriving plants fight them off. Give your plants the soil, sun and moisture conditions they prefer to keep them healthy and thriving. Consider native plants that naturally grow in your region or in a similar climate. If you've an established garden, replace the unhappy campers with plants that have a 'can-do' attitude. Use the observation and planning steps in Chapter 3 to create an inventory of what your garden has to offer, and then find plants with needs that match.

Using Organic, Slow-Release Fertilisers

Many synthetic fertilisers contain highly soluble nutrients that force plants into quick, lush growth. Although this growth may seem like a good thing, believe us when we say that it's not; succulent growth is attractive to insect and disease pests. Also, any fertiliser that plants don't take up immediately can run off and pollute waterways.

In contrast, most organic fertilisers are the slow-release kind. The nutrients are bound up in large molecules and released slowly through the action of micro-organisms. Therefore, plants receive a slow, steady diet of nutrients, and the risk of runoff is minimised. See Chapter 7 for details on fertilisers.

Encouraging Beneficial Organisms

Each harmful insect has a predator or parasite that attacks it, making your work easier. You can cheer on these helpmates by planting flowers and other plants that attract them and by avoiding the use of pesticides. Other garden visitors – including birds, bats and toads – can also help you in your pest control efforts, so welcome them into your garden.

Many crops require pollination by visiting insects, and the populations of many native pollinating insects are in decline. Invite in these important garden denizens by providing food and shelter, in addition to avoiding pesticides. Chapter 17 gives you more information on beneficial creatures.

Practising Integrated Pest Management

Integrated pest management (IPM for short) is the practice of looking at all the costs and options before deciding on a course of pest treatment. Instead of eradicating pests, you manage them. With IPM, you do the following:

- ✔ **Watch the weather carefully.** The appearance of many insects and diseases is tied closely to the temperature, humidity and time of the year.

- ✔ **Monitor pests.** Don't treat for pests unless they're causing serious damage. A few pests may be insignificant and tolerable in the big picture. Remember that pests are dinner for all kinds of wildlife!

✔ **Keep everything clean.** Practise good cultural techniques: rotate crops, destroy harmful weeds and clean up infested plant debris.

✔ **Use the least invasive and least toxic control methods.** Using simple techniques at an early stage is often all you need. Dislodge insects with a strong blast of water, or use finger, thumb and foot to squash!

Check out Chapter 1 for much more on IPM.

Trapping and Blocking Pests

Sometimes, protecting your crops from insects is as easy as throwing a fleece or fine mesh cover over them. If the cabbage white butterfly moths can't reach your broccoli to lay their eggs, for example, you don't find caterpillars in your vegetables. A circle of matting at the base of each brassica foils cabbage root flies and mini-cloches made from cut-up large plastic bottles keep slugs and snails from tender young plants. Chapter 18 has more ideas.

You can also use insects' own attractants against them. *Pheromones* – scents that insects secrete to attract a mate – are among the most powerful tools. Pheromone baits combined with traps cause the downfall of codling moth, plum moth and raspberry beetle. These baits attract only the pests you want to eradicate, and so they're safe to use around beneficial insects.

Avoiding Toxic Pesticides

Commonly available synthetic pesticides are some of the most toxic materials that homeowners use. As an organic gardener you can use organic alternatives. Even organic pesticides, however, such as pyrethrum and neem, can harm beneficial organisms. Always follow the label directions precisely if you choose to use pesticides, and use them as a last resort. See Chapters 17 and 18 for more information on managing pests without pesticides.

Promoting Diversity

Natural plant populations contain many species scattered over a large area, making them less vulnerable to attacks from pests and diseases. Use the same concepts in your garden by mixing crops within a row and avoiding large patches of the same variety. Instead of planting a long hedge made up of a dozen or more specimens of the same species of shrub, for example, consider designing a mixed border that includes a variety of evergreens and perhaps some flowering and fruiting small trees and shrubs.

Chapter 23

Ten Ways to Be Eco-Friendly

. . . .

In This Chapter

▶ Allowing things to be

▶ Observing the three Rs: Reduce, reuse, recycle

▶ Planning and planting for the future

. . . .

*B*eing eco-friendly means more than simply not spraying chemicals. You can minimise your ecological footprint, both in what you do and in what you don't do. In this chapter we describe ten ways to conserve resources, reuse and recycle, and minimise the environmental effect of your activities in your home and landscape.

Letting Perfection Go

In the past many gardeners sought perfection – unblemished red apples, long straight stems topped by curvaceous rosebuds and a lawn with nary a dandelion in sight. Now most gardeners understand that perfection just isn't worth the work, the resources required and the harm the methods do to the environment. If you tend to be a perfectionist, consider a change of perspective. Instead, seek perfection in other things, such as a balanced ecosystem of plants, insects and micro-organisms that benefit one another.

If you must have perfection in your garden, concentrate on one area and nurture it well, but let the rest be what it will. Concentrate on something manageable, such as a collection of beautifully tended container plants.

Reducing, Reusing and Recycling

Before you buy a product, consider its useful life and what's going to happen to it when you're finished with it. Is it going to last a long time? Can you reuse or at least recycle it? Reducing the number of throwaway products is an important part of an eco-friendly lifestyle. Similarly, look for products with minimal or at least recyclable packaging.

Before you throw anything away, consider whether someone else can use it. Used plastic pots, for example, may be rubbish to you, but organisers of a local school garden may welcome them. The web-based organisation Freecycle (www.freecycle.org) is a fantastic way to keep good stuff out of landfill.

Composting Kitchen Scraps and Garden Debris

Although more enlightened councils now offer food and garden waste collections, why throw away all that potential nourishment for your garden? Compost is dead easy to make: simply layer uncooked kitchen scraps, crumpled envelopes and shredded paper with lawn clippings, chopped dry leaves, shredded twigs and plant stalks and other garden debris to make rich compost.

You can also compost food waste in smaller, enclosed compost containers, to avoid enticing the neighbourhood rodents to set up home in your garden. Or create a wormery, and watch thousands of wiggly friends transform your kitchen scraps into ultra-rich compost.

Flip to Chapter 6 for details on how to make your own compost.

Reducing (Or Eliminating) Your Lawn

Reducing or even eliminating your lawn is a great way to improve the biodiversity and sustainability of your garden. Of course, doing so depends to some extent on your approach to lawn care, but if you like the bowling-green look a smaller lawn cuts your water bill, reduces fertiliser use and boosts your garden's wildlife value.

Even if you live where water is plentiful, making your mown lawn smaller makes ecological sense. Keep a well-mown area close to the house, for sitting and relaxing, but let areas further away develop into meadows that are cut just two or three times a year. Think of the fuel savings from your mower too. For more information on relaxed lawn care and wildflower meadows, turn to Chapter 16.

Planting a Tree

The list of reasons why trees are good for the environment is long, and you've probably heard many of them before: wildlife habitat, shade, erosion control, increased property value, wind protection and carbon dioxide trapping, to name a few.

Trees are also beautiful in their own right. To plant a tree is to plan for the future – your children's future, your neighbourhood's future and your planet's future. Check out Chapter 15 for information about good trees and how to plant them.

Choosing Human-Powered Equipment

Whenever possible, choose tools powered by old-fashioned elbow grease. Think rakes and brooms instead of leaf blowers, for example. Although electric- and battery-powered equipment creates less on-site pollution than gasoline-powered tools, keep in mind that the electricity they use has to be generated somewhere, invariably causing some degree of pollution – just not in your garden.

If you've a small lawn, consider a new, high-quality version of the traditional push mower. This type of mower is quiet and easy to use.

Minimising All Forms of Pollution

The fumes from your petrol-driven appliances such as mowers, strimmers and hedgetrimmers – and the loud noise they make – are obvious sources of air and noise pollution. Keep your eyes out for more subtle tools that do the same job. Reappraise the amount of outside lighting you need, and eliminate unnecessary lights to decrease light pollution; or switch to motion-detector lights that go off automatically.

Consider solar-powered lighting and quiet, solar-powered pumps for fountains.

Teaching Your Children Well

Helping children to discover the pleasures of gardening and connecting with the natural world ensures that future generations become eco-friendly, too. Start small by sprouting seeds together or talking about the plants you see on a walk. Name the vegetables and fruits in the supermarket, and talk about where and how they grow. The Internet contains lots of great ideas about gardening with children at home and in schools (for example, check out www.rhs.org.uk/children).

Sourcing Your Food Locally

Most people can't grow all their own food, but you can strive to eat locally produced foods harvested at the peak of flavour and nutrition. That's right, you can become what's called a 'locavore'! Support local farmers by buying direct from farm shops and at local farmers' markets. To grow more of your own food locally, join a CSA (Community Supported Agriculture) organisation, a community orchard or a local food group, sharing the work and the harvests with many other like-minded people.

Many small farms are organic; but even many that aren't often use ecologically sound practices. Ask the farmers, and they're usually happy to tell you about their farming philosophy and techniques. For products that can't be grown locally, such as coffee and chocolate, look for organic options. Also, some companies sell products described as 'fair trade' or 'sustainably grown' that benefit the environment and give fair prices to farmers in their native countries.

Considering the Seventh Generation

According to The Great Law of the Iroquois Native Americans, 'In every deliberation we must consider the impact on the seventh generation.' When you look at all your decisions through this long-term lens, you choose activities and products that have a minimum negative effect on the environment. After all, surely you want your great-great-great-great-great-grandchildren to inherit a vibrant, ecologically diverse Earth that's able to sustain them and their progeny? Maintaining your gardens by using organic techniques is one step towards this goal.

Index

• A •

absorbent material, 254
acaricides, 248
activators (compost), 73
adult insects, 252
aerating lawns, 227–228
AGM (Award of Garden Merit)
    varieties, 116
Agraland Limited (website), 259
air circulation, 164, 180
alfalfa, 122
alliums, 135–137
all-male plants, 137
Allotment Gardening For Dummies
    (Wombwell), 117
allotments, 115, 117
almond trees, 187
amphibians, 246
animal diversity, 11–12
animal pests
  birds, 296
  cats, 293–294
  deer, 289–291
  dogs, 294
  grey squirrels, 292–293
  mice, 295
  moles, 297–298
  preparing for, 288
  rabbits, 292
  rats, 295
  types, 289–298
  voles, 295
annuals, 97–98, 106–107, 131, 190,
    193–194, 300
anthracnose, 276
ants, 260
aphids, 260–261
appearance (plants), 116
apple scab, 277
apple trees, 182–183
arable land, 23
aromatherapy, 153

artichokes, 149
asparagus, 137–138
aubergines, 141–142
Award of Garden Merit (AGM)
    varieties, 116

• B •

baby plants, 105
bacteria, 270, 272
bacterial fungicide, 275
bactericides, 248
badgers, 291
bagged compost, buying, 58–59
balanced fertilisers, 84
balled and burlapped, 208
balled plants, 99
BAP (Biodiversity Action Plan), 22
barberry shrub, 213
bare-root, 98–99, 107–108, 180, 202
barriers, 242, 254–256, 288
basil, 154
Bat Conservation Trust (website), 246
bats, 246
beans, 139–140
bee-attracting plants, 195
beetroots, 144–145
beneficial fungi, 275
beneficial insects, 92, 243–246
beneficial microbes, 55
beneficial nematodes, 257–258, 265
beneficial organisms, 317
berries. *See also* soft fruits
  buying plants, 165–166
  choosing locations for, 164–165
  weed control, 165–166
biennials, 98, 300
bindweed, 301
biochar, 90
biodiversity, planning for, 30
Biodiversity Action Plan (BAP), 22
biodynamic agriculture, 25
Biodynamic Association (website), 25

biointensive mini-farming, 25
biological controls, 14, 242, 257–258, 291
birch trees, 212
birds, 246–247, 296
blackberries, 167–168
Blackburne-Maze, Peter (author)
  The Complete Guide to Fruit Growing, 175
blights, 279
blood, as organic fertiliser, 89
blossom-end rot, 147
blueberries, 166–167
Bokashi system, 77, 90, 295
bone, as organic fertiliser, 89
bonemeal, as organic fertiliser, 89
botrytis, 174, 277
branch collar, 210
brassicas, 127, 138–139
Brazil nuts, 47
British Trust for Ornithology (website), 247
broad spectrum, 248
broccoli, 138–139
brown rot, 277
buckwheat, as cover crop, 309–310
bud scars, 179
bud union, 200
buds (fruit trees), 179
building
  compost bins, 67–69
  healthy soil, 8–9
  wormeries, 76
bulbs, 196–198, 231
burlapped plants, 99
bush trees, 176
butterfly bush, 213
butterfly-attracting plants, 195
buying
  organic fertilisers, 88–89
  plants, 103–105
  roses, 200
  soft fruit plants, 165–166

● **C** ●

cabbage, 138–139
cabbage white butterflies, 261
cabbage whiteflies, 262

calcium, 86
calendars, 249–250
calendula, 154
canes, 172
canker, 277
capsaicin, 141
caraway, 155
carbon-rich materials, 70
cardboard, 71, 303–304
care and maintenance
  alliums, 136
  asparagus, 138
  aubergines, 141
  basil, 154
  brassicas, 138
  calendula, 154
  caraway, 155
  chamomile, 155
  chives, 156
  coriander, 156
  dill, 157
  emerging plants, 103
  fennel, 157
  flowers, 192–193
  fruit trees, 179–182
  horseradish, 158
  lavender, 158
  legumes, 140
  lettuce and leafy salad, 140
  mint, 159
  oregano, 159
  parsley, 160
  peppers, 141
  potatoes, 143
  root crops, 144
  rosemary, 160
  sage, 161
  spinach, 146
  sweet marjoram, 161
  sweetcorn, 145
  swiss chard, 146
  tarragon, 162
  thymes, 162
  tomatoes, 147
  turf, 222–223
  vining crops, 149

carrot flies, 262
carrots, 127, 144–145
castings, 45
caterpillars, 252
cats, 293–294
cauliflower, 138–139
CCD (Colony Collapse Disorder), 21
celeriac, 149
celery, 149
centipedes, 243
chafer grubs, 262
chamomile, 155
chemical controls, 14
cherry trees, 183–184
chicken manure, pelleted, 89
chickpeas, 122
chipped bark, 303
chitting, 142
chives, 155–156
chlorophyll, 84
choosing
  crops for raised beds, 130–131
  fruit trees, 182–186
  grass, 220
  ingredients for composting, 70–71
  pest- and disease-resistant plants, 237
  right plant for right place, 29
  trees and shrubs, 211–217
  turf, 221–222
circulation, for fruit trees, 164, 180
citrus peels, 76
clay particles, 42–43
clay soils, 43–44
climates (regional), 28
cloches, 123
closed system, 24
club root, 277
cobnut trees, 187
cocoa shell, 303
codling moths, 262–263
cold frame, 122
cold tolerance, 183, 185
collars, 255
Colony Collapse Disorder (CCD), 21
colour (design element), 31
comfrey, 73, 91–92

Community Supported Agriculture (CSA), 322
companion planting, 157
complete fertilisers, 84
The Complete Guide to Fruit Growing (Blackburne-Maze), 175
composted manure, 56
composting
  about, 55, 58, 65
  activators, 73
  benefits of, 66
  compost bins, 66–69
  'cooking', 72
  importance of, 320
  ingredients for, 70–71, 77–79
  leafmould, 73–74, 303
  location for, 66–70
  in small spaces, 69–70
  types, 58–59
  worm, 74–77
conifers, 215–217
conserving water, 15, 24
containers, 102, 106–107, 118, 152, 202
convenience, planning for, 30
conventions, explained, 1–2
'cooking' compost, 72
copper bands, 256
coral spot, 278
cordons, 120, 176
coriander, 156
corms, 198
cosmetic uses for herbs, 153
cost benefits, of edible gardens, 114
cotoneaster shrub, 213
cotton clothing, for composting, 71
couch grass, 301
courgettes, 148–149
cover crops, 92–93, 123, 309–310
covers, 229
craft uses for herbs, 153
Crawford, Martin (author)
  Creating a Forest Garden, 25
Creating a Forest Garden (Crawford), 25
creeping buttercup, 301
cress, 121
crop monitoring (IPM), 13

crop rotation, 126–128, 238
crops
  cover, 92–93, 123, 309–310
  cultivating in containers, 118
  growing mix of, 115
  requirements for, 116–118
  windowsill, 120–122
cross-pollination, 19, 178
crown, 219
CSA (Community Supported
     Agriculture), 322
cucumbers, 148–149
cultivating
  about, 45, 59
  cover crops, 93
  crops in containers, 118
  digging, 61–63
  for lawns, 220, 226–229
  mechanical, 63–64
  necessity of, 60
  timing for, 62
  weeds, 306–308
cultural considerations (design element), 31
cultural controls, 13
currants, 168–170
Cutler, Karan Davis (author)
  Herb Gardening For Dummies, 154
cutworms, 263
cypress, 216

damping off, 103, 278
damson trees, 186
dandelion, 301
dappled shade, 29
days to maturity, 116
deadhead, 192
debris, cleaning up, 239
deciduous trees, 32
decomposers, 50
decomposing mulches, 302
deep shade, 29
deep-rooted plants, 10
deer, 289–291
deer-resistant plants, 195, 290–291
deficiency (of nutrients), 84
dense shade, 29

designing your garden
  about, 30–31
  basic principles, 31–32
  brainstorming, 33
  landscaping and arranging, 32–33
  making a map, 34–35
  tips, 35–36
dessert apples, 183
determinate varieties, 146
deterring pests, 237–239
diatomaceous earth, 254
digging, 61–63
dill, 156–157
disease resistance, 116, 183, 185, 199,
     237, 316
disease triangle, 271
disease-control techniques and products,
     274–276
diseases, 8, 312. *See also* pests and
     diseases
diversity
  animal, 11–12
  encouraging, 8
  plant, 10–11
  promoting, 318
DIY stores, for buying plants, 103
dock, 301
dog poo, 77
dogs, 294
dormant root, 180
double digging, 61–63
drainage, 51–52, 118, 164, 220
draw hoe, 307
drink uses for herbs, 153
dutch hoe, 307

Easiwall, 119
EcoCharlie (website), 94, 259
eco-friendliness, 319–322
Ecology Action (website), 25
ecosystems, 9
edging, 193
edible gardens
  allotments, 115, 117
  extending the season, 122–124
  plants for, 114–116

requirements for crops, 116–118
selecting varieties, 116
in small spaces, 118–122
edible landscaping, 12
educating children, 322
effective micro-organisms (EM), 77, 90
eggs (insect), 252
eggshells, crushed, 71
elephant garlic, 136
EM (effective micro-organisms), 77, 90
Emorsgate Seeds, 232
energy conservation, 31, 32
environmental benefits, 20–24, 114
environmental problems
lawn-mower and strimmer damage, 283
leaf scorch, 283
nutrient deficiency, 284
salt damage, 284
weedkiller damage, 282
environmental safety, 249
ericaceous, 119, 166
erosion, 8, 64
espalier trees, 120, 177
evergreen trees, 32

● *F* ●

F1 hybrid seeds, 101
false cypress, 216
family type, 119
fan trees, 177
farm livestock, 57
fast-release fertilisers, 83–84
fatty acids, 309
feeding, 46, 110–111, 118, 226–227
fences, 288, 290, 292
fennel, 149, 157–158
fenugreek, 122
ferret dung, as mole deterrent, 297
fertilisers
about, 81–82, 317
applying, 87–88
avoiding trace element deficiency, 86–87
boosting soil, 90–91
buying organic, 88–89
fast-release compared with slow-release, 83–84
for flowers, 192

green manures and cover crops, 92–93
liquid, 91–92
mineral-based, 89
organic, 82–83, 88–93
primary nutrients, 84–85
roses, 203
secondary nutrients, 86
sustainable sources of, 93–94
synthetic, 82–83
threat to water from, 22
trees and shrubs, 210
vegetable gardens, 133–134
fertility (soil), 7, 46–48, 164, 220
filbert trees, 187
finnochio, 149
firethorn shrub, 214
firing weeds, 308
fish, as organic fertiliser, 89
Fisher, Kathleen (author)
Gardening For Dummies, 211
Herb Gardening For Dummies, 154
flame guns, 308
flea beetles, 263–264
florence fennel, 149
flower garden, herbs for, 152
flowering and foliage shrubs, 213–215
flowering crab apple trees, 212
flowering trees, 212–213
flowers
about, 189–190
aftercare, 192–193
annuals, 193–194
bulbs, 196–198, 231
cut for composting, 71
foliage, 197–198
for meadows, 231
mixed borders, 190–191
perennials, 194–196
planting, 192–193
roses, 198–204
soil preparation, 191–192
types, 193–198
foliage, 197–198
foliar feeding, 87
food miles, 114
food uses for herbs, 153
food waste, composting, 77–78
forest gardening, 25

Forest Gardening (Hart), 25
fragrance uses for herbs, 153
frames, 120
Freecycle (website), 320
freshness benefits, of edible gardens, 114
frost injury, 284–285
frost pockets, 115, 180
frost-tender plants, 98
frost-tender vegetables, 131
fruit cage, 164, 296
fruit pots, 119
fruit trees
  bare-root, 180
  buds, 179
  cross-pollinating, 178
  grafting, 178
  size and shape, 176–178
  soil fertility, 164
fruits, 71, 163–166. *See also* soft fruits
full sun, 29
fungicides, 248
fungus, 270, 271, 275

• *G* •

gage trees, 186
garden centres, for buying plants, 104
garden compost, 303
Garden Organic (website), 26, 114, 276
garden waste, for composting, 71
Gardening For Dummies (Fisher,
    MacCaskey and Marken), 211
garlic, 135–137
Gear, Alan and Jackie (organic gardening
    pioneers), 26
genetically modified organisms (GMOs),
    19–20, 101
glass mulch, 304
GMOs (genetically modified organisms),
    19–20, 101
Google Earth (website), 117
gooseberries, 168–170
grafting, 132, 178
granular fertilisers, 87
grapes, 170–171
grass, 219–232, 303, 309–310, 320
gravel mulch, 305

Green Gardener (website), 259
green lentils, 122
green manure, 57, 92–93
greenhouses, 123
grey mould, 174, 277
grey squirrels, 292–293
ground beetles, 243
ground covers, 152, 229
ground elder, 301
growing
  extending seasons, 122–124
  green manures and cover crops, 92–93
  in greenhouses, 123
  plants vertically, 119–120
  salads, 121
growth boosters, 83
growth habit (design element), 31–32
grubs (insect), 252

• *H* •

habitat, 9
habitat pile, 78
hair, as deer repellent, 289
half standards, 176
half-hardy, 98, 191
handpicking pests, 242, 253
harden off, 122, 133
hardiness of cherry trees, 184
hard-neck alliums, 136
hard-to-kill perennials, 195
hardy, 98, 131, 191, 207
harlequin ladybird, 245
Hart, Robert (author), 25
harvesting
  asparagus, 138
  aubergines, 141
  brassicas, 139
  legumes, 140
  lettuce and leafy salad, 141
  peppers, 141
  potatoes, 143
  root crops, 144
  spinach, 146
  sweetcorn, 145
  swiss chard, 146
  tomatoes, 148

vegetables, 134–135
vining crops, 149
hawthorn trees, 212
hay, as mulch, 304
hazlenut trees, 187
heading cut, 210
health (soil), 7, 18
health benefits, 17–20, 114
heating compost, 72
heavy-feeding vegetables, 133
hedgehogs, 247
heirloom seeds, 101
heirloom varieties, 114
Henry Doubleday Research Association,
    25–26
Herb Gardening For Dummies (Cutler and
    Fisher), 154
herbaceous perennials, 98
Herbal Remedies For Dummies
    (Hobbs), 153
herbicides, 248, 309
herbs
  calendula, 154
  caraway, 155
  chamomile, 155
  chives, 155–156
  for companion planting, 157
  container gardens, 152
  coriander, 156
  dill, 156–157
  fennel, 157–158
  horseradish, 158
  invasive, 153
  lavender, 158–159
  mint, 159
  oregano, 159–160
  parsley, 160
  reasons for growing, 152
  rosemary, 160–161
  sage, 161
  sweet marjoram, 161
  tarragon, 162
  thymes, 162
  types, 154–162
  using, 153
heritage varieties, 114

high-rise composter, 68
Hills, Lawrence (gardener and journalist),
    25–26
Hobbs, Christopher (author)
    Herbal Remedies For Dummies, 153
hoes, 307
holly bush, 214
Holmgren, David (student), 25
home test kits, 52
honey fungus, 278–279
honeydew, 260
horseradish, 158
horses, 57
horticultural fleece, 254–255
horticultural oils, 258
hosing off pests, 242
hover flies, 244
human manure, 57
human urine, as mole deterrent, 297
human-powered equipment, 321
humus, 45, 56
hydrangea bush, 214

• *I* •

icons, explained, 4
indeterminate varieties, 146
insect mesh, 254–255
insect pollinators, 21–22
insecticidal soaps, 258–259
insecticides, 248
insects
  about, 251–252
  beneficial, 92, 243–246
  as biological control, 257
  diversity, 11–12
  relationship with weeds, 311–312
integrated landscape, 33
integrated pest management (IPM), 13–14,
    317–318
Introduction to Permaculture (Mollison), 25
invasive herbs, 153
invasive roots, 206
'in-vessel' compost units, 78
IPM (integrated pest management), 13–14,
    317–318

• J •

Jeavons, John (biointensive techniques innovator), 25
juniper, 216

• K •

Knotweed, 302

• L •

lab tests, 53
lacewings, 244
ladybirds, 244
landscape fabrics, as mulch, 305
landscaping, 12, 32–33
larvae (insect), 252
lavender, 158–159
lawn-mower damage, 283
lawns
  alternatives to, 229–232
  choosing grass, 220
  clippings, 303
  drainage, 220
  feeding, 226–227
  maintaining, 224–229
  mowing, 224–225
  planting, 221–224
  reducing or eliminating, 320
  roots, 219–220
  soil preparation, 220–221
laying turf, 222
leaders, 215
leaf miners, 264
leaf scorch, 283
leaf spots, 279
leafhoppers, 264
leafmould, 73–74, 303
leafy salad, 140–141
leatherjackets, 264–265
leaves, 71, 273
leeks, 135–137
legumes, 127, 139–140, 309–310
lettuce, 121, 140–141
light shade, 29
light source, for seeds, 102

light-feeding vegetables, 133
lilac bush, 214
lily beetles, 265
lime, 54
limestone, 54
liquid fertilisers, 87, 91–92
livestock, farm, 57
local water patterns, 30

• M •

MacCaskey, Michael (author)
  Gardening For Dummies, 211
macronutrients, 47
maggots (insect), 252
magnesium, 86
mail-order catalogues, for buying plants, 104
maintenance, 30. *See also* care and maintenance
mangetout, 139
manure, 56–58, 71, 73, 89, 303
mapping your garden, 34–35
marjoram, sweet, 161
Marken, Bill (author)
  Gardening For Dummies, 211
marrows, 148–149
meadow, 230–231
measuring
  soil acidity/alkalinity, 48
  soil pH, 52–53
mechanical controls, 13
mechanical cultivating, 63–64
mechanical damage, 208
medicinal uses for herbs, 153
mice, 295
microbial treatments, 91
microclimates, 28–30
micronutrients, 47, 86–87
micro-organisms, 92
mildew, 279–280
minarette trees, 177
mineral nutrients, 46
mineral-based fertilisers, 89
mint, 159
miticides, 248
mixed borders, 190–191
mixed plantings, 238

mixed populations, 10
mixed salad leaves, 140
mixing compost, 72
mizuna, 121
mole smokes, 297
mole spurge plant, 297
moles, 297–298
Mollison, Bill (ecologist), 25
mould, 174
mowing lawns, 224–225
mulch mats, 305
mulching, 16, 203, 273, 302–305, 316
multistems, 212–213
mung beans, 122
mycorrhiza, 91

• *N* •

National Society of Allotment and Leisure
    Gardeners (website), 117
The National Wildflower Centre, 232
natural acids, 309
natural features, 34–35
nectarine trees, 184–185
neem, 256
nematodes, 257–258, 265
nettle, 301
newspaper mulch, 303–304
nitrogen (N), 84–85, 92
nitrogen fertilisers, 22
nitrogen-fixing plants, 11
nitrogen-rich materials, 70
no-dig beds, 128–131
noise, as mole deterrent, 297
non-compostables, 78–79
non-decomposing mulches, 304–305
nonorganic fertilisers, 18
nurseries, for buying plants, 104
nut trees, 186–187
nutrient deficiency, 284
nutrients
  phosphorus (P), 85
  for photosynthesis, 46
  potassium (K), 85
  primary, 84–85
  secondary, 86
nuts, 47
nymphs (insect), 252

• *O* •

offsets, 198
oils, for pest control, 258–259
okra, 149
onions, 127, 135–137, 280
open pollinated seeds, 101
orchards
  caring for fruit trees, 179–182
  choosing fruit trees, 182–186
  nut trees, 186–187
  tree anatomy, 176–179
oregano, 159–160
organic fertilisers
  boosting soil, 90–91
  buying, 88–89
  compared with synthetic fertilisers, 82–83
  green manures and cover crops, 92–93
  liquid, 91–92
  mineral-based, 89
  types, 88–93
organic gardening, 7–8, 24–26. *See also*
    specific topics
Organic Gardening Catalogue (website), 94
The Organic Gardening Catalogue, 232, 259
organic herbicides, 309
organic matter, 45, 54–56, 221
organic pesticide
  safety, 248–249
  types, 248
organisms, 45, 317
oriental vegetables, 149
ornamental trees, 212–213
over-fertilising, 239
overgrown ground, clearing, 310–311

• *P* •

pan, 64
paper, for composting, 71
parent rock, 40
parsley, 160
parsnips, 144–145
partial shade, 29
particle barriers, 254
pathogens, 272
peach trees, 184–185
pear trees, 185–186

peas, 139–140
peppers, 141–142
perennials, 99, 106–107, 190, 194–196, 300, 301
permaculture, 25
Permaculture Institute (website), 25
personal safety, 248–249
pest resistance, 116
pesticides, 20–21, 247–249, 318
pests and diseases
  about, 235, 251, 270–271
  of alliums, 136
  animal pests, 246–247, 287–298
  aphids, 260–261
  of asparagus, 138
  attracting beneficial insects, 245–246
  of aubergines, 142
  bacteria and viruses, 272
  barriers, 254–256
  biologically, 257–258
  of brassicas, 139
  cabbage white butterflies, 261
  cabbage whiteflies, 262
  carrot files, 262
  chafer grubs, 262
  codling moths, 262–263
  common, 276–282
  cutworms, 263
  diagnosing, 269–270
  disease-control techniques and products, 274–276
  encouraging natural predators, 246–247
  environmental problems, 282–285
  establishing thresholds, 241
  flea beetles, 263–264
  for fruit trees, 181–182
  fungus, 271
  harlequin ladybird, 245
  identifying and attracting beneficial insects, 243–246
  identifying problems, 239–241
  insects, 251–252
  in lawns, 229
  leaf miners and sawflies, 264
  leafhoppers, 264

leatherjackets, 264–265
of legumes, 140
of lettuce and leafy salad, 141
lily beetles, 265
managing insect pests, 252–260
nematodes, 265
organic pesticide, 247–250
organic solutions, 235–242
of peppers, 142
plant-based insecticides, 259–260
of potatoes, 143–144
preventing and controlling pests, 8, 237–239, 241–242, 253–268, 272–274
raspberry beetles, 265
removing manually, 253–254
repellents, 256
of root crops, 145
rose sawflies, 265
scales, 265
slugs, 266
snails, 267
soaps and oils, 258–259
spider mites, 267
of spinach, 146
of sweetcorn, 145
of swiss chard, 146
thrips, 268
of tomatoes, 148
trapping and blocking, 318
traps, 256–257
types of pests, 260–268
vine weevils, 268
of vining crops, 149
whiteflies, 268
wireworms, 268
pets, domestic, 56
pH, 48, 220
pheromone-baited traps, 182, 257
phosphorus (P), 85
phosphorus fertilisers, 22
photosynthesis, nutrients for, 46
Pictorial Meadows, 232
pinch, 192
pine needles, 303
pine trees, 216

planning
  design, 30–36
  microclimates, 28–30
  region's climate, 28
  soil assessment, 27–28
  vegetable gardens, 125–126
plant extracts, 256
plant safety, 249
plant-based fertilisers, 89
plant-based insecticides, 259–260
planting
  about, 9–10
  alliums, 136
  asparagus, 137
  aubergines, 141
  basil, 154
  brassicas, 138
  calendula, 154
  caraway, 155
  chamomile, 155
  chives, 156
  companion, 157
  container-grown perennials, annuals, and
    vegetables, 106–107
  coriander, 156
  deer-resistant plants, 290–291
  determining date for, 132
  dill, 157
  diversity of animals and insects, 11–12
  edible gardens, 12
  fennel, 157
  flowers, 192–193
  fruit trees, 180
  green manures, 93
  horseradish, 158
  lavender, 158
  lawns, 221–224
  legumes, 140
  lettuce and leafy salad, 140
  mint, 159
  oregano, 159
  parsley, 160
  peppers, 141
  plants, 105–110
  potatoes, 142–143
  root crops, 144

  rosemary, 160
  roses, 200–202
  sage, 161
  seeds, 102
  shrubs, 108–110
  spinach, 146
  sweet marjoram, 161
  sweetcorn, 145
  swiss chard, 146
  tarragon, 162
  thymes, 162
  tomatoes, 147
  trees, 108–110, 321
  vining crops, 148–149
plants
  all-male, 137
  annual maintenance, 111
  annuals, 97–98, 131
  bare-root, 98–99, 107–108
  bee-attracting, 195
  biennial, 98
  buying, 103–105
  caring for emerging, 103
  diversity, 10–11
  for edible gardens, 114–116
  feeding, 110–111, 118
  genetically modified, 101
  growing vertically, 119–120
  herbaceous perennials, 98
  location for, 316
  mapping existing, 34
  planting, 105–110
  roots, 99
  setting out, 133
  short-cutting seed-sowing process, 105
  size and appearance, 116
  soft fruit, buying, 165–166
  soil requirements for, 46–47
  staking, 111
  starting from seeds, 99–103
  tips for buying, 104–105
  transplanting, 103, 133
  types, 97–99
  watering, 103, 110, 118
  woody perennials, 99
plastic sheeting, 305

plugs, 105
plum trees, 186
pollination, 19, 21–22, 178, 183–185
pollution, minimising, 321
polytunnels, 123–124
pores, 43
potash, 85
potassium (K), 85
potassium bicarbonate, 275
potatoes, 142–144
potting compost, 102
powder fertilisers, 87
powered scarifier, 227
prevailing wind, 28
prevention (IPM), 13
primary nutrients, 84–85
propagator, for seeds, 102
prune trees, 186
pruning, 181, 210–211, 238, 274
pumpkins, 148–149
pupae (insect), 252
pyrethins, 259–260

• R •

rabbits, 292
radishes, 122, 144–145
rain gardens, 24
raised beds, 128–131
raking soil, 221
raspberries, 171–172
raspberry beetles, 265
rats, 295
ready-grown seedlings, 105
recycling, 15–16, 78, 319–320
reducing, 15–16, 319–320
region's climate, 28
'relaxed lawn', 230
repellents, 242, 256, 288–290
replant disorder, 199
reusing, 15–16, 319–320
Rhizomatous Tall Fescue (RTF) turf, 222
rhizomes, 153, 198, 278
rhizomorphs, 278
RHS (Royal Horticultural Society), 53, 175, 276, 278
rhubarb, 172

Ribes, 168–169
root balled, 208
root crops, 144–145
root damage, 285
root rot, 280
root zone, 210
roots, 99, 153, 219–220
rootstock, 119, 185, 200
rose blackspot, 280–281
rose sawflies, 265
rose sickness, 199
rosemary, 160–161
roses
  buying, 200
  choosing, 199
  disease-resistant, 199
  fertilising, 203
  mulching, 203
  planting, 198–204
  rose sickness, 199
  troubleshooting, 203–204
  underplanting, 281
  watering, 203
rotating crops, 126–128, 238
rotovating, 45, 63–64
Royal Horticultural Society (RHS), 53, 175, 276, 278
Royal Society for Protection of Birds (website), 247
RTF (Rhizomatous Tall Fescue) turf, 222
rubber mulch, 305
runners, 173
runoff, 22, 44
rust, 281, 282

• S •

safety, from organic pesticides, 248–249
sage, 161
salad leaf mixtures, 121
salt damage, 284
sand particles, 42–43
sandy soils, 44
sawdust, 71, 304
sawflies, 264
scale (design element), 32
scales, 265–266

scarify, 227
scion, 178
Scottish Allotments and Gardens Society
    (website), 117
season of bloom (design element), 32
season-extending attributes (design
    element), 32
seasons, for trees and shrubs, 207–209
seaweed, 89–91
secondary nutrients, 86
seed potatoes, 142
seeds
  creating lawns from, 223–224
  of herbs, 153
  planting, 102
  sowing, 133
  sprouting, 121–122
  starting from, 99–103
  starting indoors, 102–103
  types, 101
self-fertile, 119, 178
self-watering, 119
serviceberry trees, 212–213
shade, mapping, 34
shade-loving perennials, 196
shallots, 135–137
shaping
  beds, 129–130
  fruit trees, 176–179
shavings, 304
shelter, supplying, 116–117
short-cutting seed-sowing process, 105
short-term care, for trees and shrubs,
    208–209
shredding, for compost, 78
shrubs, 108–110. See also trees and shrubs
silt particles, 42–43
silt soils, 44
single digging, 61
size
  apple trees, 183
  beds, 129–130
  fruit trees, 176–179
  plants, 116
  starting small, 115
slope, mapping, 34
slow-release fertilisers, 83–84
slowworms, 247

slugs, 266
small spaces
  composting for, 69–70
  edible gardens in, 118–122
snails, 267
soaps, as repellents, 258–259, 289
soft fruits
  blueberries, 166–167
  currants, 168–170
  gooseberries, 168–170
  grapes, 170–171
  raspberries, 171–172
  rhubarb, 172
  strawberries, 172–174
soft-neck alliums, 136
soil
  about, 7, 39–40, 49–50
  adding organic matter, 54–56
  adjusting pH, 54
  assessment of, 27–28, 52–53
  boosting, 90–91
  building healthy, 8–9
  checking drainage, 51–52
  compost, 58–59, 73
  conditioners for fruits, 164
  cultivating, 59–64
  digging, 61–63
  enriching, 315–316
  excavating components, 40–41
  fertility, 7, 46–48, 164, 220
  health, 7, 18
  humus, 45, 56
  manure, 56–58, 71, 73, 89, 303
  mapping, 34
  mechanical cultivators, 63–64
  moisture for fruits, 164
  preparing for flowers, 191–192
  preparing for lawns, 220–221
  preparing for seeds, 100
  preventing erosion, 23
  raking for lawns, 221
  supplying, 116–117
  testing, 50–53
  tips, 60
  topsoil, 23, 40, 42–45
  warming, 123
  wet, 45
Soil Association, 23

soil organisms, 45
soil profile, 40–41
solution, 87
sorbus trees, 213
special uses
  for basil, 154
  for calendula, 154
  for caraway, 155
  for chamomile, 155
  for chives, 156
  for coriander, 156
  for dill, 157
  for fennel, 158
  for horseradish, 158
  for lavender, 159
  for mint, 159
  for oregano, 160
  for parsley, 160
  for rosemary, 161
  for sage, 161
  for sweet marjoram, 161
  for tarragon, 162
  for thymes, 162
spider mites, 267
spiders, 244
spinach, 145–146
spirea shrub, 214
spray, as deer repellent, 289
spring-blooming bulbs, 196
sprouting seeds, 121–122
spruce trees, 217
spurs, 179
squash, 148–149
staking trees, 111
standards, 176
starter plants, 105
Steiner, Rudolf (philosopher), 25
stepover trees, 177
sticky traps, 257
stirring compost, 72
stolons, 153
stone mulch, 305
straw, as mulch, 304
strawberries, 172–174
strimmer damage, 283
structure of topsoil, 44–45
subsoil soil, 40

sulphur, 54, 86, 275–276
summer-blooming bulbs, 197
sun, 34, 116–117, 164
supersweet varieties, 145
supports, 120, 192
sustainability, 20, 31, 93–94
swan neck hoe, 307
sweet marjoram, 161
sweetcorn, 145
swiss chard, 145–146
synthetic chemicals, alternatives to, 18
synthetic fertilisers, 82–83

• T •

Tamar Organics (website), 94, 259
tarragon, 162
taste benefits, of edible gardens, 114
tender plants, 98
terminal bud, 179
thatch, 227
thinning cut, 210
thin-walled bins, 67–68
thresholds, establishing, 241
thrips, 268
thymes, 162
tilling, 63–64
tines, 63
tomatoes, 127, 146–148
tools, for weeding, 306–307
top-dress plants, 87
top-dressing lawns, 228
topiary, 215
top-size bulbs, 197
topsoil, 23, 40, 42–45
tots, 105
trace elements, 47, 86–87
transplanting plants, 103, 133
traps (insect), 256–257
tree protectors, 255
trees and shrubs
  choosing healthy plants, 208
  conifers, 215–217
  fertilising, 210
  flowering and foliage shrubs, 213–215
  flowering and ornamental trees, 212–213
  long view for, 209–211

planning, 205–207
planting, 108–110, 321
pruning, 210–211
seasons, 207–208
short-term care, 208–209
staking, 111
varieties, 211–217
triploid varieties, 183
true bulbs, 198
trunk protectors, 292
tumbler compost bins, 67–68
turf, 221–223

• u •

ultrasonic mole deterrer, 297
underlying rock, 40
underplanting roses, 281
unstructured soils, 44

• v •

vacuum cleaner contents, for
    composting, 71
vector, 272
vegetable gardens
  alliums, 135–137
  asparagus, 137–138
  aubergines, 141–142
  brassicas, 138–139
  determining planting dates, 132
  fertilising, 133–134
  growing herbs in, 152
  harvesting, 134–135
  legumes, 139–140
  lettuce and leafy salad, 140–141
  'no-dig' beds, 128–131
  onions, 135–137
  peppers, 141–142
  planning garden, 125–126
  potatoes, 142–144
  root crops, 144–145
  rotating crops, 126–128
  setting out plants, 133
  sowing seeds, 133
  spinach, 145–146
  sweetcorn, 145

swiss chard, 145–146
tomatoes, 146–148
types, 131–132
varieties, 131–132, 135–149
vining crops, 148–149
watering, 134
weeding, 134
vegetables
  container-grown, 106–107
  grafted, 132
  oriental, 149
  uncooked for composting, 71
ventilating compost, 72, 78
'Vermicompost' fertiliser, 89
VertiGarden, 119
viburnum shrub, 215
views, mapping, 34–35
vine weevils, 268
vining crops, 148–149
viruses, 270, 272, 282
voles, 295

• w •

walnut trees, 187
warming soil, 123
waspinator, 244
wasps, 244
water and watering
  conserving, 15, 24
  flowers, 193
  lawns, 225–226
  local patterns, 30
  mapping, 34
  minimising contamination, 22
  plants, 103, 110, 118
  roses, 203
  vegetables, 134
websites
  Agraland Limited, 259
  Bat Conservation Trust, 246
  Biodynamic Association, 25
  British Trust for Ornithology, 247
  for buying plants, 104
  EcoCharlie, 94, 259
  Ecology Action, 25
  Emorsgate Seeds, 232

websites *(continued)*
  Freecycle, 320
  Garden Organic, 26, 276
  Google Earth, 117
  Green Gardener, 259
  National Society of Allotment and Leisure
    Gardeners, 117
  The National Wildflower Centre, 232
  Organic Gardening Catalogue, 94
  The Organic Gardening Catalogue,
    232, 259
  Permaculture Institute, 25
  Pictorial Meadows, 232
  RHS (Royal Horticultural Society),
    276, 278
  Royal Society for Protection of Birds, 247
  Scottish Allotments and Gardens
    Society, 117
  Soil Association, 23
  Tamar Organics, 94, 259
weedkiller damage, 282
weeds and weeding
  about, 299–300
  annuals, 300
  biennials, 300
  clearing overgrown ground, 310–311
  controlling, 165
  cover crops, 309–310
  firing with flame guns, 308
  flowers, 193
  as harbourer of diseases, 312
  as homes for insects, 311–312
  Knotweed, 302
  lawns, 220, 228
  mulching for weed prevention, 302–305
  organic herbicides, 309
  perennial, 301
  pulling and cultivating, 306–308
  types, 300–301
  vegetables, 134
well-rotted manure, 56
western red cedar trees, 217
wet soil, 45
whiteflies, 268
wild animals, 57
wild-flower seeds and plants, 232
wildlife, protecting, 20–21
wind, 34, 180
windowsill crops, 120–122
windrows, 79
winter injury, 284–285
wire bins, 69
wire composter, 68
wireworms, 268
Wombwell, Sven (author)
  Allotment Gardening For Dummies, 117
wood ash, for composting, 71
wood chips, 304
wood shavings, for composting, 71
wooden bin system, 69
wooden pallet bins, 69
woody perennials, 99
woody stems and branches, recycling, 78
wool clothing, for composting, 71
worm composting, 74–77
wormcast, as organic fertiliser, 89

yew trees, 217

FOR DUMMIES®

Making Everything Easier! ™

UK editions

BUSINESS

978-0-470-97626-5

978-0-470-97211-3

978-0-470-71119-4

REFERENCE

978-0-470-68637-9

978-0-470-97450-6

978-0-470-74535-9

HOBBIES

978-0-470-69960-7

978-0-470-68641-6

978-0-470-68178-7

Asperger's Syndrome For Dummies
978-0-470-66087-4

Boosting Self-Esteem For Dummies
978-0-470-74193-1

British Sign Language
For Dummies
978-0-470-69477-0

Coaching with NLP For Dummies
978-0-470-97226-7

Cricket For Dummies
978-0-470-03454-5

Diabetes For Dummies, 3rd Edition
978-0-470-97711-8

English Grammar For Dummies
978-0-470-05752-0

Flirting For Dummies
978-0-470-74259-4

Football For Dummies
978-0-470-68837-3

IBS For Dummies
978-0-470-51737-6

Improving Your Relationship
For Dummies
978-0-470-68472-6

Lean Six Sigma For Dummies
978-0-470-75626-3

Life Coaching For Dummies,
2nd Edition
978-0-470-66554-1

Management For Dummies,
2nd Edition
978-0-470-97769-9

Nutrition For Dummies, 2nd Edition
978-0-470-97276-2

Available wherever books are sold. For more information or to order direct go to www.wiley.com or call +44 (0) 1243 843291

30093 (p1)

FOR DUMMIES®

A world of resources to help you grow

UK editions

SELF–HELP

 978-0-470-66541-1

 978-0-470-66543-5

 978-0-470-66086-7

STUDENTS

 978-0-470-68820-5

 978-0-470-74711-7

 978-1-119-99134-2

HISTORY

 978-0-470-68792-5

 978-0-470-74783-4

 978-0-470-97819-1

Origami Kit For Dummies
978-0-470-75857-1

Overcoming Depression For Dummies
978-0-470-69430-5

Positive Psychology For Dummies
978-0-470-72136-0

PRINCE2 For Dummies, 2009 Edition
978-0-470-71025-8

Psychometric Tests For Dummies
978-0-470-75366-8

Reading the Financial Pages
For Dummies
978-0-470-71432-4

Rugby Union For Dummies, 3rd Edition
978-1-119-99092-5

Sage 50 Accounts For Dummies
978-0-470-71558-1

Self-Hypnosis For Dummies
978-0-470-66073-7

Starting a Business For Dummies,
3rd Edition
978-0-470-97810-8

Study Skills For Dummies
978-0-470-74047-7

Teaching English as a Foreign Language
For Dummies
978-0-470-74576-2

Time Management For Dummies
978-0-470-77765-7

Training Your Brain For Dummies
978-0-470-97449-0

Work-Life Balance For Dummies
978-0-470-71380-8

Writing a Dissertation For Dummies
978-0-470-74270-9

**Available wherever books are sold. For more information or to order direct go to
www.wiley.com or call +44 (0) 1243 843291**

FOR DUMMIES®

The easy way to get more done and have more fun

LANGUAGES

978-0-470-68815-1
UK Edition

978-1-118-00464-7

978-0-470-90101-4

MUSIC

978-0-470-97799-6
UK Edition

978-0-470-66603-6
Lay-flat, UK Edition

978-0-470-66372-1
UK Edition

SCIENCE & MATHS

978-0-470-59875-7

978-0-470-55964-2

978-0-470-55174-5

Art For Dummies
978-0-7645-5104-8

Bass Guitar For Dummies, 2nd
Edition
978-0-470-53961-3

Criminology For Dummies
978-0-470-39696-4

Currency Trading For Dummies
978-0-470-12763-6

Drawing For Dummies, 2nd Edition
978-0-470-61842-4

Forensics For Dummies
978-0-7645-5580-0

Guitar For Dummies, 2nd Edition
978-0-7645-9904-0

Index Investing For Dummies
978-0-470-29406-2

Knitting For Dummies, 2nd Edition
978-0-470-28747-7

Music Theory For Dummies
978-0-7645-7838-0

Piano For Dummies, 2nd Edition
978-0-470-49644-2

Physics For Dummies, 2nd Edition
978-0-470-90324-7

Schizophrenia For Dummies
978-0-470-25927-6

Sex For Dummies, 3rd Edition
978-0-470-04523-7

Sherlock Holmes For Dummies
978-0-470-48444-9

Solar Power Your Home
For Dummies, 2nd Edition
978-0-470-59678-4

The Koran For Dummies
978-0-7645-5581-7

FOR DUMMIES®

Helping you expand your horizons and achieve your potential

COMPUTER BASICS

978-0-470-57829-2

978-0-470-46542-4

978-0-470-49743-2

DIGITAL PHOTOGRAPHY

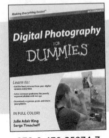

978-0-470-25074-7

978-0-470-76878-5

978-0-470-59591-6

MICROSOFT OFFICE 2010

978-0-470-48998-7

978-0-470-58302-9

978-0-470-48953-6

Access 2010 For Dummies
978-0-470-49747-0

Android Application Development
For Dummies
978-0-470-77018-4

AutoCAD 2011 For Dummies
978-0-470-59539-8

C++ For Dummies, 6th Edition
978-0-470-31726-6

Computers For Seniors For Dummies,
2nd Edition
978-0-470-53483-0

Dreamweaver CS5 For Dummies
978-0-470-61076-3

Green IT For Dummies
978-0-470-38688-0

iPad All-in-One For Dummies
978-0-470-92867-7

Macs For Dummies, 11th Edition
978-0-470-87868-2

Mac OS X Snow Leopard For Dummies
978-0-470-43543-4

Photoshop CS5 For Dummies
978-0-470-61078-7

Photoshop Elements 9 For Dummies
978-0-470-87872-9

Search Engine Optimization
For Dummies, 4th Edition
978-0-470-88104-0

The Internet For Dummies,
12th Edition
978-0-470-56095-2

Visual Studio 2010 All-In-One
For Dummies
978-0-470-53943-9

Web Analytics For Dummies
978-0-470-09824-0

Word 2010 For Dummies
978-0-470-48772-3

**Available wherever books are sold. For more information or to order direct go to
www.wiley.com or call +44 (0) 1243 843291**